THE LANGUAGE OF COLOR

THE LANGUAGE OF COLOR

Rudolf Steiner's Painting and Glass Windows in the First Goetheanum

by
Hilde Raske

RUDOLF STEINER PRESS

Rudolf Steiner Press
Hillside House, The Square
Forest Row, East Sussex RH18 5ES

www.rudolfsteinerpress.com

Reprinted by Rudolf Steiner Press, 2023

Originally published in German under the title *Das Farbenwort* by Verlag Freies Geistesleben, Stuttgart, 1983
First English edition by Walter Keller Verlag, Dornach, 1987

A catalogue record for this book is available from the British Library

ISBN 978 1 85584 660 9

Cover by Morgan Creative. Cover art: 'Atlantis' by Rudolf Steiner
Typeset by Symbiosys Technologies, Visakhapatnam, India
Printed and bound by Halstan & Co. Ltd., Amersham, Bucks. HP6 6HJ

Table of Contents

Illustrations

Foreword to the English Edition

Sixty-four years ago, late in the night as the year changed from 1922 to 1923, a building of enormous proportions was burned to the ground in the foothills of the Jura Mountains in Switzerland. Except for some local excitement, the event passed relatively unnoticed.

The building had not yet been officially opened. It was not quite complete. Although widely visible because of its immensity and unusual design, a few finishing touches remained to be made before its doors could be opened to public view. Work on the building had begun shortly before World War I. In September of 1912, hundreds of people – artisans, craftsmen, lay carpenters, artists and just plain helpers among them – converged on an obscure, rural point in Switzerland to begin construction of an edifice unlike any other that had hitherto been built. Nothing of its sort has been constructed since.

While most of the countries of Europe were at war with one another, men and women – indeed, during the war years, mostly women – from those same warring countries, worked hand in hand, year after year, sculpting away layer after layer of wood; painting layer upon transparent layer of color; engraving depths of light through colored glass – all in an effort to create an artistic edifice which, in its design, forms and colors, would open everyone's eyes to a whole world of experience that, for most people, otherwise remains unseen and unknown. However, shortly before the building was to be opened to view, it was burned to the ground.

What did so many people labor over a ten-year period to create, which ultimately – so to speak, unseen and unheard of – succumbed to flames?

Their work, if indeed it was reproducible, was never recreated. A second building was constructed soon after, which related to the first in its basic architectural design. But this progression of design from the first to the second edifice is not something easily recognized by a casual observer. It is a feature pointed out by Rudolf Steiner, the man who designed both buildings.

Rudolf Steiner called the buildings *Goetheanum*, confirming thereby a connection to the endeavors of the great German poet/scientist, Wolfgang von Goethe. The second Goetheanum still stands today. Unlike the first, which was literally carved out of wood, the second Goetheanum was poured in concrete to massive dimensions. Rudolf Steiner, however, died at a very early stage of its construction, so that the carved forms and expansive paintings he created for the first Goetheanumn never found their echo in the second.

It is precisely their loss from view that Rudolf Steiner lamented after the tragic fire of New Year's Eve 1922/23. The carved forms, the engraved motifs in colored glass tryptichons, the flowing tableaux painted on the ceilings of both intersecting cupolas, all relating and harmonized as an integrated, unified, living work of art: to view this environment promised a special experience.

A sense of this experience – buried in the midnight flames of arson – is what Hilde Raske, with this book, strove to convey.

Hilde Raske, artist and eurythmist, devoted years of study and experimentation to fathoming Rudolf Steiner's paintings and art of painting. She grew so conversant with these unusual works of art that she could describe them almost as events in color and light-and-dark. What might otherwise escape the unpracticed eye was so vividly and clearly described by her that it became self-evident even to the casual observer. Years of study, practice, and painting taught her that a wealth of experience can be found in these art works, and that this experience can best be attained if these art works are not explained and analyzed but allowed to speak for themselves.

Rudolf Steiner's own colors, his own words on the first Goetheanum, are what Hilde Raske labored for years to compile in this volume. She sought to present a panorama of the veritable deeds of red and blue, light and dark in the building's two cupolas. The colors said something; they spoke to each other and something of that language, even though concealed by the New Year's flames, can still be heard in the preparatory sketches that remain.

This language is what Hilde Raske wanted to convey through this book. Often through the years, in the course of preparing the manuscript, she would turn aside and remark, "I can *hear* my paintings. And if I don't hear them, then they're just not quite right yet!"

This sense of listening to colors is the technique that permeates this book and guides the reader in deciphering 'The Language of Color' in the First Goetheanum.

Acknowledgements

Literally decades of study and research preceded the compilation of this volume. Throughout, Hilde Raske's staunch friend and associate, Bertha Wolfe, gave whatever and as much support as was needed to help this work mature. The *Vorstand* of the Goetheanum, as well as the directors and editors at the *Rudolf Steiner Nachlassverwaltung*, provided materials indispensable to the subject matter. Waldemar Kumm, curator at the Goetheanum, was extraordinarily generous of time and assistance in comparing printed proofs with original sketches for color accuracy.

Throughout the years, many people helped by providing encouragement, lending a critical literary ear, or checking for typographical or other errors. Their efforts resulted in a refining of wording, clarifying of obscure details and other improvements that made the text more 'reader friendly'. Hilde Raske was ever concerned not only with the material she had to present, but with the person who would read and study it. John Meeks, who assisted editorially and in gathering research materials for a time while still in Switzerland, contributed several passages in the book, notably those concerned with the Babylonian time period, historical notes on the 'Faust' motif, and thoughts on *Meister Eckhardt.* Peter Sagal worked closely with Hilde Raske for the final five years of manuscript preparation, researching, editing, footnoting and, in general, bringing the German text together in its final form, with much responsibility to bear in particular for the concluding chapters. This, regrettably, resulted in an undue Americanization of the original German manuscript, requiring scores of hours of correction and amendment by Dr. Wolfgang Niehaus of *Verlag Freies Geistesleben*, publisher of the German edition, who deserves the unqualified gratitude of European readers. It was Hilde Raske's deepfelt wish that this work be made available to English-speaking people, a task Peter Sagal took on himself to secure. This could only be accomplished thanks to the enthusiastic, perservering personal support of Heidi Keller-von Asten, who, through *Verlag Walter Keller*, was kind enough to underwrite publication of this edition.

The translation was born of the unremitting efforts of several people who worked dedicatedly for years, sometimes far apart from each other, to complete the task. Christl Hoffmann worked long, long hours she hardly had to spare to translate the entire sections on the large and small cupola. Peter Sagal worked primarily on the Introduction and editing the aforementioned sections. His work, in turn, was edited in part by the poetic pen of Theodore van Vliet. M.E. Ormiston supplied valuable insights, material and some spare, but choice, prose.

The task of completing the entire remaining portion of the translation fell to Thomas Decker, who did the Notes and several chapters, and Dorit Winter, who translated 'Painting Out of the Color', 'The IAO', and 'After the Fire'. Coralee Roth-Frederickson edited the whole, reworking and re-editing the entire first parts and producing as unified and flowing style of language as circumstances permitted. The editor also wishes to thank Theodore Mahle who has served as a consultant in the latter stages of this project. Special words of gratitude are owed Karen Myrin, whose generous support catalyzed the entire translation, and Dietrich von Asten, whose substantial contribution made it possible for the Anthroposophical Press to participate in the publication and distribution of this English-language edition.

Peter Sagal
New Year's Eve 1986/87

INTRODUCTION

"Color is a whole world; it is itself a cosmos and has something creative within it. One can elicit the form out of what the colors say to each other in the universal expanse. This is the language of color, the conversation of color, the creative Word of Color. When one feels this in a truly artistic way, then – just as the world is properly described as having been brought forth from the Word – when color is heightened to Color Word, human, superhuman and subhuman forms arise out of it." (September 7, 1921)*

How do the paintings in the first Goetheanum fit into the situation prevalent in the world of art at the turn of the century? How did they unfold in the course of their creator's life?

The beginning of the century saw a groping for new paths in painting, a dissolution of the traditions that had prevailed since the Renaissance, a breakthrough into a new realm of color – a light blazed in the turbulent souls of artists in east and west.

Monet, approaching his landscape impressionistically, allows but a breathing of colors: a subtly differentiated rose-violet drops into an expanse of reflecting green – *Lake with Wisteria.*

The young Kandinsky, looking at one of Monet's *Haystacks* at an exhibition of impressionists in Moscow, found himself for the first time "face to face" with a real painting which, by artistic means alone, made the pictured object itself uninteresting. In this meeting with late impressionism, doubt as to the importance of the formal object engraved itself negatively in his consciousness, while the belief in the invincible power of the colors on his palette established itself positively." (W. Haftmann)[1] He ceased painting Russian city moods and began large tableaux with generous surfaces of color: pink, green, black. *Blue, Pale and Delicate* and *Blue, Deep and Profound* became themes of his work.

Kandinsky talks about blue in his book, *On the Spiritual in Art*: "Blue's inclination toward a deepening of its hue is so great that it becomes more intense and characteristically inward just there where its tone deepens. The deeper it becomes, the more it calls forth in the beholder the impression of endlessness, arousing in him a yearning for something pure and, ultimately, supersensible." He characterizes himself as the first painter to eliminate formal objects from his pictures, as a chronological comparison of his life's work reveals: first, the dissolution of purely formal objects; then, the immersion in color; later, a return to formal elements, albeit geometrical and symbolical.

Van Gogh gave up the grey tonality of early works like *Potato Eaters* and increasingly embellished his paintings with brilliant colors which, at first, shocked his contemporaries. The play of colors surrounding his portraits became ever more expressive as, for example, in his famous self-portrait of 1877. Subdued tones also appeared: light green and faint rose – the scent of apple blossoms. The complementary tones of orange and blue, ordinarily harmonious and peaceful, became dramatic. Orange opens up to a world of light; in the blue, black crows shudder in ominous foreboding. Van Gogh himself describes his technique: "I do not follow any system in laying on the colors. Sections, uncovered areas of canvas here and there, completely unfinished corners, parts overworked, others coarse; in short, the result – and I have reason to presume this – is sufficiently unnerving and irritating to arouse displeasure among people with prejudiced ideas about technique."[2] R. Neumayer comments, "Van Gogh enthusiastically sings the song of Veronese green, of yellow in its variations from lemon to orange, of Prussian blue and vermilion, of cadmium and of ochre. The beauty of pure colors and their harmonies is the 'Song of Songs' of Van Gogh and the *Wilden*."[3]

The development of modern art is difficult to comprehend if one fails to grasp the effects of such startling works of art and of the beautifully balanced paintings that Gauguin brought back from his stay in the South Pacific.

An exhibition in Paris in 1905 caused a major stir in the art world. A circle of young artists took a deliberate stand against traditional painting. A critic called them *Fauves* – 'wild beasts'. They adopted this insult as a title of honor, thereafter calling their movement *Fauvism*. Matisse, Derain, Marquet, Vlaminck and Roualt belong to this group.

* *Dated quotes are passages by Rudolf Steiner, excerpted from his numerous lectures. A chronological list of references to these lectures begins on page 279.*

Franz Marc writes about Germany's *Fauves* (*Wilden*) in *The Blue Rider.* "In this age of the great battle for a new art, we fight as 'savages', unorganized, against an old, organized power. The battle appears unequal; but, in spiritual things, it is not the number, but rather the strength of the ideas that triumphs. The dreaded weapons of the 'savages' are their *new thoughts*; they kill more surely than steel and shatter what was believed to be unbreakable .... It is impossible to explain the latest works of the 'savages' as a formal development and re-interpretation of impressionism ... . Their thinking has a different goal: to create, through their work, *symbols* for their time that belong to the altars of the coming spiritual religion, behind which the products of technique disappear."

In the second edition of *The Blue Rider*, Marc adds, quoting Daubler, " 'On earth, everything that is to be, can only be begun.' This statement of Daubler's can stand for our entire creative effort and intent. Fulfillment will follow some time or other in a new world, in a new existence. On earth, we can only set the theme. This book is only the prelude to a new theme. Whoever listens to it attentively will find that the jumpy, restless way it moves betrays the kernel out of which it was conceived. Its source is a region of springs that bubble in a hundred places simultaneously, now hidden, now openly singing and murmuring. We took the divining rod through the art of past ages and the present. We pointed only to what is alive, unmolested by the compulsions of convention. Everything in art that is born of itself, that lives of itself and not upon the crutches of habit, gained our devoted love."

In the same volume Roger Allard, in seeming contradiction to this, raises the question of a theoretical foundation for painting. "In 1807, Goethe said that 'for a long time now, painting has lacked knowledge of a figured bass, of a tried and tested theory, such as exists in music.' "

Kandinsky returns to this question several times. "These presumed rules that ought some day to amount to a 'figured bass' of painting are nothing other than knowledge of the inner effects of particular agents and their combinations." He points out that "all of the arts are deeply related, especially music and painting. Surely Goethe based his thought that painting should have a 'figured bass' on this obvious relationship. This prophetic statement of Goethe's is a kind of premonition of the situation in which modern painters find themselves .... Given the characteristics of today's harmonics, it is self-evident that in our time it is less possible than ever before to construct a fully-rounded theory, a figured bass for painting .... Still, it would be premature to claim that painting will never have firm rules or principles reminiscent of the musical figured bass, or that such principles would only lead to academicism."

Interested in spiritual exercises, Kandinsky attended a number of Rudolf Steiner's lectures at the *Architektenhaus* in Berlin during the winter of 1908. Inspired by the lecture on 'Sun, Moon and Stars' (February 26, 1908) in which Rudolf Steiner spoke of the spiritual nature of colors and of the Ariel scene in Goethe's *Faust*, Kandinsky painted an Ariel picture, which he gave to his student, Maria Strakosch-Giesler. Several colored woodcuts, including *The Pointer*, also appear to have been at least partly inspired by Rudolf Steiner.[4]

The new art movement expanded rapidly throughout Europe. Groups banded together for exhibitions, seeking "to create a new canon that endows our lives with beauty and style." (Allard) Marc says, "We are struggling for pure thoughts, for a world in which pure thoughts can be thought and spoken without becoming impure. For only we, or others of a higher calling, shall be able to reveal the other side of the Janus head, whose glance, now hidden, looks counter to the times."

Thus it is probably no mere coincidence that in Munich, at the same time that artists in the *Bauhaus* were seeking new directions in art, Rudolf Steiner's *Mystery Dramas*[5] portrayed – in the figure of the painter Johannes Thomasius – an individual path to the experience of and creation out of the soul-spiritual nature of color.

Kandinsky, visiting Lothar Schreyer in his studio, saw *House of the Dead*, a religious painting that Schreyer had just completed. Deeply moved, he said, "As a Russian, I can never forget my 'Christ is Arisen'. But at the same time I know that the resurrected Christ lives in the Holy Spirit, in his divine and human nature. And Christ expressly left to us the Holy Spirit and sent us the Holy Spirit as the third person of the Godhead ... . I see the realm of spirit drawing up in light and want to proclaim it as well as my art permits me. That is why I do not paint pictures of Christ, do not paint the Son of Man, who can be depicted as a human being. The Holy Spirit cannot be grasped in material form, but only immaterially. This is my goal: Light from light, the flowing light of the Godhead – to proclaim the Holy Spirit. Are the people capable of comprehending this annunciation, of seeing the Light? When?" He then turned away, saying bitterly, "My paintings reach – the art dealer!"[6]

In the founding manifesto of the *Bauhaus* in April, 1919, Gropius expressed the following goal: "Let us create together the new building of the future, where everything – architecture and sculpture and painting – will form a unity, rising toward heaven from the hands of a million workmen as a crystalline symbol for a coming, new religion."[7] Then he went to America and designed mammoth industrial projects.

Feininger, well-known for his woodcut *The Cathedral of Socialism*, also went west and gained fame. Macke, "who, of all of us, brings forth the purest tonality of color" (Marc), fell in the autumn of 1914, just a few weeks after World War I began. Marc himself, whose paintings speak perhaps most directly to the heart, and who hoped to see his pictures, as well as those of his contemporaries, on the altars of a new generation, was killed in 1916.

The deeds and destinies of the painters at the turn of the century, with their expressed search for artistic balance (Schreyer and Itten) and "the spiritual in art" (Kandinsky), amplify the tragedy of the destruction of the great paintings in the cupolas of the first Goetheanum, with their portrayal of a new Christ experience, in the conflagration of New Year's Eve, 1922/23.

Rudolf Steiner also shared intensely in the spiritual struggles and searching and the questions that arose out of the times and moved the artists at the turn of the century. His early efforts were philosophic and scientific, resulting in books, lectures and essays that often touched on Goethe's unique way of apprehending the world of phenomena. Later, as destiny confronted him with new tasks, he worked as architect, sculptor, painter, playwright, and choreographer.

In Vienna, where he studied mathematics and physics at the Institute of Technology, he saw paintings by Boecklin, "works of art that gave me cause to sustain my preoccupation with ideas about painting."[8]

His role as editor of *Goethe's Treatises on Natural Science* in Vienna and Weimar, 1883–1897[9] entailed many years' study of Goethe's research on the metamorphosis of color, including the significant expositions of how color arises out of light and dark. He describes Goethe's approach in an introduction to the *Treatise on Colors*:

"Goethe advances from regarding color as an attribute of the world of appearances to regarding color itself as appearing within those attributes. He does not stop there, but in the chapter on 'The Sensory-Moral Effects of Color', goes on to examine the still higher relationship between the world of colored objects and the soul."[10]

In *Goethe as the Father of a New Aesthetics*, Rudolf Steiner quotes from Schiller's letter to Goethe of August 23, 1794: " 'You bring the whole of nature together in order to illuminate the single instance; in the universality of its modes of manifestation, you seek the basis from which the individual case may be explained. Step by step, you rise from the simpler organization to the more developed, in order at last to construct the most developed of all – the human being – genetically, out of the entire edifice of nature. In recreating him according to nature's own process, you seek to penetrate to her hidden technique.' " Rudolf Steiner goes on to say, "In this re-creation lies a *key* to understanding Goethe's world-outlook. If we really want to attain to the archetypes of things, to the inalterable in the midst of eternal change, then we ought not to concentrate on what has already reached completion, since this no longer fully corresponds to the idea which expresses itself therein; rather, we must go back to the *becoming*, must listen to nature in the process of creating. That is what Goethe means when he says in his essay, 'Contemplative Power of Judgment', 'If, in the sphere of morality, through belief in God, virtue, and immortality, we should raise ourselves to a higher sphere closer to the primordial Being, then the same should obtain in the sphere of the intellect: namely, that by contemplating an ever-creating nature, we make ourselves worthy of participating spiritually in her creations. Indeed, I strove untiringly towards what is typical and archetypal, albeit at first unconsciously and out of an inner drive.' Thus, the Goethean archetypes are no empty schemes; rather, they are the driving forces behind phenomena."

This way of looking at things, which leads from their sensory appearance to an experience of their spiritual reality, may find a corresponding expression in art.

"Beauty is not the divine dressed in the garb of sense-reality; no, it is sense-reality dressed in the garb of the divine. The artist does not bring the divine down to earth by letting it pour down into the world, but rather by lifting the world up into the sphere of the divine. Beauty is *semblance* because it conjures before our senses a reality which, as such, presents itself as an ideal. Consider the *what*, but even more, consider the *how*, because the crux of the matter lies in the *how*. The *what* remains *sensory*, but the *how* of its appearance becomes *ideal*. Where this ideal mode of appearance appears to the best advantage, there the dignity of art appears at its highest. Goethe says about that, 'The dignity of art appears perhaps most eminently in music because no account has to be taken of a material factor there. Music is all form and content, exalting and ennobling all that it expresses.' To be sure, an aesthetics proceeding from the definition that 'beauty is sense-reality that appears as if it were idea' does not exist yet. It has to be created. It could even be called 'The Aesthetics of a Goethean World-Outlook'.

And that is the *aesthetics of the future*."

During this Weimar period, Rudolf Steiner had much contact with actors and painters. In *The Course of My Life*, he reminisces about one of them, the artist Otto Froehlich.

"The soul-life of this young man was all light and color. What others expressed in ideas, he brought forth as 'colors in light'. Even his intellect functioned in such a way that, through it, he brought together the things and events of daily life as colors combine, not as mere thoughts that connect with each other as ordinary people fashion the world .... When we were together, Otto Froehlich would 'paint' in his mind. One could forget in his company that the world contained anything else besides light and color .... And the young painter really brought things to a point where he could guide the brush and lay on the colors in such a way that his pictures reflected to a great extent his exuberant, vibrant, light-filled, color fantasy. When he painted the trunk of a tree, the linear form of the object did not appear on the canvas, but rather what light and color reveal out of themselves when the tree trunk offers them the opportunity to come to visible life."

Frequent lecture tours gave Rudolf Steiner the opportunity to become thoroughly acquainted with the art treasures of the leading European museums and galleries. In London, he saw how far Turner had advanced in bringing the wonders of nature onto his canvases with pure, fleeting colors. These trips, with the opportunity they presented for contemplating a great variety of artistic impulses in the company of Marie von Sivers, a personality of great artistic sensitivity, amounted to "a higher education in art" for him.

On November 25, 1905 he wrote the following to Marie von Sivers: "Our ideal should be this: to create forms as an expression of the inner life. For an age that cannot see forms, nor create them with inner sight, must necessarily reduce the spirit to an inessential abstraction, and in the face of this merely abstract spirit, reality must appear as an aggregation of matter devoid of spirit."

Rudolf Steiner shared with keen interest the questions that moved the painters of his time and their struggles to find new artistic paths and forms of expression. At the Congress of the Theosophical Society in 1907, he presented forms gained from his own spiritual view, "forms born of spiritual seeing and spiritual hearing" – sketches for each of the seven Seals of the Apocalypse and for the execution in sculpture of particular motifs for the capitals of seven columns in metamorphic progression.

When, towards the end of 1909, Rudolf Steiner was asked about a theme for the summer activities of 1910, he replied that he would like to present the 'Fairy Tale'[11] – Goethe's story of 'The Green Snake and the Beautiful Lily'. Instead, however, he presented his first drama, *The Portal of Initiation* – the culmination of a long, inner transformation of the images in Goethe's tale.

The premiere of this play, subtitled 'A Rosicrucian Mystery', took place in August 1910 in Munich. Marie Steiner von Sivers describes the preparations for the performance:

"That was the most beautiful time of the year, festival-time in Munich. Then it was possible to concentrate fully on just one task for a period of about two months. During the day we rehearsed; at night, Rudolf Steiner wrote the text of the drama that had already fully formed in his mind. In between he supervised the carpentry, painting, modelling, sewing and embroidery, all done according to his specifications. He had new ideas for everything and could lend a hand everywhere. His talented fingers would quickly produce a pattern to guide the artists in their work. He went from one workshop to another and new life budded everywhere, taking on surprising configurations. Here, in the huge bins of the Schrannen Hall in Munich, lay great lengths of linen from which the backdrops were to be made; there, he gave the dimensions of the columns for the Sun Temple, for the Subterranean Temple, and explained their ornamentation. He designed the cloud formations of the region of spirit, the chasms, crags and crystals of Ahriman's domain, and the enchanted forms of Lucifer's realm. Landscapes with Balde's little round house and Hilarius' oval country home gradually took shape upon the canvas, forms that would later be realized in wood at the construction site of the first Goetheanum. Here stood the furniture whose beautiful contours and hues matched the colors of the walls and the soul-configurations of the people for whom they served as home surroundings. The stage was always colorfully lit according to the traits of individual characters or the functions of the rooms."[12]

A new play was performed in each of the following three summers: *The Soul's Probation* (1911), *The Guardian of the Threshold* (1912), and *The Soul's Awakening* (1913).

And what is portrayed in the first drama? A painter's destiny! A painter's destiny in its sorrows and joys, a painter despairing at his waning artistic powers, at his inability to create out of a feeling for nature, for the changing moods of light and dark. After experiencing something of the world of the elements and gaining insights into his own personal destiny and its interweaving with that

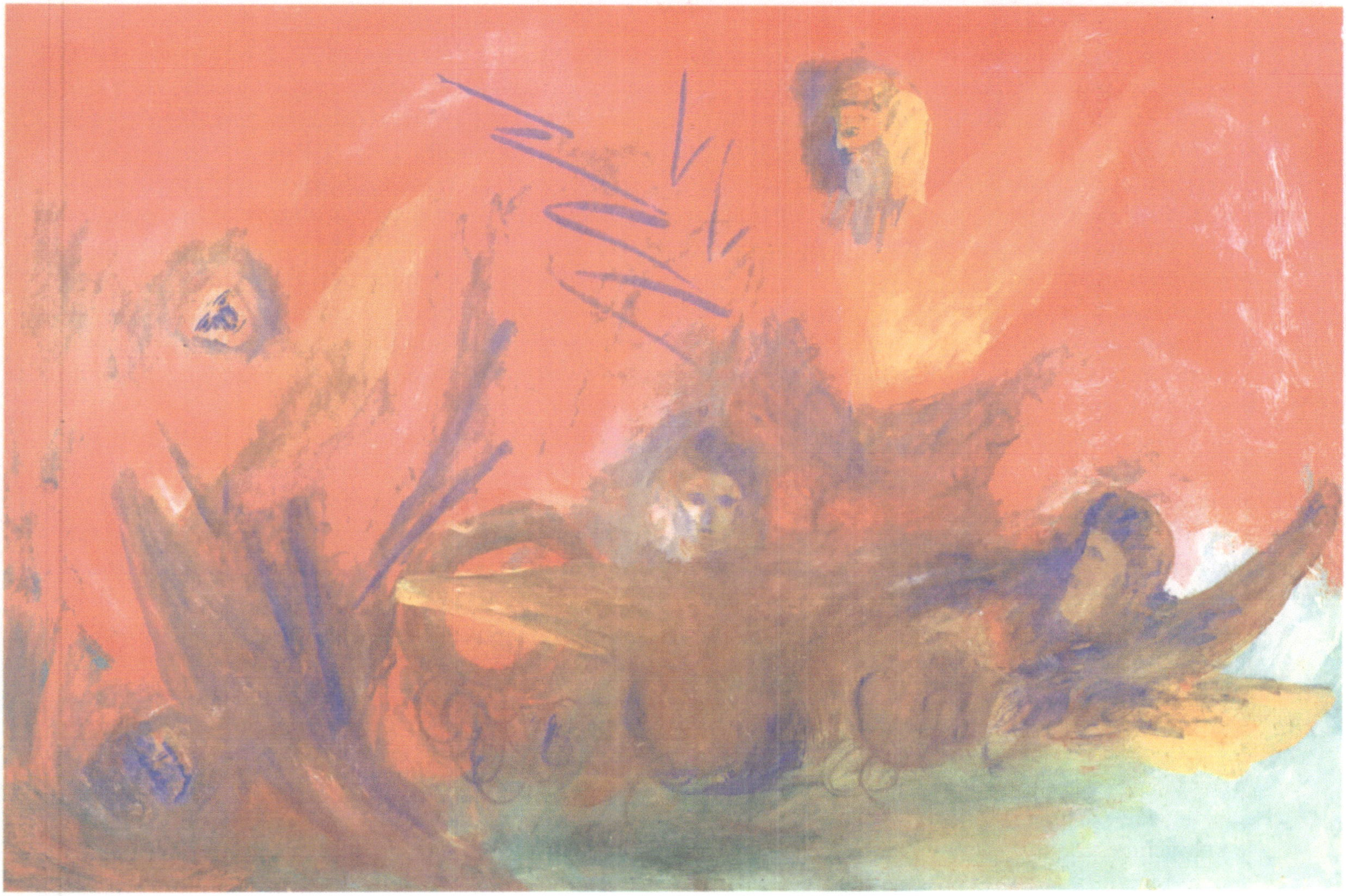

Light-Beings

of others, he experiences within a new awakening of his creative forces.

In the eighth scene, the painter appears as a creative artist. A visiting friend, an engineer, sees a portrait he has just completed of a mutual acquaintance, a researcher. Startled, the friend cries out,

> "The canvas – I want to smash right through it,
> to find that which I should seek!"

and he utters the following words of crucial significance for this new way of painting:

> "These forms, which seem to be produced by
> the color ... ."

Rudolf Steiner repeatedly refers to this line as expressing the point of departure for a new art of painting, where the artist fashions form out of a grasp of the very life of color itself.

The circle of painters in Munich, including Jawlensky and Kandinsky, knew Rudolf Steiner from his public lectures and books. The congresses, with their artistic events, took place at first within the closed circles of the Theosophical Society. Already in Berlin and again in Munich, Rudolf Steiner took a personal interest in the work of several artists, having conversations with them and gaining understanding of their search for new creative ideals and paths. Thus an inner relationship may be presumed to exist between his meetings with significant artists and his dramatic characterization of the destiny of a modern painter, through whom Rudolf Steiner expresses his own view of the future task of painting.

In the second play, *The Soul's Probation*, the artist stands before a new painting and says:

> "Then in the gentle ether-red of spirit worlds
> I tried to densify what is invisible,
> by sensing how the colors nurse a longing
> to see themselves in souls transfigured into
> spirit."

The actress rehearsing the role of Johannes, the artist, felt it too abstract to speak such words before a blank easel, and so asked Rudolf Steiner to provide an appropriate painting.[13] He immediately took up the suggestion and painted *Weaving of Light* (see page 13) in tempera, probably dipping his brush in the colors at hand which were used for painting the backdrops. Marie Steiner describes that moment: "For *The Soul's Probation*, in just about half an hour, Dr. Steiner sketched spirit forms in the peach-colored billows of the ether sea, a picture that the professional artists themselves did not dare to draw; it was his first painting."[14] Rudolf Steiner was fifty years old at the time. There is no known record of his ever having painted before.

The stage directions for the scenery and costumes of the individual scenes of this drama call for an unusual intensification and lively alternation of color. Already in the first play, the scene indications range from the yellow-red mood of a living room to a rose-colored meeting room for people seeking knowledge of the spirit, and on to a series of color impressions corresponding to the soul moods of various characters.

Two great antagonists appear, each in his own realm: Lucifer, the spirit of light, in an atmosphere of fiery red; and Ahriman, the spirit of darkness, in a cold, blue, crystalline environment.

The scenery in *The Soul's Awakening* depicts the contemporary world more strongly: work in offices, the crass demands of everyday life, and the attempt to shape these in a dignified way. In contrast to this, Rudolf Steiner depicts the path of spiritual sight in the conscious experience of the cosmic midnight hour and a look back into the events of a previous earth-life in an Egyptian mystery center.

In these plays, through the medium of color, Rudolf Steiner expands the possibility of stage scenery from the ordinary set to a panorama of the highest imaginative vision, leading the viewer into the soul and spirit of the events. The colors and forms are attuned to the words and experiences of the characters, whether they be in sub- or super-earthly realms, in the etheric or astral world, in elemental or spiritual domains, or simply involved in the ordinary affairs of daily life.

Thus color can be seen as an integral part of the dramas, accompanying the characters as they tread the path of knowledge between two powerful spiritual adversaries. In their search they penetrate deeper and deeper into the spirit; the task of the stage settings is to display these ever-deepening experiences in color and form.

"A landscape which, in its special character, should express the soul world ... . A landscape of fantastic forms, majestic, composed of swirling masses of water on one side and erupting whirlpools of fire on the other. In the center a chasm, out of which fire is spurting and towering up as if to form a portal in front of the mountain-like formations of fire and water ... . This is the realm of the spirit. The scene appears as a significant flood of color; above reddish, coursing in fiery red, and transmuting to blue, dark blue, and violet below. At the bottom a globe of the earth, as if symbolic. The characters coming onstage should appear as if part of the entire color set." (Scenery directions for the *Mystery Dramas*) Such scenery ought not be regarded as naturalistic, but rather of the stuff of natural *forces*, imaginative pictures of creative, soul-spiritual powers in their various manifestations. Here are the threads that lead the human being from one earthly life to another. Such threads reveal themselves as spiritual decisions gleaned from previous earthly deeds to be transformed into new deeds in later lives. Thus, the imaginative scenes of the characters' former lives on earth arise here of inner necessity. Just as the persons in these plays must be surrounded by colors and forms that reflect what lives in their souls, words, and deeds, so do the dramas themselves need to be surrounded by an environment corresponding to *their* inner content.

"Let us consider for a moment that the world-view gained from spiritual science should come to life in the artistic. Would it not be natural, then, that the need would arise to have a kind of architecture, a kind of artistic setting, wherein the soul could picture: When you reach for what is near you, what surrounds you here, should it not be something drawn directly from your own spiritual-soul life? When you want to merge with your immediate surroundings, should they not provide you with something you want to experience? Thus it necessarily follows that the surroundings must have very special forms, a very special configuration of spatial relationships. When we make a physical gesture, we are satisfied insofar as the hand or arm takes on the form of that gesture. When we speak of that spiritual relationship that the soul enters into through spiritual cognition, then what happens is that the gesture comes out of us and directly inhabits our immediate surroundings. That which comes out of us, which otherwise, insofar as we are physical beings, lives within our skin, comes out of us in spiritual cognition; one should like to say, it becomes a spiritual gesture that lovingly embraces its surroundings. What this gesture wants to embrace, what it wants to come into contact with, what it wants to look upon, the colors in which it wants to live, that is what has to provide the underlying conception for a building in which spiritual science is to be pursued. The forms, the colors, everything artistic, have to result directly from what can be experienced of the world when it is spiritually-scientifically embraced. Thus a building that should serve spiritual science is, in its forms and colors and everything that is artistically produced, directly related to the essence of spiritual science itself in such a way that this spiritual science must transform its ideas and words into artistic forms. And in transforming itself into artistic forms, it creates the necessary environment for that which must be pursued within the building." (April 10, 1915)

The occasion, or one might better say, the necessity, for constructing a building to house the *Mystery Plays* arose during the rehearsals for the first drama in 1910. The premiere took place in a rented theater. Limitations on rehearsal time, coupled with the wish to create an environment appropriate to the dramas, led some members of the Theosophical Society to begin preparations toward construction. A building society was formed, plans drawn up, models worked out, and a suitable property acquired in Munich. When official pressure against the project mounted in 1912, friends offered their land near Basel as an alternative site. Thus did the Goetheanum come to be built on the Dornach hill.

"Green and unmolested, the hill lay there, rugged with original growth ... . The landscape lay at our feet in radiant autumn glow; the cherry trees in the valley flamed red like fire, like burning blood, in the sun's play of light ... . The mountains and hills gleamed in every shade of yellow, those October days ... . A year later, the shovels had begun to turn over the clay soil. The protective covering of grass was removed and the hilltop flattened. The day approached when the foundation stone would be laid.

"Actually, the night, the 20th of September when darkness sets in early, was stormy. The elements conspired; the wind howled; the rain poured down; our feet sank in the clay. The great torches that illuminated the pit into which the stone was to be lowered continually spewed burning fragments into the depths, creating a scene of tremendous, somber earnestness, and unfathomed grandeur, for Rudolf Steiner's words resounded powerfully above the commotion of the elements in clear, full, destiny-laden tones." (Marie Steiner)

STAGES IN THE DEVELOPMENT OF THE GOETHEANUM

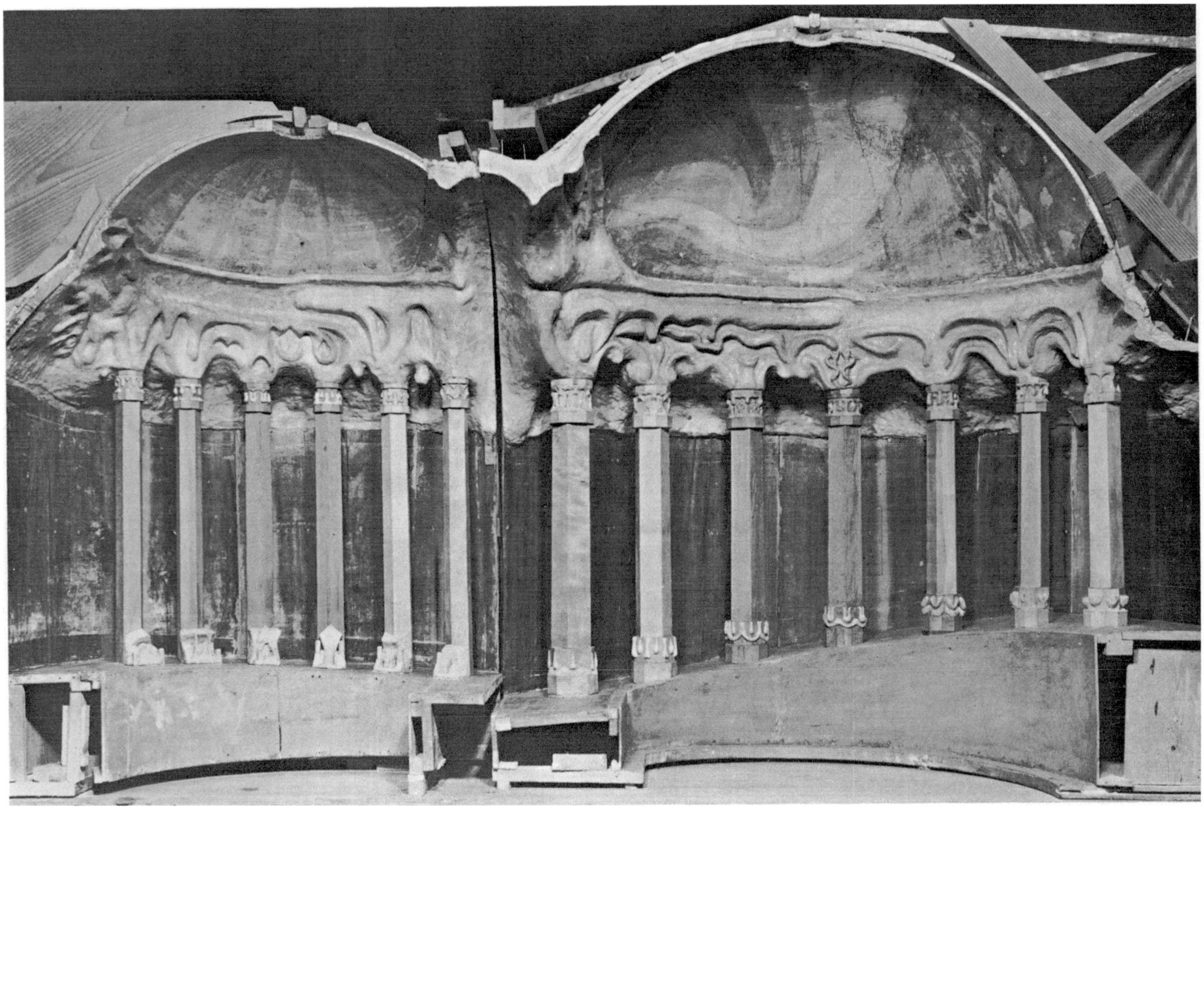

The Model of the Interior

THE MODEL OF THE INTERIOR

"This model is the very embodiment of the architectural concept of the Goetheanum. It is born entirely of artistic feeling, just like the content of spiritual science is grasped with feeling. It is, in its own way, yet another expression for what otherwise is expressed by spiritual science itself." (February 28, 1921)

Immediately after the foundation stone was laid, Rudolf Steiner made the model of the interior of the first Goetheanum. It is kept on display in the second Goetheanum, in the room containing his large wooden sculpture, called *The Group* or *Representative of Man*.

The model, a one and a half meter long cross-section showing the southern halves of the two interlocking cupolas, contains a multitude of form elements. Assja Turgeniev described her first impression of it. "This model – the only one from that time that has been preserved – yes, you just breathed it in; you did not dare to approach it with your thoughts. Convinced that thoughts could not comprehend it, you let go of everything you believed you already knew."[1]

Today, the model affords the best means for gaining a clear picture of what the interior of the first Goetheanum looked like and for visualizing the interpenetration of the large and small cupolas. In addition, its living, metamorphosing forms provide the basic elements of a training in sculpture.

"One becomes a sculptor by reaching back, with full consciousness, to the formative forces that once led man to the plastic arts. One must regain cosmic sensibility; one must re-acquire a feeling for the all-encompassing universe and be able to see a microcosm – a little world – in the human being." (April 9, 1922)

Rudolf Steiner describes a kind of archetypal space out of which the sculptor or architect can gain creative impulses for his own work.

"This [sculptural] space, everywhere shaped and everywhere capable of creating forms out of itself, can be seen with Imagination; and out of the perception of this space, one can actually create forms in the plastic arts, be they sculptural or architectural." (April 9, 1922)

Working with surfaces, with the tension between concavity and convexity – in short, with the polarity of forces – opens up the secret of creating forms out of the non-spatial and can lead one to a grasp of the spiritual. Definite laws are at work here, as exemplified in the forms of the columns.

"The essential thing is the transition from one form to the other, since what underlies this transition is the same law-guided process of cosmic becoming underlying the transition from the formation of Saturn to the formation of the sun in the universe. Not that these forms are like symbolic imprints of Saturn and the sun; rather, underlying Saturn and the sun is an inner lawfulness that can actually be seen. And it is this same inner, observable lawfulness that has been developed in the forms here." (January 24, 1920)

This intrinsic lawfulness, to which Rudolf Steiner repeatedly drew the sculptors' attention, reflects the formative forces out of which the motifs were created.

"Everything that one experiences artistically like this takes shape in the fantasy, the imagination, as something quite self-evident; one cannot do otherwise; it simply comes about in this way. And one can hardly say anything else about it either. Yet the remarkable thing is that when one simply lets one's own experience flow into the forms, one comes to feel that one is creating in accordance with nature's own process of creation." (June 12, 1920)

The Large Cupola

The movement embodied in the metamorphosing forms of the sculpted reliefs progresses from west to east in the large cupola and from east to west in the small one. The immediate impression – even the photograhs convey something of this – is that of music in motion. The eye palpately follows each form as it shoots upwards or curves around, bends smoothly or corners sharply, tautens or relaxes. It skims across the surface, pondering the

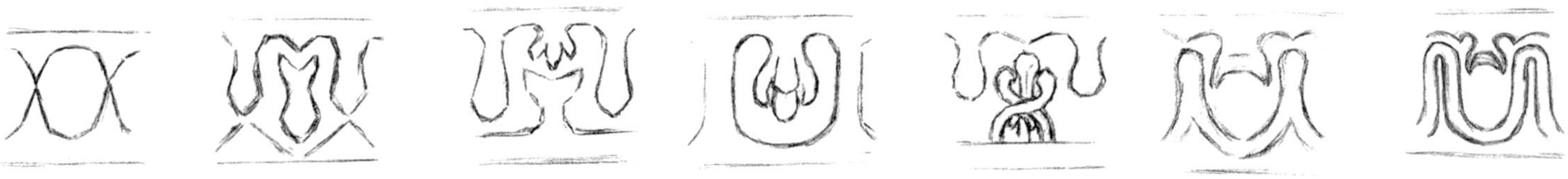

Capital Motifs in the Large Cupola

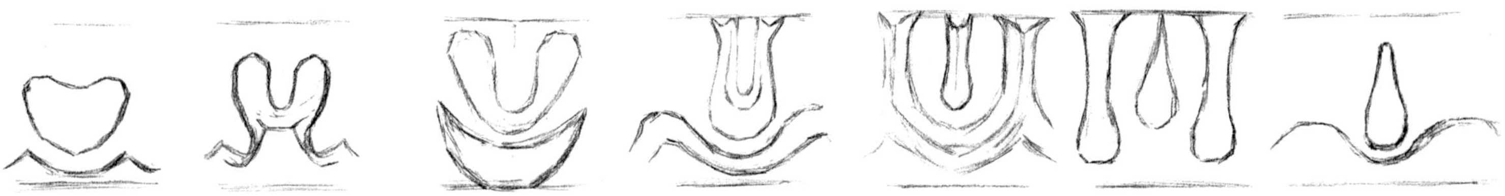

Pedestal Motifs in the Large Cupola

Drawing by Carl Kemper

sheen and hue of the several woods of the columns. The varieties of wood used in constructing the model are the same as those later employed in the Goetheanum itself: white beech, ash, cherry, oak, elm, maple and birch.[2] Here, the capitals and pedestals have been modelled in plasticine on the wood, as has the cupola-bearing wreath of architraves above the columns.

"The two columns flanking the organ gallery at the back of the hall have the simplest capital and pedestal motifs: forms which seemed to strive from above downwards, countered by others striving upwards from below. This form of the interaction of above and below, here in its most primitive state, is metamorphosed in the subsequent architrave, capital, and pedestal forms. I arrived at this progressive metamorphosis while working on the model literally in the following way: by trying to sense artistically what it is that comes to form in the forces of nature when, in the development of a plant, at first something primitive – a smooth-edged leaf with primitive forms – takes shape below; then, the higher one goes, the more markedly this primitive state becomes metamorphosed into a differentiated, indented, more complexly-formed leaf, even changing into petal, stamens and pistil." (August 28, 1921)

The Motifs of the Pedestals

The first column expresses a primeval condition fraught with latent becoming. Germinating and sprouting begin in the second. The third column opens to the light, receiving the light, moon-like. There is a contraction and swelling below in the central form. The germinating form contracts, the periphery reverberates in like gesture in the fifth form. The contraction intensifies further in the sixth. The seventh form appears almost seed-like, crystalline.

The Motifs of the Capitals

Simple, austere configurations above and below approach each other in the almost crystalline gesture of the first capital. This swells out and opens up in the next one, while an inward concentration takes place in the third. In the fourth and central capital, the forms achieve a degree of self-containment. The transition from the fourth to the fifth results in a complete reversal of forces. The staff, with snake-like forms winding around it, stretches from below upwards. In the sixth capital, the staff of the fifth spreads out below and the drop-like form above enlarges to form a chalice facing downwards. In the seventh everything is vibrant, musical movement.

The Architraves

The forms of the architraves can be compared with musical intervals. From the austere saturnian arches by the west entrance, the movement dissolves into a questioning, like that aroused by the interval of the second, and then into the rhythmic undulation of the third. Here the flow of movement abruptly ends, making room for the two interweaving staffs of Mercury above the fourth column, where the architrave forms advancing from west to east meet those coming from east to west. Whereas the forms of the first three motifs appear to be guided and held from above, the forces of the last three seem to work from below.

"Misunderstanding may arise in that, for example, in the capital of the fifth column and again in the architrave above the fourth column, something makes its appearance which seems to resemble a Staff of Mercury .... The motif that you see on the fifth column evolved entirely out of metamorphic transformation. I did not in the least think of moulding a staff of Mercury; it arose [out

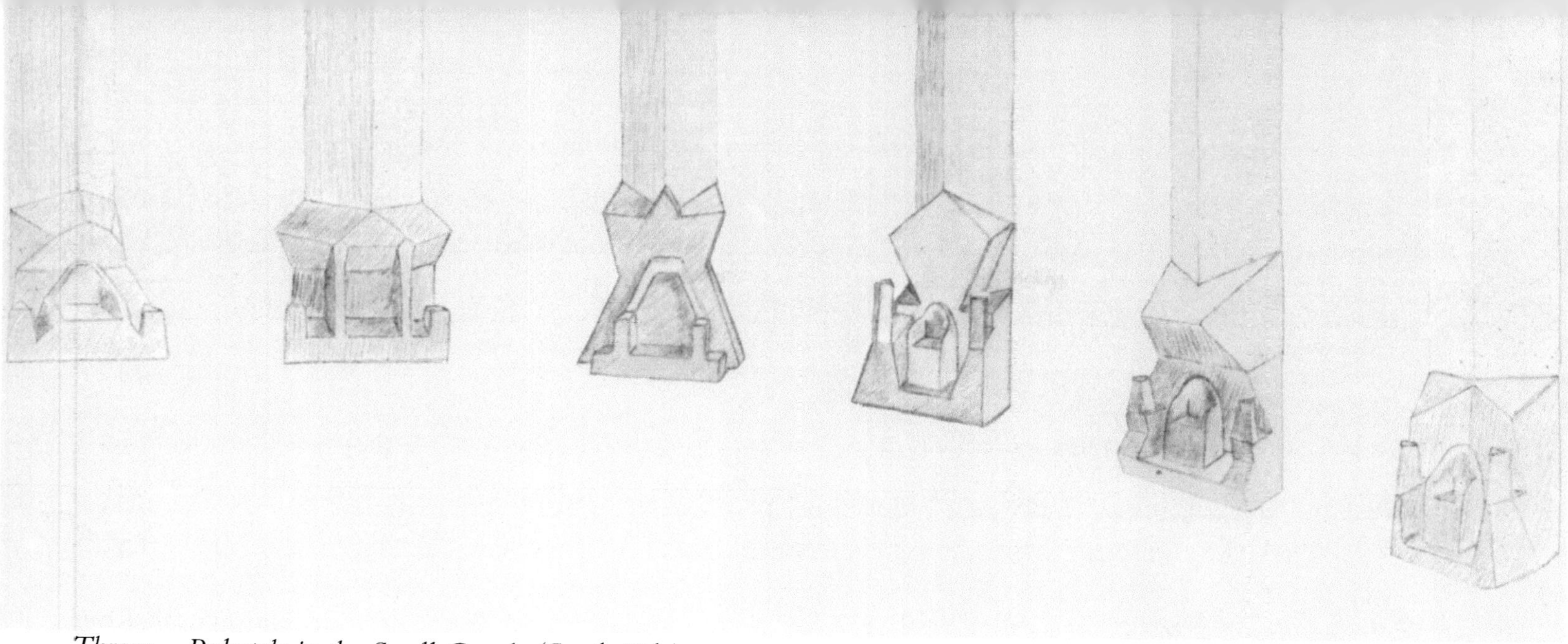

Throne – Pedestals in the Small Cupola (South Side) *Drawing by John Meeks*

of the previous form] like the petal arises from the leaf of the calyx." (August 28, 1921)
Due to the inclination of the floor of the auditorium – lowest by the stage in the east and highest at the entrance in the west – the columns and architraves correspondingly increase in height and thickness from west to east.

The Small Cupola

The small cupola exhibits a completely different character than the large cupola. First of all, the twin series of seven columns in the large cupola face two groups of six in the small one. Moreover, whereas the forms of the pedestals in the large rotunda seem to accompany those of the capitals, in the small one the forms of the pedestals – also called throne-pedestals or thrones – are shaped by an austere but expressive treatment of the surface. The first throne-pedestal, starting in the east, has rounded, lightly-swelling forms. The second brings a dualistic element to expression. The third is fashioned from two interpenetrating triangles. Thus far, the seats, which are strongly geometric and architectonic, appear to be determined and bound by cosmic forces. In the subsequent three pedestals, they appear more independent of their surroundings, and the formative forces are more in the background. Thus, a pentagram appears in the fourth throne, with the fifth and sixth freely corresponding to the second and first, respectively.
In addition, the central motifs of the architraves in the small cupola do not occur directly above a column, as do the motifs in the large cupola, but *between* the third and fourth columns. This would suggest a division of the twelve into four groups of three. Whereas the progression of motifs in both cupolas emphasizes the east-west or west-east axis, the central forms of the architraves accentuate, in their conjunctive function, the north-south axis. Indicated in the model are the southern halves of the architrave forms above the west entrance, the stage arch, and the 'baldachin' in the east (beneath which Rudolf Steiner's sculpture, *The Group*, was to have been placed). Their northern counterparts must be imagined as a symmetrical continuation of the forms.
Although Rudolf Steiner spoke at length about the reliefs in the large cupola, he said very little about those of the small. The following description was given as a response to a workman's question about the throne-pedestals. "There the world of the stars has descended, and the living-organic has been pushed up to the architraves." Assja Turgeniev who communicated this statement, adds, "... a reply which can open up far-reaching insights into the relationship between the two cupolas."[3]
The connection between the seven columns of the large hall and the world of stars had already been indicated in the first sketches, where the columns bear the names and the symbols of the seven planets (see page 24). These seven columns strove toward the spatially smaller but spiritually more comprehensive chamber of the Twelve, the small cupola.
Unlike the sculpted surfaces of the walls and columns, the ceilings of the two cupolas were smooth, primed for painting. In the west ceiling of the model, Rudolf Steiner painted the streams of color that were to serve as a chromatic background for the motifs of the large cupola (see page 51). Above the entrance can be seen a sketchy suggestion of the first two motifs, 'Elohim' and 'Eye and Ear'. In some of the sketches, the correspondence between the forms of the throne-pedestals and the motifs to be painted above them is evident.

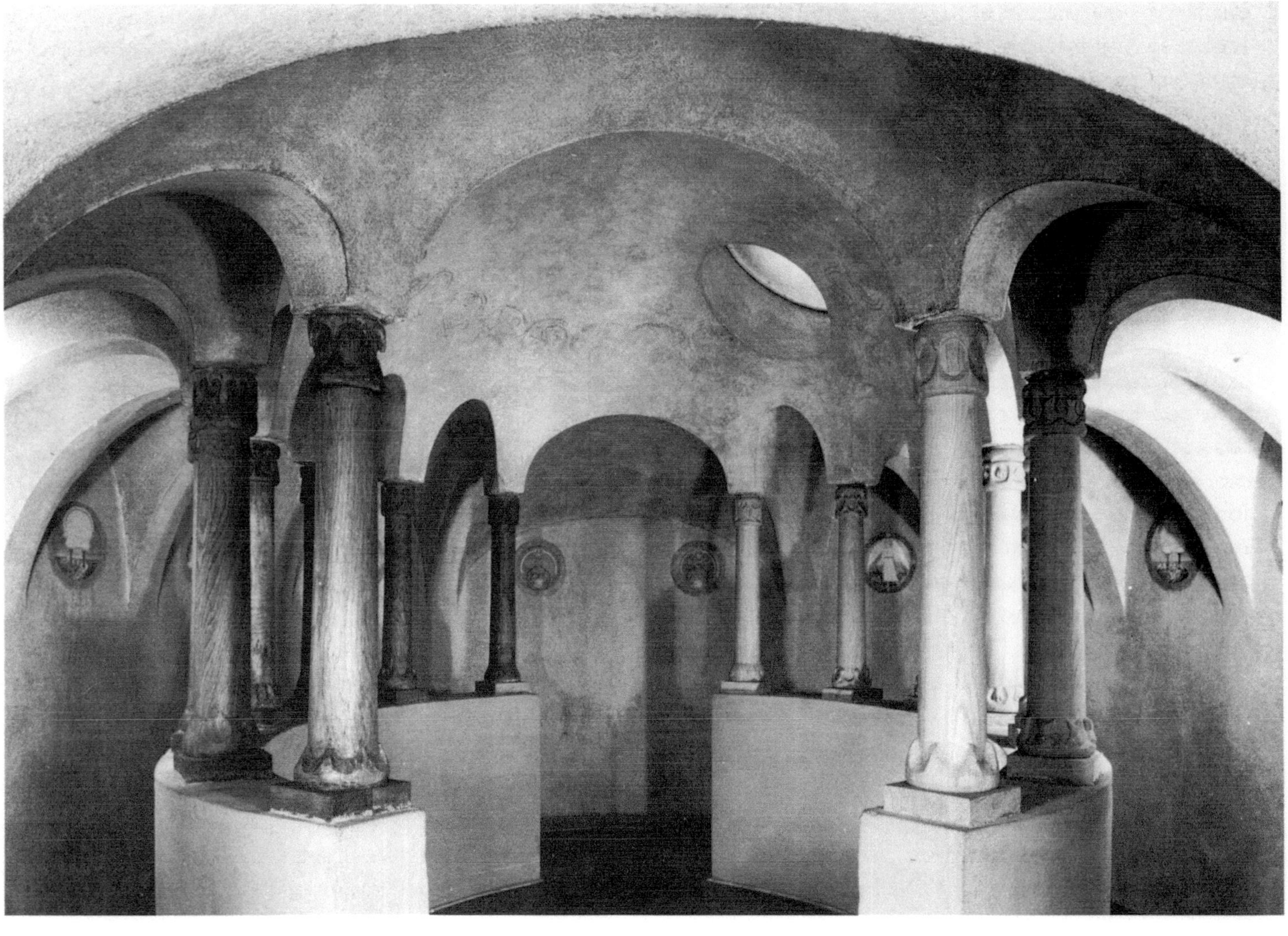

Scale Model building in Malsch

PRECURSORS

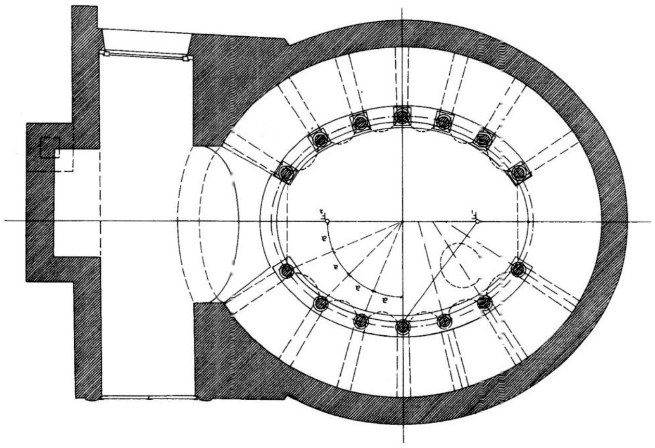

Floor plan of the scale model building in Malsch
Drawing by Albert von Baravalle

What led to the creation of this incomparably harmonious, richly-sculpted model? What circumstances enabled its translation into an edifice housing a theater with nearly a thousand seats? To answer these questions, several important stages preparatory to the development of the Goetheanum must be taken into account.[1]

1907: The Congress in Munich

The first major occasion providing Rudolf Steiner with an opportunity to present new artistic forms arose at a congress in Munich in May 1907. These forms were an expression of the inner life, born of "spiritual hearing" and "spiritual sight". The seven "planetary" columns stem from spiritual hearing and the seven "apocalyptical" seals, seal-like designs from the Revelation of St. John, were derived from spiritual sight.
Because of time limitations, the columns were simply painted on narrow boards about two meters high. Each was topped with its own, unique capital and bore a planetary symbol, one after another expressing a major evolutionary stage of the world and man. These "columns" were placed against the wall all around the hall in alternation with paintings of the seven apocalyptic seals. The walls themselves were covered with red cloths. Rudolf Steiner had wanted to drape blue material across the ceiling to give the impression of arches, but had to forego the idea because of limitations imposed with the rental of the hall. This intention, to imbue the hall with a polarity of red and blue, found expression in the colors of two columns placed at the front of the auditorium. One, red, bore the letter 'J'; the other, blue, bore 'B', the initials for Joachim and Boas, the two pillars of Solomon's Temple.[2]

Busts of Hegel, Schelling and Fichte, representative of individualistic, middle-European striving for knowledge, were placed in front of the podium. In the Goetheanum several years later, the paintings immediately above the speaker's pult depicted a powerful imagination of the "Thinking, Feeling, and Willing I."
At this congress, lasting but a few days, Rudolf Steiner gave the first impulse towards a renewed and spirit-imbued art, an impulse that came to fruition in the first Goetheanum.

1909: Scale Model Building in Malsch

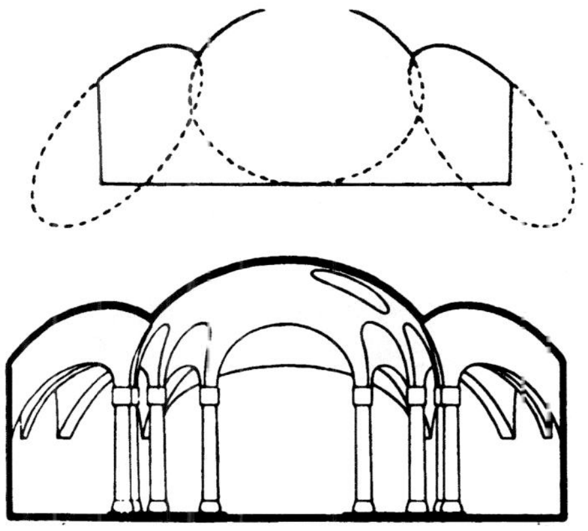

Elliptical construction of the building in Malsch
Drawing by Erich Zimmer

"Columns want to stand three-dimensionally in space; they want to be built!" thought Karl Stockmeyer, a mathematics student, upon seeing the cardboard drawings of pillars at the congress in Munich. He asked Rudolf Steiner to describe the architecture of an edifice that would suit actual columns of such design and, in response, was given several indications for an elliptical

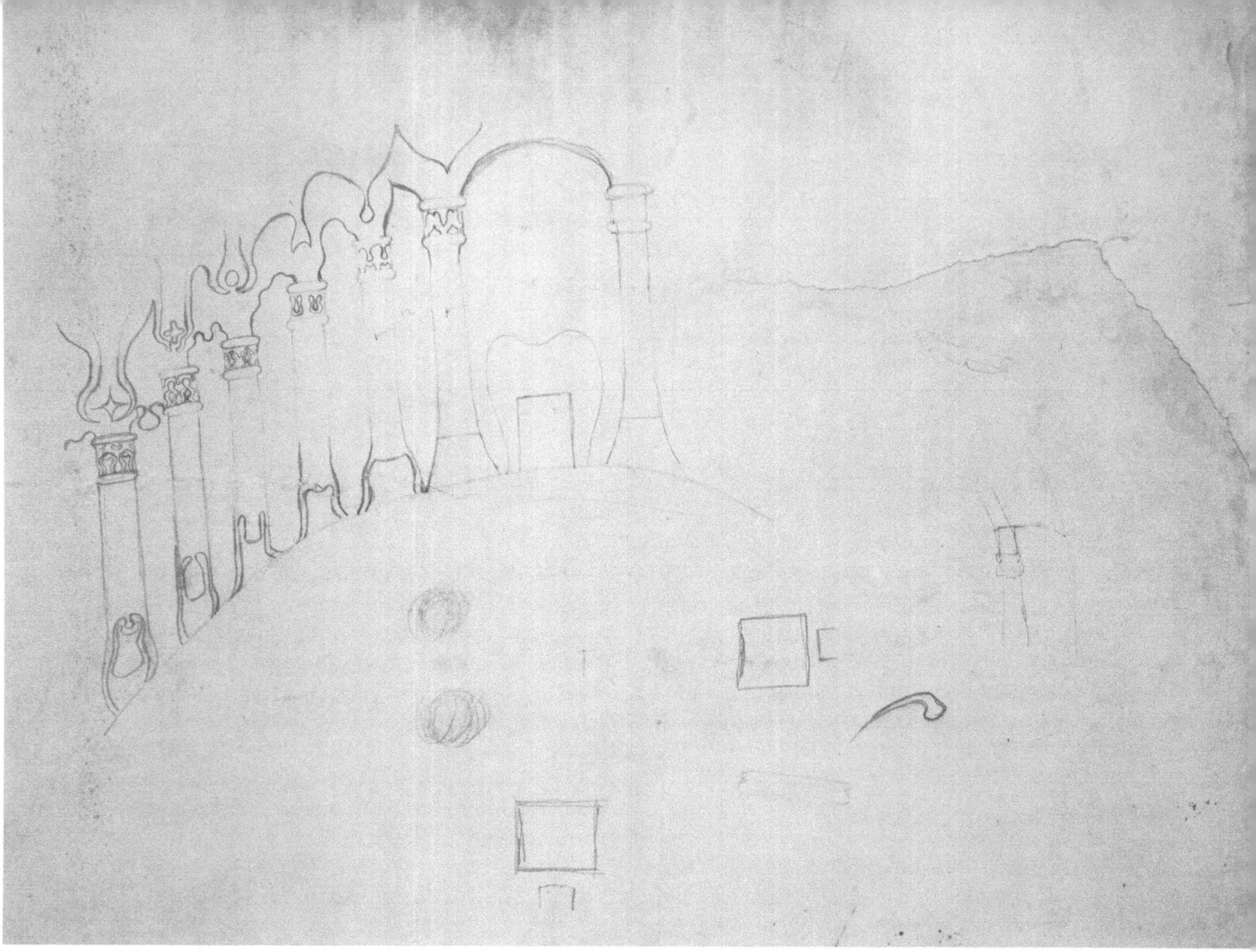

Rudolf Steiners' first sketch for the columns and architrave on the north side of the Small Cupola

structure. He and his father then undertook construction of a small, scale model building in Malsch, near Karlsruhe.

The building, which still stands today, is about $3^1/_2$ meters high. Two rows of seven columns, complete with capitals and pedestals and carved out of oak, support the elliptically arched ceiling. The entrance lies in the west; the speaker speaks from the east.

The apocalyptic seals have been painted directly upon the red-madder walls, with the signs of the zodiac painted in gold upon the arched, indigo-blue ceiling.

Karl Stockmeyer and his father were unable to finish the project. Architect Albert von Baravalle undertook its completion in 1958, even painting the walls and ceiling, seals and zodiac signs; Gertrude Hahn, the sculptress, then finished the columns, of which only one row had been carved.[3]

The pairs of seals and columns mirror each other in the succession from west to east. The colors of the seals shine between the wooden columns. Rudolf Steiner had suggested carving the columns out of Siberian syenite, which has a greenish hue. The green of the stone would have been magnificent against the red of the walls.

At the spring and autumn equinoxes, a ray of light passes through a small window in the ceiling and falls upon the first, the Saturn column. All in all, the little building gives the impression of a strong, self-contained work of art and awakens a festive, sacred mood.[4]

1911: Festival Hall in Stuttgart

In 1911, Rudolf Steiner designed an auditorium and a festival hall for the fledgling anthroposophical movement's building in Stuttgart. The former was painted blue, a color Rudolf Steiner considered appropriate for regularly scheduled work; the latter was done in red and blue, arousing a mood of festive gathering. For the first time, Rudolf Steiner described the difference in the effects of transparent and luminous colors.[5]

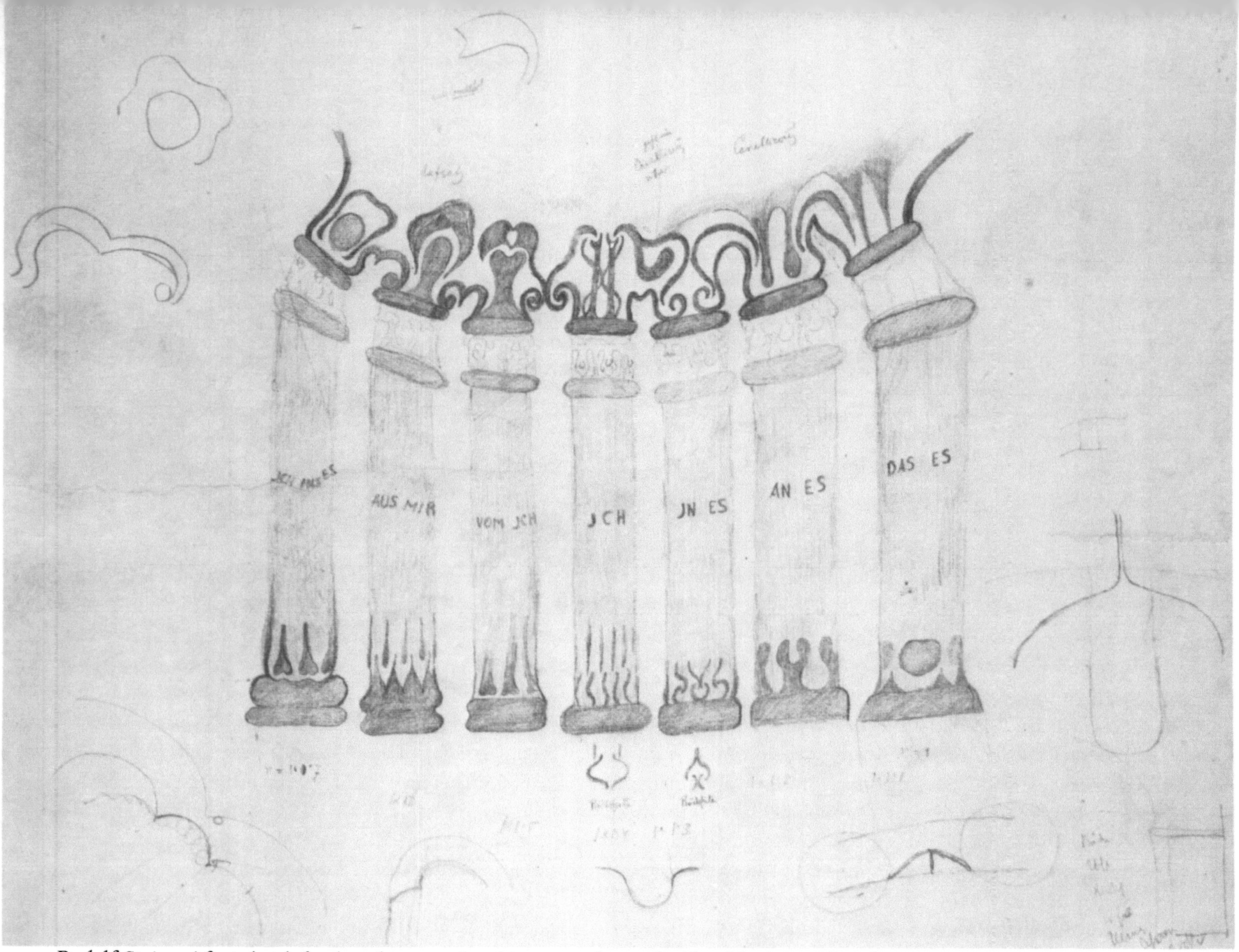

Rudolf Steiners' first sketch for the columns and architrave on the south side of the Large Cupola

The festival hall was built into a large room of the house along the lines of the Malsch model, but adapted to the existing, almost square structure so as to form a wide-bodied ellipse approaching the dimensions of a circle with a diameter of about ten meters. Drawings of the apocalyptic seals were placed on the red walls and Imme von Eckardstein painted golden zodiac signs on the indigo-blue ceiling, according to pencil sketches and suggestions by Rudolf Steiner.[6]

1911–1913: Berlin and Munich

On the twelfth of December 1911, Rudolf Steiner gave a lecture in Berlin about the Johannes Building, a double-cupola theater and center for the Anthroposophical Society planned for construction in Munich. That lecture remains one of his fundamental expositions on an architectural style unfolding from a new cognition of the spirit.[7] In it, he fully expounds on the basic architectural concept of two interpenetrating cupolas; however, no indications are given for the exterior design, probably because plans called for surrounding the building with apartment houses.

Two sketches he drew of the interior, one for the large cupola, the other for the small one, show the strong, expressive movements of the architraves and faintly suggest the color ground of the cupolas.

Upon the seven columns of the sketch for the large rotunda, he wrote a sequence of words in mantric form that echo stages in the development of the 'I'. The columns in the sketch for the small cupola show, for the first time, forms for the throne-like pedestals.

The building in Munich was to be constructed of concrete. Prolonged hindrance by local authorities prevented its execution.[8] Rudolf Steiner then moved the whole project to a plot of land donated in Dornach, Switzerland, where the first Goetheanum was then constructed: a double-cupola building carved out of wood and standing on a concrete base.

A NEW BUILDING;
A NEW IMPULSE IN ART

Construction began immediately after the foundation stone was laid on September 20, 1913. First the terrace was poured in concrete, then the wooden framework built on top of it. The stages of construction can be followed in dated photographs.

The magnitude of the project remains vividly inscribed in the memories of elderly townspeople of Dornach who still tell of the days when enormous wagonloads of timber drove through the village and on up the hill, astonishing everyone. Hundreds of carpenters, many of them shipbuilders, came to help with the work.

The building planned for Munich was to be hidden by surrounding apartment houses. Consequently, although its interior was minutely designed, its outer face was left bare. The Goetheanum in Dornach, however, was to stand freely in the open landscape, presenting Rudolf Steiner the added challenge of working out an organic design for the exterior.

Carl Kemper's drawings show how this 'organic style' comes to expression in the forms of the west facade, how static forces like weight and support, push and pull are carried over into the sphere of living forms.

Intense artistic activity developed at the construction site. There was carving in the *Schreinerei*, a new technique for glass engraving, new priming, plant colors, and a special lasur technique for painters, as well as the further unfolding of the new art of eurythmy from its first beginnings. Rudolf Steiner suggested and demonstrated new approaches to the manifold areas of endeavor.

Woodcarving

Carving the capitals, pedestals, architraves, as well as the exterior architecture entailed a tremendous amount of work. The capitals alone were about one meter high and the architraves above them looked like mountains. Although some of the workmen were experienced sculptors, most had never held a mallet and chisel in their hands. Natalie Turgeniev-Pozzo describes their first attempts at carving the capitals.

"On the first day of our job as sculptors, a row of wooden blocks stands before us. They are more than a meter in height and in breadth. Dr. Steiner had made small models of the capitals. [We were to hew their forms out of these prepared blocks.] We take hold of the chisels and mallets. Most of us timidly begin cutting away at the corners. The wooden mallets are very light; unpracticed hands could not hold heavier ones. It takes a big effort to split off just a couple of chips. We turn to each other for advice, tap again on the wood, and we are already tired. Even the few sculptors among us have never tried anything like this before. Our arms ache, and there is nothing to show for the work. The second day, Dr. Steiner comes, picks up a mallet and chisel, steps up, as we did, onto an overturned crate and begins to work. It is the first time for him, too, but after just a few blows he is completely oriented in the work and steadily cuts off one little chip after another. He hammers away like that for ten minutes, an hour, without pause. Without even moving off the crate, he continues for nearly two hours. We stand around him at a light distance, pale with fatigue, our eyes staring wider and wider in speechless astonishment, unable to move. We had already experienced ourselves how difficult it was."[9]

Assja Turgeniev described the work on the architraves. "It was wonderful to chisel out the big, soft curves of the architraves and to watch Rudolf Steiner work among us. He cut a lengthwise plane into the curvature at the right side of the central form and suddenly deepened it concavely, saying, 'This is like the shoulder – an arch within the arch. One should sense warmth and love in the concave.' We learned to cut convex surfaces as flatly as possible. 'Astral fat' was the term he employed to describe unduly round forms. Aiming towards that flatness, Jan Stuten carved his forms almost geometrically. Rudolf Steiner praised these the most. 'One must cut from the plane to the edge, not conversely; the edge should be determined by the plane; one should await it with curious expectation'."[10]

On one occasion he described the woodcarving process in the following way: "In the left hand is the feeling; feel the form with the chisel; in the right is the power. The most important thing is that the two work together."[11]

Convex and concave, outward curves, and inward curves, cold and warmth as formative forces in the process of sculpting the curved plane that is curved again – all this can help us to experience the relationship between our inner world and the outer world of nature.

"One will find, for example, that if one curves a plane and then doubles the curve so that the curve is curved again, one arrives at the simplest archetypal phenomenon of inner life. A plane that is curved in such a way that the curve is again curved can be used in a multiplicity of ways, so that – of course, this has to be worked out further – the inner life of what is experienced as surface arises out of the surface itself. These things show us that a relationship exists between nature outside and the inner nature of man which, in truth, has a sensory-supersensory character." (February 17, 1918)

Often the corrections were humorous: the form looked like a reptile or mollusk, or was too fat. Further indications came then in lectures.

"Very, very much in the nature of sculpted relief will be found carved into the wood in the interior of our building. It will be full of pure forms that otherwise are not to be found in the physical world – forms, however, that express a progressive development, as if one were to begin with strong, individual beats between the Saturn columns at the back [of the hall] and so go forward symphonically in harmony to close with a finale in the east. Forms these are, forms that are so little present in the outer, physical world, as melodies are so little present. These forms are walls that have been brought to life. Physical walls do not come to life, but etheric walls, spiritual walls, they shall come to life!" (June 17, 1914)

The Goetheanum and Eurythmy

Rudolf Steiner worked on shaping the forms of the first Goetheanum and, at the same time, on the development of eurythmy. His statements leave no doubt that, for him, a direct relationship exists between the two. 'Eurythmy probably could not have been found without the work on the building. Before the Goetheanum was architecturally conceived [eurythmy] existed only in a very rudimentary stage."[12]

Rudolf Steiner already had given the first elementary lessons in this new art of movement to Lory Smits in 1911. These came about as a result of a question the young woman's mother had asked him in December of the same year. "Wouldn't it be possible, through certain rhythmical movements, to heal, strengthen and regulate the physical body by way of the etheric body, which is the home of everything rhythmical, as well as of health and illness?" Rudolf Steiner answered enthusiastically in the affirmative and spontaneously offered to give the necessary instruction. Thus Lory Smits was given the first exercises from which the practice of eurythmy then developed: stepping, alliterative stress, and the first indications for the sound gestures.

In 1912, in the sixth scene of *The Guardian of the Threshold* eurythmic gestures were demanded by a dramatic work for the first time. There groups of luciferic and ahrimanic beings were to move in a dance-like fashion in 'thought forms', like snakes and lightning, one group in fiery red and the other, belonging to Ahriman, in bluish green. At first, only a few choreographic forms and gestures were given for the contrasting character of the movement of the two groups.

In April 1912, Rudolf Steiner gave lessons to three beginning eurythmy students in the gestures, showed the rod exercises and built up the basic elements of eurythmy, so that small performances became possible.[13] Later, more young people came along to learn the elements of the eurythmic art under the direction of Marie Steiner. Rudolf Steiner gave them ever new suggestions for experiencing the sounds of vowels and consonants. These should be experienced and formed in colors: every stretching as light, every bending, as darkness, as for example, the light-imbued *EE*; the warm, embracing *O*, the dark *OO*, tending towards blue; the sheltering, enveloping *B*; the opening, receptive *AH*.

The sensory-moral experience of color, movement and sound then grew into the expression of tone, and of the chord, that then became visible in the performing eurythmist. An essential aid in this regard are the eurythmy figures Rudolf Steiner created to show the colors of the sound gestures. They provide inexhaustible material for studying the experience of sounds and the musical moods of major and minor in movement, feeling, and character.

The rehearsals provided a fresh stimulus to new tasks. Tone eurythmy was born. To 'visible speech' was added 'visible music'. The poetry and music performed onstage were accompanied by, and sheathed in, a colored lighting corresponding to the inner quality. 'Light eurythmy' or 'color eurythmy' came into being.

"When the human being reveals his soul through speech or song, he is present with his whole being. He is, one could say, *in his natural tendency*, in motion throughout his body. But he does not bring this tendency to expression. He arrests this motion as it emerges and concentrates it in the organs of speech or tone. Looking at this with – to use the Goethean expression – sensory-supersensory vision, one can see which tendency of motion in the human being's entire bodily constitution underlies a musical sound, spoken sound, harmony, melody or speech image. Thus it is possible to have people, or groups of people, perform movements that bring musical or spoken sound to *visible* expression in exactly the same way that the organs of speech or song make this *audible*. The whole person, or group of people, becomes a larynx; the movements speak or sing like the larynx sings or speaks."

In the year 1915, eurythmy was integrated into some scenes of Goethe's *Faust*; at Easter, in the 'Burial' and 'Easter Night' scenes and at Whitsun, in the 'Ariel' scene.

In August of the same year, 'The Twelve Moods of the Zodiac' was performed for the first time. These verses by Rudolf Steiner, written expressly for eurythmy, reach into cosmic spheres, to the zodiac and planets. They are fundamental not only to eurythmy as an art, but also to the relationship between eurythmy and the Goetheanum building itself, as expressed through the efficacious forces in the numbers seven and twelve.

"The world of forms governs the physical body; the

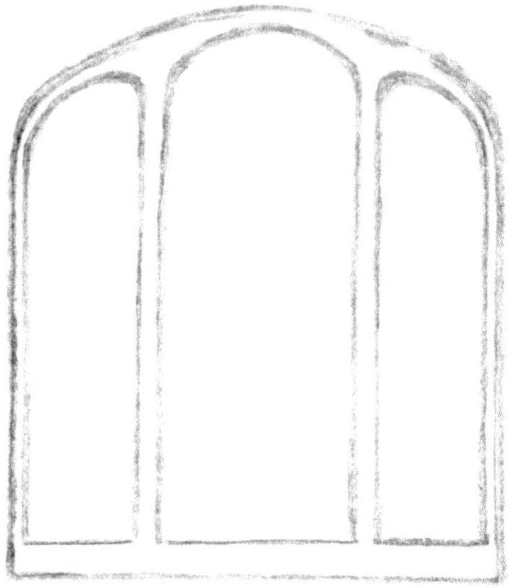

The Form of the Windows in the Large Cupola

world of movement governs the etheric body. Thus one has to find the etheric body's innate movements. The human being must be taught to bring to expression, through gestures and movements of his physical body, what is natural to the etheric body ... .
That is attempted in eurythmy. It will become apparent there that the human being, in his movements, is really an intermediary between cosmic letters, cosmic sounds, and that which we employ in the sounds and letters of our poetry. A new art will emerge in eurythmy. It is an art for everyone. And one would like to see humanity filled with understanding for this art ... . I have already spoken, in connection with many things, about the relationship of the large rotunda to the small one, the relationship between that which is in the large rotunda and [that which is in] the small one. Now, someone could ask: How do the smaller forms of our double-cupola building come forth from the larger ones? The answer is that if someone were to try to dance the forms of the large structure according to eurythmic laws, the forms of the small structure would come of it. If one pictures to oneself that someone were to unite his eurythmic movements with everything that comes to expression in the forms of the large rotunda, then dance into the smaller room and, dance what streams out from there, then the twelvefoldness of the columns and the cupola would emerge of themselves. And then I hope that still something else will dance eurythmically in the building, something invisible: The Word. *That* will provide a good acoustic experience." (October 7, 1914)

The Colored Windows

In the history of art, the technique of bringing pieces of colored glass into a composition, a picture, is well known. For the windows of the auditorium, Rudolf Steiner not only gave sketches for the motifs but also indications for a new technique. The windows, formed out of a solid piece of thick colored glass, were etched so that the motifs could shine forth "in confederation with the sun." The etching was done by means of a fine electric drill fitted with corundum.
A special atelier building for working on the windows, known as the Glasshouse, was constructed. Its window frames were made the exact size as those in the Goetheanum. Because of this it is still possible today to experience the proportions of the windows.
The colored windows had the following order: red for the ante-room in the west; then green, blue, violet and peach-blossom on the north and south sides of the auditorium. (see page 227)
Rudolf Steiner said that since each window had a different place, it should also have a different color. "By doing this, a musical and spiritual organization in the interrelation of outside and inside could be expressed. The only differentiation possible in a single colored window would be between thicker and thinner surfaces. Matter would present itself to the viewer in a thicker or thinner state. Light would shine more strongly through the thinner sections of the window and more weakly through the thicker sections. In this way the interplay between spirit and matter could be demonstrated." (June 17, 1914)
He spoke of the experience of light and the forming of this light experience out of color as a way into the spiritual world. "And the windows should show us while we look at what is represented by colored light and dark, 'Thus, O man, do you find your way to the spirit.' We will be shown how the soul stands in relation to

the spiritual world when during sleep it is out of the body. We will be shown the soul's relation to the spiritual world when, between death and rebirth, it is disembodied. We will be shown how man experiences the abyss when he reaches the threshold to the spiritual world. The stations on the way into the spiritual world will be shown. They will arise, as it were, like creations of the light coming in from the west and showing the mysteries of initiation. What is characteristic is that we create walls which cancel themselves, which obliterate themselves, through the way in which they are formed. What is portrayed in the windows must show, 'how we break through the wall'. We are shown representations of beings we meet when we seek the way to the spiritual world or, if we go unconsciously, what conduct we must show towards the spiritual world." (June 17, 1914)
The windows of the first building were done by six artists under the direction of Thaddäus Rychter. We must thank the willpower and dedication of Assja Turgeniev for the windows of the second Goetheanum.

Painting

In the painting, Rudolf Steiner strove to realize a new glazing technique (lazuring) in which the auric luminosity of color would be brought into appearance. He formulated this intention most clearly after the fire. On June 9, 1923, he said, "Color must be something which has emancipated itself from cumbersome matter. It is repugnant for color to be bound by heavy matter, particularly when it is used artistically. That is why it is incongruous to paint from a palette. When brought to the surface, the colors will always have something heavy to them. It is also difficult to establish a living relationship with them. One can really only establish such a relationship with fluid color. A color experience, a real comprehension of color, is achieved in the living interplay between the painter and a fluid color brought onto the surface. There the world arises out of color. Only in that moment when color gleams with the quality of revelation, emanates life and is vitally comprehended does the painterly arise. What then happens on the surface becomes creative; it becomes of itself a world. Then color is understood, understood as one of the ingredients of the world."
In order to attain this living luminosity, plant colors were manufactured and used. Because they are won from the realm of the living, they stand closer to life than synthetic or mineral colors. This is demonstrated by the fact that plant colors are not made of one chemically pure substance but a mixture of many substances. In this way light, which has also formed the plant, comes into a living interplay with a whole complex of substances. The technique of layered painting supports this vitality even more.[14] Roughly 650 m^2 of the combined surface area of both domes were given a ground and painted. The height of the different motifs varied from six to eight meters. In the smaller buildings which preceded the Goetheanum, color appeared only as a wall covering or on paintings. It was different in the cupolas. There the intention was to create a color space, to use color perspective. "We must not merely glance at color and use it as a covering, something superficial. We must again gain the possibility of living with color. We can only do this if the weaving and streaming of color becomes an immediate experience and we can submerge our soul in the way, for example, red or blue flows." (July 26, 1914).
On the inside of the model, Rudolf Steiner painted a rainbow which arose between blue and red. He also gave a hint how the first and second motifs could arise out of the colored background. The painters were astounded. Something entirely new in the history of painting had happened. For the first time streams of color formed the basis out of which the motifs blossomed. Arhild Rosenkrantz wrote, "What Rudolf Steiner had in mind for the painting in the large cupola can best be seen in the small model in which he painted his color conceptions. As is often the case with sketches, he was able to convey with a few prominent strokes a spontaneous expression of the whole as well as a vivid impression of what he intended. If it were possible to incorporate this concept into the finished work, the ideal Rudolf Steiner was striving for would have doubtlessly been achieved. But this was an overwhelming task for the small group of painters who dared to attempt to harmonize their diverse artistic talents into a single colossal composition."[15]
The first pencil and pastel sketches of the single motifs were given to the painters in the summer of 1914. The artists who stood before the enormous task of painting the cupolas were all different, not only in origin and temperment, but also in artistic ability and empathy. Rudolf Steiner endeavored to help each of them. Arhild Rosenkrantz described how personal and suited to the individual Rudolf Steiner's corrections were.
"Those lucky enough to work under Rudolf Steiner's direction in the first Goetheanum had special opportunities to ask his advice. He spoke personally with everyone

about how they could best find the right path. Although he gave much instruction and advice in countless art lectures during the construction of the Goetheanum, his personal help was of inestimable value.
No artist could ever have found a more sympathetic adviser than he was. It was a tremendous experience to entrust one's own work to Rudolf Steiner's opinion. He never expressed negative criticism, but rather he always looked for the positive in order to help the artist expand on the living elements in his work. Whenever one showed Rudolf Steiner an example of one's work, one sensed his extraordinary respect for the freedom of the other person. He never tried to talk the artist into anything, but rather he gave him indications which were helpful to his work."[16]
Margarita Woloschina also wrote about the first years of working together: "Nothing in this building was an imitation of the already actualized world. It was more like a creation out of the archetypal word and this word was in the world of color and received life in the glow of red and shone in yellow in the blue-green darkness as the light of the spirit."[17]
What was the intention? The colors and forms that arose out of the interplay of the color were like touching another world which was entirely new but not strange. In the large cupola, pictures of world development and the creation of man were to arise out of the streaming colors of the rainbow.
The sketch for the first motif arising out of the blue stream in the west shows, in a reddish-blue violet peachblossom, the Elohim at the beginning of the world. Alert, resonant and breathing, they are directing streams of light towards the depths, calling forth life through effective activity. Innumerable pictures of the creation have been painted but here, with the simple means of pastel and a few pencil marks an insight into the creative activity of spiritual beings is given. "Color must express that which it is able to express, so also the line. Here the attempt has been made to reach the macrocosmic, to overcome the limits of the borders of the cupola. Everything that is painted there belongs actually to the macrocosm. This intention is placed physically before the eye." (July 3, 1918)
The painters worked on the sketches of their motifs on small panels in a model of the cupolas and then eventually on the cupolas themselves. At the same time, Rudolf Steiner created in the beginning of 1917 a 9 ½ meter high model of the statue of 'The Representative of Man'. When the painters saw the middle figure they were disturbed by the discrepancy between their own endeavors and those which arose out of a direct spiritual experience. They asked whether they could rub out their own work. Arhild Rosenkrantz, the artist who painted the middle motif in the small cupola, was no longer in Dornach. He wrote saying that there could be no greater pleasure for him than having Rudolf Steiner paint over this work.[18] So it came about that Rudolf Steiner repainted or in parts overpainted the middle motif as well as the southern section of the small cupola. The painters were astonished how quickly Rudolf Steiner mastered the techniques of working with a brush. He could immediately take up working where he left off on the previous day. (see the quote of Luise Clason on p. 133)
Tatiana Kisseleff, the eurythmist who handed up the paint, tells how he painted broad surfaces with a sweeping gesture and then would stop and set strong accents. The countenance of the thinker became young, relaxed completely devoted to the activity of painting.[19] Surface was painted over surface, transparent, each flowing over the next. Eventually a motif would become recognizable. In this way a fiery flaring red became Lucifer; a hardened brown and blue-black became Ahriman and in a shining yellow between the two, the resurrected Christ appeared.
Rudolf Steiner stressed again and again that this kind of painting was still in its beginnings. He nevertheless expressed his satisfaction that he managed to paint the central motif entirely "out of the color".
Color photos were made. Even though color photography was at that time primitive, it is still possible to recognize how the surfaces were treated and to see how surface was laid over surface. A color depth arose which hitherto had never been seen in painting. The colors became windows and doors into a direct experience of the spiritual world. The impulse that "form be the deed of color" became visible reality. With this an entirely new direction was given for the development of the art of painting.
In 1918–19, Rudolf Steiner worked on his new picture of Christ. At the same time, he was intensively engaged with the need and questions of social renewal. The breadth of his work and its intensity can hardly be measured.
1918 brought the end of the First World War. Along with the collapse of Germany came revolution and social distress. The social question became a burning issue. During this time, Rudolf Steiner lectured in many cities, often in large factories before thousands of workers, on the reformation of the social organism. He also spoke

about the social question with many important public figures. Along with this, he provided teachers with the fundamentals of a pedagogy suited to the needs of the child and prepared the foundation of the Waldorf school. It lay in his heart that education should be built in such a way that the capacity for moral intuition be awakened, so that each human being would feel, "I am not only of the earth. I am not merely a product of heredity. I have descended from the spiritual world onto the earth and have as an individual a task to fulfill ... . This is ... what should be felt in the depths of the heart as the fundamental impulse underlying the social question of today. When we have learned how as human beings we can discover the other,then we have the possibility to bring something beneficial into social life." (August 29, 1922)

It was during this struggle for a new impulse in social life that Rudolf Steiner, after long absences of a month or more, would return to Dornach and once again climb the scaffolding in order to bring forth in luminous color the picture of Him who is love incarnate.

THE FIRE

In the autumn of 1919, the scaffolding inside the Goetheanum was dismantled. This gave an unhampered view of the architecture, sculpture and painting inside the building. Gropius had declared his goal to be "the building of the future". At the same time, the realization of Gropius' vision stood for all the world to see, but it remained unknown to a Europe devastated by war. Three years later this building was destroyed by fire.

There are many accounts of the fire. Each person who witnessed it experienced it differently. Heinz Müller spoke about the festiveness of the last lecture held there on New Year's Eve. The sky was clear and the stars shone brilliantly as he went to his room in Haus Friedwart. Suddenly there was a telephone call, 'The Goetheanum is on fire!' He rushed up the hill and went along to examine the heating and electrical systems, which were in order. Other evidence pointed to arson. They went for an axe. "Then we hastened onto the terrace. Rudolf Steiner pointed to a section in the wall where the south wing separated from the west wing. 'Chop a hole here.' I chopped a hole into the wall of the Goetheanum. I am not sure if you can understand what it meant to hew the beloved Goetheanum with an axe. I heard Rudolf Steiner say, 'More! Firmly!' Finally, a piece about the size of a brick broke away and fell inwards. In the same instant, the air was sucked in by the flames within. It howled. We retreated with horror. We heard Rudolf Steiner say in a choked voice, as if covered with ash, 'There is no possibility to save it.' ...

"The building had been burning a long time before flames were visible from the outside. The roof was by then almost completely destroyed. The walls on the side glowed. We had to make a large curve through the cherry orchard on the south side in order to reach the carpenters' sheds. The cupolas collapsed with terrible crackling. Soon the pillars peeled open through the intense heat. They stood like glowing lilies against the night sky."[20]

"By the dawn of New Year's day 1923, the ring of the double architrave, ... transparent as glowing glass, rested upon columns that had become light. The sky served as cupola. There were no longer single motifs left; they had all been consumed by the flames. The entire ground-plan rose up in radiant gold against the blue of the night." (Assja Turgeniev)[21]

The next day, a notice on the door of the carpentry workshop let it be known that every event on the program, including the eurythmy performance, the Three Kings' play and the lecture by Rudolf Steiner would be held. "Here the determination of the spirit was shown against the scene of destruction where the stumps of the columns were still burning on the concrete substructure."[22]

A year later Rudolf Steiner compared the burning of the Goetheanum with that of the Temple of Ephesus: "A year ago, on New Year's Eve, we looked upon the devouring flames which blazed against the sky. Dark blue and yellow-red lines of fire, from the melting metal instruments, darted in and out of the common sea of fire, a gigantic sea of fire glowing with the diversest colors. This sea of flame with its colored lines spoke to the suffering soul looking upon it. And there could be clearly read, 'The Envy of Man'. That which speaks from epoch to epoch in the development of mankind connects together, even in the greatest disaster. There is a common thread linking one of the disasters of antiquity and our own misfortune. At that time, a yet unfree mankind looked up to the gods. 'The Envy of the Gods' was written in the flames. Here, where mankind must find the quickening power of freedom within himself, 'The Envy of Man' was written in the flames. The statue of the god stood in Ephesus. The statue of 'The Representative of Man' was to have stood in the Goetheanum, reminding us of Christ-Jesus in whose wisdom we in all humility strive to unite ourselves, just as the aspirants in Ephesus strove to unite themselves with Diana of Ephesus.

The pain does not become weaker when the event of last New Year's Eve is brought into historical light. As I stood upon the podium for the last time, the inner gaze of the audience was directed toward the ascent out of physical regions into the regions of the stars where the Will, the Wisdom, and the Light of the spiritual cosmos is." (December 21, 1923)

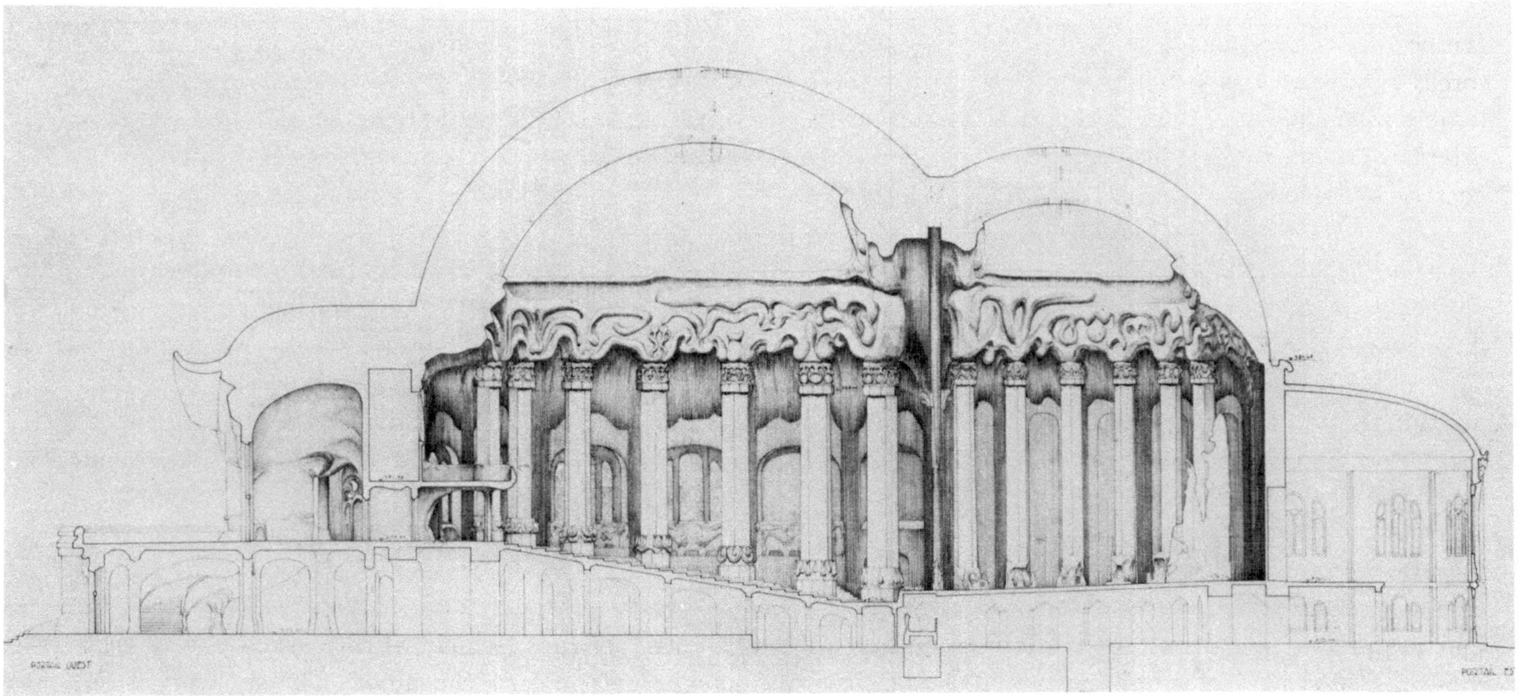

Drawing by L. Witta

AFTER THE FIRE

Is it possible to recognize and to grasp the basic spiritual forces which gave rise to this building, a building entirely new in the history of art? This task had been established by Rudolf Steiner even before the fire, for he repeatedly indicated its encompassing human and worldly character. Designs, models, sketches, Rudolf Steiner's own words, and reports of his co-workers still remain. Also spared by the fire were the interior model and the great wooden statue, which were still in the *Schreinerei*. The color sketches, which arose out of the immediate needs of the painters, appear to be even more important today than they were at the time of construction, in as much as it was possible to work directly under the guidance of the creator.

Repeated observation, appraisal and recreating of the color-tone, rhythm and experience of the thematic content give rise to questions about the relationships of these elements to one another, and of the relationship of colors to motifs. How did the image of threefold man glowing through the reddish streams in the east respond to the pictures of creation carried by the blue stream of color over the western architrave? How does motif relate to motif? How does column echo column? How does the large cupola speak to the small one and the small one to the large?

It becomes a search and an exercise, a task, to find the building from within, with the forces out of which it was formed. This building, which has been lost to outer view, will be experienced as spiritually present to the extent that the soul grasps and experiences the image of the human being given by anthroposophy.

Just as the architectural forms of earlier epochs reflected the corresponding levels of development, so the organism of forms and colors of the Goetheanum created a space in which modern man's inner need for the expansion of consciousness into spiritual vision became possible. There the spiritual was made 'visible', built out of the forces of thinking, feeling and willing.

"Let us ... observe a motif which would represent four columns covered by a cupola. One observes each such motif too narrowly if one looks at it as though it were self-sufficient. Nothing in the world is self-sufficient, no flower, no animal, no human being, but also not such a motif. For it is very much a part of such a motif that forces are present, which are independent of the geometric relationships within this motif. Geometrically, there are four columns which are covered by a cupola. But this geometry is only a part of it. That which belongs to it is a sum of forces active in the building up of the entire cosmos, which work in such a way that the columns can carry the cupola. The cupola rests on the columns. The columns stand on the earth. Gravity is involved.

"When we perceive such a motif, we perceive not only the one-sided *geometrical* element, but also the other. I have often called it the *dynamic*, the forceful: being placed in the force-filled configuration of the entire world, namely the earthly.

"If you now consider this motif, you will find this characteristic – that you can observe its symmetry from all points along the periphery. This motif is symmetrical on all sides, in all spatial directions, at least as far as the cupola is concerned. Thus we can say: A motif has been placed upon the body of the earth so that this motif spreads gradually upward and is symmetrical along the periphery.

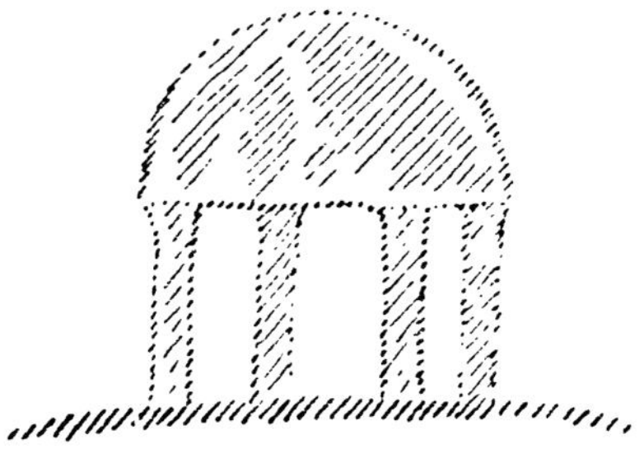

Now, it is a matter of perceiving such a motif. For to perceive such a motif artistically, that is the point. If we try to perceive such a motif properly, then we will realize – of course, it is a matter of really steeping oneself in the character of the form, steeping oneself in that which the form can say – then we will realize that this motif, which rises up from the earth and is symmetrical in all directions of space, at least in its upper part, this motif exercises an influence on us, as though we were to go into ourselves, and to experience our feelings inwardly." (October 24, 1914)

This sustaining feeling realm could be experienced in the first Goetheanum when one followed the columns from below upward, from the pedestal to the capital motif and onward to the form of the architrave above.

If one passes from standing to walking, if the feeling sphere is broken by active pacing, then one enters the will sphere. In the architecture of the building, the calm of the all round symmetry of the cupola is set into forward moving motion through the joining of two cupolas with only one axis of symmetry.

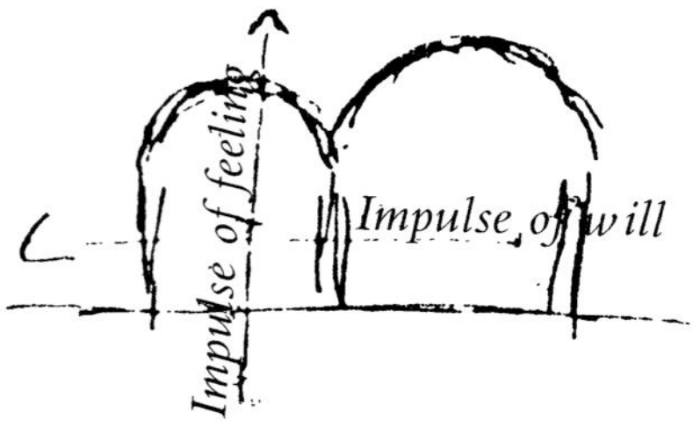

"In that moment, in which we transform the motif of the building into one which has only one axis of symmetry, the building expresses not only the experience of a transition from rest into feeling, but also the transition, within the human being, from feeling into willing, into walking. A striding motif is the motif of the will." (October 24, 1914)

Striding motifs were given in the pedestals, capitals and architraves as their forms moved from west to east. In feeling and willing one experiences two directions, one of which moves from below upward, the other striding forward. The sphere of thinking comes to expression when a conclusion is reached.

"You might also consider the staff of Mercury. If you carry it forward, it strides; if you raise it, it is uplifting; if you constrict the spiral at the top, or let it stiffen, then you will have its conclusion at the top. This conclusion towards the top represents the thinking sphere just as the forward striding represents the will sphere and the upward moving represents the feeling sphere."

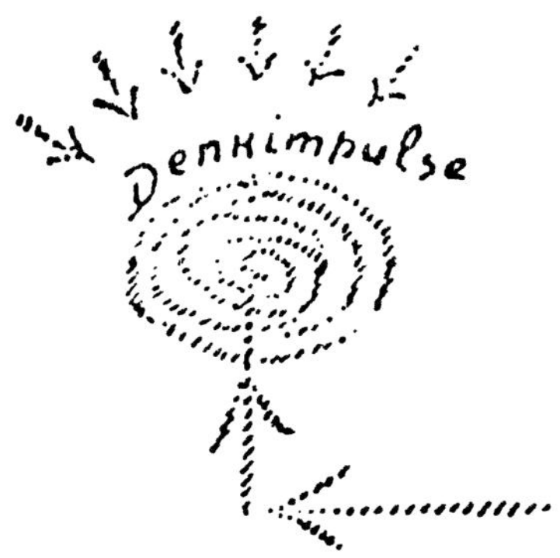

Impulse of thinking

The human being will arrive at a secure feeling about the entire evolution of mankind, if he absorbs that which lies in the form motifs of our columns and architraves, in as much as they raise themselves from below upwards. One might say: therein lie the motifs of mutual understanding of the earth's various cultural epochs." (October 24, 1914)

The conclusion of the upward movement is formed by the cupola paintings: the mighty pictures of human evolution in the large cupola, of spiritual guidance in the small one.

"Therefore, someone entering the building from west to east will receive in the striding movement, in the sequence of columns, that which expresses the will. In perceiving what moves from below upward, he will receive the European cultures and much else. What will he find in that which comes to meet him from the cupola?

He will receive what lives on earth in the secrets of spiritual development of all of humanity. Therefore, one will have to look up at this cupola and one will see on one side the secret of ancient Indian inspiration: how the Indian Rishis let flow into humanity that which was to enter ancient humanity during the Indian culture. In other words, that which was to enter mankind in the ancient Indian character, that is to be painted at one place in the cupola. How Zarathustra formed the ancient Persian culture, how the sunlight battled with the darkness, that will be seen at a second place. How the Egypto-Chaldean culture then gradually advances into the physical plane, while, however, astrological-spiritual conditions still permeate it, that will be found at a third place on the cupola. And as though standing at the abyss, the Greek, living in the rising intellectual or rational cultural epoch: how that which man is arises; how man is placed before the necessity of solving the riddle of the sphinx; how, because of the solution, he is thrust into the abyss, i. e., into himself; that will be represented at a fourth place. How the eternal divine powers and forces work into this evolution of humanity, this will come to expression through the depiction, in all four directions of space, of that which lies even further back than the post-Atlantean impulse of human evolution, namely that which lies in the Atlantean and Lemurian times: the Atlantean development will be in the south of the cupola, the Lemurian in the north.

And, finally, the result of the Lemurian and Atlantean times will be represented: that which our time should be, which will come to meet us out of the manner of the representation if we look from west to east toward the small hall to receive the impulse which is there in world evolution, and which expresses itself in the IAO. Not that this IAO is expressed symbolically; rather it finds expression in the motif. And if one looks from east to west, that will reflect what also speaks out of the depths of the cosmos into the evolution of culture, how the IAO speaks in the evolution of the soul from within. Man will perceive all that I have portrayed if he takes this cupola for his head which arches over his brain, if he frees the etheric body of the head and looks from within outward, where all I have described will reveal itself to him as a mighty imagination." (October 24, 1914)

Just there where the building found its final form, boundaries were once again overcome, for one's glance was not bound, rather it was led over into the spiritual. The building stood there as highest spiritual content, born of deepest artistic soul experience, ready to speak to the thinking, feeling and willing ego of the modern man who seeks the highest ideal.

"This painting on our cupola is not meant merely to cover a surface; rather, it should call forth this idea. If you strive upward, up to the surface of the cupola, you will find something. One must forget that there are physical walls. The physical aspect of what has been painted must be penetrated; one must see beyond the surfaces into the widths of the spiritual world. Perhaps one will not yet be able to achieve this with our building, but as the principle develops, perhaps mankind will be able, in the future, to see, out of what it has gained through spiritual science, a mighty cupola, but such a one as will, through its configuration, indicate the eternal in spiritual life." (October 25, 1914)

Thus the Goetheanum stood as the foundation stone building of a new era. Built amidst social chaos, out of the fullness of humanity, it wanted to show man a path to his higher self, a path to freedom, love and harmony. Yet unfinished, the building fell victim to human envy. The words which Rudolf Steiner spoke in Berlin in December of 1911, to express the building's impulse, indicate the needs of the soul, out of which mankind's future buildings will be wrought. The inner space should "be so formed, that every glance falls upon something that signifies the following. This expresses in color and form, in its entire language of color and form, in all that it is, in all its vitality, the same as that which is done and spoken in this place, as that which man can attribute to his own physical body, namely, the most spiritual within himself. And *one thing* will be in this building, which speaks of wisdom, of prayer concerning the human riddle, and of that which encloses the space. And in conformity with nature, it must be this: that the Word which pushes outward into space is so limited that it falls against the walls, and meets at those walls something which is so akin to itself, that it gives back to the inner space what will be given by man himself. A dynamic will spread out from the center of the Word to the periphery of the Word and that which offers itself as inner space should be a peripheral echo of spiritual knowledge and a spiritual message, not a breaking through as a window, but a limit, so that it is both limited and freed toward all the widths of spiritual eternity." (December 12, 1911)

THE LARGE CUPOLA

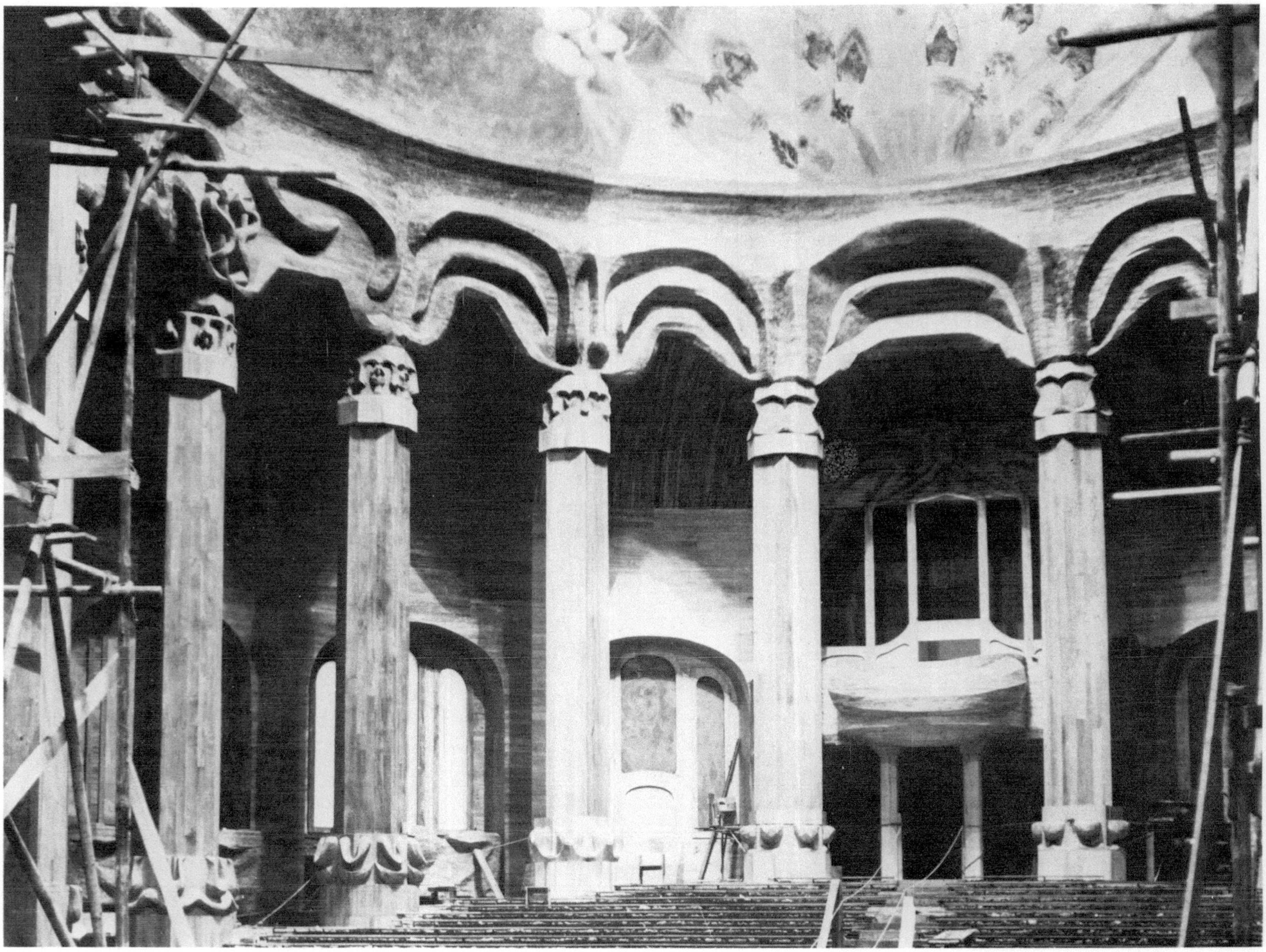

The Large Cupola

A SPACE FILLED WITH COLOR

Entering the building in the early evening of a sunny day and climbing up the stairs to the red beech antechamber, one would come upon the illumined west window and the room bathed in a glowing ruby red that was enhanced by the reddish wood.

The large auditorium answered the red in the antechamber with the green of the first window, followed by the blue, the violet, culminating in the peach-blossom window, whose light reached right up to the lectern. The three-part windows were set into the outer walls. Their light streamed in upon the different colored woods and filled the space, the brown oak reacting differently from the light shimmering birch when illuminated by violet or peach-blossom light.

This wealth of color was further heightened by the circular arrangement of the windows, the light of one window brightening another, and thus bringing about an intensive interplay of colored shadows. Heinz Mueller describes this experience as follows:

"What made the greatest impression on me ... was the color that lived both inside and outside the first Goetheanum. It was magnificent to see, for example, how the two cupolas reacted to each mood of sun and cloud, responding to the delicate morning tints or the powerful evening glow. Quite apart from the drama played out upon the blue-grey surface of the curved slate roof, there was the whole miracle of color that was revealed inside the building itself.

"It was a clear, bright sunny afternoon in high summer when I, quite alone, entered the south portal for the first time. At first, the eye had to get used to the dim light of the cool, concrete lower level. Then, passing through the colonnade and up the wide, curved double staircase, I entered the red beech antechamber of the large auditorium whence one could continue further up to the organ loft. Just a few steps in, deep red light streamed toward me from the mighty window over the west portal.

"This light filled the antechamber with its large-surfaced forms carved out of warm-hued wood, and it engendered a mood of reverence. This mood was deepened further when one looked upon the earnestly gazing countenance carved into the carmine red* window. Now one entered the large auditorium under the organ loft. Anyone who has not experienced this himself will find it difficult to imagine the ensuing miracle of color. The whole room, with all its objects, pillars, seats – yes, even the visitor himself – was enveloped in the radiant hue and gleam of the sunlight streaming in from the south through the three-part windows. Quite overpowered, I stood there for a while in deep awe until I began inwardly to understand the color the light took on as it poured through the etched windows: green, blue, violet, peach-blossom.

But even more astonishing! Where, for example, did the orange, the red, the yellow, in this intensity come from? Taking a few steps toward the Saturn pillar on the right, the one nearest the door, and then turning immediately to the second, the Sun pillar, a fleeting recollection came to my mind of the two weeks I had spent shortly before this visit at Goethe House in Weimar. There, I had especially studied the question of colored shadows, repeating Goethe's experiments with use of his own instruments. But here, all the colored lights and

---

**Translator's Note: 'Carmine red' is a translation of the German 'Purpur' which, as used in Goethe's Color Theory, refers to a red that has neither yellow nor blue in it. It is the exact middle, a pure red.*

shadows were living and weaving simultaneously, at once inviting the visitor to enter into their world. Almost involuntarily, I extended my hand, twisting and turning it in order to study the color phenomena playing upon it. As I did this, deeply involved in the play of color, I turned around to face the auditorium. Now the blue radiance from the second, the blue window, played across the back of my hand, and at the same time, an orange shadow appeared underneath! Then, a delicate green veil of color from the first window met the inside of my outstretched hand and a delicate rose shadow played upon the back of my hand. This prompted me to return a few steps to the Saturn pillar and immerse myself in the interplay of the complementary colors of red and green. Afterwards, I felt an urge to allow the colors streaming from the second, third and fourth windows and their shadows to quite systematically work on me.

This was relatively easy with the blue window and the accompanying orange shadow. However, the closer one came to the lilac and the peach-blossom windows, going down several steps, the further one moved away from all the windows. Thereby, the colors of the first windows were superimposed on the original lilac/yellow, pink/yellow-green. On the one hand, this newly created interplay of colors was richer in nuances but, on the other, it became weaker in intensity.

After I had observed this play of color upon myself for a long time, I turned back to the Sun pillar. Now with both hands, I followed this light-weaving interplay, and I realized that by sensing my way into this space, I could somehow begin to perceive the everywhere flowing, though at first invisible, light. As I experienced these overwhelming color harmonies, the following feeling began to take shape in my soul. Here the soul and the heart are receiving a gift. And the learning of the head is warmed by the heart. 'The Love of the Cosmos is at work'."[1]

Margarita Woloschin, the Russian painter, wrote in her memoirs, "It was as though the sun itself conjured these drawings out of the three-part windows which gleamed like gems beneath the dark, curved arch between the architrave and the wall ... . Colored light flooded the building, transforming the three-dimensional space into a richly differentiated, alive space and creating colored shadows on the surface of the columns and sculptured surfaces. The rows of wooden seats with their rounded backs shone like scales of mother-of-pearl, and each person who moved through this life-filled space appeared in ever new aspects."[2]

J. Lothar Gartner, who visited the building only a few days before it succumbed to fire, described his impression. "At the heart of the building, all colors and complementary colors in constant change converged upon the person walking towards the east. Because the building was circular, the flooding light met in the centre of the auditorium as in an ocular. Anyone who had the good fortune – as I had a few days before the fire – to walk through the building on a sunny winter afternoon, when the snow-covered landscape all around reflected the light to an even greater degree, entered into a sphere of weaving light. When he looked up, the changing forms of the pillars, capitals and architraves followed him. Looking at the stage, he saw the interplay of colors on the eurythmists. Had the building been completed, one knew that the striding Christ figure of the great, wooden sculpture in the background would have come towards the student enveloped in an interweaving play of color."[3]

Sketches for the Painting of the Large Cupola

- *The position of the Motifs in the Large Cupola (W. S. Pyle, circa 1929)*
- *Layout for the Color Movements of the Large Cupola (east on the top)*
- *Layout for the Window Motifs and Painting Motifs of both Cupolas*
- *Color layout for both Cupolas (the small cupola above, the large one below)*
- *The Model showing the Large Cupola*
- *The Elohim Work Creatively into the Earth; Light-Beings Radiate Light into it*
- *The Senses Arise, Eye and Ear Become*
- *Jehova and the Luciferic Temptation — Paradise*
- *Lemuria*
- *Atlantis*
- *The Ancient Indian*
- *The Ancient Persian*
- *The Ancient Egyptian*
- *Greece and the Oedipus Motif*
- *The Wrath of God and the Yearning-Grief of God – 'I'*
- *The Round of Seven – 'A'*
- *The Circle of Twelve – 'O'*
- *Study for the Position of the Motifs in the Large Cupola (Louise van Blommestein, 1951)*

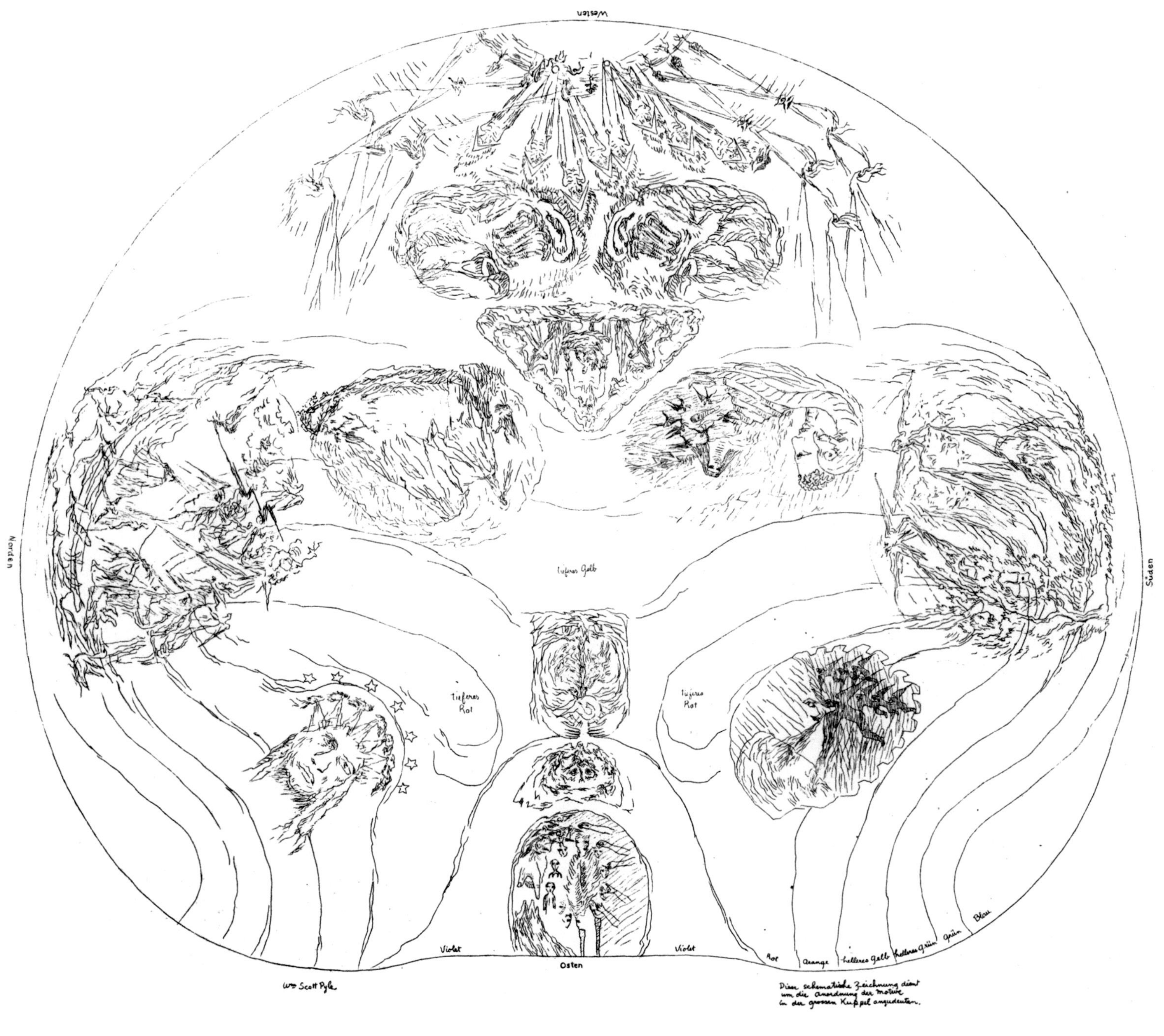

The position of the Motifs in the Large Cupola (W. S. Pyle, circa 1929)

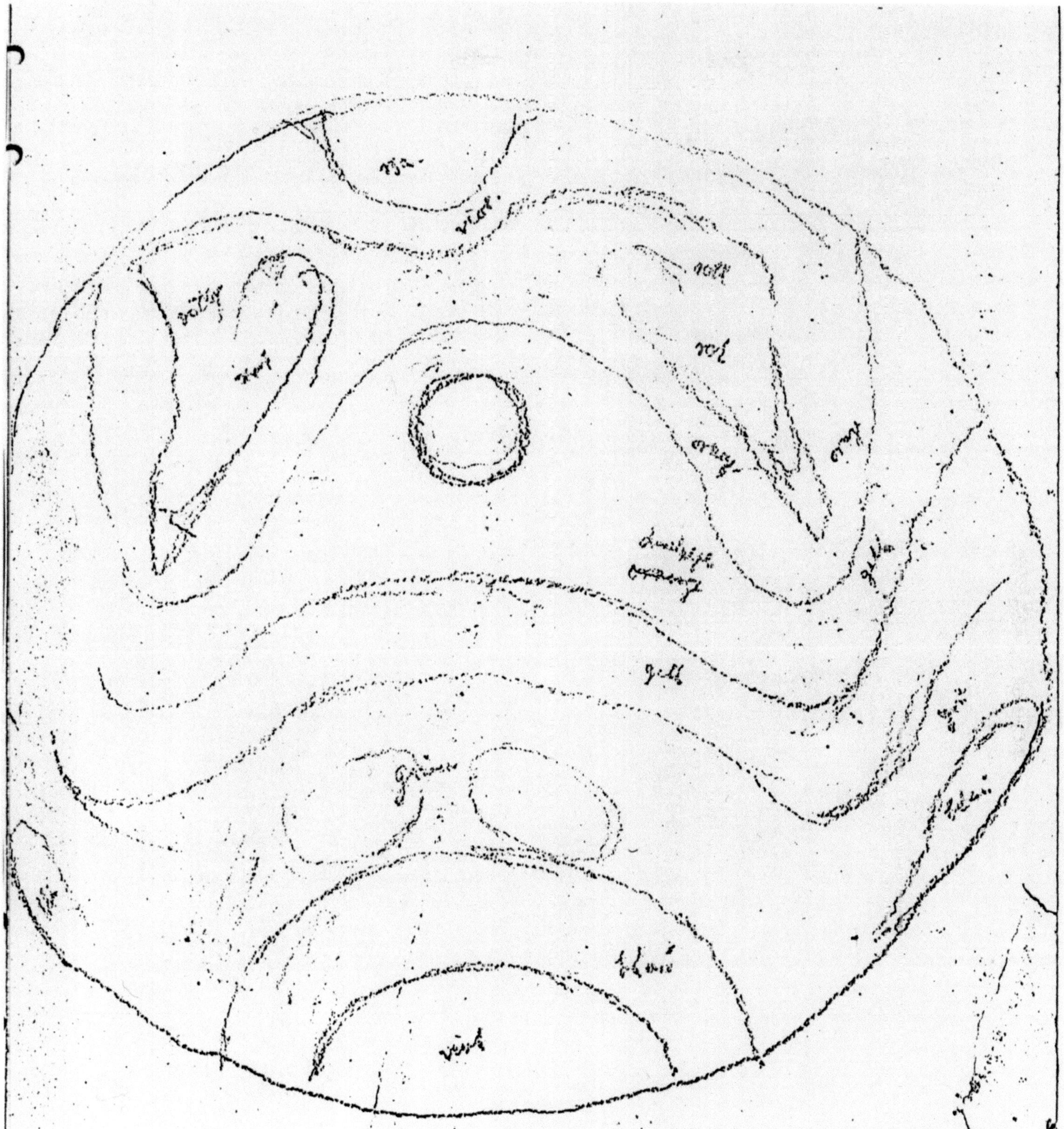

Layout for the Color Movements of the Large Cupola (east on the top)

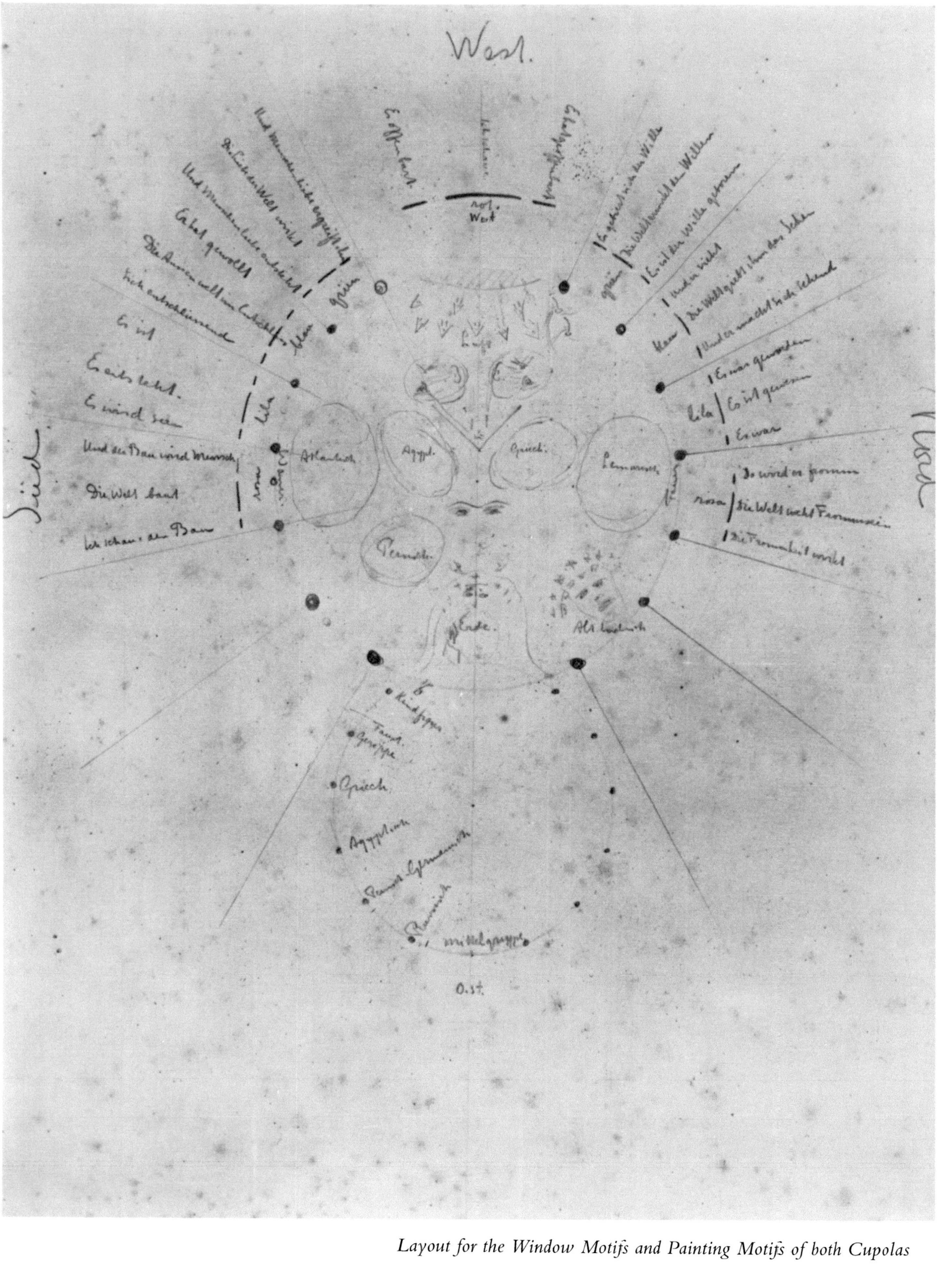

Layout for the Window Motifs and Painting Motifs of both Cupolas

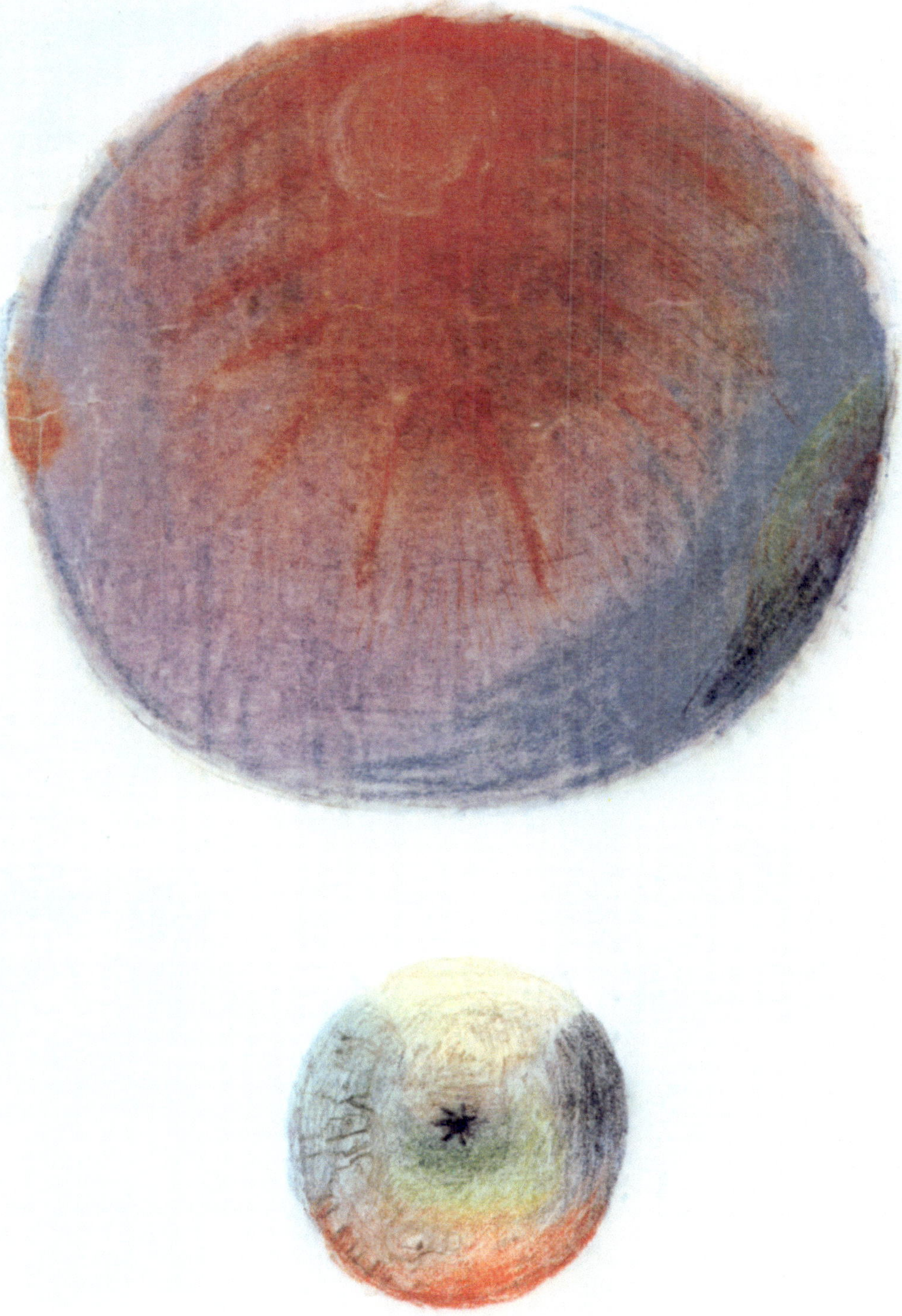

Color layout for both Cupolas (the small cupola above, the large one below)

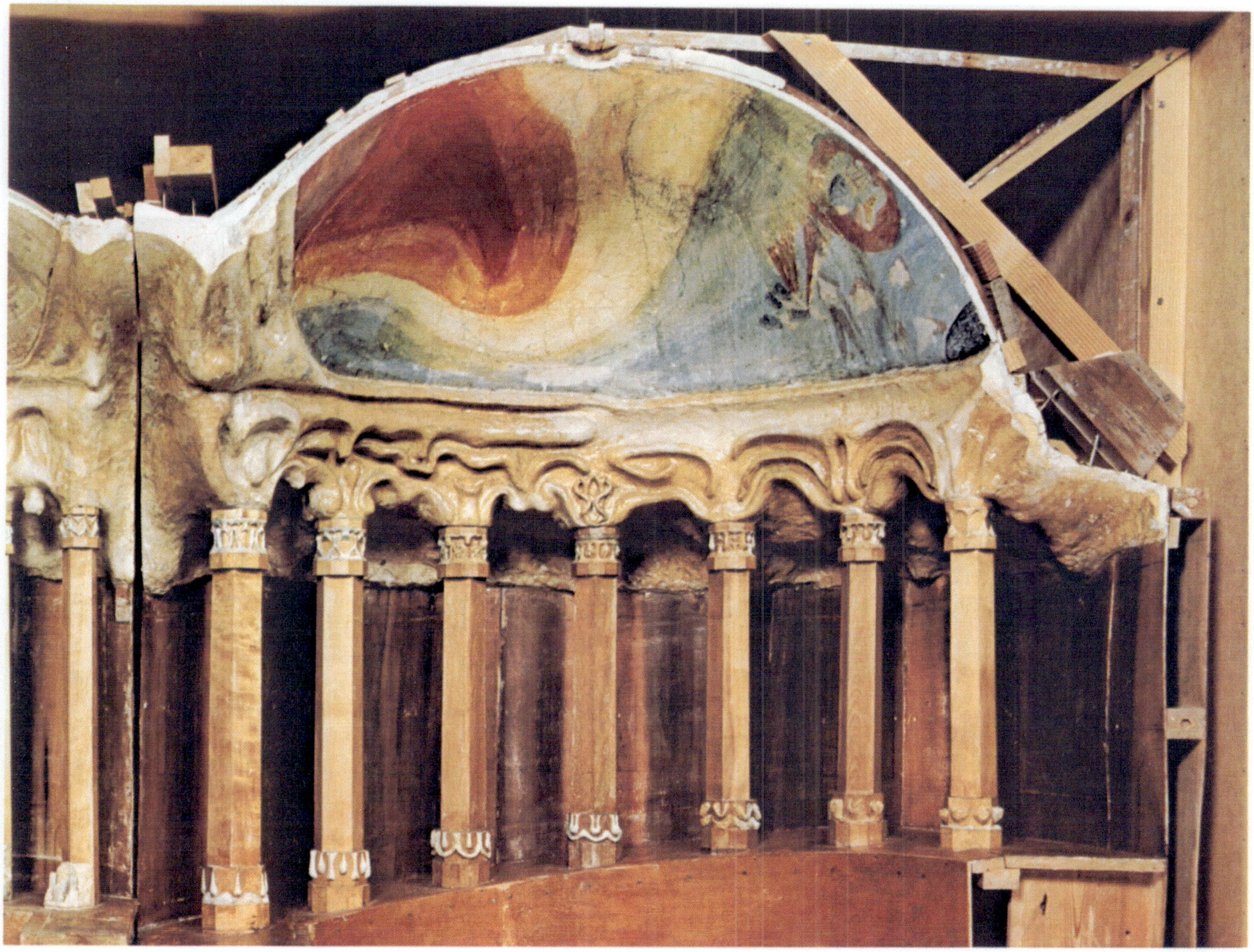

The Model showing the Large Cupola

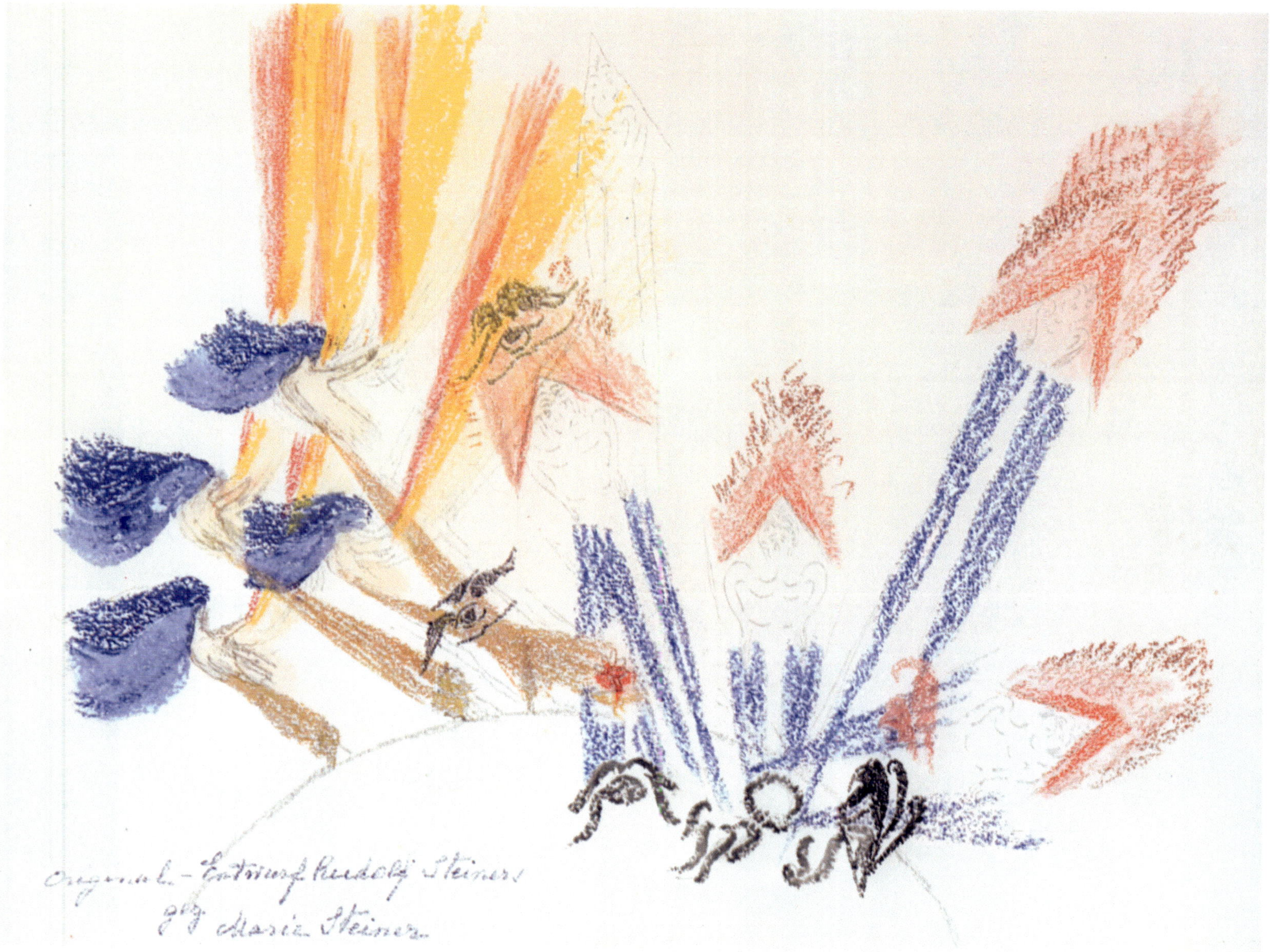

The Elohim Work Creatively into the Earth; Light-Beings Radiate Light into it

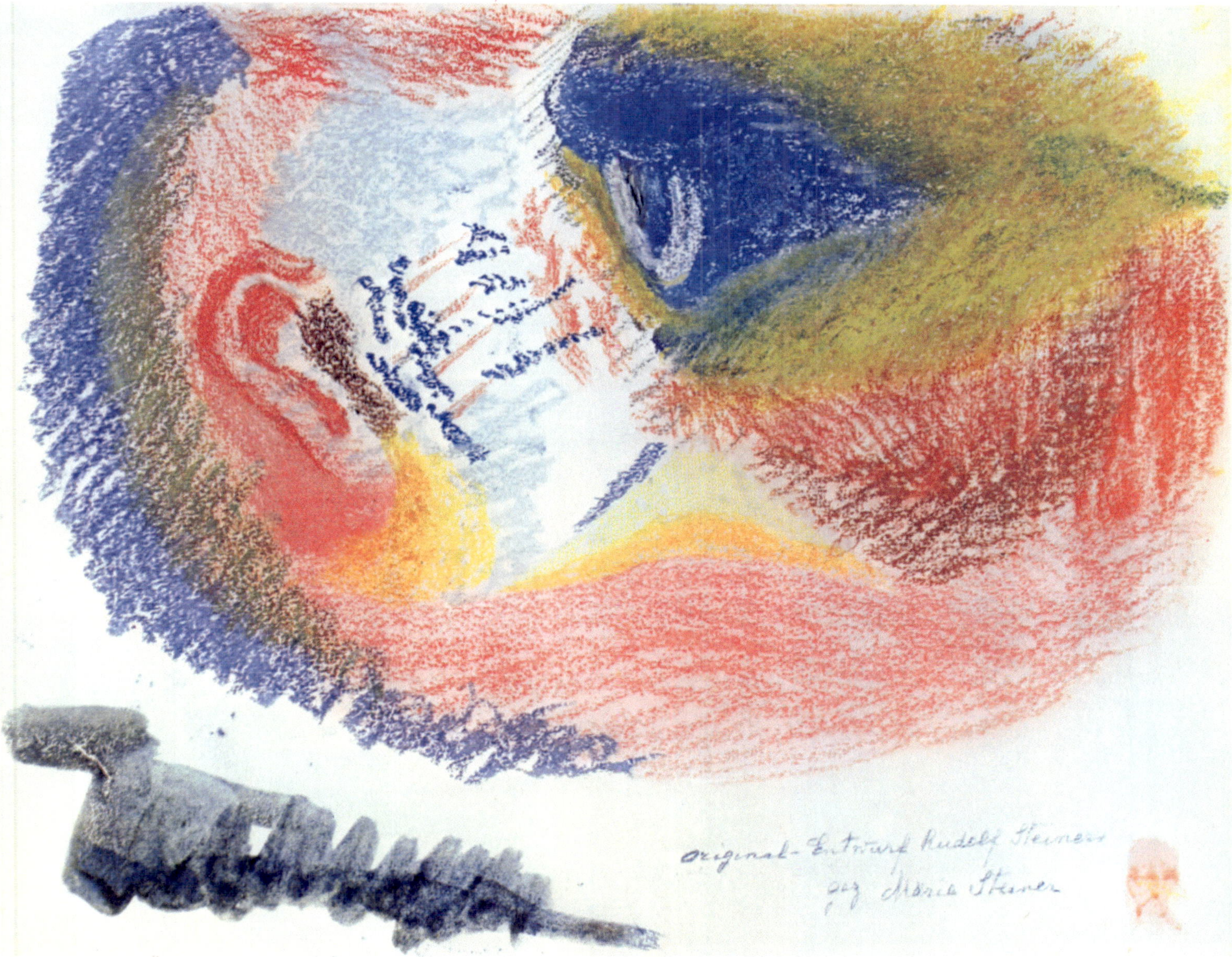

The Senses Arise, Eye and Ear Become

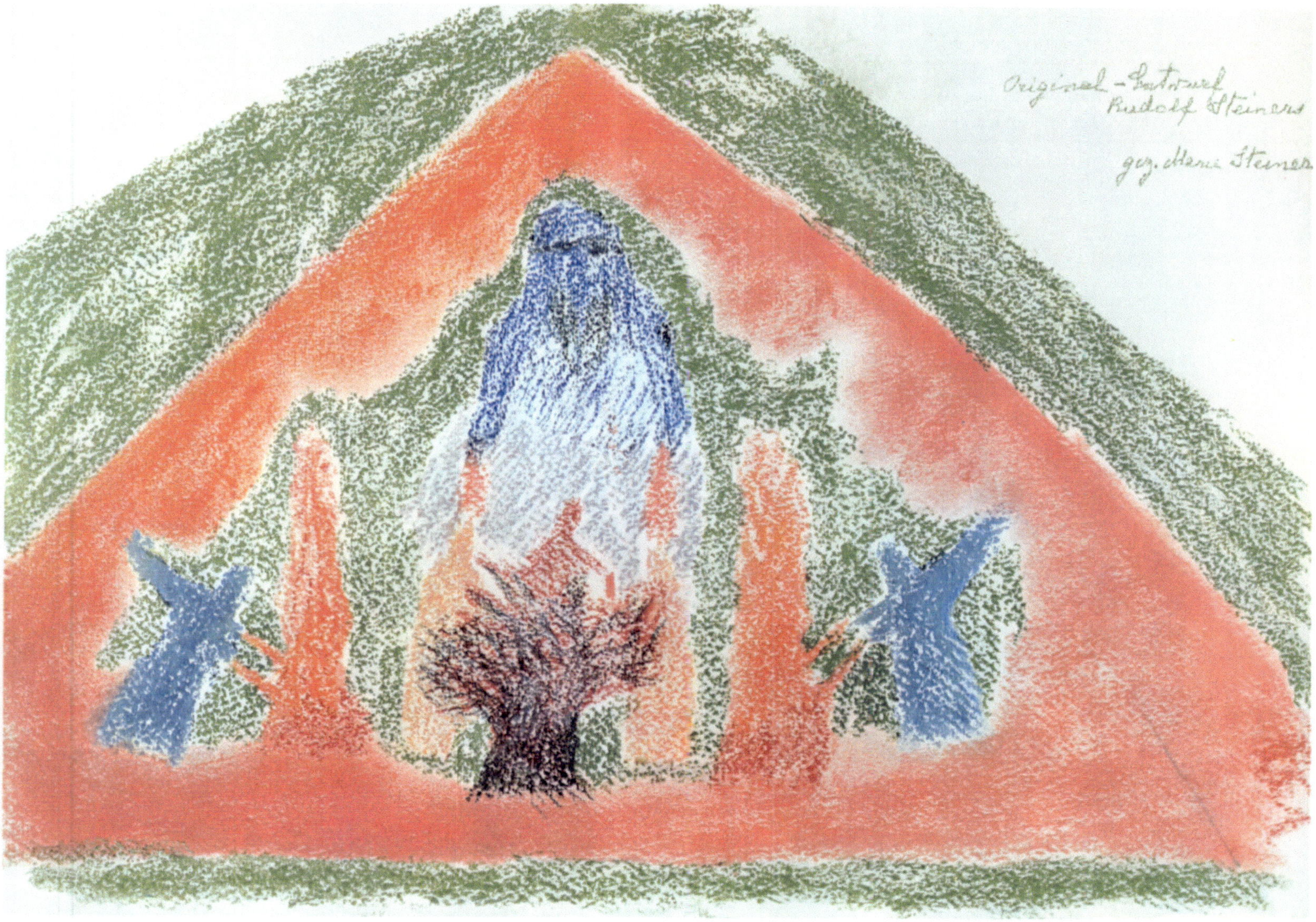

Jehova and the Luciferic Temptation – Paradise

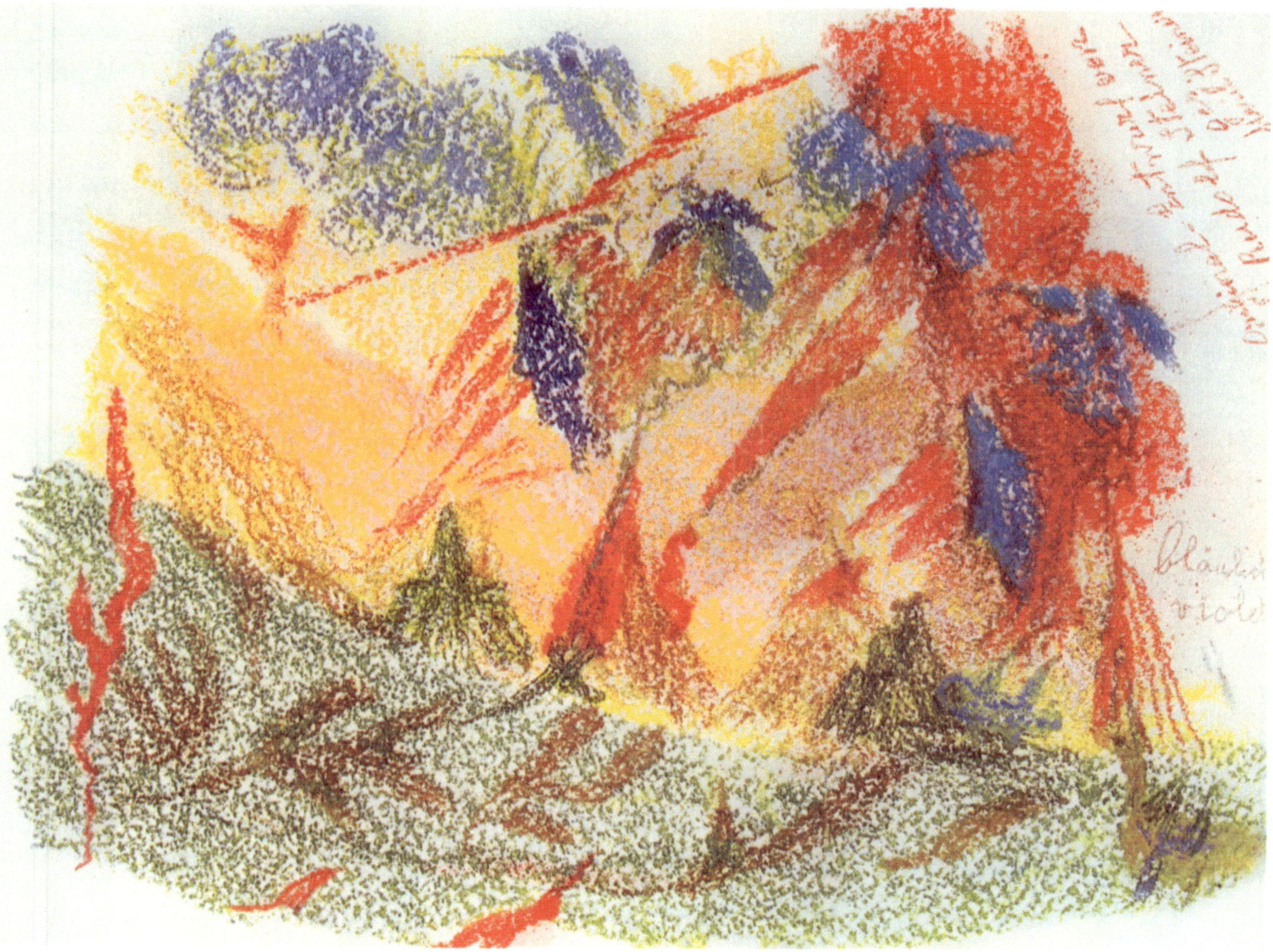

Lemuria

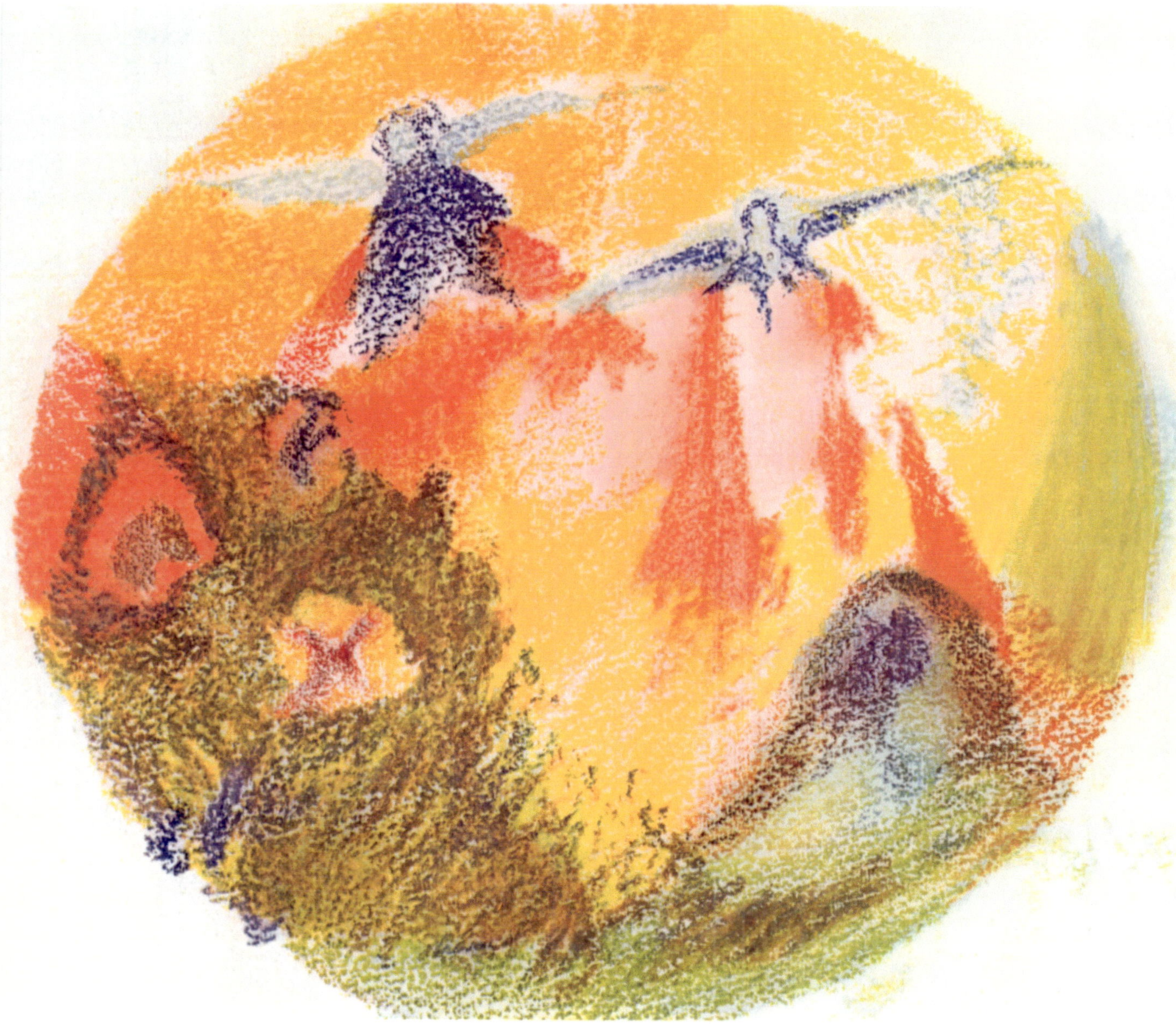

Atlantis

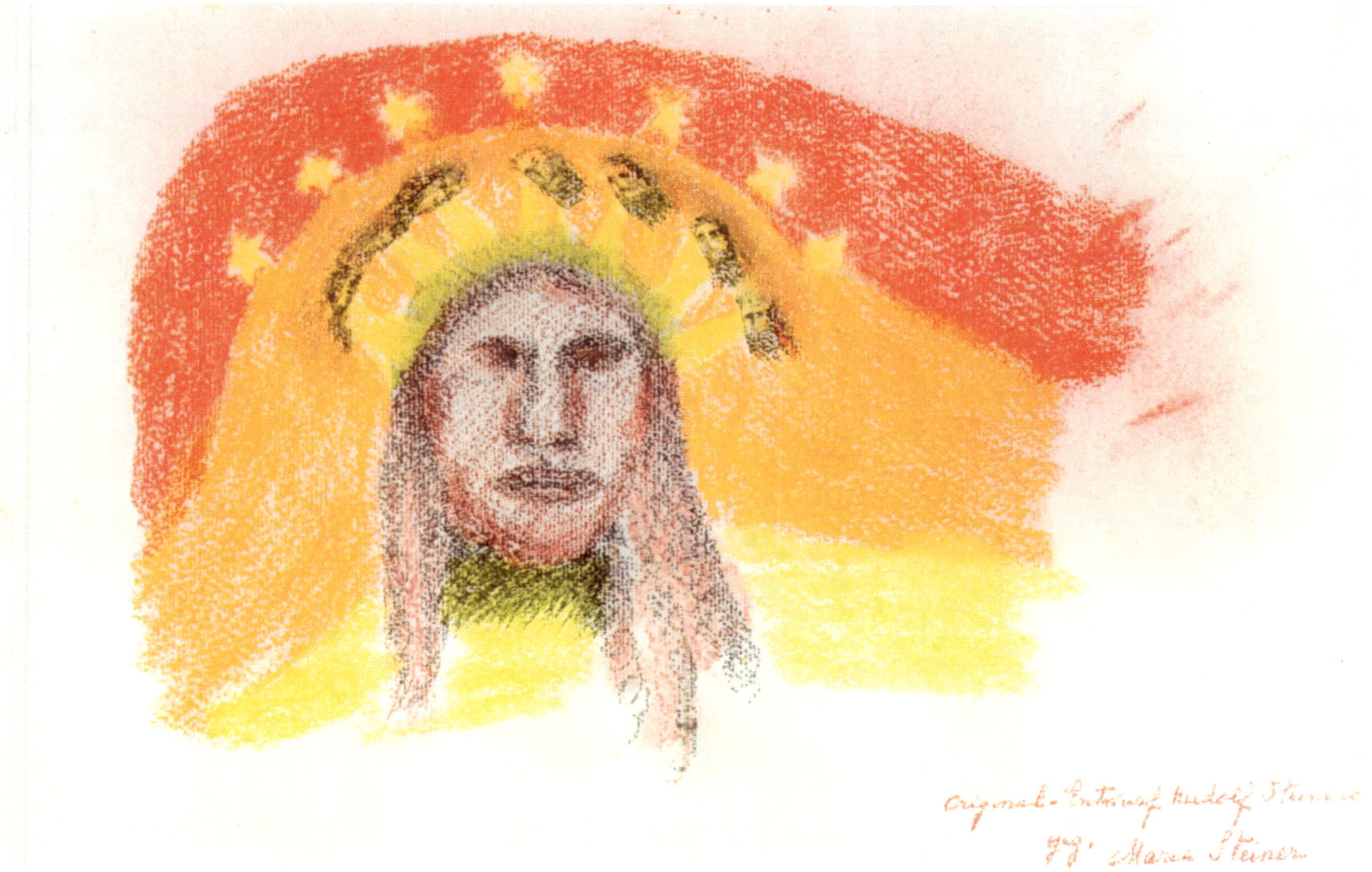

Tne Ancient Indian

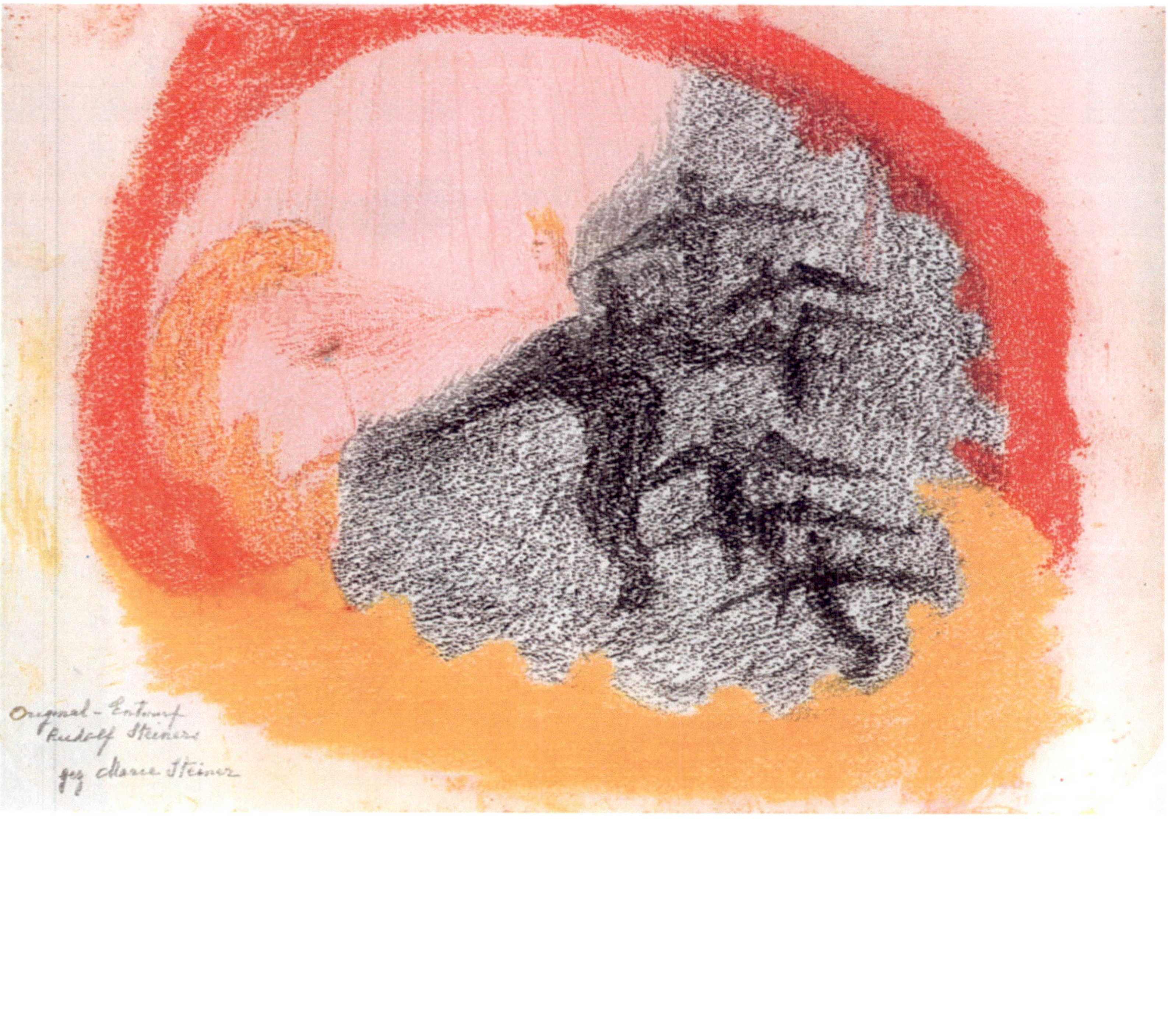

The Ancient Persian

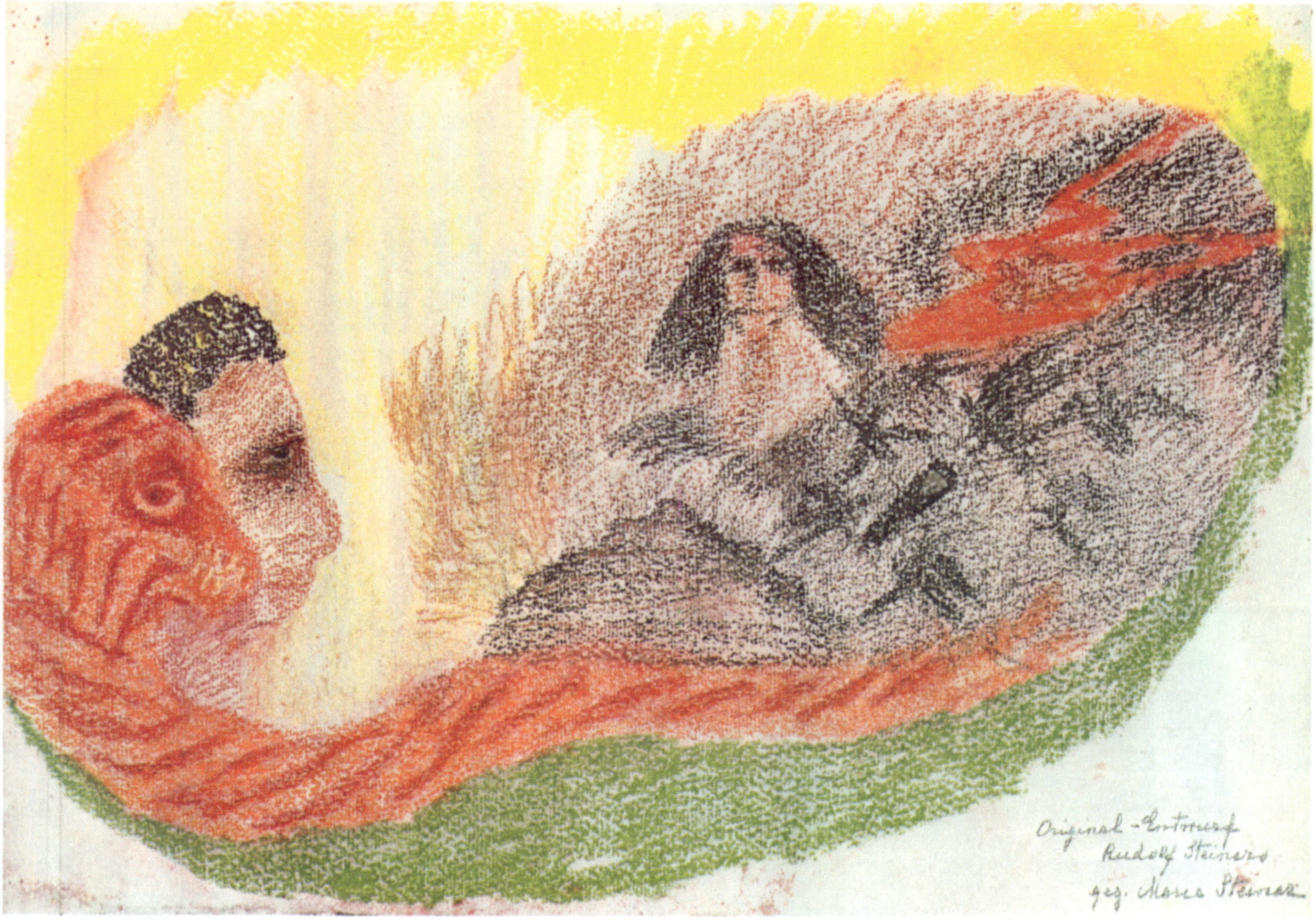

The Ancient Egyptian

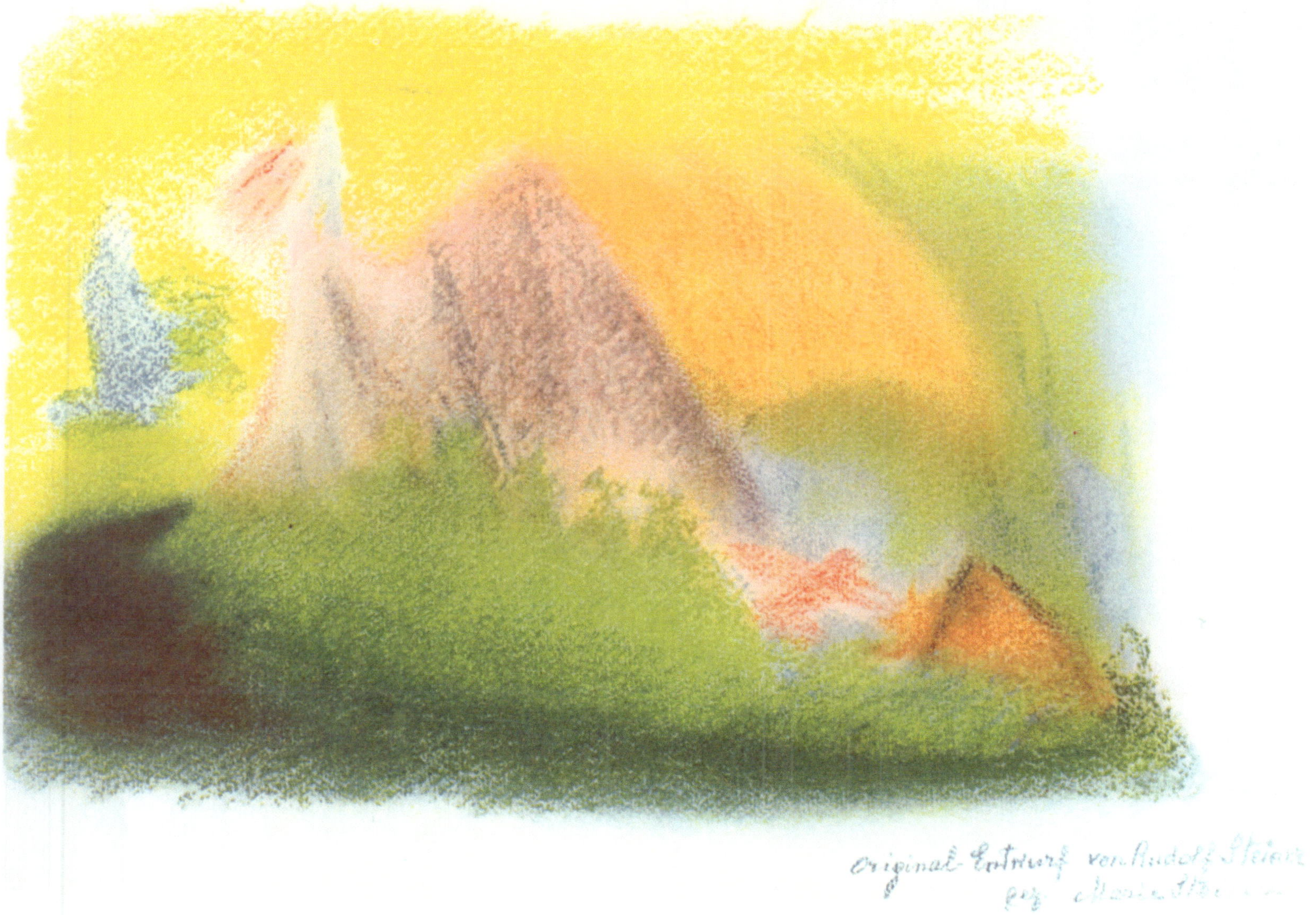
Original-Entwurf von Rudolf Steiner

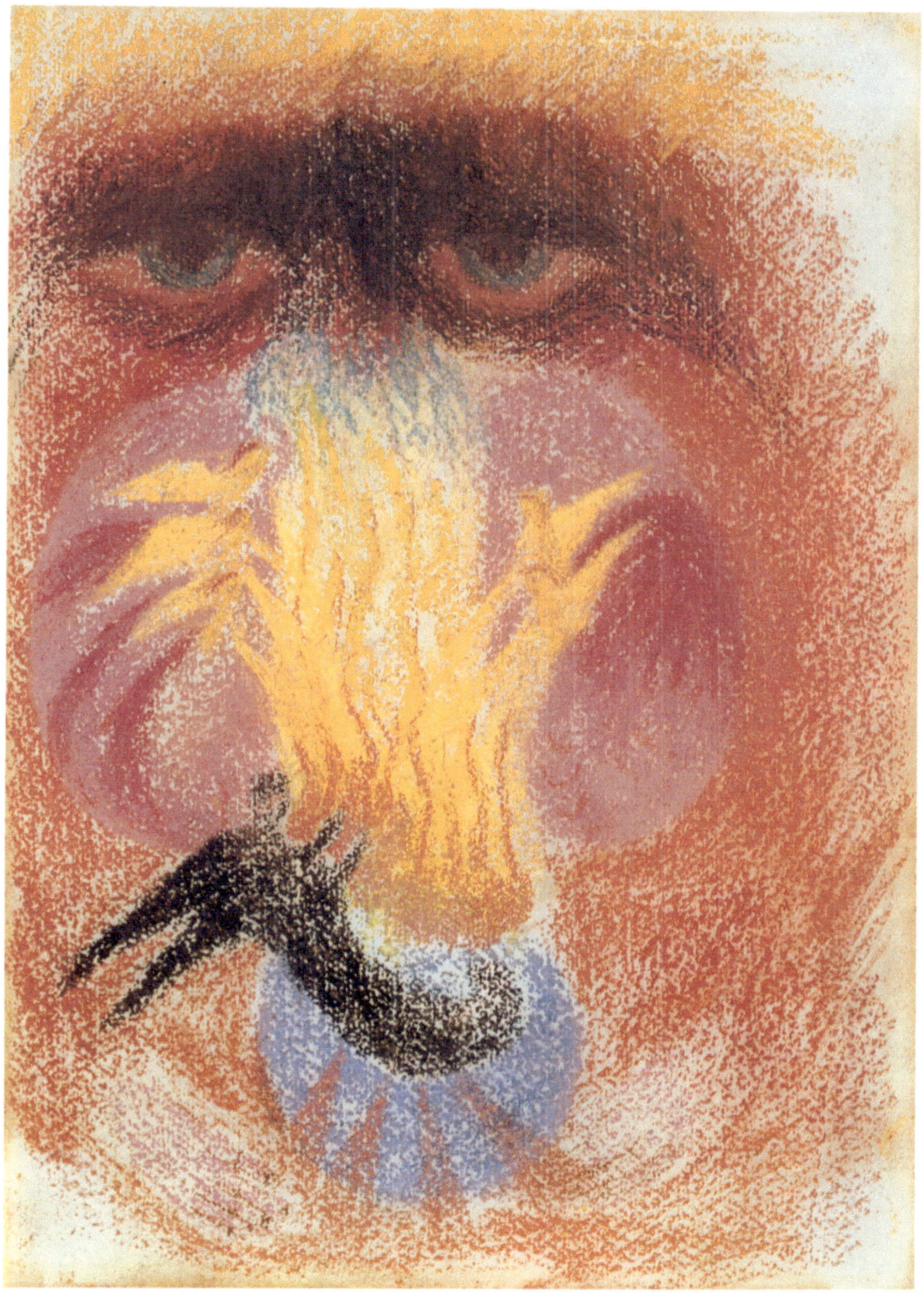

The Wrath of God and the Yearning-grief of God – 'I'

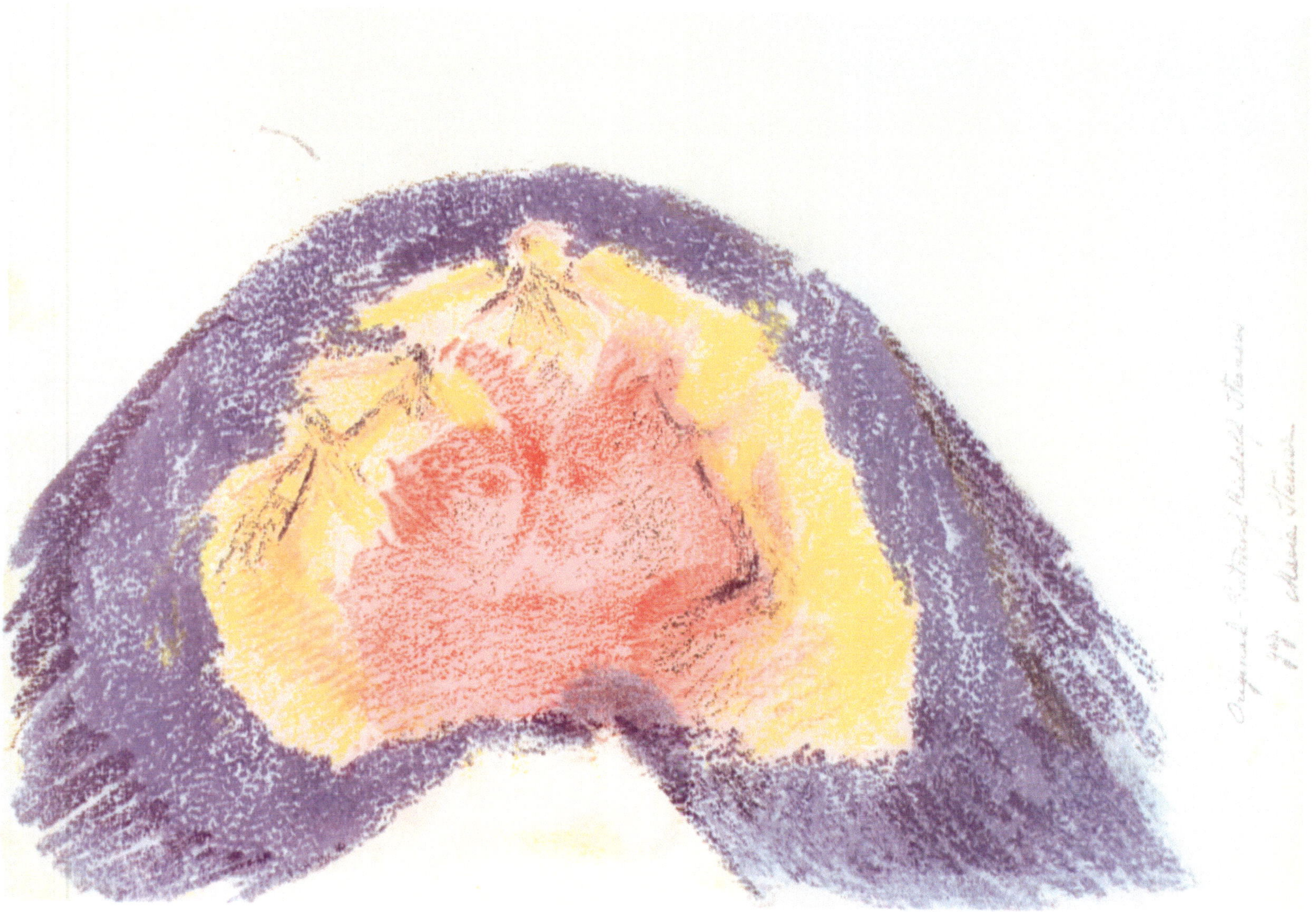

The Round of Seven – 'A'

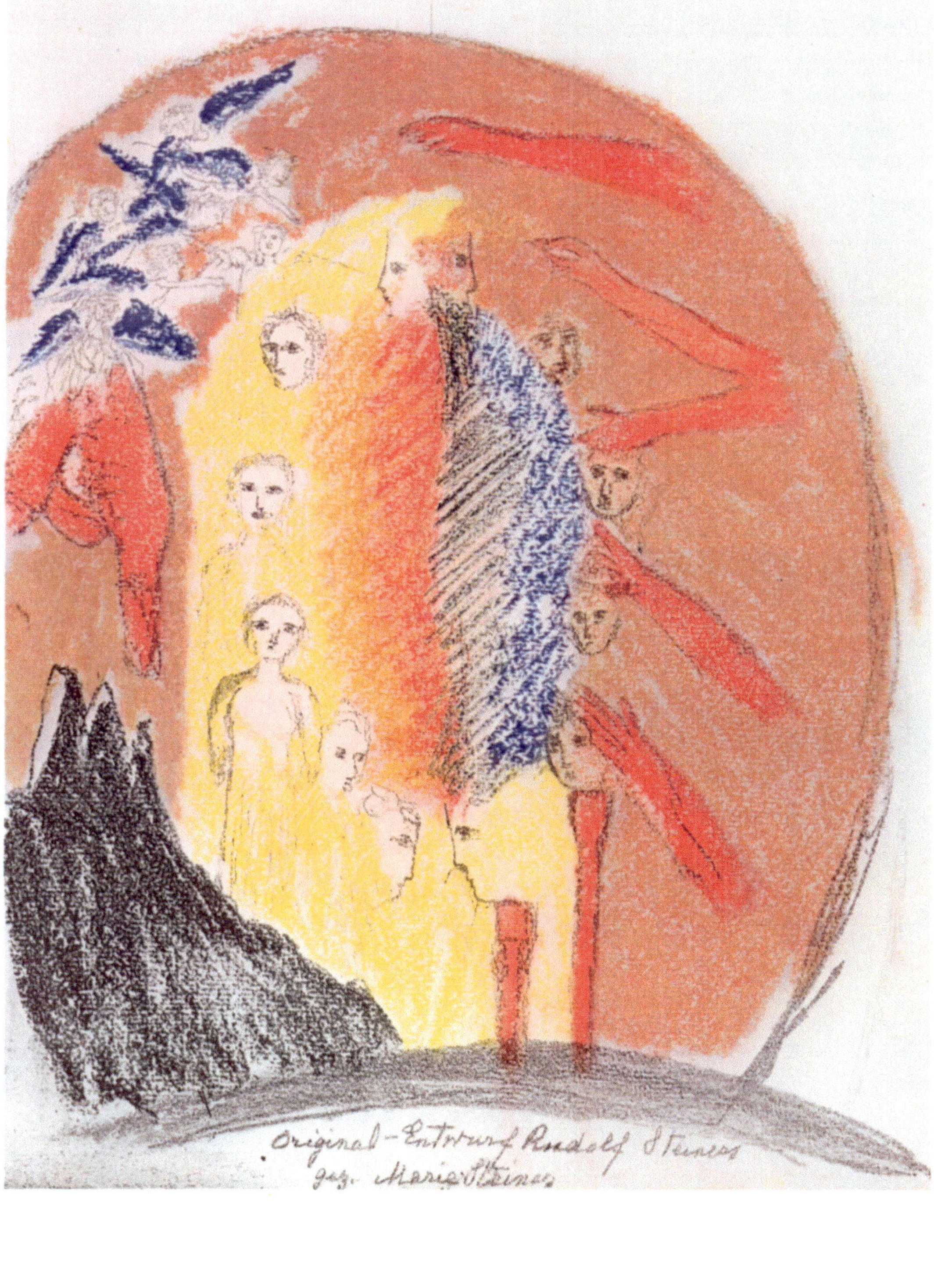

The Circle of Twelve – 'O'

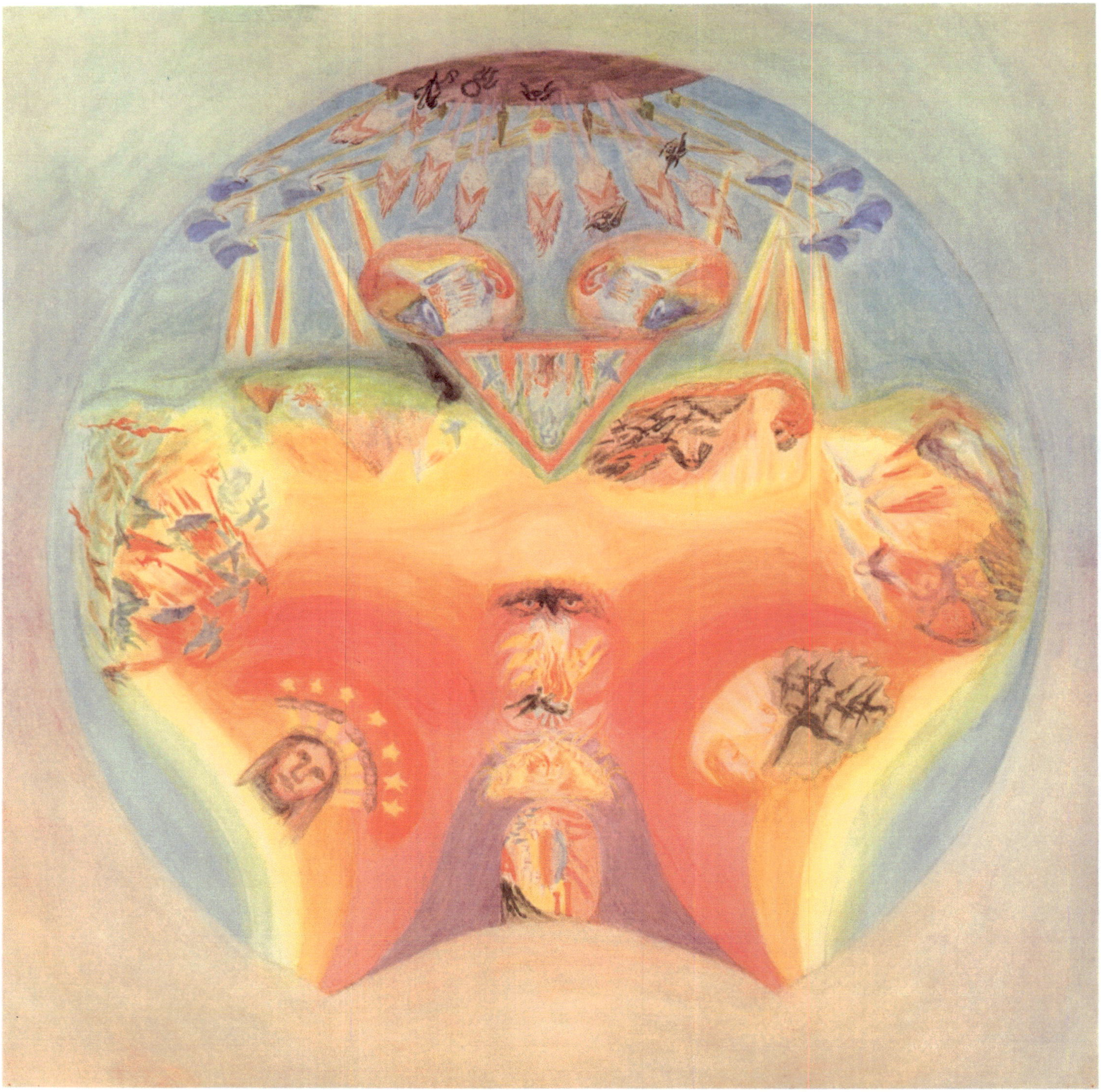

Study for the Position of the Motifs in the Large Cupola (Louise Blommestein, 1951)

THE POSITIONS OF THE MOTIFS IN THE LARGE CUPOLA

The motifs in the large cupola were borne on the streams of the rainbow while the motifs in the small cupola seemed to emerge from different nuances of the incarnadine (cf. Rudolf Steiner's indications for both cupolas on p. 49). Rudolf Steiner made a pencil sketch of his indications for the color streams in the large cupola: from the west – violet, blue going over into green; from the east – pink, violet, red, orange, yellow. This is complemented by a sketch by William Scott Pyle, which shows how the motifs were arranged in the streams.

Years after the fire, Louise van Blommestein painted a picture in which she attempted to reconstruct the overall positions of the motifs in the large cupola. The threefold creation motif appeared above the severe arches of the Saturn architrave in the west. Here violet lightened to blue as it ascended, and even higher up it went over into green. In violet: "The Elohim Work Creatively into the Earth"; in blue : "The Senses Arise, Eye and Ear Become"; in green: "Jehovah and the Luciferic Temptation". Opposite this in the west was the threefold cosmic picture of man, the IAO, which shone forth in various shades of red: The I, also called "The Wrath of God and the Yearning-Grief of God" in warm red facing towards the middle of the cupola; beneath this in shades of violet "The Round of Seven – A"; above the arch of the stage "The Circle of Twelve – O".

The expansive pictures "Lemuria" (in the north) and "Atlantis" (in the south) appeared above the middle architrave formations, where the cool colors of the west meet the warm flowing colors of the east. The cultural motifs of "The Ancient Indian" and "The Ancient Persian" were conveyed in the streams of red working from above, while "The Ancient Egyptian" and the Greek Oedipus motif both rested on the green.

ELOHIM

"The Elohim work creatively into the earth;
Light-Beings radiate into it."

The mighty shapes of the architrave over the west portal of the auditorium are supported to the left and right of the organ by two pillars. The capitals of these pillars, as the forces work simultaneously from above and below, create a basis for the seven-part metamorphosis in the seven pillars, progressing from west to east. The austere lines of the three arches of the architrave appear like an image of the world-bearing trinity prior to the primeval beginnings on Saturn.

Ascending above the architrave in deep blue, which below blends into violet and above densifies into green, is the motif of the earth's beginnings, its light coming in as though from a distant past. "The Elohim Work Creatively into the Earth; Light-Beings Radiate into it."[4] This motif is indicated blossoming forth from the blue background of the model of the interior.

"You will find when you live in blue and gradually feel your way into it that the blue has a quality that draws the soul. Our souls want to lose themselves in it, long for it, want to continue to long for it. Then you will also discover that out of it figures arise, expressing the secrets of the cosmos, expressing the soul of the cosmos. From the creative power of the color itself, a world will come into being, a world will form itself, inwardly differentiate itself, a world enjoying its own being. The form will be born out of the color. You will feel yourself not merely living in the color, but that the color gives birth to the form, so that the form becomes the deed of the color." (October 25, 1914)

The paintings in the cupola were executed in plant colors. In comparison with other synthetic colors genuine indigo blue has the special quality of not only creating light/dark values but also of differentiating nuances of hue when it is used in a veiling technique.

Pastel Sketch

Shapes appear. A reddish color emerges. Reddish peach-blossom shades interplay in vivid iridescence. Vermilion lights up actively and above the vermilion weaves a gentler red, protectively shaping and intensifying to a deep, dignified carmine red. Peach-blossom is the breathing center. Bluish-lilac rays, aimed willfully into the depths, stream out, awakening rejuvenating seed forces and life in the darkness of the violet earth.

Largely-drawn black eyes look out from the point where the rays cross one another. Plant forms are sprouting from the ground. Black forms appear mysteriously. Are they eyes? limbs? the movement and formation of the senses? Does a delicate red suggest a human being?

At the side, pale beings surrounded by blue with blue hovering over them receive the intense sun-like yellow and red and direct them, softened, toward the earth. Their light calls forth a blossom-like red out of the violet ground. In the experience of the colors, in sensing and following stroke and movement, one can get close to the language of the sketch.

The divine heads ray forth in dignified carmine red, their will forces calling forth life in the depths of the earth. The barely indicated weaving of peach-blossom plays rhythmically in and out, ordering and forming matter, much as the tone forms cladmic music patterns. Worlds of light and sound emanate from these forms. Forces become directly visible, form-creating Beings called 'Spirits of Form' or 'Elohim' in the Hebrew of Genesis and 'Exusiai' in the Greek of Dionysus' *Areopagita.* Rudolf Steiner's drawing actually shows only the south side of this widely spread motif. The northern part

and the southern part were to be executed as symmetrical mirror-images to create the whole.
A photograph of the pillars of the large cupola (see page 40) shows beings hovering in the region of the sun pillar, taking the light of the sun realm and directing it down to the earth, an expression of harmony between the visual and plastic arts.

The Motif

A premonition of primeval beginnings awakens in one when a reddish color arises out of a deep blue ground. This mood, like the first moment of awakening from a full, sleep-like consciousness, is expressed in Fercher von Steinwand's poem, 'Archetypal Impulse'.

In the unconfined expanses
Of our ancient Mother Night,
Hear – how 'gainst itself there clashes
The most enigmatic Might!
Hear we premonition's paces?
Has our longing's sleep now ceased?
Was a spirit-flash released?
Is it dreams that glide through space?

In the Indian *Vedas*, this moment is described as a kindling "through the power of fire".

Then was no not-being, and no being,
No air-filled space, no heaven above.
What stirred itself and where? In whose protection?
What turbulence was in the chaotic depths?
There was no death, nor was there immortality,
Nor light of day, nor twinkling of the stars.
It breathed within itself, breathless, the That
To which no other found its way.
Dark was the dark when time began.
A lightless to and fro – the All.
The one life-seed within its sheath,
Enkindled was it through the fire's might.[5]

People of each cultural epoch experience the creation of the world in different images arising from primeval memories. In Genesis we read, "In the beginning, God created heaven and earth." For a modern conception, Rudolf Steiner describes the process of creation as follows:
"Let us try ... to bring the following picture before our eyes: a weaving, primeval element, and weaving within this, the fiery, gaseous, and watery. Within this elemental weaving and working live spiritual beings, a group of brooding spiritual beings. They are engaged in productive reflection, and through their productive reflection emerges the intention to channel all activity towards the image of man. The first thing to arise from this reflection is an image of something manifesting outwardly, making itself known, and a stirring within, inwardly animated. Within the elemental shell, the primeval beings thought out what manifested outwardly, what stirred inwardly.
Try to realize in these words the significance of what is said in the first lines of the Bible and you will have a foundation for understanding such things as we shall contemplate in the next few days as the true meaning of the monumental, archetypal words through which is revealed to humanity one of the greatest of all things, namely, its own origin." (August 17, 1910)
"B'reschit bara Elohim haschamayim v'et ha'aretz. What is it, then, that is so special about these archetypal words? Formerly, when a letter sounded through the soul, it awoke a picture. ... *Bet*, the first letter, evoked the mate-

rial weaving of the shell; *Resch*, the second consonant, called forth the countenances of the spiritual beings weaving within the shell; and *Schin*, the third sound, evoked the prickly force which worked its way up to manifestation from within." (August 17, 1910)

"How can one, then, imagine the cosmos; how can one develop an inner feeling for the form of macrocosmic man? When one begins to feel how sound bursts forth into form! ... This is an absolutely objective language, a language which crystallizes into images the sounds that are produced if the soul allows itself to be stimulated by it." (August 18, 1910)

"In everything that was carried over from the Saturn, Sun, and Moon existence, the Elohim in their cosmic activity thought out what reveals itself outwardly and stirs inwardly; and over that which stirs within, and through that which stirs within, deep darkness rules. But spreading itself out into it, brooding over it, permeating it with warmth was the creative spirit of the Elohim Ruach." (August 18, 1910)

The days of creation in their metamorphosis and unfolding live on in deeds and sufferings of light. Color theory is the history of the creation, and the history of the creation is reflected in the theory of color. "My theory of color is as old as the world," said Goethe to Eckerman.[6]

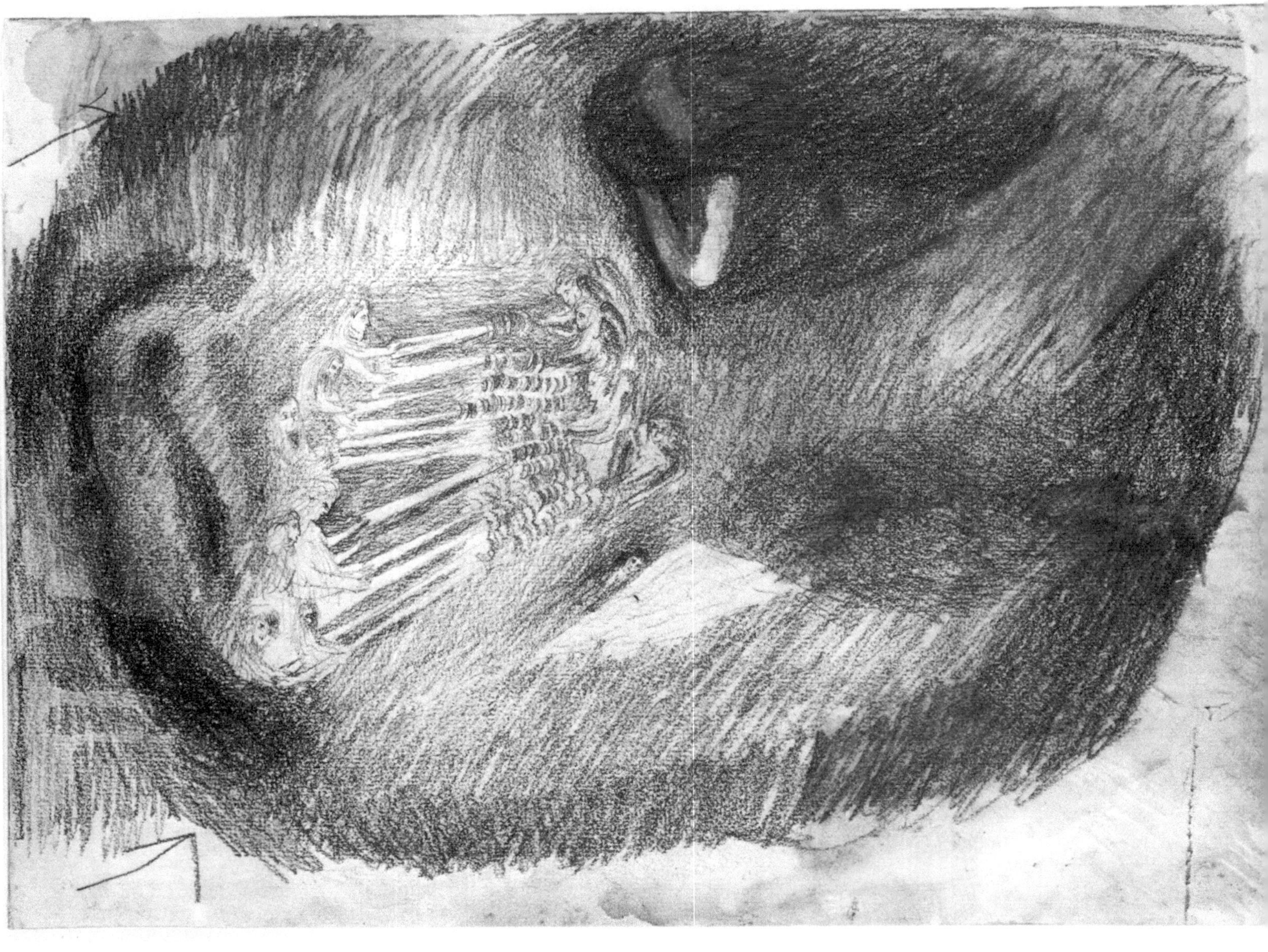

EYE AND EAR

"The senses arise; eye and ear become."

Pastel Sketch

Ultramarine blue and warm red confront each other. The blue, distinctly formed into an eye, rises out of broken yellow and red tones. The red densifies into an ear-like shape and is surrounded by a dull blue.

The sketch originates in the tension between blue and red, the tension that brings about the movement and spatial orientation of the colors and allows depth and perspective to arise in the color area.

Blue and red together create a transparent area of light in tones of delicate blue. Red rays emanate from the region of the eye, sound waves from around the ear. Rays and waves interpenetrate each other in lively interplay. Below this play of light and sound, a human figure in blue rests on a yellow elevation. Is he listening to the colors and sounds?

Drawing

The pencil drawing contains a wealth of light and dark values of unique beauty. The world of light between eye and ear is crowded with an abundance of figures, as if opening up from the depths of space. What is more sensed than perceived in the pastel sketch becomes visible here. Out of a more suggested and undefined life in color, a world of spiritual beings now becomes perceptible. Around the eye, figures send out rays of light from the contained force of the red; on the opposite side, light-colored forms, delicately enveloped in blue in the pastel sketch stream out harmonies of sound in hovering, gliding motion, their noble figures turned toward the center. A reciprocal giving and receiving of the forces of light and sound takes place between the two columns of figures.

Margarita Woloschin reports a conversation she had with Rudolf Steiner about this motif. "He said, 'On the one side, we see blue in the center that gradually goes over into red at the periphery; on the other side, red in the center leads through various gradations to blue at the periphery. The strength of the composition rests on the contrasts, on the struggle, between cold and warm.' At the time I was not conscious of the color language. I asked about the pictorial content. Which beings were represented here, which hierarchies? The answer was: 'These are thoughts of the second hierarchy.' I asked whether one might add shadowy repetitions to these figures (seven on each side) to connect them with the color background. 'You can certainly do so because the etheric world is a mirror-image, so a being can appear as a manifold manifestation.' I asked how I should paint. 'I want you to remain absolutely free.' "[7]

In the sketch, the eye is on the right side, the ear to the left. In the final execution, the motif of the eye and ear appears twice in mirror reflection above the widespread creation motif. Thus, the eyes are on the *outside*, the ears *inside*. The powerful blue eyes look from right and left towards the center, towards the red.

The Motif

The symmetrical, mirror image arrangement not only corresponds outwardly to the way man's sense organs were formed. Rudolf Steiner describes the formative forces participating in the creation of the sense organs. Particularly the symmetry of the eyes and ears manifests the directions in which two opposing currents meet. One current, that of the forces forming the 'organs of life', provides the organic foundation for perception; the other, that of 'the forces forming the sense organs', makes this foundation suitable for receiving impressions from the outer world. "You only need to look at the sense organs of a person facing you to see, for example, that the right ear has been formed from left to right, inasmuch as it owes its origin to that stage of development dominated by the forces forming the organs of life and it then became a sense organ through the opposing forces that formed the sense organs by working from right to left. For the left ear, the opposite applies. Similar relationships exist in the other symmetrically organized sense organs."[8]

The motif 'Eye and Ear' is the only one in the large cupola created entirely as a mirror image, expressing thereby an essential feature of the sense organs. For Goethe, it was obvious that the eye originated in forces of light, as the ear did in forces of sound. He characterized their relationship as follows: "Color and sound are like two rivers which, although having their source on the same mountain, flow under very different conditions in opposite directions, so that along their entire course no single spot can be compared with any other. Both are, in general, elemental effects, active in accordance with the general law of separating and coming together, rising and falling, retreating and reappearing, but on different sides, in different ways, in different senses."[9]

Considered deeply, these words throw a special light on the motif 'Eye and Ear'. They are like a glimpse into the sources of tone and color where, although distinctly differentiated from each other, they "can be related to a higher formula."[10]

From the point of view of archetypal, phenomenological processes, the color blue arises when a lit, semi-transparent medium passes *in front* of complete darkness, and the front of the eye, with cornea and lens, relates similarly to the darkness of the eye-socket. Indeed, the process of seeing can be said to take place in front of the eye. Red, on the other hand, always has light in the background, with semi-transparent darkness passing in front. Similarly hearing is a process that takes place much more 'within', behind as it were, the physical organism of the ear. Hearing takes place deep in man's rhythmic organism.[11]

As blue relates to red, so sight relates to hearing. The inner tensions, brought to expression through effects of color, begin to *sound*. An artist who daily experiences how color harmonies stimulate an inner listening might say, "I *hear* my pictures, and if I do not hear them, they are worthless."

Meditating deeply on the sun-like nature of the eye and the sound nature of the ear, one can not only experience the forces living *within* the sense organs, but also the forces which participate in their creation. The cupola motif stimulates such a perception.

"When you look, for example, at the large cupola, you will clearly perceive how on the western side we tried to grasp the inner nature of the eye, the microcosmic that reveals itself in the inner eye. Not what the eye sees in the outer world, and not the physicality of the eye, but that which is inwardly experienced when one is *within* the eye with the eyes of the soul, which, of course, is only possible when one has given up using the eye in the usual sense as an instrument for external sense perception, and instead beholds the inner nature of the eye in the same way one usually sees external objects." (December 29, 1918)

During a guided tour of the building, this experience was further described. "And so you can see, for example, above the organ motif, how something is painted which anyone working in a banal way in the sense world will find insane. You will, however, no longer find it insane when I tell you the following. When you close your eyes and more or less sense your way into the inner eye, you will see something like two eyes looking at each other. That which takes place inwardly can in a certain way be further developed. Then something takes shape which, in a primitive way, lights up in the darkness like two eyes facing you. This inwardly experienced seeing, if projected beyond, will be so experienced that one sees in it a great beyond, a world coming into being. And this was what we attempted to create out of the color: what the closed eye experiences when it looks into the dark and beholds itself. You need not read the mysteries only with the intellect; you can see them; suddenly they are there. This is the struggle that goes on in the act of seeing." (August 28, 1921)

In another lecture, Rudolf Steiner said, "When we as human beings look with closed eyes into our forces of light, into our own seeing space, we see something before us that appears like the beginning of creation. You meet this beginning of creation here in the west of the large cupola. And it is not just a fantasy picture in which the Tree of Paradise and above it a kind of Father-God and then these two eye-like forms appear. It is all something that arises before the inner eye, the eye of the soul, if you deepen your inner feeling." (December 30, 1921)

The process described here opens up the possibility of seeing the three parts of the motif of the creation in its comprehensive greatness and to experience its unfolding. From its beginning in the creation by the Elohim to its end in the Paradise picture, this motif shows the history of the creation of man. The central motif of eye and ear demonstrates a more inward aspect of the creation, and at the same time, serves as a gateway through which other worlds can be seen.

In a lecture given in 1906, Rudolf Steiner connects the origin of the senses with the great stages in the evolution of mankind.

"At the first stage, man had come so far that the ears were fully developed in accordance with their predisposition. Actually they were already present in an archetypal form when man came over to Saturn from quite different worlds .... That ancient sense of hearing which man possessed when he entered planetary evolution was quite a unique sense of hearing. It could best be characterized by saying that his physical body was basically only a large ear .... Man hardly differentiated himself as a physical body from his environment. He heard in his whole body what lives as sound outside in the cosmos. As a string vibrates when another is plucked, so every tone sounded in the world had a related vibration in the human physical body.

Man entered the Saturn evolution with a predisposition for hearing. On Saturn he added the sense of warmth. In the subsequent Sun evolution, he acquired the sense of sight. The predisposition for the sense of sight during the Sun evolution is, therefore, the third phase in which the other senses transform themselves correspondingly so that on the Sun, the human being is a hearing, feeling and, in a way, a seeing being." (October 19, 1906)

The three senses here discussed all have a certain relationship to the polarity of warm and cold. Just as we speak of warm or cold colors, so a voice, a sound or tone can be felt to be warm or cold. The warmth sense stretches over the entire physical body without concentrating in any isolated organ. In the tension between the colors red and blue in the motif 'Eye and Ear', the sense of warmth flows freely as an actively creative element, not just as an element that manifests in outer form.

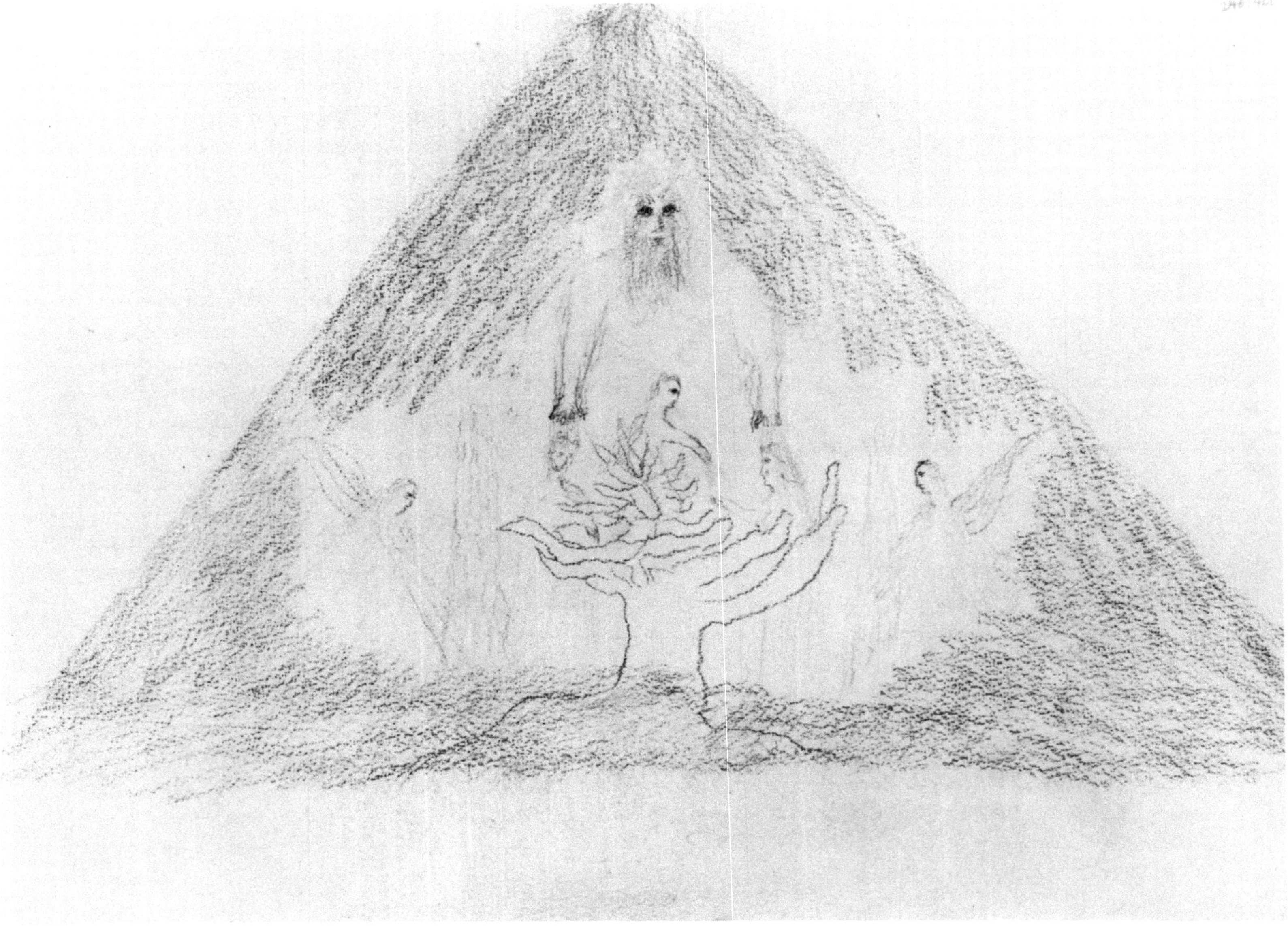

PARADISE

"Jehovah and the Luciferic Temptation — Paradise"

Pastel Sketch

Within the supporting stream of expansive green, red lights up and spreads downward, encompassing the motif in a triangle. A dialogue begins between green and the red that goes over into peach-blossom. Adam and Eve are lightly sketched in the peach blossom. Green painted over the red and peach-blossom produces a gnarled, held effect. From the tree a red shape winds its way upwards – Lucifer! Inclined toward Eve, the tempter gives her the light that awakens the senses.
As though protecting the center, columns of flame rise on both sides, sustained by blue angels. The blue at the top forms itself into a sublime countenance. The very blue which formed the space out of which the first two creation motifs were born has become 'image' – the image of Jehovah. "For the Rabbis, one of the names of God is also space." (September 20, 1918)

Drawing

Jehovah's countenance is mighty, his eyes blaze with wrath, and tongues of flame emanate from his hands. The expressions of the angels seem noble and sorrowful. Serpent-like, Lucifer emerges from the tree. With an expressive gesture, he reaches toward Eve with his left arm and showers her with the light of knowledge. "Then their eyes were opened." (First Book of Moses)
"It lay in the original intention of the divine spiritual beings to give man to himself in such a way that, by looking through himself, he assimilated the world inwardly. Through Lucifer's interference, man was, in this respect, torn away from himself and now looks at and perceives the world round about him. This means that Lucifer gave man to the world, placed him into earthly existence, led him out of himself." (August 18, 1915)

The Motif

It was Lucifer who awakened the tendency to perceive the external world, the physical objects. With this descent, man awoke to a quite different relationship to the sense world and to a different way of thinking than had been intended.
"Profoundly significant are the words in the Bible: 'You will be equal to the gods, your senses will be opened,' for they had not been intended to be opened but to be left in a condition that would have allowed man to look back in his thinking to his old Moon existence and through this thinking grasp what the macrocosm brought about on his periphery, what was given to him by the gods." (August 8, 1915)
In lectures on painting,[12] Rudolf Steiner described the Moon stage of the earth as a state of surging, flowing soul-life in which the mysteries of color have their origin. Before Lucifer's influence, man's perception was so alive that he was able to experience direct impressions of the spirit.
"He would have looked at that which could make impressions on him from outside. But not only colors and sounds came to him, not only what are impressions from outside, but everywhere spirit flowed out from objects: with the color green, the spirit of green, and so on. Spirit would come to him everywhere, a condition Goethe had only a premonition of when he said, 'If this plant is to be an idea only, then I see my ideas; then they surround

me just as colors do ... .' But if the outer impression had come to man in such a living way, then ... every outer impression would have been met by the breathing process. Red, the impression, comes in from outside; from inside, the breathing comes to meet it, which, however, would then be sound. Every single impression would evoke a sound from man. There would not be a permanent language. Every object, every impression would be directly answered from within with a sound-gesture .... We are reminded of this original spirit, when man had eyes not only to see, but eyes to perceive the spirit; when he answered the perception of his eyes with a sound gesture from within his breathing processes; we are reminded of this being one with the spirit by the words: 'In the beginning was the Word.' The beginning of the Gospel of St. John speaks of this life in the divine." (April 12, 1917)

The senses, created by the gods as gateways through which what is within or without could flow in and out, were altered by Lucifer to a way of experiencing that led to mirror-image perception. Through this interference, the contact between man's inner breathing life and the outer world was dimmed.

"The pre-luciferic nature of man is contained in the elemental presence of warmth and air; the luciferic influence crept into the fluid and the firm substances of man. He penetrated into these and lives in them. The luciferic influence is alive in everything that is firm or liquid. This is not meant simply as a picture but describes the facts of the case rather clearly, when I say that through this pressing together of man's body, which is the effect of the luciferic influence, man has become heavier and has sunk from the circumference to the earth. This was the exodus from Paradise as it is pictorially represented. We can say that man first received weight, the force of gravity, in order to sink from the earth's circumference down to the earth." (August 24, 1910)

The expulsion from Paradise, condensed in Genesis into an event that has again and again been painted by many old masters, and that can still be a moving experience in performances of medieval plays, was described by Rudolf Steiner as a process carried out over eons, i. e., man's descent from etheric realms, the densification of his corporeality and his arrival on the earth. Among other medieval paintings, Rudolf Steiner points to Master Bertams's *Fall of Man* (Kunsthalle, Hamburg) where Lucifer is represented as a serpent with a human head. He calls this representation "spiritually correct"[13] in contrast to a merely realistic drawing of a snake.

In the painting of the two cupolas, Rudolf Steiner did not take his starting point from imaginations given in this way. The task of modern painting is that "the form be the work of color"; the motif is not the starting point, but rather the result of the experience of color.

The colors in the sketch 'Jehovah and the Luciferic Temptation' speak clearly and distinctly: red in green, peach-blossom in green, blue in green; red, attacking and pronounced; blue, calm and retiring; and peach-blossom, bringing as always a breath of soul.

Rudolf Steiner said, "Green can be said to be in a rhythmic state of equilibrium ... going in, coming out. That is why a wide, green field is so refreshing." (February 16, 1916)

Is it possible to fathom the origin of the motif from the colors of this sketch? Rudolf Steiner described the process of color perception in general for an understanding of a new theory of colors at a point in time (1916) when the artists were trying to master the new painting style for their work in the large cupola so that the connection between color perception and the practice of painting is readily evident.

"To begin with, blue affects our eyes. We do not immediately perceive it, but it flows a certain time; only then do we first become conscious of it .... Thus in this time, we do not yet experience the color blue in the sense of a blue impression, but we do already experience the moral impression of the color. This is already taking effect in us. How the soul streams into the blue, the way this is received with a feeling of comfort, this is already part of us. The soul quality of color is experienced earlier, but it remains in the unconscious. The human being does not perceive it. And the human being only begins to become conscious when color appears. He does not notice what precedes the experience of color." (February 16, 1916)

Between the effect of color on the eye and the perception of color itself lies an area of experience that is a gateway to the creative process. "Where real painting is involved, one works out of the soul impression of color. Then one does not work like an artist depending on a model, that is, simply copying a model; rather one knows that to call forth a certain soul impression, red is required. Somewhere else one will use blue to evoke a different impression. This is how all the paintings in our Dornach building are carried out. This is painting out of the color context with its source in that soul nature as it ought to come to expression through the colors. Therefore, it was necessary to experience the building, in the highest sense of the word, as a soul-being. How the building will stand before the world will reflect how it

has grown out of the experience of the building as a soul-being. People will perceive that out of which the Dornach building has grown if they can use the short time that passes between when the building affects the sense organs and when this impression is brought to consciousness. But anyone who participates in the construction must create out of just this short span of time, must create everything in the way of color and forms in this building out of this short time-span." (February 16, 1916)
The sketch 'Jehovah and the Luciferic Temptation' was done during the winter of 1914. In three lectures delivered seven years later,[14] Rudolf Steiner gave additional material for the study of color. He started out describing the tonalities of red in green, blue in green, peach-blossom in green, which are the very same colors used in this sketch.
Peaceful green, the balance between the warm and cold tones, and peach-blossom, the utmost intensification of the warm and cold colors, were designated as 'image colors', green, seen everywhere in the earth's plant life, as the 'dead image of life', peach-blossom, nearest to man's 'incarnated' color, visible in the healthy skin of a person whose soul forces are alive and incarnated, as the 'living image of the soul'.
Rudolf Steiner contrasted these with the basic colors red, blue, and yellow, which are mobile in themselves and endowed with forces that lead over to form, and these he called 'lustre colors'. He characterized warm, active, advancing red as 'lustre of life', inwardly weaving and reserved blue as 'lustre of the soul' and radiant yellow as 'lustre of the spirit'.
This view of image and lustre colors results in a new differentiated handling of the painter's medium. One learns to sense one's way up through the kingdoms of nature from black, the 'spiritual image of death', to life, to soul, to white or light, the 'soul image of the spirit'.
"So, if I take the realms of nature, the dead realm, the living realm, the realm of the soul, and that of the spirit, I ascend; and just as I ascend from death to life, soul, and spirit, I ascend from black, through green and peach-blossom to white ... .
I have a world before me: mineral, plant, animal, and spiritual kingdoms to the extent that man is spiritual. I ascend through realities, but nature itself provides me with the images of these realities. It forms its own likenesses. The color world is not a reality; even in nature, the color world is an image, and the image of death is black, the image of life is green, the image of the soul is peach-blossom, and the image of the spirit is white." (May 6, 1921)

The Three Creation Motifs

The three creation motifs unfold in three color stages of increasing intensity. In the first stage, a red peach-blossom color appears out of a blue background; in the second, the polarity of two colors: red and blue; in the third, the interplay of image,and lustre colours: peach-blossom, green, red, and blue.
Elohim: Red appears within an enveloping, protective lustre of a wide blue background: a "dialogue and alternating play of forces" brings the configuration of the picture into being.
Eye and Ear: Red and blue in polarity. The tension creates a color space in the same way as two opposing currents meet in the sense organs. Out of this tension, man develops his capacity for perception.
Jehovah and the Luciferic Temptation: Peach-blossom, the 'living image of the soul', has sunk into green, the 'dead image of life'. The blue that had filled a wide expanse and provided the foundation for the creation out of which everything was born is now densified into the image of Jehovah and has also become 'image' in the figures of the two angels.
The motifs were to arise out of the streams of color, were to appear as though born out of these streams.
"No one will fully experience this dialogue and interplay of forces unless he can feel the colors as waves of the sea, rising and falling, unless he can experience the elemental beings playing upon these waves, the elemental beings who spontaneously develop their forms out of themselves in these waves of color." (January 15, 1920)
The sketch for the first motif belongs to the south side. The extensive motif was also carried out on the north side in symmetrical mirror images forming a great unified picture of the Creation. The second motif was as a whole executed twice in symmetrical mirror image.
The composition of the third motif is dominated by strict symmetry in the columns of fire and the gestures of the blue angels. However, in the center, around the Tree of Paradise, the red of Lucifer brings movement and unrest, something new that breaks through and dissolves the symmetry.
"In the paintings that will fill out the cupolas, we attempted to treat color in a very special way. Naturally, I can only give partial indications of these things. Regarding the treatment of color in creating figures something was attempted that is not usually attempted with color. An attempt was made to experience color directly. Everything that comes to the soul through spiritual research ought to be here inwardly experienced. Color

should not be merely on the surface revealing just anything that is beneath; rather, color should have inner life and this inner life should be developed out of the color itself so that out of the corresponding color and placing of colors life itself appears.
One should so regard the painted art work that immediately, in the interaction of color and what flows out of the color into the form, one has the feeling that one lives immersed in that which is alive in the color. One then grasps the reality that stands behind the color. Color should have its language; forms should have their language; not something *through* color nor something *through* form. Then life with the spiritual worlds leads precisely to this: when color and forms present pictures, we only present them as we artistically experience them in every moment, so that one need not hold oneself directly to a model; rather one brings that which lives and weaves in spiritual reality and in spiritual being into the weaving of color and the life of forms which one then brings onto the surface." (January 14, 1916)

LEMURIA AND ATLANTIS

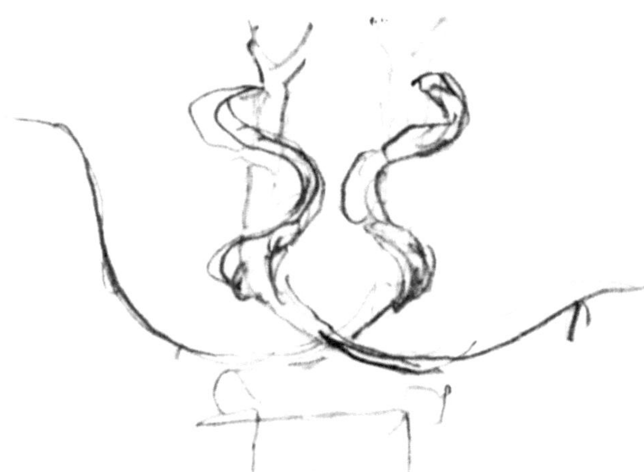

Drawing by Carl Kemper

Above the middle or the fourth of the seven planetary pillars in the north and south, the metamorphosis of capital forms comes to a kind of completion – the Earth stage. A new impulse is announced with the fifth column. Above the central column we see the movements of the architrave from west to east intertwining in the double Staff of Mercury. Here, above the fourth column, restful blue colors meet the warm colors pouring in from the east, creating green and yellow-green tones. This interaction and interweaving of passive and active colors forms the color foundation for the two motifs, 'Lemuria' in the north and 'Atlantis' in the south.

"The figures which you see here on the left and right, and which seem to represent mythological figures, are meant to convey something of the situation as it was before the great Atlantean catastrophe. To spiritual investigation, the materialistic theory of evolution proves itself entirely incorrect. If we go back in human evolution, we arrive first of all at the Graeco-Roman period which began approximately in the eighth century B. C. Going further back, we come to the Egypto-Chaldean period, beginning at about the turn of the fourth and third millenia B. C. We come to still older periods, finally arriving at a time which, speaking in spiritual-scientific terms, we must call the time of the Atlantean catastrophe. Great redistributions of continents took place at that time. One looks back clairvoyantly to a time in earth evolution when the area that is now covered by the Atlantic Ocean was land. But at the same time, one returns to a period of the earth's evolution when the human being could not exist in his present shape with muscles and bones as we have them today. If one considers such creatures of the sea as jellyfish which can hardly be distinguished from their environment, one comes to the material form in which man once appeared on earth during the time of Atlantis when the whole earth was covered constantly by a dense mist in which man lived and because of which he was a very different organic being. The forms that have been painted here to the left and right of the ceiling appear to the seer, the clairvoyant, if you know what I mean." (December 30, 1921)

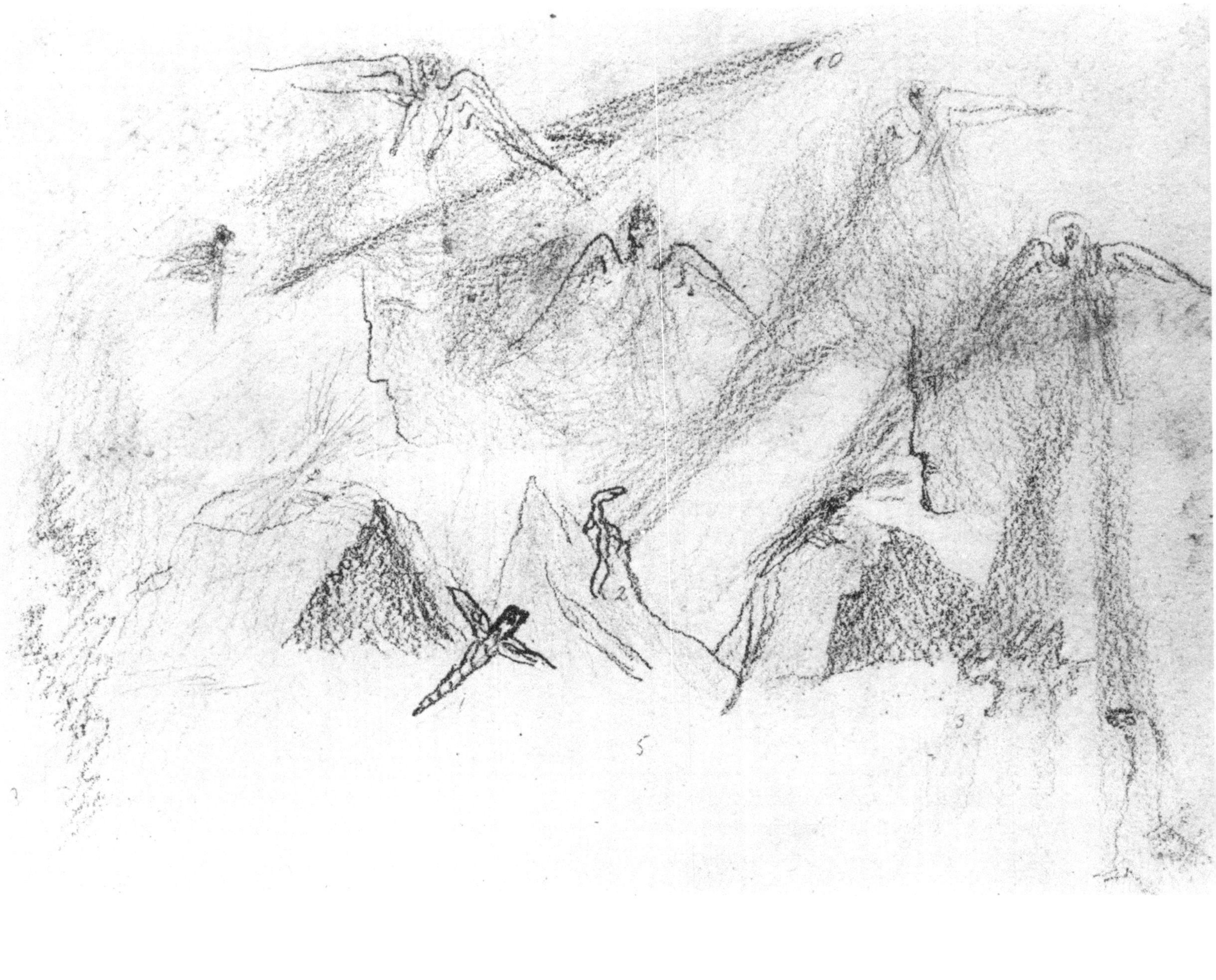

LEMURIA

Pastel Sketch

Red and yellow interpenetrate each other in a glowing, steaming atmosphere. Fiery breath, fiery air. Flashes of lightning, whirling dragons. Deep ultramarine holds all this turbulent movement and lends protective forces. Solemnly, earnest contenances and winged figures take shape.

Down below in the dull green, reddish seaweed or algae shapes drift about. Green painted over red results in broken brownish tones. Elevations arise out of the green dampness. Upon these solidified areas, a gentle red appears straining towards the great blue profiles which send back helping rays in response to their effort.

Drawing

What appears in the pastel sketch merely as gentle, red flecks is recognizable in the drawing as delicate shapes of etheric currents, still open, without completion or skin. Half gliding or swimming, supporting themselves upon the elevations, and rising out of the mud of the earth below, they abandon themselves to the forces streaming towards them from the divine countenances. The first impulse towards the vertical! Surrounding nature also reflects this. Lizard-like animals attempt to move upwards; prototypal saurians, with comb-shaped backs, are bound to gravity.

Below, forces of gravity and density; above, lightning, spiritual beings with large wings in regions of fire, tremendous mobility fills the whole picture.

The inner content of the motif is the contact, the dialogue between the as yet delicate indications of a human disposition and the beings who are awakening the breath and ego forces expressed by deep blue in the pastel and accentuated by lines in the drawing.

The Motif

The Lemurian continent was situated "deep down in the south, stretching from northern Africa to southern Australia". (April 1, 1902). It came to an end through fire catastrophes. The subsequent Atlantean evolution unfolded in the area between America and Europe, which today is covered by water.

"Preceding the times of the Atlantean continent and the great Atlantean race from which all European and Asian races have developed, there was yet another continent and another race, submerged even more deeply into animal nature: the Lemurians. Science ascribes it a merely hypothetical existence. Still, certain islands south of Asia and north of Australia bear witness to its reality because they are remnants of the ancient Lemurian continent." (June 9, 1906)

"At that time the earth looked very different. What are now hard cliffs then floated along like water. There was no air as we know it today; the entire earth was enveloped in hot steam. Many of the metals that are hard today existed either in the form of steam or they flowed like water. The steamy atmosphere was permeated by etheric currents as today with air currents. Man already lived on this earth, but he was a kind of fish-bird, floating, swimming forward."[15]

Rudolf Steiner vividly described this early condition of the earth to the workmen on the first Goetheanum, dramatically characterizing the picture of how the earth was covered by a "greenish-brown mud" and giant lizards swam and waded in this mud, and how in other places, the mud had hardened "like a horse's hoof" and how animals had settled on the elevations: Ichthyosauruses, and fish-sauruses so large that a modern man would require a ladder to mount them. "These beasts" had heads like dolphins, but not so hard, and teeth like crocodiles. Their long tails were covered with strong thick scales. But in the air, in the "fire-air" above, which was filled with hot steam and flickered with flashes of lightning, dragonbirds darted with very flexible bat-like wings and sharp eyes. Rapturously, they threw themselves into the mouths of the mighty saurians who swallowed them as nourishment. (cf. September 20, 1922)

Man was the last to enter the earth. The lower animals, the creatures of air and water, were already living on the earth while man was still waiting in the spiritual circumference of the earth until he had become sufficiently dense and could descend and later assume his human, physical form. This form did not yet exist. A man with today's senses could not have perceived it.

"If we were to go back to the very early times of Lemuria, we would see people moving about the earth with a very different form than that of present-day man. Their shape could not be called human because they did not yet have the seed of the human soul which first enabled man to ascend to higher stages of development. We would find human shapes which had only sheaths for a human soul, human beings who only possessed physical, etheric and astral bodies. The astral bodies, pictorially speaking, had a kind of "indentation" for the incorporation of the ego-consciousness. Basically, the four parts of man's being were already present, but that to which you today say 'I', what lives in you today, was then still within the bosom of the Godhead." (April 1, 1907)

"One must be quite clear about the fact that man first took on dense substance much later and then quite gradually. If we want to get an idea of his physical nature at the stage of development under discussion, we can best do so by imagining something like steam or a cloud floating in the air. But of course this idea approaches reality only quite *externally*. For the fire-cloud, 'man', was inwardly alive and organized. Compared with man's later development, however, his soul-being must be imagined as being asleep, or only dimly conscious. He lacked everything that could be called intelligence, understanding, or reason. He moved – it was more floating than walking – by means of four limb-like organs, forwards, sideways, backwards, in every direction."[16]

In Genesis it says, "In the beginning God created heaven and earth. And the earth was waste and void and it was dark in the depths and the spirit of God moved upon the waters." Only the sixth day of creation – a 'day' meaning an aeon of cosmic evolution – brings the creation of man after the Word of God had called forth the previous stages. The mighty words of the Elohim sounded forth: "Let us make man an image like unto ourselves."

"The Adam-Man, 'the earthy one', man as such is the earth-being *kat ex-ochen*, the crown, as it were, of all earth-being, and that which came last as the fruit of the earth being." (August 24, 1910)

Embedded in the activities of the Elohim and the Beings subservient to them, he matures to the stage where Jehovah-Elohim could fashion his earthly corporeality and breathe air into him. "And Jehovah-Elohim breathed into him the living breath ... and thus man became a living soul."

"Indeed, at that time, not only was the stream of air breathed into man, but also that which lived in him as spiritual being ... . When you experience the air, you must make clear to yourself that this is the physical body of the surrounding spirit, and that with every breath, you take in not only physical air, but you also breathe in spirit. It is completely true that at that time, with the breathing-in of physical air in the way it occurs with man in his present form, all this sank into his physical sheath – for this is what is indicated in the Bible." (April 1, 1907)

The warmth of the blood was necessary for the development of the ego. Individual life could not begin until this stage was reached.

"So you must imagine that then, when actual human evolution began in the Lemurian era, on the one hand, the spirit belonging to the air descended upon man, and that then that higher spirit, which is within the warmth of the blood, the actual earth spirit, began to descend. These two spirits stand in such a relationship to one another that one might say that that spirit whose body is the air enabled man to attain to speech, for the organization in the human organism that makes our breathing process possible also makes speech possible. Speech developed during Atlantean times and the highest expression of speech, which occurred already towards the end of that era, was man's ability to say 'I'." (April 1, 1907)

Rudolf Steiner's pictorial motif 'Adam Kadmon in early Lemuria' from the series of studies for artistic training can give further insight into man's development during Lemurian times. In this pastel sketch, peach-blossom and carmine weave above. The earth in gentle warm red is surrounded by a dull blue in which green plays and sprouts. A human head, the crown of the skull turned

down as though rooted in the earth, looks up to a divine countenance woven in bright yellow which calls forth and bestows light and life forces from ether regions.
Adam Kadmon is the archetypal cosmic man unified with the beginning stage of the earth, early Lemuria. "Man felt an intimate relationship to everything plant-like. He did not feel the same relationship to the higher animals, for he knew that he could only make his way to the earth by overcoming the animal nature, by leaving the animals behind on his evolutionary path."(December 28, 1923)
The eyes of the human being are impressive as they receive consciousness from the spiritual world. In the lower part of the picture, the animal's dim, dreamy gesture gives the appearance that they bear the earthly round in humility. During a lecture given on September 30, 1922, Rudolf Steiner drew many blackboard sketches illustrating the subject 'Man and the Earth'. He mentioned Adam Kadmon, as archetypal man was called in the Old Testament, and the giant Ymir in Germanic sagas: "The earth once was a giant human being, the giant Ymir." Blackboard drawings, executed in color during the lecture given on December 28, 1923, although done quickly and sketchily while speaking, are, in movement and content, similar to the training study.[17]
The cupola motif, 'Lemuria', man forming himself between fire-air and earth-mud, inspired by sublime gods to stand upright, is situated above the fourth, the Mars column and the interwining staffs of Mercury in the architrave on the north side of the cupola. Directly opposite, on the south side, the Atlantis motif answers to it.

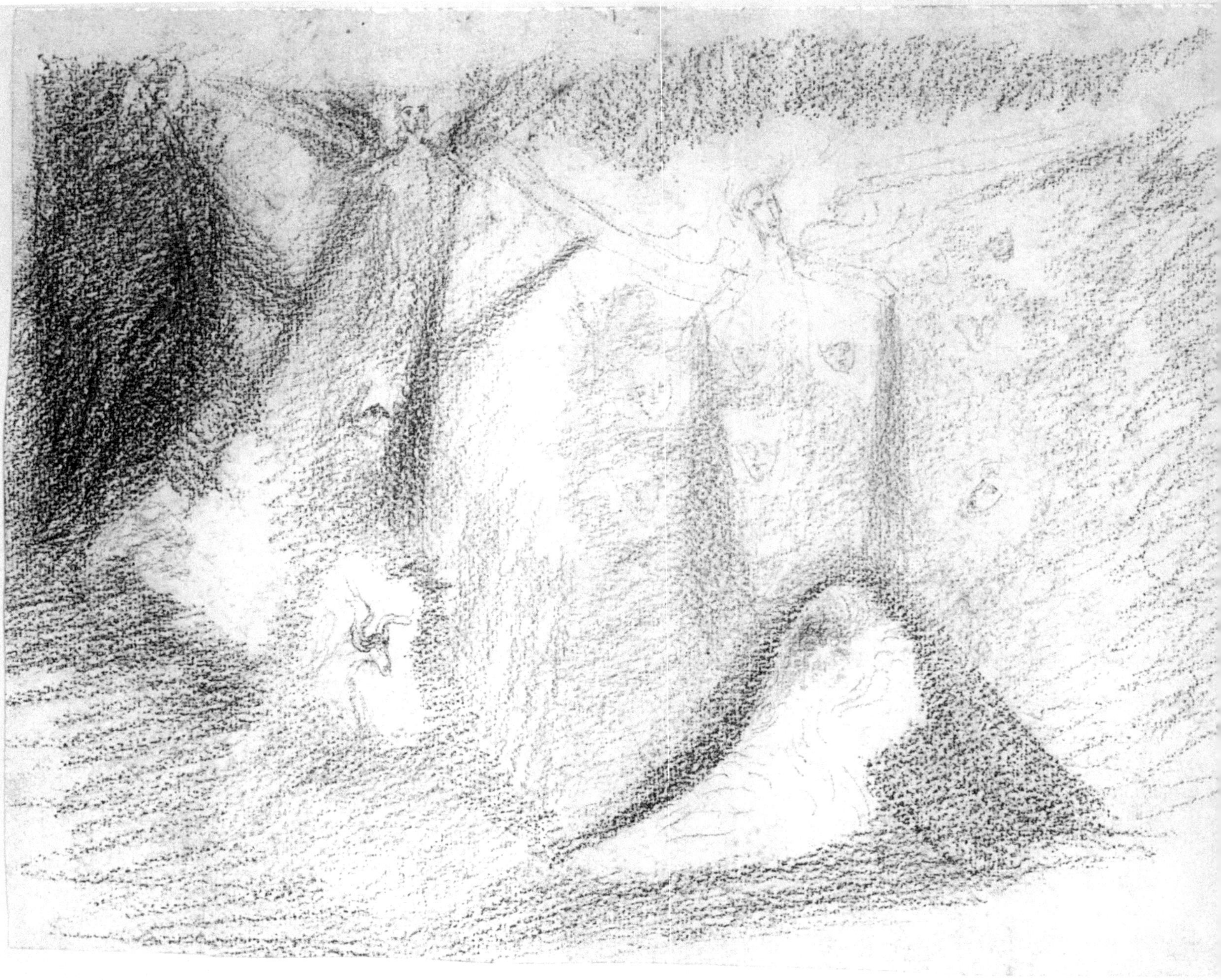

ATLANTIS

Pastel Sketch

Violet speaks strongly in a golden yellow background. Blue is brought to it and spreads out in wide wings. Lighter blue, as though emanating from the distant heavens, gives a sense of coming life within the protection of the gods. Red works powerfully downwards. From the sides, green and violet weave across the warm yellow, which still shines through. Blue, reddish and brown are supported by the weaving, violet-tinged green. The blue becomes a bird-being, the red lion-like and the brown bovine. Across from the animals, dark purple shapes a kind of cave enclosing a hidden, streaming inner life.

Drawing

The pencil drawing for the 'Atlantis' motif contains an incomparable wealth of light and dark values. The region of the animals shows bird and lion as though emerging from areas corresponding to their natures. Strokes characterize a horned cow nobly and sorrowfully experiencing earth existence. Light currents in cave-like darkness arouse a sense of inner life that belongs only to man. The upper part of the picture contains an area of light with great depth. Noble beings – their expression speaks of Apollonian clarity and purity – protect and guide a multitude of shapes born of the light. The heads of souls pressing toward incarnation are delicately indicated. What appears as powerful red in the pastel is here obviously pathways of will clearing the way.

The language of this drawing can be experienced more intensely and convincingly when retraced with a pencil. There is nothing naturalistic. Even the smallest line, e.g., in the widespread wings, is a sustaining, rhythmically ordering force, opening up spiritual spaces.

The Motif

Volcanic eruptions brought about the end of the Lemurian era through fire. The major part of the land inhabited at that time was destroyed in this way. Only a small number of people were able to escape.

"The part of mankind that was saved migrated to the land we know as Atlantis, situated essentially between present-day America and Europe; there, the human race continued to increase. Gradually the earth atmosphere changed to such an extent that the remnants of the old 'smoke' cleared away and the air only remained impregnated with mighty masses of fog. In the Germanic saga, a memory of this lingers in the description of *Niflheim* or *Nebelheim**, a land continuously permeated by such dense fog." (June 4, 1907)

At that time, man was quite different than he is today. His physical body was of very delicate substance. Rudolf Steiner describes the way the objects the Atlantean perceived through his body did not have clear outlines but were blurred, surrounded by color borders as though framed in auras.

"Firm contours formed themselves only gradually. If we had had a rose before us in the early stages of old Atlantis, we would have seen a misty shape arising, a pink-red circle in its midst, and only gradually the outer

**Editor's Note: The German Nebel (Old German Nifl) means fog; Heim means home; consequently the legends surrounding Niflheim (Nebelheim) refer to man's home in the fog; i.e., the Atlantean times.*

colors would have settled over the surface. Objects received their clear-cut contours only later." (June 23, 1908)

Man perceived the events about him in dream-like pictures, at times dimly, at others more clearly, in accordance with the rhythmic sequence of day and night.

"If we imagine for a moment that we go out for a walk in a thick winter fog and see the streetlights in the evening as though surrounded by an aura of light, we will have an approximate idea of the Atlanteans' consciousness of the objects around them. For man at that time, everything was surrounded by such a mist; everything was as though within mist. This was the way things were seen by day. Nights presented something quite different. The night perception was, however, also not the way it is today. When the Atlantean left his body, he did not sink into unconsciousness but found himself in a world of divine spiritual beings, of ego beings whom he recognized around him as his companions. True as it is that today man does not see beings during the night, it is also true that in those times man dove into a sea of spirituality in which he indeed perceived the divine beings. During the day, he was a companion of the lower kingdom; at night, he was a companion of higher beings. Thus man lived within a spiritual consciousness, albeit a vague one; even though he had no consciousness of self, he lived among these divine spiritual beings." (September 3, 1908)

Today, man quite naturally wakes in the morning and falls asleep at night. At that time, it was almost the opposite. During the night, while moving among sublime spiritual beings, he felt himself more awake; during the day, he entered into his physical body and rested.

The ego of the man of Atlantis was still embedded in a kind of group nature. Rudolf Steiner differentiates four archetypes of such group souls. "One can see them quite distinctly when looking back clairvoyantly to the times when man had no corporeality and had not yet descended to the earth. For now we must describe more clearly the moment when man descended out of spiritual regions into his body. We can describe this moment only in terms of great symbols.

"There was a time when our earth consisted of much softer matter than it does today, when rocks and stones were not so solid as today, when plant forms looked different; when everything, as in a primeval ocean, was embedded in caves of water; when air and water were not separate; when all the beings living on the earth today, animals and plants, developed in the water. As the mineral beings began to take on the form they have today, then one could say that man stepped forth out of invisibility. So he appears to the one on the threshold of initiation. Surrounded by a kind of shell on the outside, he descended from the regions which are today regions of air. Man did not yet have a dense, physical body like the animals which were already present in the flesh. He was a being of delicate air substance, even in the Lemurian times. And he took form in such a way that the clairvoyant image represents him with the four group souls: on the one side as an image of a lion; on the other as the image of a bull; up above as the image of an eagle, and below in the middle, something already akin to a human being. This is how it appears to clairvoyant vision. In this way man emerges from the darkness of spirit land." (June 19, 1908)

These three animals and their union in the human form belong to the oldest imaginations of man. Already in the old Sumerian zodiac, in which Scorpio was represented by the eagle[18], this four-part image represented the turning points in the yearly cycle. The picture of the Sphinx, a winged being with the body of a bull, the chest of a lion and a human head, is an artistic expression of this imagination of man's cosmic origin. It accompanies the whole Egyptian period and re-emerges in early Christianity. We find four beings – the fourfold animal being – as a motif in the second seal created by Rudolf Steiner for the Munich Congress.[19]

"As our fingers are connected to our egos, so human beings felt themselves as part of the group souls which were clairvoyantly seen as the four heads of lion, bull, eagle, and man depicted in the Apocalypse of St. John. Man felt himself placed into one of these group souls." (June 23, 1908)[20]

The Atlanteans' extraordinary memory is also connected with this. "Man's memory today is such that he can only recollect the times of his youth. But there was a time when a different kind of memory existed, when a man remembered not only his own deeds, but also those of his father and grandfather, as though they were his own. Memory reached far back through the blood-relationship with the ancestors, right back to the founder of a line, whose blood flowed down through the generations." (May 22, 1908)

As the air became more and more cleared, the Atlantean participated less and less in the memories of his ancestors. Gradually his memory became more individual and formed itself into images which bore the stamp of personal experience.

"If we want to characterize the events of those days, we should think of man as if he were crawling out of his corporeal snail shell into the spiritual world. There he lives among divine spiritual beings. There he hears his name, what he is, sounding to him from outside. Towards one group sounded the word which was in the archetypal language the word for this group; another group heard a different word. Man could not name himself from within; he had to receive his name by hearing it called from outside. When he crawled out of his corporeal snail shell, he knew what it was because the sound of his name had been called into his soul. Now in his physical body, he learned to perceive the physical environment; he learned to sense himself as an ego; he learned to feel within himself the divine force which previously had come to him as sound from outside; he learned to feel God within himself. This God, who was closest to him, and who simultaneously indicated his ego, he called Jehovah, the guide to the ego. Man felt the strength of this God unfolding within his ego." (June 23, 1908) In this way, man descended from one of the divine group-souls to the experience of an individual earthly soul.

In the sketch for 'Atlantis', the three animals, eagle, lion and bull, are like words spoken out through the creative power of the red rays of the gods. Man, meanwhile, is at rest, receiving and experiencing celestial language in earthly existence.

The process of emerging from group-existence lasted aeons. Finally, the pouring flood-waters flowed over all of Atlantis and caused, as the story of the Flood depicts, the end of the Atlantean epoch. Only a small band of human beings could save themselves. For them, the spiritual light had darkened. But outside a colorful sign appeared that signified at the same time separation from and union with the divine.

"There was no distribution of rain and sunshine as there is today. For that reason, what we know as the rainbow could not exist in ancient Atlantis. You could search the whole of Atlantis and you would rarely find one. Only when the densification of the water had led to the flood, when the great flood has passed over the earth, was it physically possible for a rainbow to occur. And here we have a point where spiritual science will evoke the greatest reverence for religious documents. For when you are told that after the Flood, Noah, the representative of those who saved the human race and brought it over, was the first to see the rainbow, that is really a historical happening. After the flood, humanity saw the first rainbow; before that, its appearance was physically impossible ... . When the old Atlantean was thus immersed in his physical body, he looked up into celestial space and, as I said, he did not see a real rainbow there, but there was something like a circle of color, where later the sun would appear. The sun did not yet fully penetrate the mist with its power, but it shone through the mist. It worked upon earth with its power impeded and checked by mist. It emerged more and more, so that everything that has been described, this beginning of outer consciousness, was connected with the emergence of the sun out of the mist. What was up there where the other six spirits dwelled who, together with Jehovah, had guided the evolution of the earth, gradually emerged and shone down upon the earth in their deeds." (June 23, 1908)

The motifs of the sketches of the following four cultural epochs after the appearance of the rainbow seem like weavings in the colors of the rainbow.

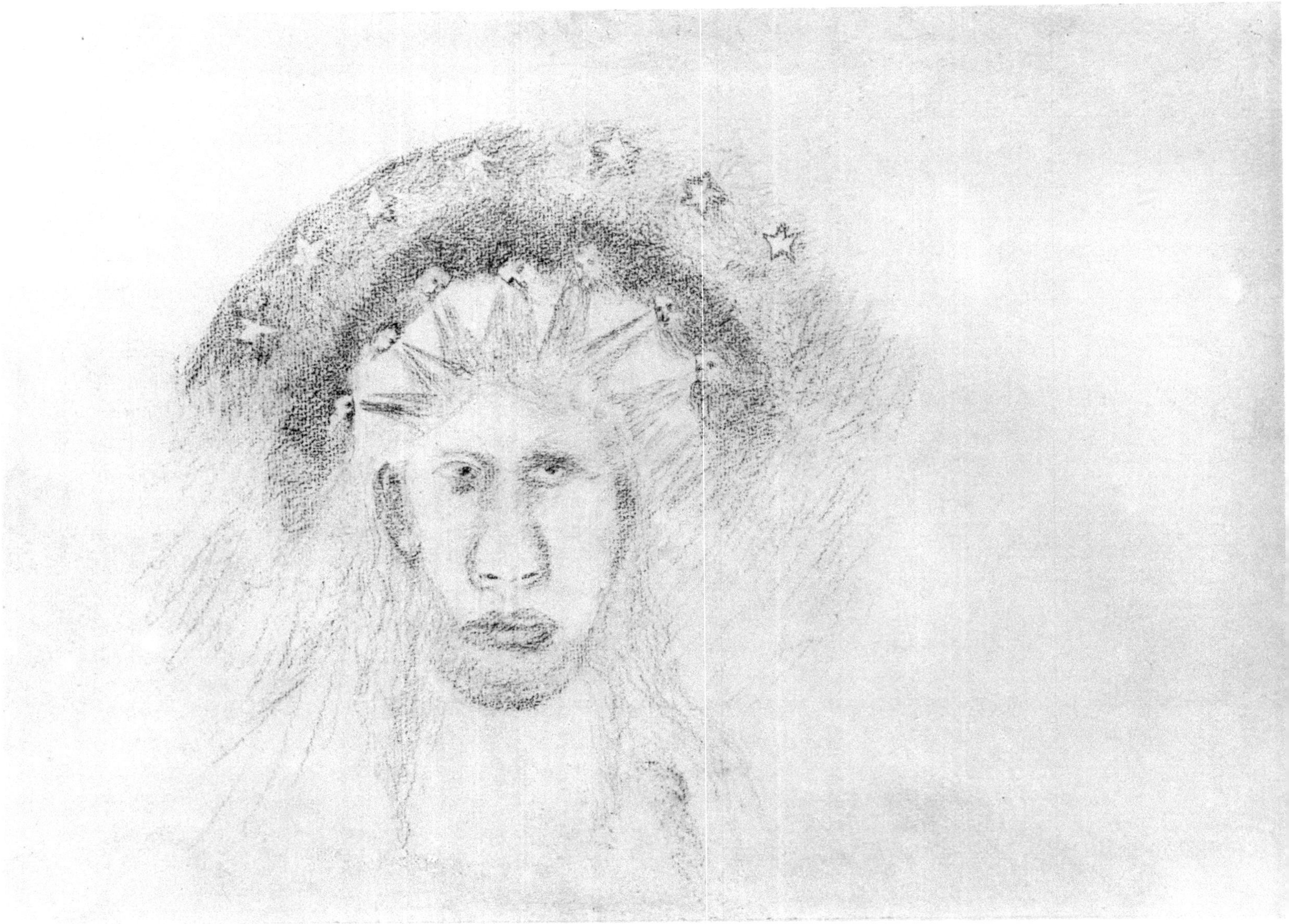

MAN IN ANCIENT INDIA

"The mystery of the ancient Indian inspiration is how the Indian Rishis directed to mankind that which was to come into primeval humanity from spiritual spheres during the Indian civilization." (October 24, 1914)

Pastel Sketch

Peach-blossom shapes a large countenance, completely abandoned to life's fullness in the warm colors, and listening to the wisdom-filled, instreaming yellow. Within the red, 'lustre of life', the yellow, 'lustre of the spirit', lights up as seven bright stars.
Red, orange, yellow and peach-blossom-incarnadine determine the motif. Details are clarified by small additions of black: the eyes that look inward, pronounced lips, the listening attitude of the ear. Seven wise heads allow the forces of inspiration to stream into the human being reverently sensing the wisdom of the stars. There is a mood of majestic repose that had been given to man as an inner force. The head, as an image of the heavenly sphere, is open, not yet closed off.

Drawing

The rays of the stars and the devotion of the soul receiving them weave into one another in the interplay of light and dark. The seven Rishis, the great teachers, grouped into three and four, guide the language of the stars to the head of the Indian. The expressions of inner listening is even stronger than in the pastel sketch.

The Motif

During a guided tour of the Goetheanum, Rudolf Steiner said that this motif of 'Man in Ancient India' appears as if "... coming over from old Atlantis, enlightening him. There was not one being who lived within his skin but a sevenfold being. His soul forces were, so to speak, made up of the seven soul-rays of the holy Rishis, and what he then revealed to the world did not come out of his own spirit but out of the spirit of the seven holy Rishis.
"The more one works out what is said here, the closer one comes to what has been painted here. The feelings were first of all transported back to ancient India, to ancient Atlantis. What could be seen there has been painted on the wall here, and only afterwards, when it is actually there, can one begin to speculate about it. So the communication is in proportion to artistic creativity. And, actually, everything in this building should arise like this." (August 28, 1921)
No naturalistic style of painting could have expressed the immediacy of experience that speaks in the sketch and the drawing. Thus Rudolf Steiner took new paths which he himself called risky.
"And here the risk had to be taken not to close the head at the top but to leave it open. For indeed, when protraying the Indian as he was in his time, he appears as though connected with the heavens through his primeval wisdom. I would like to say that for him the top of his physical skull was lost in unconsciousness and he felt his soul extending into the expanse of heaven. This is set down here in artistic form." (December 30, 1921)
"To paint the ancient Indian with the head open at the top and those inspiring him, the seven holy Rishis, who in turn were inspired by the stars, if one does that abstractly, that is actually nonsense; I say this quite openly. And yet when you experience what was experienced in the ancient Indian culture in the pupil's relationship to the guru, the teacher, you feel he had no skull, that it had fled away." (August 28, 1921)
After the submersion of Atlantis, a part of the earth's inhabitants migrated from the region of Ireland through Europe to Central Asia. The first post-Atlantean civili-

zation developed there under the guidance of great leaders. According to Rudolf Steiner, this ancient Indian culture goes back eight or nine thousand years, much further back than the *Veda* texts.

"That was the ancient Indian people, a race then living in the Far East. They were concerned far more with the memory of past times than with the present. The greatness and power of that civilization, of which written reports such as the *Vedas* and *Bhagavad-Gita* are mere echoes, are that its people lived within the memory of experiences they themselves had had in Atlantis." (June 20, 1908).

They remembered the times when man lived among gods in harmony with the spirit. They saw the world around them as mere 'maya', illusion.

"Thus the land that had just arisen before man's physical eyes, the rocks which only now had become visible, though formerly they had been seen spiritually, all the external phenomena appeared to him less important than what he could remember. They called all that could be seen with the physical eye 'maya', the great illusion, and they wanted to escape it. The best among them in this first epoch were raised to the stage of their ancestors through a method of initiation, a remnant of which survives in yoga. A religious undertone emanated from this, which may be put in these words: worthless, vain illusion surrounds us in the appearances of the senses. The true, the real is up there in the spiritual world that we have left behind. The spiritual leaders were those able to raise themselves into the regions in which they had formerly lived." (June 20, 1908)

"In ancient India, the 'gurus' or teachers did not teach in the real sense of the word; they worked 'magically' from personality to personality directly upon the ether bodies. They lowered their own day-consciousness, and 'exalted beings' who formerly had spoken to their spiritual ancestors spoke through them."

Through the power of the Rishis, the mysteries of the cosmos were opened up to mankind. It was a planetary wisdom, the wisdom of earth evolution, sounding in harmonious "accord with the wisdom of the various oracles of Atlantean times"[21] that streamed down from the Rishis under the leadership of the great Manu.

"All of the planets have effects upon man. But to begin with, the effects had to be mediated and this was done through the great Manu who initiated the seven Rishis in such a way that one individual Rishi understood the mysteries of one of the planets in its influences. And since there were seven planets, these seven Rishis together represented a seven-part lodge able to impart to its pupils knowledge of the mysteries of our solar system. Many old occult scripts point to this, as for example in the following: There are mysteries to be sought beyond the Seven; they are those guarded by the holy Manu himself about times preceding the separation of the planets.[22]

The same forces the planets held were hidden within the secrets of the seven Rishis. And this choir of the seven Rishis worked in complete unity with Manu within that wonderful wisdom, passing it on to their pupils. If we wanted to characterize this, we might say that this archetypal teaching contained approximately what we know of today as the evolution of mankind through the planetary conditions of Saturn, Sun, Moon, Earth, Jupiter, Venus, Vulcan." (September 5, 1908)

According to Rudolf Steiner, the seven Rishis must be sought in relationship to what is represented in the constellation of Taurus.

"They were initiated into the Sun mysteries in such a way that, for us, the symbol of their initiation is the standing of the sun in Taurus; and what we can see in the sky when the sun is in Taurus actually expresses the mystery of the specific initiation of the Rishis. This initiation worked down through the seven personalities who were the seven holy Rishis. This comes to expression in the fact that the seven stars, the Pleiades, shine down from the same place. That is the place where our entire solar system entered our cosmos. Thus the initiation into the various kinds of Sun mysteries can be expressed by taking the forms of expression from the position of the sun in a constellation." (December 18, 1910)

The significance of the Pleiades, which are a uniquely beautiful and impressive spectacle to the senses, goes far beyond the sequence of the cultural epochs, bound, as they are, to temporal evolution. They are, as it were, an archetypal phenomenon in the starry heavens, which pictorially unites the being of the fixed stars with that of the planets. The seven-part wisdom of ancient Indian inspiration sounded in archetypal harmony "for behind it stood the basic wisdom of the prophetic Christ initiation", the wisdom of the descent of the primeval Word.

"In the first culture of the post-Atlantean epoch, the Rishis brought those sublime teachings, teachings that lead mankind into the high, lofty, spiritual worlds, up to higher Devachan. In the following cultural periods, that which was seen was brought down onto the physical plane until, in the fourth post-Atlantean epoch, One came down onto the physical plane who was known as Brahma in the Indian cultural period, and whom we call

Christ, the One who no longer mediated the spiritual, but Himself became a man in order to spread to all men the mysterious might of the primeval Word.
Thus the primeval Word descended in order to raise man again. And man must understand how this came about so that he can make an instrument of himself through which, in the future, he may become effective. We must learn to know what worked before our times so that we may participate in the ever higher transformation of what is around us that was created for us.
In the future, we must create a spiritual world. In order to do this, we must first understand the cosmos." (September 5, 1908)

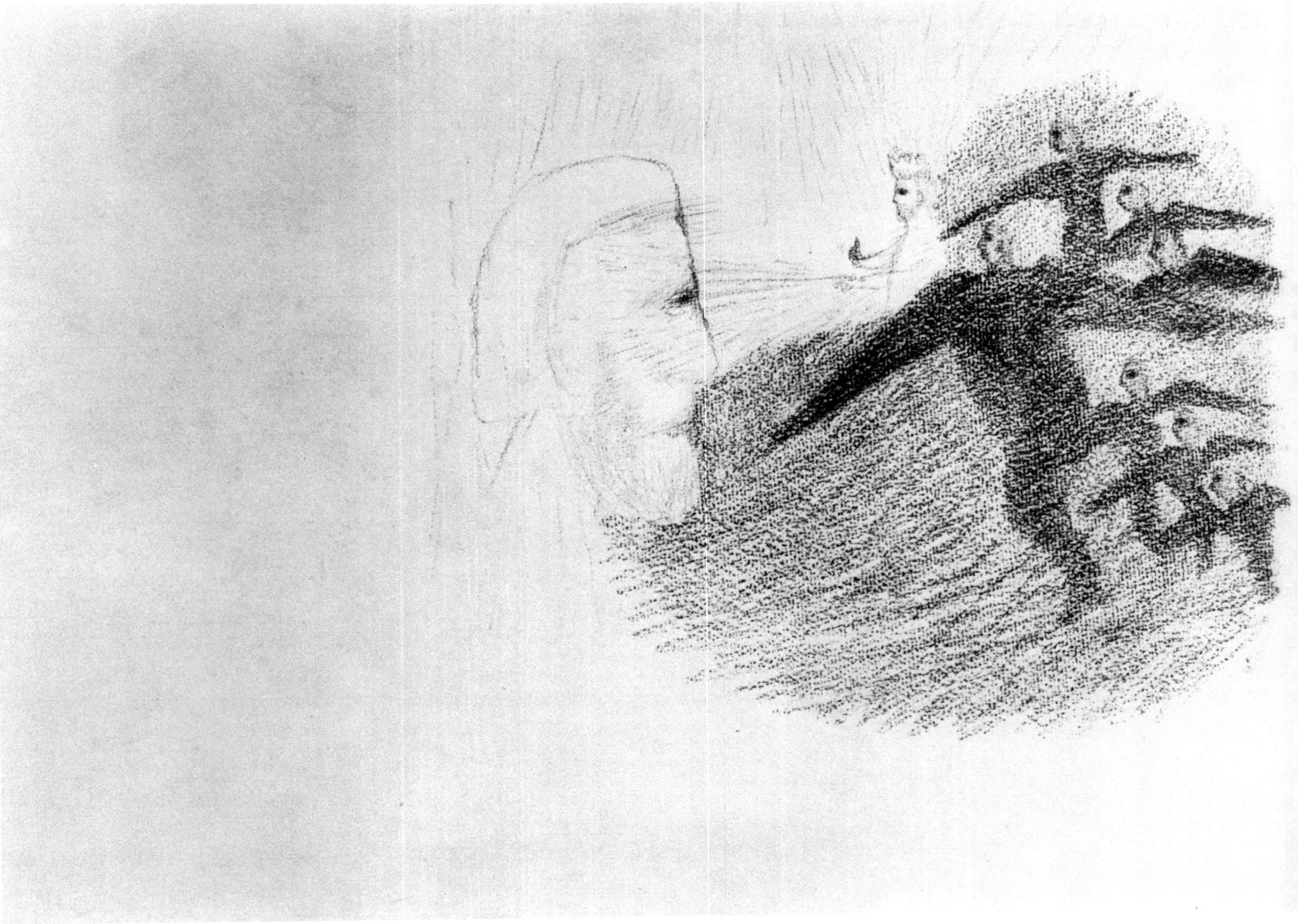

MAN IN ANCIENT PERSIA

"How Zarathustra shaped the ancient Persian culture, as though it were the sunlight fighting the darkness." (October 24, 1914)

Pastel Sketch

Yellow and peach-blossom stream in – etherically invigorated light. Black, fighting back against it, fills a large area of the sketch. Dark beings with barely formed wings and dragon-like bodies follow the leader of darkness.

In the center is a priest-king clothed in light carmine and gold. A beam of light emanating from his hand awakens the eye of the Persian with noble features and light hair – awakening him to the contemplation of the outer world and teaching him to stand fast in the battle between light and darkness.

Unlike the Indian motif, the forces of the stars are not visible here. Neither does Ormuzd himself appear in the picture, but the light is still ensouled and enspirited by his divine life.

Drawing

As in the pastel sketch, the area is slanted, divided almost diagonally. The Persian looks on the universal battle between light and darkness and he sees the storming hosts of Ahriman in deep black, following their leader. Also here, as in the pastel, their wings and bodies are only indefinitely shaped.

In the middle stands a crowned form in a priest-like posture. He receives the light out of the heights and guides it to mankind, awakening the eye, the seeing, so that he can hold himself in the battle against the adversary.

The primal opposition of light and darkness determines the composition and characterizes this motif of the confrontation between good and evil, the mission and destiny of man in ancient Persia as it also comes to expression in Persian mythology.[23]

The Motif

Within the red, orange and yellow currents of color lies, to the north, the picture of the ancient Indian and, to the south, that of the ancient Persian. The Indian is deeply engrossed in inner contemplation, listening to the inspirations of the holy Rishis, resting in the unified world-foundation, in Brahma. In the streams of red and orange, two contrasting realms appear to the Persian: that of light and that of darkness. Inspired by Zarathustra's raying wisdom, he learns to recognize the spirit behind outer phenomena.

Thus two differently orientated spiritual currents can be experienced in these first two motifs. The one, developing in the south in India, turned its gaze away from the outer world in order to dedicate the inner life to the spirit; the other, originating in the north in the highlands of present-day Iran, in the "focus of the world's most beautiful light"[24], sought the revelation of the spirit in the penetration and transformation of the physical sense-world.

"The ancient Persians – and here we are speaking of the prehistoric Persians whose roots go back to a colony founded by the last Atlanteans to emigrate – these Persians already had a different consciousness; they experienced the physical plane as a reality. The physical plane no longer appeared foreign to the ancient Persian. He said to himself, 'On this physical plane there are possibilities for planting and nurturing the Spirit.' He already took notice of the physical world; he did not study it yet, but he took notice of it. The ancient Persian still experienced a hostile element in it, but in such a way that he could overcome it. He became a friend, a companion, of the God Ormuzd in order to redeem matter. He worked into the physical, gradually beginning to realize that this world is not merely maya, not merely illusion without substance, but a reality to be reckoned with."

The ancient Persian became a farmer and a cattle-breeder. In the wild beasts, in all of nature, he saw an evil, a fallen world that had once been good but had not developed further and so remained frozen in an earlier form.[25]

Consequently, he had to take up the golden dagger and change nature, tame the wild beasts and guide them again towards the good. According to legend, he received this dagger from the Turanians, a people living further north who failed to cultivate the earth.

"Along with the golden dagger, given to the Iranians by King Demshid, who had developed his people out of the indolent mass of Turanians, the aspiration for the wisdom bound to outer human forces was given; this striving for wisdom re-develops forces that had become decadent, penetrating and interweaving them with those spiritual forces that man can gain on the physical plane. Used as a plough, this golden dagger dug the earth, turned it into fertile fields and brought man the first primitive inventions. Its effects remained and continue to work in our own times in all the cultural achievements that man is proud of today. It is quite significant that King Demshid, who had come down into Iranian territory from Turan, received this dagger from Ahura Mazdao, for it gives man the power to win over the outer, physical world through his work." (September 1, 1910)

The Turanians were a nomadic people, still clairvoyant, who simply accepted what was available on the earth without cultivation. They hunted wild animals but neither tamed nor bred them. Thus they simply took what the Iranians regarded as the gifts from higher worlds that had become decadent and allowed them to descend still further. The Iranians, on the other hand, felt that nature had to be changed.

"Everything man can do to ennoble the forces of nature, to raise them, can be achieved if man unites himself with Ahura Mazdao, with the power of Ormuzd. Ormuzd is an ascending current. But when man leaves nature as it is, then one can see how everything drifts into savagery. This stems from Ahriman! And then the following mood evolved in the Iranian land: To the north of us many people roam around. They are in the service of Ahriman. They are the people of Ahriman, who only wander around in the world and only take what nature offers them; they do not want to lay a hand on nature to spiritualize her. We, on the other hand, want to unite ourselves with Ormuzd, with Ahura Mazdao." (September 1, 1910)

There were great battles between the Iranians and the people given over to the power of darkness. Iran and Turan fought for centuries in "one of the greatest wars ever fought in the history of the world." (September 1, 1910)

It was Zarathustra who taught the Persians to see the spirit behind everything perceptible by the senses: the spirit-man behind physical man, a spiritual Being behind the sun's body of light. A comparison can be drawn between the physical body of man as an expression of his spirit-man, his aura, and the radiating body of the sun as an expression of the great aura, Ahura Mazdao. And against the spirit of Light, so Zarathustra taught, fights Ahriman, the spirit of darkness, who works against the purification of the human soul, who tries to make the countenance of the light become clouded for mankind.[26]

"And so, while the Indians directed their gaze mystically inwards in order to reach Brahma, to reach the eternal which shines out as from a point within man, Zarathustra directed his pupils toward the great periphery of existence and showed them the presence of the great sun-spirit, Ahura Mazdao, in the sunbody. And just as in man, the actual spirit-man strives towards perfection but has his lower passions, desires and the possibility of exposure to the illusions of lies and untruths working against him, just as man has within himself the opponent of his own impulse toward perfection, so Ahura Mazdao is opposed by Angro-Mainyush, Ahriman." (January 19, 1911)

Ahriman's power, "which corrupts man's soul-life through its influence if he succumbs to it one-sidedly,"[27] echoes through the following words taken from later texts of the Persian religion.

> Seven they are, messengers of King Anu are
>   they;
> Wherever they go they cause darkness.
> A tornado they are, grimly chasing across the
>   sky;
> Dense clouds they are, causing the sky to
>   grow dark.

In the purifying power of fire, the Persian found a way to the sun spirit which animates everything on earth, warming it and filling it with light. The sun spirit was worshipped in the fire ritual. The flames consumed everything impure, while the warmth protected the pure who advanced through the region of the fire to the spirit.

Through the fire's activity, we first draw
near you,
Master of Wisdom, Lord of Life,
Through Your Holiest Spirit that reigns
within fire,
That will become pain for him whom You
have predestined for pain.
May You meet us as the richest in delight,
Oh fire of Ahura Mazdao!
At the time of the trial, with the delight of
the richest in delight,
With the reverence of the most reverent,
May you find us, at the greatest of all events,
Oh Lord of Life, Whom we know as the Sun.[28]

In the motif, 'Man in Ancient Persia', the head is shown in profile; the eye, awakened by the light of Zarathustra, sees the spirits who battle within and about him. Light and darkness appear in their pure effects, as forces underlying the senses.

"The Persian people were to be made aware that a battle is taking place in the human soul, insofar as the soul is devoted to activities and strivings in the physical sense-world, a battle between the power of the God of Light and that of his adversary. Mankind was shown how to conduct itself so as not to be led into the abyss by the adversary, but instead to direct his influence to the good through the power of the God of Light."[29]

To receive the light from cosmic, etherically quickened heights and give light to direct mankind, this is the teaching of the great leader of the Persian epoch, represented here in the priest-like figure with the crown in the center of the picture.

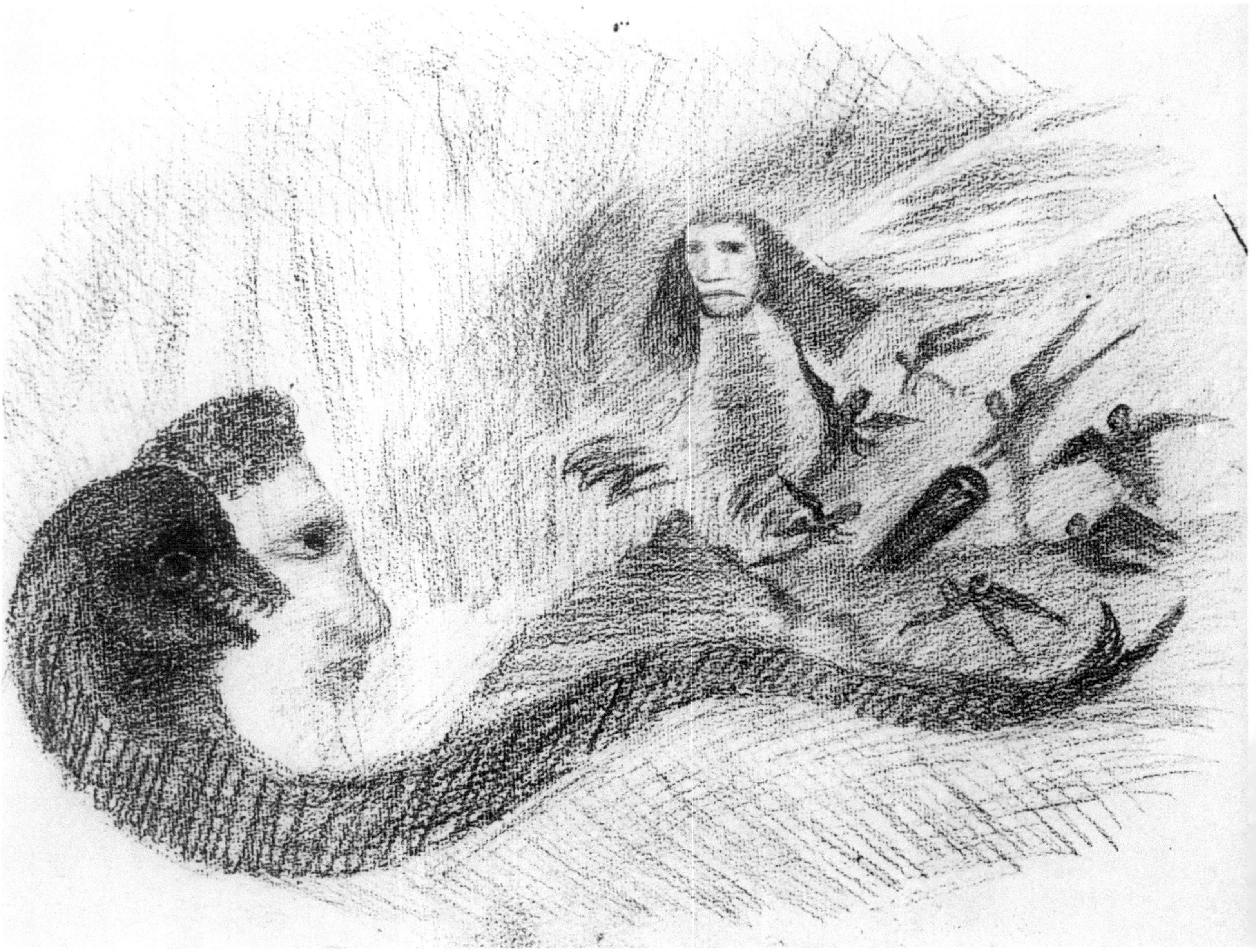

MAN IN ANCIENT EGYPT

"How, then, the Egypto-Chaldean culture gradually comes out onto the physical plane still penetrated, however, by astrological and spiritual relationships ... ." (October 24, 1914)

Pastel Sketch

Warm, deflected yellow, "a glowing half-tone",[30] sets the basic mood. Red flares up and flashes boldly into the picture; black brings structure and pictorial content.
Compared to the light-filled incarnadine of the Persian, the Egyptian appears to be formed out of red overlaid with black. His kinky hair is dark and so is the eye, and his countenance is dreamily directed towards the pyramid, looking upon it as if from outside. He sees the mighty sphinx with the lion's claws, but the music of the sun no longer sounds; he beholds the mummy, surrounded by winged beings who want to seize it.
Red, which cradles the motif below and elevates it from the supportive green, densifies into a snake-like monster. With its large, glossy sinister eyes and dangerous sharp teeth, it cuddles enigmatically against the Egyptian's profile.

Drawing

The profile of the Egyptian is Hamitic, the forehead slightly receding, the eyes warm, dark and full of feeling. His gaze encompasses and takes hold of all the essential elements of the ancient Egyptian epoch: the pyramid, here the step pyramid of early times; the mummy, in this drawing enveloped by ahrimanic beings with pointed wings and greedy arms; and finally, the large, mysterious sphinx.
Here, the snake-being appears as a bringer of danger as well as inspiration even more strongly than in the red of the color sketch: dangerous if the feeling with which the spirit is received is not pure, and the most noble power of inspiration, when the feeling soul (the Egyptian is the image of the 'sentient soul') opens to the spiritual world with inner devotion.

The Motif

Dark is the look of the ancient Egyptian. What had been maya for the Indian, a task for the Persian, now for him takes on increased reality. Whereas once the etheric light was visible, whereas once Osiris could be found, now his greatest hope is simply to be reunited with Osiris after death. He sees the pyramid as an image of the hoped for ascent into the spiritual world after death.
"He wanted to see with his senses how the soul made its way out of the dead body into the higher regions. He wanted to have this constructed before him and so he built these thoughts into the pyramids: the path of the soul, how it rises, how it comes out of the body, how it is still partially fettered, and how it is led out to higher regions. In the architecture of the pyramids, we can see the attachment of the soul to the earthly; in its mysterious forms it confronts us like an image of Kamaloka. We could say that seen externally, it is a picture of the soul bereft of the body and drawing into higher regions." (August 4, 1908)
The pyramid rests on a wide plane. Its apex points to the heavens, to which the body-free soul strives for the union with Osiris. Texts from the time of the ancient empire speak with overwhelming power of this path of the soul to heaven, to Osiris.

> "A ramp will be built for you so that you
> may ascend to heaven."

"Arise, King Unas! Take up your head, gather your bones, collect your limbs, shake the earth from your flesh. Arise, King Unas, you should not be dead!"

"Come to his aid! Come to his aid! It is repugnant to King Unas to wander in the darkness without being able to see."

"The gates of heaven will be opened to you, the gates of the cool waters will be unlocked for you.

You will find the Sun-God standing; He will take you by the hand; He will lead you to the two dwelling places of the Gods in heaven; He will set you on the throne of Osiris!"[31]

How far the soul could arise after death depended upon its deeds on earth. These deeds were weighed against each other during the Judgement of the Dead. There, the soul of the deceased was placed before his judges, who decided whether he was worthy of seeing Osiris.

"According to the old Egyptian view, if after death such a soul had through its deeds been found worthy of this sight, it was allowed to unite with Osiris. Indeed, it was itself addressed as Osiris because it had been united with him. The formula was: 'Osiris was purified in the pond situated south of the field Hotep and to the north of the field of the locusts, where the gods of the green wash themselves at the fourth hour of the night and at the eighth hour of the day with the image of the heart of the gods passing over from the night to the day.' It is impossible to express all the profound relationships of this formula. It is important to understand the expression, 'from the night to the day'. Formerly, it was night; the soul, however, is led over into day, into a spiritual day where it will be united with Osiris, where it may itself be an Osiris."[32] (August 14, 1908)

The pyramid in the sketch is reminiscent of the early one at Sakkarah built in accordance with Sumerian architecture[33] about 3000 B. C. It has seven steps, an expression of the old planetary wisdom.

Next to the pyramid, mightily dominating the picture, is a sphinx. Just as the pyramid answers the question of man's further existence after death, so the enigmatic sphinx in its fourfold nature is an imagination of an earlier perception of cosmic, creative forces and speaks of the mystery of the origin of the human shape. The sphinx, familiar not only in Egypt but also especially in Assyria and Greece combined animal and human features, reminiscent of the four great human types of ancient Atlantis.

"How was it when the ancient Atlantean looked at one of his fellow men by day? He saw a strongly receding forehead, strongly protruding teeth, something akin to an animal. Then, when he fell asleep at night and the Atlantean clairvoyance began, his eyes were directed not merely to the animal-like form, but to the shape of the human etheric head, a shape much more beautiful than it is today, which grew out of the physical head .... This etheric body was much more beautiful than the physical body of today, which has adapted itself to strong, dense forces." (August 4, 1908)

The great race formations of lion-man, bull-man and eagle-man had come to full development by the third Atlantean evolutionary period. The gradual harmonization of these physical types through the interaction of the various soul forces constituted a later task of human evolution.

"And where the ego had become strong, a being had developed which may indeed be called a unification of the three other natures because the ego harmonized all three members. In this group the clairvoyant has indeed before him what is especially captured in the sphinx where the sphinx clearly has the body of a lion, wings of an eagle, and also something bull-like. In the earliest representations, there was even a reptile's tail, indicative of the old reptilian form, and, in the front, the human form which harmonizes the other parts. These are the four types over which, however, the human element predominates in Atlantean times. At first gradually moving towards greater unity, the human form shaped itself out of the eagle, lion and bull natures harmonizing these natures within itself. They were fashioned into the complete human form and this fashioned itself gradually into the form which existed in the middle of the Atlantean epoch." (September 10, 1908)

During the third post-Atlantean cultural epoch, the process of incarnation had advanced so far that it could appear as an imaginative picture directly in the form of a sphinx. In the sketches, the Egyptian's eyes rest first upon the mighty sphinx, with the chest and claws of a lion, the body of a bull, the wings of an eagle, and a visibly human head.

"Think about this recollection of ancient Atlantean consciousness, symbolically placed before man in the Egyptian time. Think how the Egyptian priest wanted to say to his people, 'In Atlantean times, your souls, when awake, beheld the human form in animal shape; during the night, however, a beautiful human head grew out of it.' This memory, represented sculpturally, is the sphinx. These forms can only be understood in this way. One must learn to understand that they are not

contrived, but that they are realities." (August 4, 1908)
Thus the ancient Egyptian's sensory-sentient sight was guided to a spiritual reality which he was unable to perceive directly, but which spoke to him through the forms of his art. The sphinx spoke of the Egyptian's former life in Atlantis; the pyramids, of his reunion with Osiris after death. In this way, he learned to recognize the laws of the spiritual world which underlie the appearance of the world and he learned that man is a being who again and again individualizes himself out of the spirit into the physical.

Just as in life he had been prepared for the spiritual world after death, so would his soul in death be again directed towards the earth. This was achieved through the mummification of the body, whereby the corpse was embalmed and wrapped, later also painted, in order to connect the soul of the departed with the physical world. When the soul looked back upon the discarded body and saw the mummy there, it was moved by the thought that its being was connected with that body. Repeated viewing intensified the deep impression the mummified body made upon the soul.

"Through the fact that in ancient Egypt the bodies were preserved for a long time, the souls experienced something quite specific during the time after death. When they looked down, they knew, 'This is my body'. They were bound to it, bound to this physical body; they had before them the form of their body; this body became important to the souls, for after death the soul is impressionable. The impression of the embalmed body was deeply imprinted upon the soul, and the soul was formed accordingly." (September 2, 1908)

In this way, the soul was strongly attracted to the earth; its feeling for the value of the physical body was intensified, a feeling that has affected subsequent epochs right down to our time.

"Imagine your soul transported back into the old Egyptian body. Imagine your soul after death guided back to higher spheres through the passage of the pyramid; your body, however, is preserved as a mummy. This had an occult consequence. The soul had to continually look down if the mummified body lay below. Thereby, thoughts became hardened, ossified, rigidified and banished to the physical world. Because after death the ancient Egyptian soul was forced to look down out of the spiritual worlds upon its preserved physical body, the thought took root that the physical body was a higher reality than it in reality is. Think of yourself in your soul of that time. You looked down at the mummy. The thought of the physical form has hardened; it has been carried through incarnations; today, this thought appears in such a way that man cannot tear himself loose from the physical bodily form. Materialism, as an idea, is in many cases a fruit arising from the embalming of the corpse." (August 4, 1908)

In the sketches, the Egyptian's eye looks upon the sphinx, the pyramid, and the mummy, around which black, ahrimanic beings swarm. The sphinx is the image of his cosmic origin; the pyramid, the image of the soul's path into the spiritual world; the mummy, a means of preserving the individuality after death for future lives.

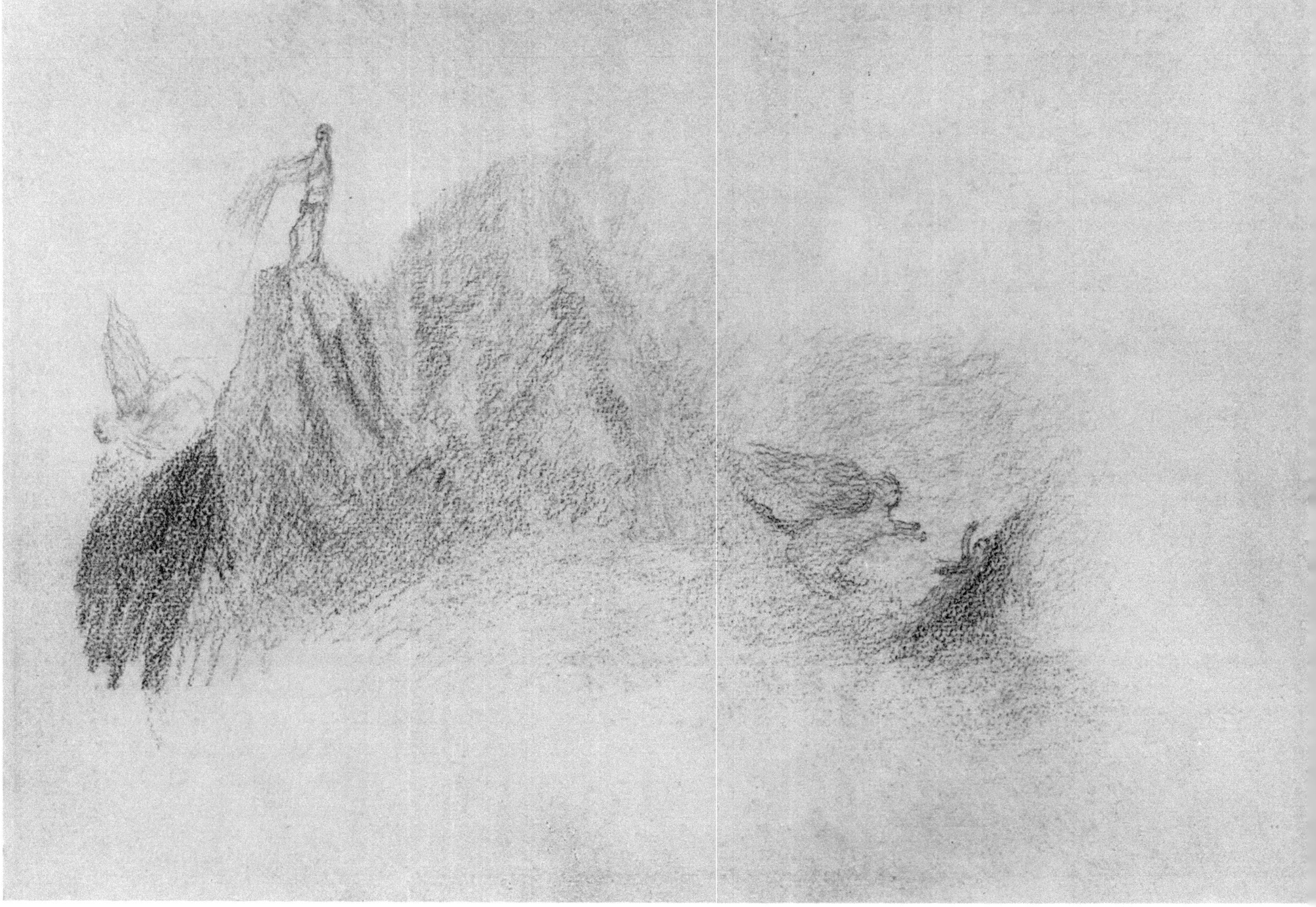

MAN IN ANCIENT GREECE

"... And, as if standing at the abyss, the man of ancient Greece, living at the dawn of the coming intellectual or mind culture, shows how that which the human being is arises; how he is faced with the necessity of solving the riddle of the sphinx; how through the solution, he hurls the sphinx into the abyss, which is to say, into himself ... ."
(October 24, 1914)

Pastel Sketch

Warm green above a supportive current of darker green passes into yellow at the top. Areas of gold-orange and pale blue produce a greenish hue in the yellow, a kind of honey color which the Greeks called *chloros.* This mood is intensified by light reddish, rising into the light like a mountain.

On the mountain, in the radiance of the morning sun, blue stands upright, suggesting a human figure. Down below, out of the darkness and surrounded by blue, the red of a winged sphinx pushes a defensive human being towards the orange-red of a pyramid. Red rays, emanating from the blue on the mountain, hurl a deep blue into the abyss: red, that depresses and encroaches; red, that radiates and creates freedom; blue, that manifests inwardness and the power of standing upright; blue, that disappears into darkness.

The *chloros* does not merely lead one to experience the beauty of green; it helps towards an understanding of the Greek way of seeing color, of his experience of the sense-world within the entire framework of his life. The colors of this sketch reveal the ancient Greek way of seeing and feeling, something difficult for modern man to imagine.

Drawing

The light/dark of the drawing shows two scenes belonging to the same motif even more clearly and in stronger contrast than the drama arising out of the *chloros* of the color sketch. At the bottom right, the sphinx, its body heavy and wings clumsy, threatens and oppresses the human being. At the top left, Oedipus, the man of ancient Greece, who has found himself and thereby also the strength of inner freedom, the freedom from the dark implications of destiny, stands upright in the morning brightness.

The Motif

"Any Greek who took his development as a human being seriously was basically in a small way more or less a conqueror of the sphinx. Oedipus merely represented in an especially typical form what every Greek had to experience." (November 20, 1914)

Ego-conscious and upright, the Greek stands in the sun-filled world, rejoicing in sense experience and abandoned to the beauty of the world. The cosmic origin of man, which his soul had once received and looked upon as the wisdom of higher worlds, is now merely a memory, living only in art and myth.

Man no longer understands the ancient Egyptian imagination of the sphinx, the etheric form of the human being which had arisen before the spiritual eye of the clairvoyant in Atlantis. Egypt has sunk into the grave, together with the mystery of the sphinx and the pyramid and the old life of pictures. The sphinx has become a riddle. Rudolf Steiner describes the riddle that she poses for man as a fundamental experience during the Greek epoch. "With the sphinx, man experiences something which penetrates him and, at the same time, tears him apart." (November 20, 1914)

The cupola motif speaks of this experience, not only of the triumph over the sphinx, but of the confrontation with it, of the human being who falls back before a powerful, approaching sphinx, defending himself and yet defenseless, pressed against the side of a pyramid, lost, fallen prey to the sphinx if he fails to hurl it into the abyss. This struggle calls upon man to unfold his powers of intelligence so that the human etheric form can draw into the physical.

"For the Greek, the sphinx-nature was something he should make an end of, something he should set outside himself. When he hurls it into the abyss, that is, brings the expanded etheric body into the physical body, then he overcomes it. The abyss is not somewhere out there. The abyss is one's own, physical body." (November 20, 1914)

Only through the training of the ego-nature, of the personality, could the Greek conquer the sphinx. The first beings to accomplish the deeds of the ego were the heroes. One of them was Oedipus. The Greek myth tells of him: A sphinx had settled on a rock beside the road to Thebes, threatening every passer-by by giving him a riddle to solve and throwing him into the abyss if he could not do so. Many had already forfeited their lives. With courage and sagacity, Oedipus approached the sphinx, heard the question concerning man, reflected and solved the riddle. The sphinx, as prophesied, hurled itself into the abyss.

"The destiny of Oedipus shows us how an individual is removed from blood relationships, is set outside them, and develops himself outside the blood bond and then, to his own ruin, is placed within it again. We have before us not merely a subjective rebel against the ties of blood, but rather a human being who is aroused to rebellion against the ties of blood by the laws of nature themselves, which are then aroused against him."

Oedipus stands at the threshold of a new consciousness, at the threshold of two eras. The old clairvoyance is fading, and the forces of thought are entering mankind. Oedipus "hears the oracle, i. e., something enters his soul that can be ascertained only through clairvoyant vision. Greek consciousness wanted to say, 'To be sure, something of this nature comes to us from past eras, but man's organization has advanced to a point where it is unfit for this kind of clairvoyance, where this clairvoyance is no longer of any use.' Because of his transformed consciousness, Oedipus interprets the oracle in such a way that it cannot but be fulfilled. This means man can no longer deal with clairvoyant consciousness in the right way; the spiritual world has receded from him; the old clairvoyance no longer benefits him." (August 29, 1909)

On the Color Perception of the Greeks[34]

It is well-known that the Greeks perceived certain colors differently than we do. Homer spoke of the 'wine-colored' Aegean Sea, of Agamemnon's 'hyacinth colored' hair. *Chloros* (green) was used to describe resin and honey, as well as the leaves of trees.

"Curiously, the Greeks used the same word, which we call green, to describe yellow honey, yellow autumn leaves, and yellow resin. They had a word which they used when they referred to dark hair; the same word was used to describe lapis lazuli, the blue stone. Nobody would be inclined to assume that the Greeks had blue hair. Such things can really be taken as conclusive proof of the fact that the Greeks, as a people, simply did not differentiate between yellow and green, that they did not perceive blue as a color in the way we do, that they saw everything more alive, tending towards red or yellow. All this is further corroborated by accounts of Roman writers who tell us that Greek painters had painted with only four colors, with black and white, yellow and red. If we judge according to our present day experience of color, we must say that an intrinsic characteristic of the Greeks was their blindness to blue; they also did not see the blue nuance in green, only the yellow nuance. For the Greeks, the entire environment was more fiery because they saw everything tinged with red. Metamorphoses in the development of mankind reach right down into this way of seeing." (March 20, 1920)

Goethe maintains that the names the Greeks gave to colors are not exact, but flexible and indeterminate, in that they were used for the colors on either side of neighboring colors. "Their yellow inclines towards red on the one side, towards blue on the other; blue tends partly to green, partly to red, red to yellow and then again to blue; carmine red hovers on the borderline between red and blue and tends sometimes towards scarlet, then again to violet. Inasmuch as the ancients not only saw colors as mobile and volatile in this way, but also had a premonition of enhancement and recession, when speaking of color, they used expressions indicative of this point of view. They allow yellow to 'redden' because, when intensified, it leads to red; or they allow red to 'yellow' inasmuch as it frequently tends to return to this, its origin."[35]

In studies of the perception and experience of color, Rudolf Steiner points to the significance man's ability to perceive the darker, the blue colors, has for him.

"It is generally thought today that the tapestry of the sense world spread out before us has always been the same as it is today. Even conventional science can demonstrate that this is not the case. The Greeks, for example, did not see the blue sky as blue, as we see it today. The Greeks had no concept of this blue of the sky. It appeared shadowy to them .... I might say that it was the blue coloring of the world, the blue tinge that first caused outer spirituality to retreat. And at the time when man's instinctive consciousness perceived outside something of the elemental nature everywhere about him, he also perceived, in his inner being, something of an elemental soul-spiritual character." (December 30, 1921)
A physiological process is connected with the change in color perception. The red colors, primarily perceived by man up to the Greek times, were taken up by the eye differently than the blue colors later on.
"With the Greek, things were so that currents went up from the bodily nature and poured into the eye. In our times, the opposite must take place. We must develop our soul-spiritual nature. The current must spread from this soul-spiritual over man's organization. We must direct these currents from the soul-spiritual into the eyes and the other senses.
"In the future, the way for mankind must be the opposite of the way that was appropriate until the middle of the fourth post-Atlantean culture. In the future, reflective man will again become spirit-cognitive in a different form, as prepared from above. We have grown into a receptivity for the blue part of the spectrum. ... As we grow into the blue part of the spectrum, as we, in a certain way, grow more and more fond of the blue and blue-violet colors, our sense organs cannot but be metamorphosed, transformed." (March 20, 1920)
The Greek experience of the world, so different from the experience of present-day man, is artistically presented in an immediate way in the green-yellow tones of the sketch, 'Man in Ancient Greece'.
"Were we, with our modern visual perception, to paint landscapes the way the Greeks saw them, we should have to use quite different colors than we are accustomed to today. That which we perceive as nature was unknown to the Greeks, and what the Greeks perceived as nature is unknown to us. The evolution of mankind proceeds forwards in metamorphoses, and it is essential to realize that at the time when intellectualism arose, when man became reflective, (the Greeks were not reflective, they lived concretely within the world of nature) was the same time that feeling changed for the dark colors, for blue and blue-violet. Not only does the inner life of the soul change, but also what emanates from the soul into the senses." (March 20, 1920)
Thus it is reasonable that the colors of the Greek motif comprise but a portion of the total rainbow spectrum, that portion corresponding to the color perception for the Greeks.
The motifs as a whole in the large cupola unite the streaming colors of the rainbow and lead ultimately to peach-blossom and violet in the pictorial imagination of cosmic man, the 'IAO', which Rudolf Steiner called the "the thinking, feeling and willing ego". (December 30, 1921)

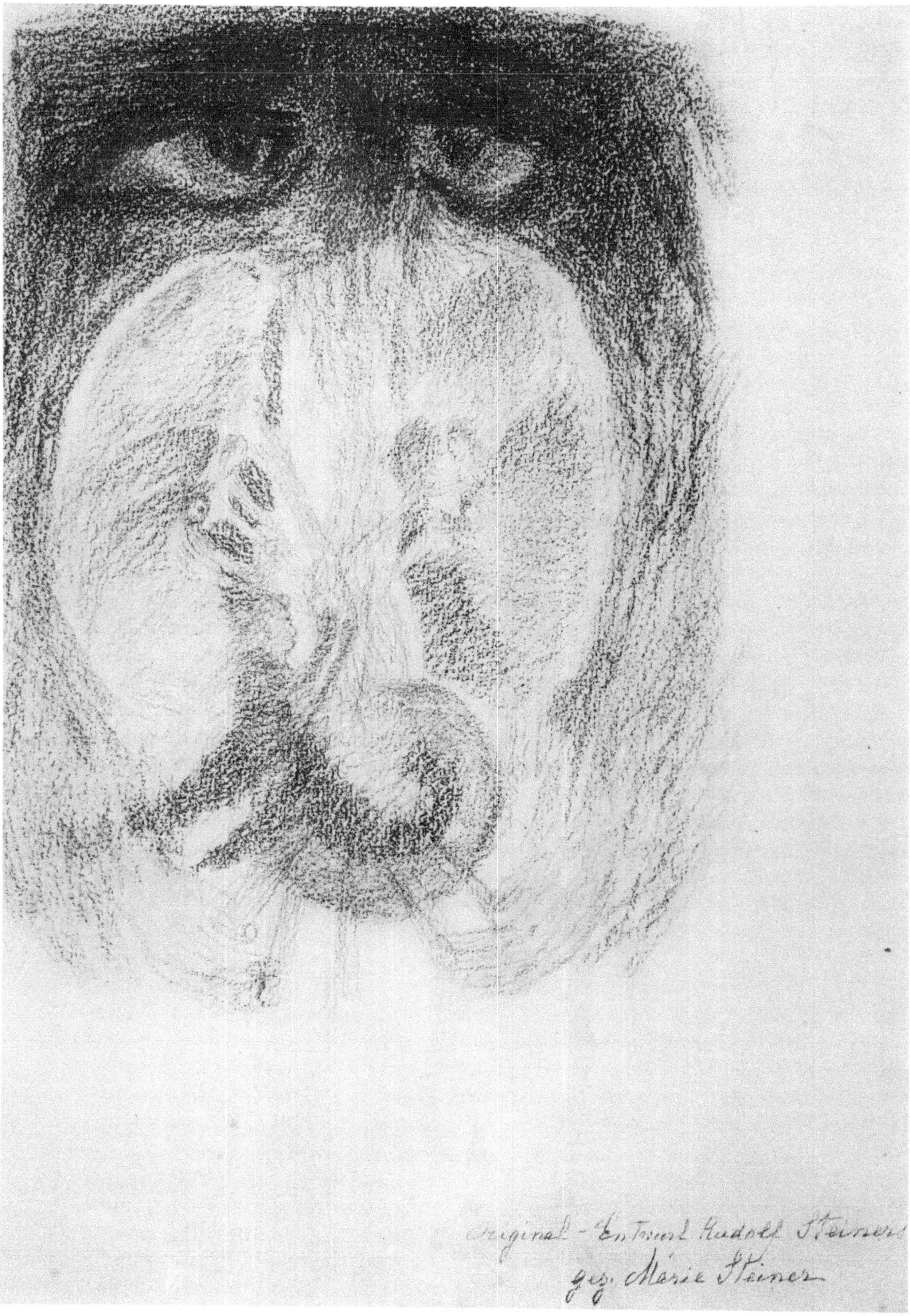

'I' – The Wrath of God and the Yearning-grief of God

IAO – THE COSMIC IMAGE OF MAN

The architrave made of birchwood, which arches over the stage, is a metamorphosis of the motif at the entrance to the building. It prepares the eye for what is happening in the small cupola, and thus opens the 'entrance' into another space.
A three-part motif, which Rudolf Steiner called the 'IAO'* rises above this architrave. The motif consists of red and peach-blossom colors, which also support and surround it.
In the west, above the Saturn architrave and the organ, there arose, "out of the depths of the cosmos", out of a distant blue, the picture of the Elohim who together share the goal of the creation of man. In the east, came the answer, out of the red, peach-blossom tones of the 'IAO' – the thinking, feeling, willing I.
"How the eternal, divine powers and forces work into the evolution of man, that is what will come to expression when an impulse even deeper than the post-Atlantean, namely the Atlantean and Lemurian times, is represented in the four directions of space. The Atlantean will be in the south, the Lemurian in the north of the cupola.
"And finally, the result of the Lemurian and Atlantean times will be represented: that which our time should be, which will come to meet us, out of the manner of representation, if we look from west to east toward the small hall to receive the impulse which is there in world evolution, and which expresses itself in the 'IAO'. Not that this 'IAO' is expressed symbolically, but rather that it finds expression in the motif. And if one looks from east to west, that will reflect what also speaks out of the depths of the cosmos into the evolution of culture – how the 'IAO' speaks in the evolution of the soul from within." (October 24, 1914)

These words were spoken when the sketches for the painters who were to work in the cupola already existed, so that the artists were led to the strongest intensification of the color experience.
"If one were to swim through the world as red, if one were to become one with this red, so that one's soul and the world were completely red, then one would not be able to deny the perception, in this world gone red, in which one has oneself become red, that this entire world of red is penetrated by the substance of divine wrath, which streams toward us from all sides, for all that is possible in us of evil and sin. At the same time, we would be able to feel, in all this endless red, as though we were in a penal court of God's and it would be possible for our moral perception to be like the moral perception of our soul in a vast, endless space. And when the reaction then comes, when anything arises in our soul, when we experience ourselves in the endless, I might say unique, red, then it can only be thus, that one calls that learning to pray. If one can see the raying out and glowing of divine wrath in this red, and with it all that the human soul can harbor of evil, and if one can then experience this learning to pray, then the experience of red will have been endlessly deepened. Then we can also feel how this red can mould its way into space.
Then we will be able to grasp how we can experience a being that emanates goodness, that is filled with divine goodness and divine mercy, a being that we want to perceive as spreading into the space. Then we will feel the necessity to allow this perception of the spreading into space of divine goodness, this divine mercy, to form itself out of the color. We will experience the need to

* *Translator's Note: 'I' is pronounced 'ee' and 'A' as 'Ah'.*

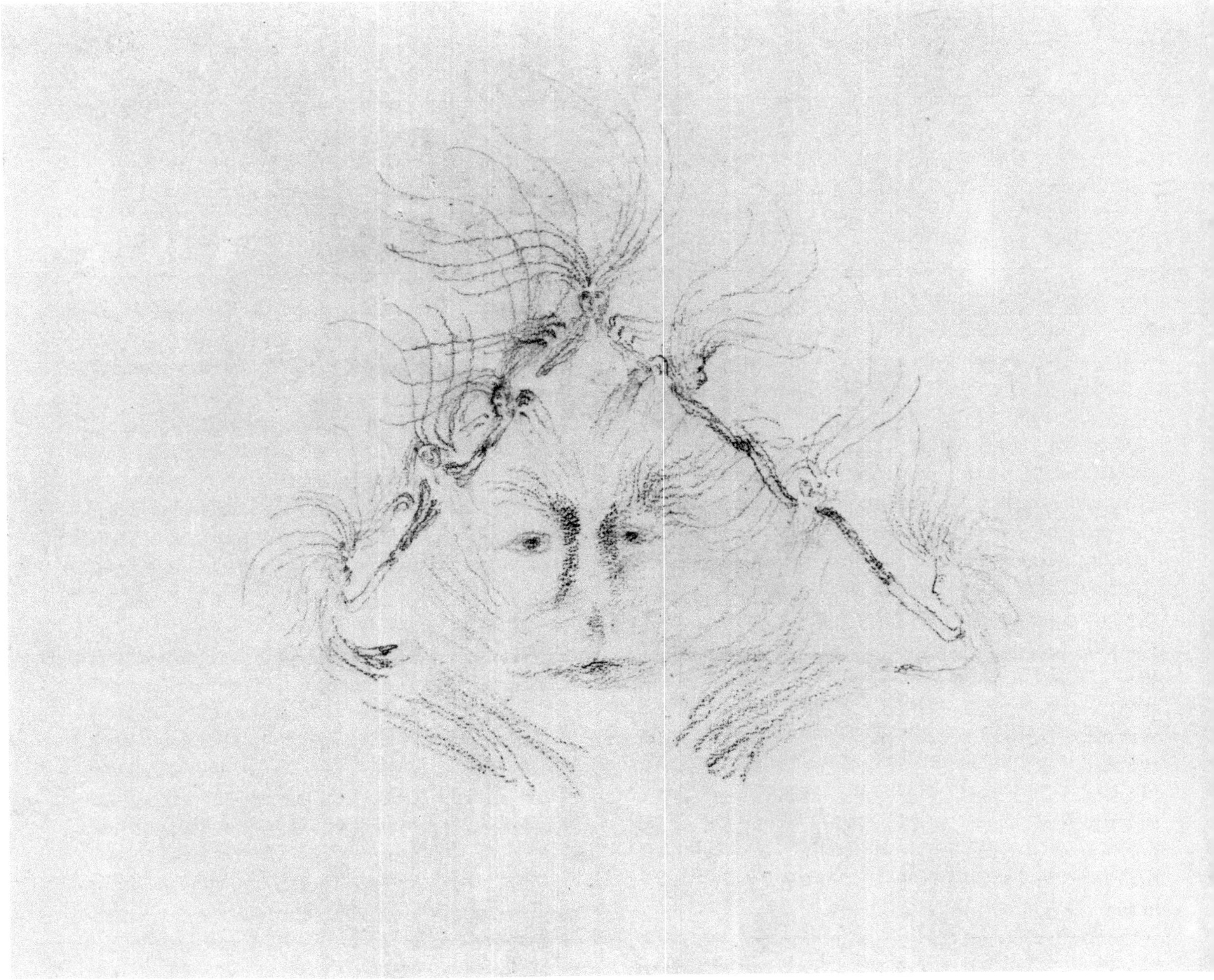

'A' – The Round of Seven

ward off space, so that the goodness, the mercy streams forth. Before the space was there, the red was so pulled together, so concentrated in the middle, and now it places itself into the space, this goodness and this mercy, and as clouds are driven apart, so it drives the red back, drives it apart, so that it must yield to the mercy, and we feel: This you must do in dispersing red. And then we will feel: Here in the middle we must lightly indicate a kind of rose violet as it streams into the dispersing red."[36] (January 1, 1915)

In the edition of the color sketches for the large cupola (1930) three motifs are given:

The I – 'The Wrath of God and the Yearning-grief of God'

The A – 'The Round of Seven'

The O – 'The Circle of Twelve'

The I – The Wrath of God and the Yearning-Grief of God

Pastel Sketch

The warm red parts and opens on an inner space of a delicate bluish red. Held by divine hands, the earth hovers in a matte blue. In the center, yellow-red rises like a pillar of flame, swelling, tongue-like. Black stretches upward, the wings pointed; dragon-like, worm-like the body, the tail coiling around the blue of the earth. Greedy arms seek to tear down the harmonizing, healing light, to conquer it for the darkness. Out of the world of the rose color, bright angels send rays of purity and ego strength in the eurythmical I-gesture. In the heights, above the rose-red, divine eyes, blue-black in the glowing red-yellow, look out, large and wakeful, at the battle of light and darkness, in which the human being builds his ego.

Drawing

In the light-dark, light and warmth intermingle. The black of the ahrimanic being, "the spiritual picture of death", becomes transparent, and the directions of the gestures become clearer. The movements stream toward the center. The drama takes place in an inner space, the space of the I-sound. The I-gesture is indicated in two ways: once as upsurging self-aggrandizement; then as noble strength, as higher self, as the angel speaks in man.

In the corresponding motif in the west, 'Jehovah and the Luciferic Temptation', it is Lucifer in red who causes confusion and snares man in matter too soon. Here God, the Father sees with earnestness and sorrow that Ahriman wants to conquer the light force of the earth.

The A – The Dance of Seven

Pastel Sketch

Violet, protective and supportive, parts to reveal a weaving yellow at the center of which red appears. The yellow, the color nearest to light, moving intensively, powerfully declarative, is held and supported quietly by the violet, the color nearest to darkness.

At the top, a winged figure in an aura of light, can be seen; others are indicated with a few strokes of red and violet in the yellow. The red in the middle seems to reveal a face. The surrounding violet has the form of a gentle curve.

Without the red in the middle, the A-mood would be merely a parting, not a receiving. The picture reveals in the movement of the light from within outward and from without inward, the creative breath rhythm of the middle man, a gift of the spirits of light, who 'bless with soul' the middle sphere of the heart.

Drawing

The composition clearly forms a triangle. Seven figures of light greet one another in a dance, as they turn, swinging, toward and away from each other. The apex forms a forward-looking figure with horizontally out-streched wings; beneath it the next two on either side turn outward; the next two look forward again; the two bottommost face the middle. There is an alternation of inside and outside, a rhythm of three and four within the seven.

More, however, is revealed in the movement, in the striving toward each other, in the interplaying streaming light. It allows us to recognize a countenance of knowing goodness at peace in itself, of beingness, which could not be experienced without the dance. Are they archangels, or spirits of wisdom, or of movement? Can we recognize a cherubim-like, cosmic lion-like being in the center?

The O – The Circle of Twelve

Pastel

Peach-blossom, surrounded by flowing violet, is the background color out of which the motif lights up. From its colors alone, this is "a gateway into the spiritual world".

"We should educate ourselves to see not only peach-blossom, but also that which moves in the incarnadine .... If we perceive the filling of our body with our soul as being incarnadine, then that will be an entry, a gateway into the spiritual world; then we will come into the spiritual world." (May 7, 1921)

On the left side, a great red hand points from above. The back of the hand forms a boundary turned away from the motif toward a black mountain range rising from below. Red from above and black from below on the side create a space, a boundary for what happens within.

Moving toward the right, a light, shining yellow turns into red and then into a darkness which opens onto blue. The darkness contains something obscured, secretly veiled. A blackish green, through which a gentle rose shimmers, lies between the deep blue and the red, which moves over into orange and yellow. Between these polar colors is the dark realm, the deep effect of a color perspective, the secret of the threshold between birth and death.

Seven blue angels extend helping forces to the seven countenances and figures appearing in the light yellow. The five who are visible in the darkness on the side are guided by supports which deepen into red out of the peach-blossom, and are like supportively carrying arms, like limbs bestowed from without. The dark and light countenances at the top, turned to right and left, act like a Janus head; the two at the bottom are turned to each other.

Thus a rhythm is created: above, two profiles, of which one looks into the light, the other into the darkness. Below, two who look at each other, one out of the light, and the other out of the darkness, speaking to one another. Apart, and then embracing each other again – the gesture of the O. It embraces the deepest forces of will, grips the depths of destiny, closes off within itself the cycle of birth and death, of coming to earth, of leaving the earth, of which the two pillars at the bottom also speak.

The twelve – seven light and five darker faces – remind us of the cosmic twelve. Yet it is not just a matter of cosmic laws in general. The faces are meant to resemble those of personalities connected to the building. Rudolf Steiner had asked the painter, Hermann Linde, who directed the painting activities, to take on the execution of the individual, portrait-like features of the twelve. Some are known by name: Sophie Stinde – much in the building existed thanks to her capacity for action and loyalty; Theo Faiss – a boy who had an accident near the Goetheanum; the poet, Christian Morgenstern.[37] "And when we consider how those who understand spiritual science as deeply as, for example, our Christian Morgenstern, remain connected even after their physical death with that which is the meaning of our building, then we will recognize in our building, a manifestation of the spiritual movement for which the boundary between what one usually calls birth and death, simply becomes irrelevant." (January 3, 1915)

The 'IAO' lights up out of the language of color across the threshhold into the space of the small cupola, as a hierarchical and fateful occurrence. The trinity which comes to expression through it was at one time characterized by Rudolf Steiner thus: "That which you see in the large cupola here in the east end is somewhat like the perception of one's own I. This I is, if one may put it like this, a sort of trinity and reveals itself to inner perception as tending on the one hand toward the light-filled clarity and transparency of the thinking I, on the other hand, to a certain extent, toward the polarity of the will, toward the willing I, and in the middle, toward the feeling I. This can be expressed abstractly, as I have just abstractly expressed it, as the thinking, feeling, willing I. Concretely it is to be perceived as a human being who is capable of observing the colors in nature lovingly; who is capable of looking with devotional love at all in nature that meets all his senses. If one experiences the I in such a way that one can at the same time let it stream forth into all of nature, then one becomes aware of the following perception: If you look at a plant in its greenness, in the green color of its bud, then that which you bring before your soul as a picture of the plant is basically really the same as that which you meet when you look, so to speak, into your own inner being. That which is spread out in nature as a tapestry of color, those are the colors that you find when you look into your inner being. And then, when you, as a person who loves the world, glance outward, glance out toward the breadths of daylight that spread themselves outward in endless breadths of space, then you will perceive yourself connected to these breadths of space. You perceive – when you connect these colors, these tones of the breadths of space, with yourself, and when you perceive all the configurations which present themselves – something which you cannot translate into a symbol with your reason, but which you can paint directly, intuitively, artistically. And again, if you allow your glance to sweep over the surface of the earth, over this horizontal plane, over the trees which cover the earth, over all that which comes to expression in the moving trees when the wind rustles through them, then you feel your feeling I – and you get the urge not to present this I by means of an abstraction, but so that you can paint it in terms of color. If you glance downward so that you feel connected to all that fruits upon the earth, then you will perceive the necessity of bringing the will-filled I to expression through a color which arises before you of its own accord." (December 30, 1921)

IAO as Mystery Word

The secret of the IAO lived as mystery word in Ephesus, Eleusis, Epidauros and other temples of Greece. The mystery of Artemis of Ephesus is portrayed as the happiest and most colorful. That was where all that sprouted, grew and lived was honored most.

"This was something which everyone experienced as if it were his own, this feeling of oneself as a figure of light, because this receiving of one's own figure of light through the moon was made so alive for the students and initiates of Ephesus. And in Ephesus, the procedure ran something like this. Whoever was able to let the procedure of the holy sanctuary work upon himself was really transported into this self-creating, moon-transforming sunlight. Then, as if sounding out of the sun, there sounded toward him: JOA.* He knew of this JOA that it quickened his I, his astral body; JO, that is I, the astral body, and in the A, the approach of the light ether body: JOA. Now he felt vibrating within himself the JOA; now he felt himself to be an I, an astral body and an etheric body.

"And then, as if sounding upward from the earth – for the man was transported into the cosmos – as if sounding upward from the earth was that which penetrated the JOA: eh, v. Those were the forces of the earth which arose in the eh, v.

"And now, in the JehOvA, he felt the entire man. Indicated by the consonants, which belonged to the vowels of the ego, astral body, and etheric body in the JOA, he felt the premonition of his physical body. This living into the JehOvA was what enabled the student of Ephesus to feel the final steps in the descent out of the spiritual world." (April 22, 1924)

Dionysus, the son of Zeus and Demeter, was called *Jacchus* in Eleusis, where he was honored along with Demeter and Persephone. The most festive day within the nine days duration of the mysteries of Eleusis was called Jacchus. On that, the fourth day, occurring in the second half of September, the picture of Jacchus-Dionysus was carried along the holy way from Athens to Eleusis in a festive procession. There, the youth become god, now as night god, led the initiates to the holy bay. In these rites, the purpose was to awaken consciousness of the presence of the newly born ego-principle, represented by Dionysus.

The sound sequence, 'IAO' also appears in the Greek words *iaomai* "I heal", and *iatros,* "the physician". The Greek knew that healing meant harmonizing the forces of thinking, feeling and willing, as happened in the Asclepios temple of Epidauros.

The three vowels also occurred in the most diverse connections and names. *Jason*, leader of the Argonauts, is, according to the name, helper and healer; he fetches the golden fleece out of the sun island Aea, and, with the help of the magician, Medea, brings it to Greece. He thereby delivers the old mystery wisdom which the young Greek race did not yet possess.

In the Hebraic world, *Joshua* is another name out of the mysteries. Originally he was called Hosea, though he was also known as 'Ben Nun', the 'son of the fisherman'. After the death of Moses ,who had experienced God in the "burning bush" – the "I am the I am" – Joshua guided the destiny of the people of Israel and led them to the promised land.

"We say 'IAO'. What does that express? It expresses the cosmic workings of three planets. If one adds a consonant, Joshua, if one brings an 's' into it, then that means one does not express only the vowels within the planets, but also the effect which the planets contained within the 'IAO' experience in their movements when a relationship develops to the star image 's'. That is, when in ancient times one spoke the name of God as vowels, then a secret of the planets was expressed. The deed of a divine being within the planetary world was expressed in the name. If one expressed a divine name in a consonantal way, then the deed of that divine being was thought upward to the representation of the fixed heavens, to the zodiac." (December 18, 1921)

The sounds which once resounded at Ephesus also sound in the name IOANNES, John the gospel writer

---

* *Translator's Note: 'J' in German sounds like 'y' in English, so the relationship to 'I' (ee) is more obvious in the German pronunciation of these than in the English.*

and author of the Apocalypse, who began his gospel of Christ with reference to the mystery of the Logos: "In the beginning was the Word."

"When we speak, we reveal, one might say, an echo of experiences which man has in connection to the entire cosmos during his life between death and a new birth, during his descent out of the divine-spiritual world. All the details of the alphabet are built on what lives in the cosmos." (December 18, 1921) Today we can achieve individually and in freedom what in the old mysteries sounded through the veils of secrets.

One path to the experience of the archetypal powers of the word is given to modern man by eurythmy. There the human figure becomes the instrument of 'visible speech' and 'visible music'. The sounds arise in movement, feeling and character in the light, ego-filled 'I' (ee); the open, wonder-filled 'A'; and the warm, will-. embracing 'O'.

That which once resounded secretly in the ancient temples, can be experienced artistically through eurythmy. But it is also a practice which can be experienced and structured in various ways, something which everyone, according to his own possibilities and strengths, may grasp in freedom.

The sequence and harmony of the sounds in their gestures and colors, both in the motifs of the cupola and in the eurythmy IAO, point toward the picture of the human being. From the west of the large cupola there rang forth, out of the distant blue background in the brotherhood of the Elohim, the words, "Let us make of man an image that is our likeness".

In the east the 'IAO' shone forth out of the peach-blossom that was surrounded by red and pointed the way to the central motif. One's glance was directed to the picture, woven by the hierarchies, of threefold man, the expression of "the thinking, feeling, willing I".

FROM THE LARGE TO THE SMALL CUPOLA

The motifs showing the creation of the world and of mankind in the large cupola are brought to a kind of conclusion in the 'IAO', the image of mankind woven from the cosmos. In the passage from the larger to the smaller, yet spiritually more comprehensive room, one sees an intensification and transformation as well as variation and individuality in the technique of painting and in the choice of subject matter.

The motifs of the large cupola are born of the color streams of the rainbow. Their vitality increases from the creation of cosmic beings to the level of consciousness where man stands upright in the sunshine on the mountain top. A quite different spiritual character is created by the painting technique of the small cupola. The motifs are not expressed by clearly differentiated realms of colors. The colors weave through each other and interpenetrate, now one color dominating, now another. Already during the preliminary painting of the model, Rudolf Steiner commented on several occasions that the motifs should have formed one picture. The motifs of the large cupola express the awakening of man in his senses. Those of the small cupola reveal a more intimate spiritual experience, corresponding to the temperaments and characteristics of the different races.

Rudolf Steiner described how Brunetto Latini, Dante's teacher, came to his view of the goddess Natura, Proserpina. What once took place in Egypt as initiation in the seclusion of the temple and under strict priestly control was experienced by Brunetto Latini directly and immediately from the spiritual world. This experience allowed him to see the whole of creation as well as to glance into the world of the senses and the temperaments, which more properly belong to the inner being of man.[38] These kinds of experiences are necessary for the inner growth of modern man, and they were directly presented in the paintings of both cupolas.

The Large Cupola

The senses are involved in the most intense way in the act of painting. Painting is concerned with the quickening of the sense processes and the spiritual penetration of the life processes (cf. Aug. 15, 1916). The training of the eye and the understanding of the seeing process are therefore paths to imagination.

"The sense organs must be transformed in their finer structure. What pours into the sense organs is the same thing that gradually and naturally educates the imagination through the eye." (March 20, 1920)

"The finer structure of the human organism goes through a metamorphosis and becomes something else in the course of human development. Modern man must be aware of such things, for he lives in an important time of transition. He lives in a time in which he must decide if he *is able* to find the transition, or if, as it were, he is able to receive the impressions from above." (March 20, 1920)

Looking at the motifs only from a single perspective, as has been here indicated for the senses – and it would be stimulating to look at it from other perspectives – can lead to the most diverse discoveries concerning motifs. In the first picture of Creation ('The Elohim work creatively into the earth'), mysterious, dark eyes appear where the rays cross. 'Eye and Ear' reveals inner life

through looking and listening, as a world creation out of red and blue.
In 'Jehovah and the Luciferic Temptation', the ability to perceive the external world, the earthly surroundings, is awakened by Lucifer – "Their eyes were opened".
In 'Atlantis', the sight of divine beings is noble. The perceptual abilities of the three animals are clearly differentiated, while man, still dreaming and perceiving in introspection, is devoted to the spiritual world.
Also the cultural motifs show the unfolding of the sense world, each in its own way. The Indian is still given to listening and inner experience. The royal priest awakens the eye of the Persian and gives him the strength to come to terms with the external world and to stand his ground against Ahriman's hordes. Then, the Egyptian seeks to grasp the fullness of the image with the perception of the darkly dreaming eye and also to maintain himself in spite of the awful, dragon-like being that clings to him. Finally the Greek stands upright in the morning sun and in the beauty of the sense world.
"In painting the large cupola, I have attempted, in harmony with the times, to reproduce in the sense world man's inner perception. This will give you a rough idea of what is meant by the 'Know Thyself' when one is in the realm of the senses." (December 29, 1918)

The Small Cupola

In the small cupola, the painting experience intensifies and differentiates the soul element more strongly.
"One learns to recognize how man is not in the inner realm of the sense world, but rather how the melancholic, the choleric, the phlegmatic, and the sanguine impulses work with one another, how people are outwardly different in that one of these four impulses dominates. One enters through the senses into the human interior, into the region of the temperaments. The difference in the observation of the sense realm and the observation of the temperaments is that when one regards the sense realm, the individual regions of the senses greatly differ from each other. When regarding the temperaments, one enters more deeply into the human element. There the universal nature of man is more revealed." (December 29, 1918)
The temperaments, being characteristics of the ether body, have a relationship to race. In this way they become a ferment for the special tasks and missions of individual races.
"The old clairvoyant forms of consciousness appeared in different ways in the most varied forms according to the gifts and temperaments of individual peoples .... We cannot understand these peoples if we are incapable of comprehending that their special individual characteristic is their mission. Now, however, the course of the greater development of mankind is such that, so to speak, each and every mission is given its own time. When this time has expired, then the respective mission has been fulfilled." (March 9, 1911)
The great leaders of mankind, as they are depicted in the small cupola, were divinely inspired and knew how to lead their people in such a way that their temperamental and elemental predispositions could find a healthy balance. (Compare with 'Turning Points in Spiritual History', 1911)
"There has been an attempt to capture at least, I would like to say, a part and only a part of this way of seeing which has been oriented toward particular directions, but on the other hand, removed from modern perception." (December 29, 1918)

Rainbow – Incarnadine[39]

A last aspect of this method of observing the paintings and colors of the large and small cupolas is the relationship between rainbow and incarnadine, which Rudolf Steiner transforms into a motif of inner schooling.
"We see colors in nature relative to the color spectrum, from the outermost red to the outermost violet, with all the nuances in between. If we were to tinge the colors into each other, they would take on life. They would then become incarnadine, the so-called human flesh tone, which presses out from man. Wherever we look into nature, we glimpse to a certain degree the extended rainbow as the sign of the Father. When we look at man, however, the incarnadine speaks from inside man in that all colors interpenetrate and take on life. They become enlivened in the process of interpenetration. What becomes quickened is gone when we look only at a corpse. The human element is thrown back into the rainbow and into God's creation. But man must also glimpse the source of the colorful in his inner being. He must perceive what makes the rainbow incarnadine, what makes it a living unity in his inner being." (September 24, 1921)
The painting of the large cupola produces the effect of God's creation, the evolution of the color spectrum of the rainbow. In the small cupola, it expresses a leading

into the spiritual out of the inner preception of incarnadine.
"When a seer encounters a person, he sees incarnadine not at rest, but rather in oscillating movement. The incarnadine in its external form is only an intermediate condition." (June 1, 1918)
"One must understand the flesh tone, incarnadine, in order to understand the other tones." (February 17, 1923)
"Because our thinking proceeds from the inner to the outer, we do not receive colors from the outer world as animals do, but rather we receive the skin coloring from within. This tone is most difficult to reproduce in painting. With the help of the blood, our 'I' actually colors our whole body with this wonderful human color. This color can only be reproduced in painting when all colors are carefully mixed in the right way." (October 8, 1923)

Sketch of a Stage Curtain for the Mystery Plays

Rudolf Steiner created a sketch for a curtain for the productions of the *Mystery Plays.* The curtain, made by William Scott Pyle, can still be seen today in the performances of the plays at the second Goetheanum. Motifs from the fairy tale 'The Green Snake and the Beautiful Lily' and the verse epic 'The Mysteries' by Goethe are interwoven in the curtain.
The pilgrim Brother Marcus approaches out of the expansive green after a long journey. The ferryman's boat will ferry him across the river to a towering mountain, which supports a structure similar in form to the Goetheanum. The rose cross hovers in fiery clouds above the structure. Spirit-beings from out of the turbulent blue are drawn to and strive for the rose cross. In 'The Mysteries' Goethe has Brother Marcus glimpse the cross adorned with roses at the gate of the monastery. The question according to esoteric Christianity is, "Who has made these roses the companions of the cross?" This motif leads into the small cupola, into the room with the twelve columns and the pictures of the great leaders of the various world epochs painted above them. The picture of the resurrected Christ shone forth in their midst. The great wooden sculpture which formed a unit with the sculptural forms of the two rooms, was supposed to stand beneath this picture.

Sketches for a Stage Curtain for Eurythmy Performances

A little known pastel sketch by Rudolf Steiner of a stage curtain for eurythmy performances shows three portal-like areas which direct one's gaze into various color areas. The first portal, on the left of the sketch, is in warm brown tones. A darting soaring flame is surrounded by warm red and orange tones. The middle portal opens into a world of light yellow. The space is limited by a dim blue, which creates a delicately protective bow. The contrast from blue to light yellow intensifies the radiant angel-like figures. The third portal on the right is in blue. The aspiring figures show more movement and differentiation than in the two other rooms. The picture of cosmic man, the 'IAO', would have been seen above this curtain in the east part of the large cupola. They complement each other artistically and thematically. The curtain, however, was never constructed.

THE SMALL CUPOLA

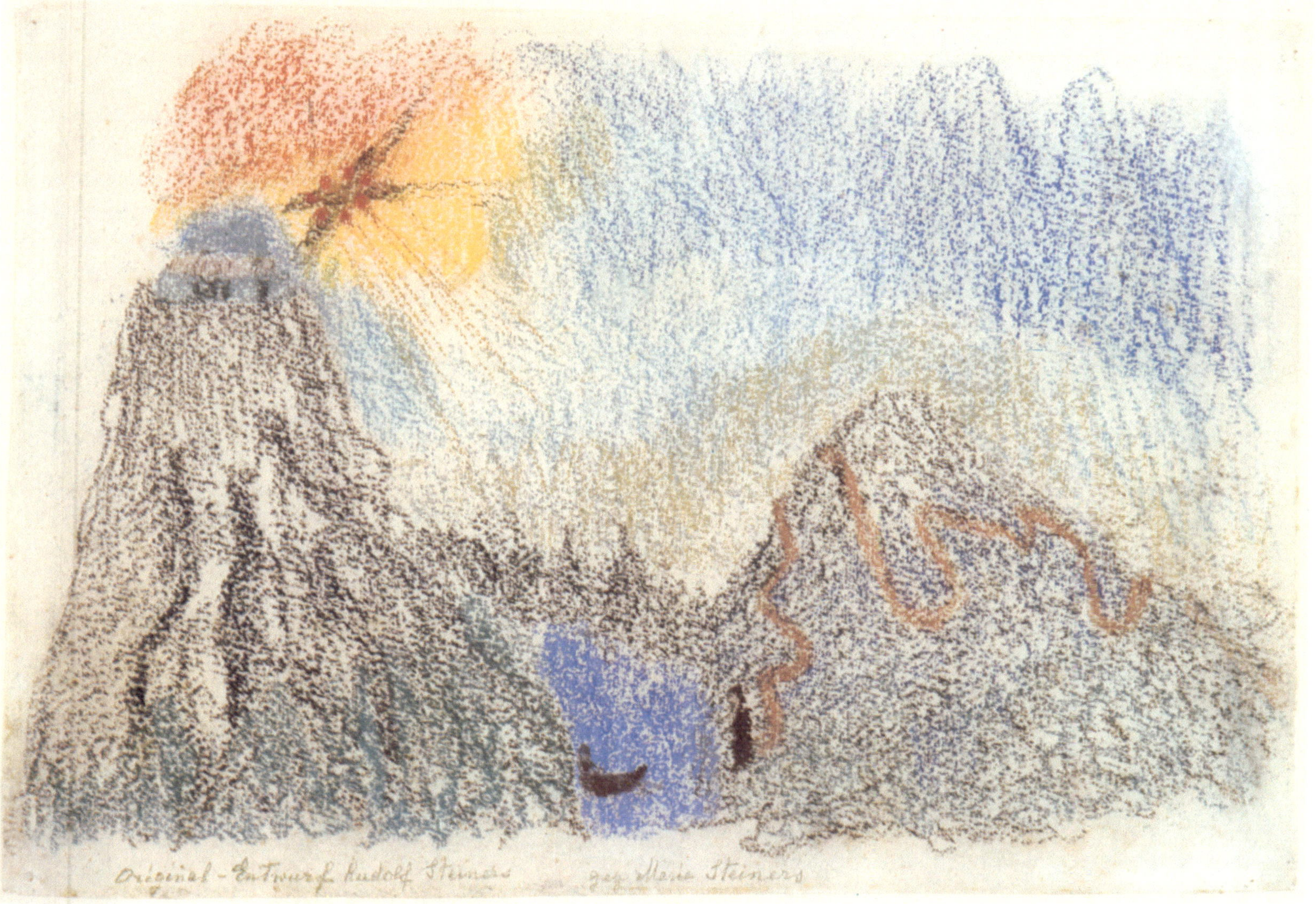

Sketch of a Stage Curtain for the Mystery Dramas

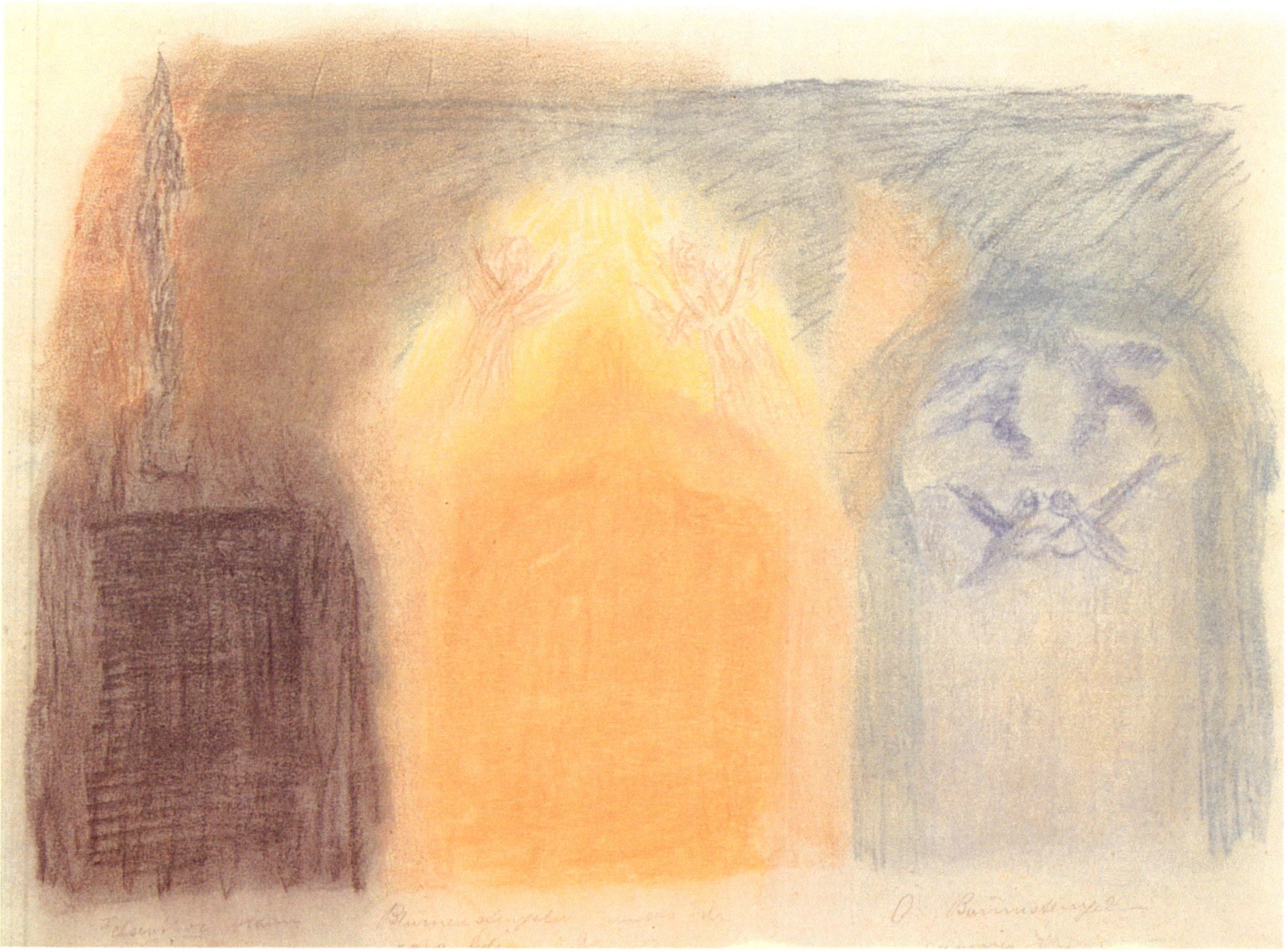

Sketch of a Stage Curtain for Eurythmy Performances

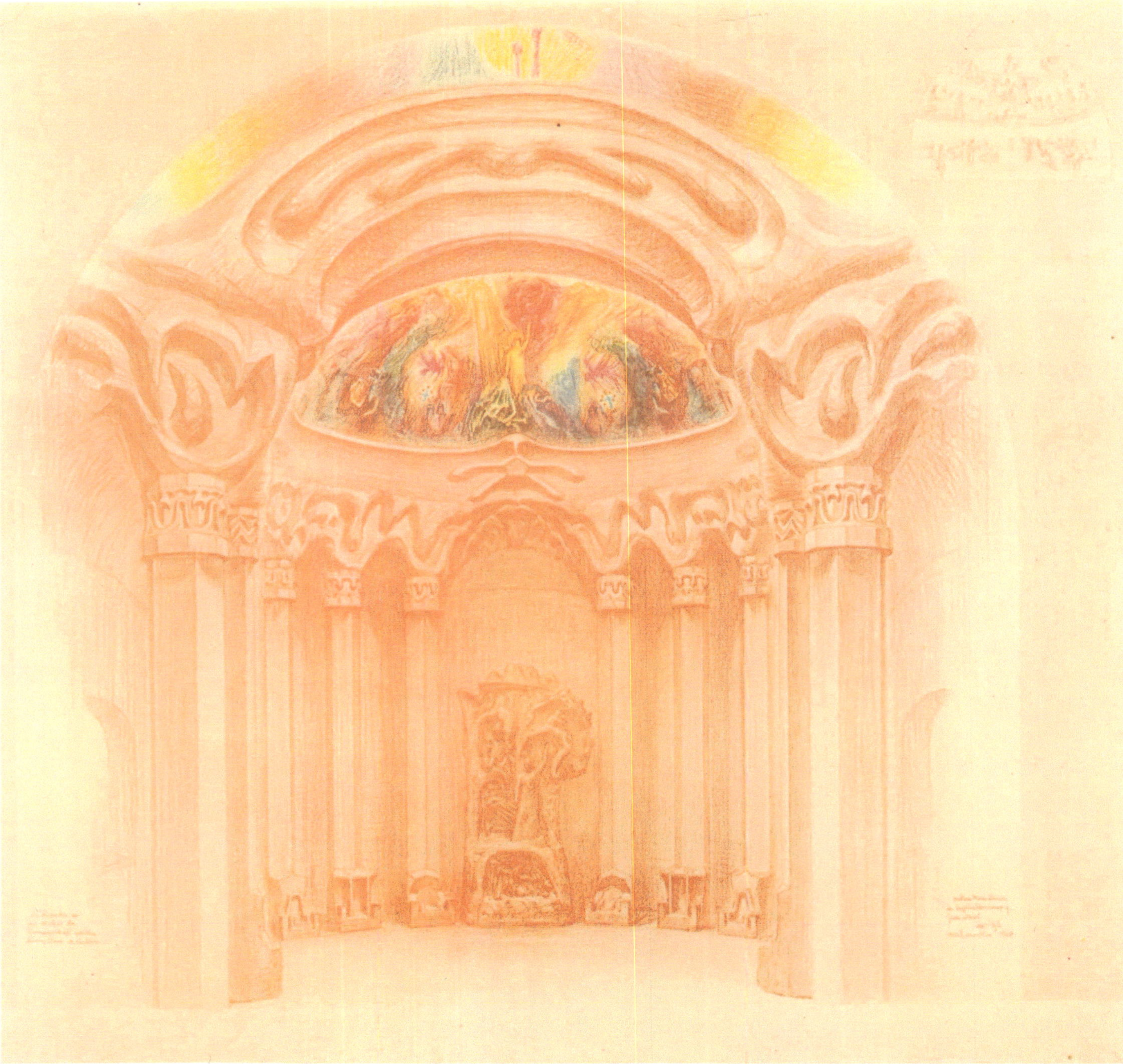

View into the Small Cupola, by William Scott Pyle

A VIEW INTO THE SMALL CUPOLA

In the painting of the small cupola figures out of the great cultural periods appear together with the spiritual background out of which they are inspired. "In this small cupola the true development of mankind has been portrayed inwardly, not in temporal order." (January 25, 1920)

All of the motifs resonated with one another, they pointed to the central motif and together with it formed a unity. This gave the impression of "surface undulating with color". (December 30, 1921)

"Now we come to the painting of the small cupola. Now I am particularly able while speaking of the painting of the small cupola to show you pictures of it. The painting of the large cupola was not entirely sucessful but what was attempted in the small cupola has realized to a certain extent what one person in my *Mystery Drama* expresses about a new art of painting: that the form should issue out of color, which means that one must really rouse oneself to a total experience of the color world as such. When one surveys the color world one realizes that it is truly a totality, a world for itself. When one intently feels one's way into color then, I would say, do red, blue and yellow speak amongst themselves. One receives with the color world something thoroughly living. One at the same time is, so to say, introduced to the world of color as having being." (June 29, 1921)

"The small cupola of the Goetheanum was painted not from thought out figures to which color was added but rather the painting began first with a color experience from which the figured was born.

Through devotion to pure color, the creativity of the soul for the figurative is strengthened. This is demanded by the colors experienced. In the creative moments of painting one feels as if the world were nothing but living weaving color which is creative and engenders being."[1]

About the actual painting of the small cupola, Luise Clason writes, "In the years when the interior decoration of the first Goetheanum could be begun, Dr. Steiner entrusted six artists with the motifs for the cupola above the stage. These were Margarita Woloschina, Luise Clason, Arhild Rosenkrantz, J. M. Brunier, Ella Dyubanjuk and Mieta Waller. These artists came from various parts of the world and had quite different artistic backgrounds. Other than Baron Rosenkrantz none of the others had ever had the opportunity to paint in such a large dimension as was required of us. Already from the beginning a very difficult task was given us. We were each given a particular motif and had together to create one enormous integrated work. When in late autumn 1914 Dr. Steiner gave Mrs. Woloschina and me the first sketches for the small cupola he said that it must be possible to create an integrated artwork together, through harmonious work. He gave this particular emphasis, pointing out that Leonardo da Vinci and his students were able to accomplish this.

Next to adjusting to work in such new media as plant color and primed boards, our major effort went towards trying to compose each of the motifs in the picture space so that they were really integrated in it and so that their proportions and tonal values mutually supported and carried each other. Only in this way could a unified whole arise. Not an easy task when one thinks that each one of us had to master and digest the motif entrusted to him. This happened step-by-step: first in small format on paper, then in the model which was one-tenth the actual size, until finally we ventured to work on the small cupola itself. Baron Rosenkrantz was the first to be finished with his motifs, the large middle section in which the figure of Christ standing between Lucifer and Ahriman was portrayed. It was time pressure that forced him to haste, as it was necessary for him to return to England immediately. A little bit later Mrs. Woloschina left us to visit Russia. It would be years before she could return and then only after the Goetheanum had become prey to fire. She never saw how her motif, that of the Egyptian culture, was completed.

These two motifs were in a certain sense complete. The other motifs, on the other hand, remained in a state of flux and steady transformation until the autumn of 1912. The time had come for the various motifs to be unified. Everything was in its place and the large contours were melded together into one picture. It was then that a seemingly insoluble problem arose. Dr. Steiner had in the meantime finished the model for his statue of Christ. This statue was to be carved in wood and placed directly underneath the painted representation of the Christ. Baron Rosenkrantz' representation, completed before his departure from Dornach, contrasted strongly with Rudolf Steiner's sculptural representation. Even Rudolf Steiner was of the opinion that the painted figure should also have similar features to the sculpted form.

It came about after much deliberation and discussion that Dr. Steiner, at our request, finally decided to repaint the Christ figure. When this was done, the necessity arose to also rework the Lucifer and Ahriman figures. We became enthused and experienced totally new worlds in respect to color and to the reality of the spiritual beings portrayed. Our own attempts were by comparison as those of 'blind' people. It was truly astonishing to see how with each session Dr. Steiner perfected his technique; how he was able to master the flowing color, and knew how to evoke the impression of spirit-being. It was our biggest wish that the rest of the small cupola should also undergo the same change. We therefore approached Dr. Steiner with the entreaty to repaint our motifs. We then with great zeal began to wash the large surfaces of the small cupola. Because of differences in handling the surface some parts were weakened to such an extent that when washed the top layer of the prime came off. We took great pains so that the color would adhere to these sections. Understandably we were in for a shock when Dr. Steiner one day took a toothbrush out of his pocket and began to work on just one of those damaged surfaces.

Over the period of a year and a half, with larger and smaller interruptions, Dr. Steiner painted, along with the middle section, the whole south side of the small cupola and on the north side the Russian cultural impulse adjacent to the Christ group. Here we were greatly surprised to see how the blue angel, the inspirer of the Russian culture was through artistic necessity transformed in the north side to the opposite color. He became orange. We painted on the rest of the motifs on the north side during the two succeeding winters. They were to be a sort of mirror image. We took great pains to keep the temperature in the closed cupola space above freezing. We had three electric ovens on day and night so that the wet color on the wall surface and in the paint pots would not freeze. One morning we were stunned to discover that the Ahriman figure upon which Dr. Steiner had painted the previous day was covered with tiny ice crystals. To our relief the color was in no way damaged. Dr. Steiner while working on the high stepladder was accustomed to paint with his fur-coat on – a very uncomfortable position for the arm holding the brush, particularly since the paint ran onto the sleeve. It was always a great event to watch Dr. Steiner paint, it was so different to what one was used to with other painters. Sometimes he came up only for a quarter or half hour, going straight to the surface he had painted the day before. He would dip the brush in the color and make a huge color curve over the entire painted surface. On the following days he would return ever again and set yet new layers of color in curves across each other. Surface by surface the whole sea of color was brought into movement. The picture surface receded and a three-dimensional space arose filled with majestic flowing color which surged and ebbed, disappearing only to re-emerge elsewhere. Within this color flow hovered beings never before seen with the physical eye. Their eyes looked at us, speaking of mysteries which waited to be revealed to understanding human beings .... When we once again came into daylight after our work on the cupola we had to rub our eyes. Such a different world received us. We loved the world up there and could only be removed by force when the scaffolding was to be dismantled and the boards one by one were taken from beneath our feet. A lost paradise ... even Dr. Steiner sensed our mood; at the first meeting below he said emphatically, 'Yes, it has now passed! One part of the work – indeed, a major part itself!' Today, the only thing that remains of this world is a memory."[2]

PAINTING 'OUT OF THE COLOR'

In painting the small cupola, Rudolf Steiner made form appear as the 'creation of the color.' He brought into being what he called 'painting out of color'. Today we have the task of ascertaining from remaining pictorial archives – pastel sketches, drawings, black and white as well as color photographs – what was meant by the expression, 'painting out of the color', and how a new way of painting was inaugurated by the phrase. Almost of necessity, Rudolf Steiner's own utterances comprise an introduction to this task. "Only in the small cupola did I succeed in accomplishing what I had indicated as the challenge of a new way of painting, so that here drawing disappears entirely behind the working out of the experience of color. I had one of the characters in the first *Mystery Drama* express it in this way: the forms appear as creations of the color." (August 28, 1921)
After the painting efforts in the small cupola ended, he often spoke during tours and in lectures of this painterly impulse. Among the descriptions given under many different circumstances and quoted here very briefly, the artistic intention is clearly defined.

The Experience of Color

In painting, "it is a matter of thoroughly rejecting any linear thinking, so that we move into the pure feeling that creates out of the color. And as strange as it may seem to someone who speaks in a falsely abstract sense of the spiritualizing of art, it must nevertheless be said, that for someone who thinks in a painterly way, the most important thing is that a particular color nuance is at a particular area of a particular surface and that when one moves to a different area of the surface, other color nuances are there. It is a matter of creating out of the color.
Indeed, the artist will be supported in this working through of what I should like to call the experience – the experience of the blue, the experience of the yellow, the experience of the red. What the artist has when he experiences yellow, or red as if it were attacking him, when he experiences blue as if he ought to run after it with his soul, as if he ought to expand, that is what changes itself in him into creativity and what then enables him to transform his perception into that which will become the work of art. If, for example, your task is to paint a particular surface, it will be a matter of finding the nuances between the so-called light, warm colors and the dark, cool colors. If you experience color, if you can work out of this experience of color just as the musician works out of the experience of tone, then it will be a matter of form arising out of the color itself, so that you do not draw – smearing color into the linear space brought about by the drawing – but instead that you begin with the color experience and out of this color experience the experience of line, of form, will arise before you." (October 19, 1920)
"[We must] make it clear that it is not the motifs which are essential to the painting of the small cupola, but rather the pulling forth of the motif from the colors. Therein lie the first beginnings of what, in all likelihood, painting of the future will have to carry. The human being will, after all, have to realize more and more that essentially, in the details of nature, there always lies something of an essence; that, for example, if one involves oneself in a color, or especially in a color combina-

tion, there will not simply be a color combination, but this color, as such, will be something which is alive, something which works out of itself, and that it is possible to educate oneself to live into this color, to educate oneself, for example, to live into the color blue. Then you will have the feeling: this blue gives me the impression of something formative, something which moves out of itself, of what moves or forms itself in space. Therefore, when you want to bring about something formative, you get something which is pulled forth out of the blue. Something that is red or yellow gives you the impression that it would like to reveal itself, come toward you, talk to you. Whereas blue glides past you, red gives you the impression that it is coming at you. In this way, one can enliven the meeting with *one* color and also with many colors. And all these things are, indeed, contained in the working of nature. This can only be understood by someone who educates himself to live into the aspects of this working of nature. Therefore, it is somewhat noticeable when, let us say, in our time, in the completely justifiable and new striving in art, certain things come to meet one which do, in fact, show that one has left the working from nature and that one is really striving in what is inartistic for new artistic things.

"When we see that all sorts of things that are expressionistic and futuristic, etc. assemble in any manner, assemble *differently*, from what appears to some extent in nature, then quite often – though of course not always – something unjustified lies in such an assembly. Someone who, for example, forms a human eye, cannot help – if he does not merely look, but knows how to live inwardly with the creative forces in nature – cannot help but set the second eye in its proper place for the simple reason that the single eye really is not anything in itself, but begins to be something only when there are two eyes. We only reach the essential, inner creative forces in nature if we can live with the phenomena of nature, such as, for example, the colors." (April 5, 1920)

Dialoque and Interplay of Forces

"To be sure, what is important is that one does not merely have a perception of the single color. The *single* color usually does no more than create a relationship between the person and the color as such. To see *blue* means to experience the urge, the longing, to stream out with the color into space where the color shows itself. Seeing *red* calls forth an experience of being attacked, of having to defend oneself against something. So it goes for the other colors. The colors also have a certain relation to that which can be formed in the color when the form is pulled out of the color. Blue, for example, will always help you when you want to express movement; red will always help you when you want to express physiognomy. For what I mean here, the important thing is not the single color but what the colors are saying to one another, the red to the blue, the green to the blue, the green to the red, the orange to the violet, and so on. In this dialogue and interplay of forces between the colors, an entire world is expressed. And you will not experience this dialogue and interplay of forces completely if you cannot experience the colors as ocean waves, rising and sinking, and playing on this color arc, yet bearing at the same time, out of these waves of color the elemental beings who themselves develop their forms out of the waves of color. Thus, it is a matter of discovering the secret, of working from nature, out of the colors in a painterly way. For indeed, a great part of what exists, of what we see, is born of the creative world of color. As vegetation sprouts forth from the ocean, so that which is alive grows out of the world of color." (January 25, 1920)

Color and the Experience of Form

"I was speaking of the creative powers of the world of color itself. When we observe something painted we really always have something reflected before us. It is just that which must be overcome. The artistic soul will have to be gripped by much more elementary perceptions. Let me express myself even more clearly about what I want to say. Let us say that I place a simple spot of color here, a spot of yellow, and to this yellow spot here, I join blue (see illustration). Anyone who really perceives color as living cannot help but see a head in profile when he perceives a yellow spot of color surrounded by blue.

"That follows of its own accord for anyone who carries the life of the colors within himself. For someone aware of the *creative* in color, two mere spots of color will lead at the same time to what is essential. And you cannot paint a face in color by saying, 'I saw a face', or even, 'I have a model and will structure this face accordingly and then it will be similar'. In the future painting will not be accomplished like that. Instead, what is colored will be experienced and quite apart from all naturalism, from all imitation, one will call forth from the color what already lies within it, that which, of necessity, one *must* call forth from the color, if one experiences a living coexistence with the life of the colors." (January 25, 1920)

"And now, you see, how can it be possible not to work out of the color itself? I would like to know, when someone says, 'I am not interested in working from a model, rather I am interested in the application of color ...' – I would just like to know why form as the creation of color should not result from this *pure* application of color. We must become independent once more of the model. We must become independent of what is naturalistic. Art worked on that long enough. Instead we must develop interest in seeing a light surface simply as a spot of color, and a dark surface beside it as a spot of color. I would really like to know how, if one has an arrangement of a light and a dark surface, one can avoid perceiving there a face turned this way (see illustration) and surrounded by hair." (April 5, 1920)

Overcoming Drawing

"Then one must strongly preoccupy oneself with the realization that mere drawing contains something untruthful. Most truthful is perception out of the color, somewhat less truthful is perception out of dark and light, and least truthful is drawing. Drawing, as such, already approaches that abstract element which is found as decay in nature. We should really only draw in such a way that we become conscious as we do so, that we are drawing what is essentially dead. We should paint with colors in such a way that we become conscious of calling what lives out of what is dead. What is the horizon line, fundamentally? If we simply take a pencil and draw

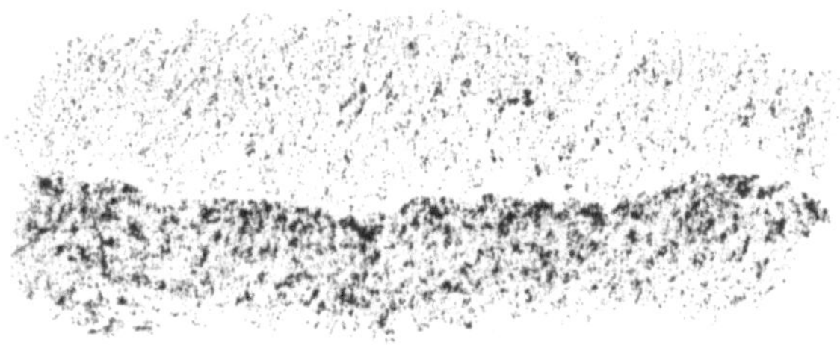

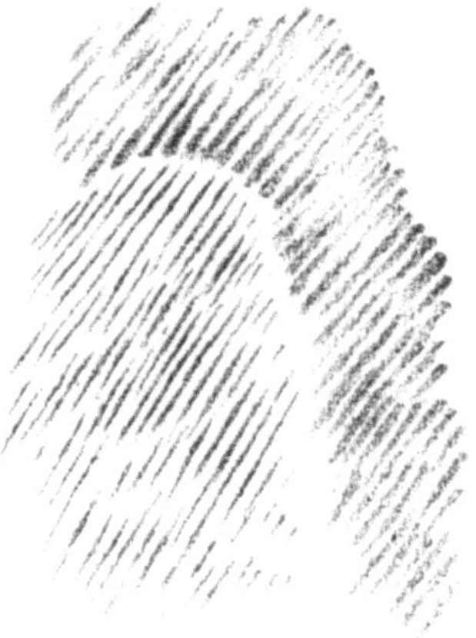

a horizon line, then that is something abstract, something deadening, something untruthful in the face of nature, which always has the tendencies toward the dead or the living. We expose the one tendency and claim that is nature. If, however, I say I see green and I see blue which separate themselves from one another, then the horizon grows out of the bordering of these colors upon one another, and then I express a truth. So you will gradually realize that the form of nature truly arises out of color, that drawing is, therefore, something abstracting." (August 23, 1919)

"Today, with the exception of the primitive beginnings inherent in impressionism, etc., and also in expressionism – which really are just beginnings – the concept of painting, the activity of painting, has been more or less swallowed by the materialism of our time. For one does not paint today; instead one copies figures by means of a sort of drawing and then fills in the surface. But those are filled-in surfaces; they are not painted, are not born of color or of dark and light.

"Do not misunderstand, though. If you get wild and simply slap the colors down next to one another and think that you accomplish what I have called overcoming drawing, you have accomplished nothing and misunderstand me. For what I mean by overcoming drawing is not having no drawing, but pulling the drawing out of the color, releasing it out of the color. And the color will give rise to the drawings. One must just know how to live in the color. This living in the colorful then leads the real artist to overlook the rest of the world, and to bear his art work out of the color itself." (June 9, 1923)

"Everything can be pulled out of the color combination, just as in modelling, everything can be pulled out of the treatment of the surface, out of the treatment of the form. Vis-a-vis the color, if painting wants to work with color, the line drawing is actually an untruth. If you paint two colored surfaces, which then of course have a border, then you speak the truth. And with such things, it is, indeed, a matter of getting used to the truth. It is because we – wanting to be naturalistic – have, in respect to art, lied so much, that we bear the misery presently, in other worldly connections as well, that so much has become frightfully untrue." (April 5, 1920)

Color and Motif – Experiencing the Harmony of Colors

"Within the world of color itself, there lies a world of creativity, and whoever perceives the colors paints what they say to one another. He need not limit himself to a naturalistic model; he can create the figures out of the colors themselves. It is a fact that nature itself and human life have a certain right, of necessity, to structure morality out of the color. Yesterday Herr Uehli indicated, with great justification, how the new painters do already perceive this way of working out of the light-dark, out of the color itself, and how they came to paint a bass fiddle next to a tin. In doing so, they really are on the right track, which is to see how the light changes in value when it becomes color or it falls upon the bass fiddle or upon the tin. That is the right idea. What is not right, however, is that this be accomplished through the naturalistic experience. Something other than a bass fiddle or tin results if one really lives into color." (August 28, 1921)

"All that is created in a painterly way must be pulled forth from the color. The world of color is a world unto itself. Whoever lives into the world of color will learn to recognize the creativity in each individual color; he will learn to recognize the creativity in the color harmonies. Whoever knows how red works upon human perception, how red speaks from within outward, who knows how blue works, formatively, structurally, will realize how to structure the painted world out of the given colors.

"That is more or less what we tried to create when we painted the small cupola in Dornach. What is always essential is – if I may express it like this now – the patch of color at a particular place. Although figurative things appear in the color, originally they are thought out of the color. Light, dark and color are really all that is justified if one represents something through painting with the help of the surface. Drawing is really a lie." (February 28,1921)

Form as the Creation of Color

"Allowing the form to appear as the creation of color, that is what wants to be brought about here. If one follows the history of painting, one will find how this principle of pulling everything painterly out of the color can now stand only at the beginning of its development. What was painterly was indeed sought in reproduction, in the naturalistic reproduction of one motif or the other because it was led astray, even in periods when painting was at its height, into representation. If one has to admit – and who would not want to admit it in the face of the creations of Raphael, Leonardo, Michaelangelo and others – that the highest painterly goal is achieved when one strives for expression, if one does have to admit that the entirely new, unspiritual as it is, could hardly do anything else but strive for expression, then because a new spiritualization of our world conception must now be sought, so a different principle, a different artistic disposition, especially in painting, must be allowed to come into the limelight.

To be sure, this artistic disposition will be sustained only by someone with an inkling of the creative totality represented by each element in the world. If one can perceive the world of color properly, then one does find in the color something of cosmic creativity. Whoever is able to immerse himself in the world of color will be able to lift himself up to the feeling that a world of being springs up out of this secret world of color, that the color wants, through its own strengths, to develop itself into a world of being.

I should like to put it this way: Just as you can see in the small child the tendency toward the grown person, so if you perceive the world of color properly, you can see the tendency toward a world of being." (January 25, 1920)

The Cupola Painting as a Gate to the Supersensible

"Take a look at the cupola paintings ... all these cupola paintings have the tendency not to respect the space on which they are painted. Instead, they have independent macrocosmic being. And selflessness on the part of the artist existed because there, too, something entirely new came to view. These figures had to glow from within, through themselves. Whereas one is accustomed to portraying the light that usually is noticeable and then reflected, here it was the aura and self-illumination which had to be grasped by the eye – in other words, this again is something which contemporary art does not at all consider to be its task. For today's painter, the human being, for example, does not glow with an aura. Instead, sunlight appears, reflects off him and he paints the reflected sunlight. We painted the glow of the human being himself from within and the connection of this glowing with the movement of light, with the light impulse of the cosmos." (October 21, 1917)

"Thus the attempt has been made to gather in the cupola that which leads to a recognition of the supersensible out of the various human circumstances – Egyptian, Greek, Medieval, past, future – out of the various temporal circumstances. And all this works out of the color so intensively that one gets the impression that the cupola surface destroys itself with something which is not limited in the soul but goes out into the spiritual, so that it lifts itself up through its artistic configuration." (April 5, 1920)

When Rudolf Steiner drew back the curtain of the small cupola in October, 1920, on the occasion of the first course for the School of Spiritual Science for a larger circle of participants, he spoke as an artist. "Above all, I would like this cupola to be understood in such a way that nothing at all of an abstract nature is fantasized into it. For in this small cupola, which I myself have been substantially involved in, the effort has for once been made to really work out of the color. This color experience is to be actually understood in such a way that one really sees the color nuance at a particular place. It could not, for example, be a case of, say, where the blue was to be especially effective, where the blue was experienced according to its location near the periphery and further away from the center and contrasting with the effect of the colors at the center – it could not, in such a case, be a matter of thinking up the Faust and of painting him there because one perceives a relationship between the Faust being and the color blue. Instead, it had to be a matter of developing the color experience of the blue at this place, in order then to allow the form, the figure, the being to emerge from the color. It had, of necessity, to become what it is. So you see that for the one who originally gave the indication it was not a matter of forming a figure here at this place out of the color experience of the blue which would then lead our perceptions back to the 16th century to the memory of the Faust figure, but rather that for him it was a matter of allowing the form and being to be born out of the living color. And if, in the end, some sort of interpretation can be imposed on things, one must realize that these are interpretations superimposed from the outside, that they can help one or the other to experience this or that from their own subjective standpoint. But what would please me most is if, in regard to this small cupola, you would forget that there is anything of a Faust likeness or an Apollo likeness or a double and so on, and rather that you would give yourself over to the pure color experience out of which the whole is born, becoming indifferent as to whether that is a Faust lurking there or some other, just as the one working out of the color was indifferent to the appearance of this figure. It emerged because the world lives in the color. One should not take the literal or symbolic parameters of the being as the motivating impulse; instead, one should take the experience of the color, the movement of the color, as the basis for painting so that the color and the harmonizing or disharmonizing of colors as such begin to live. Then one will see that one narrows the world if one tries to change that which is cognitively abstract in one's view of the world, even if it reveals itself as spiritual science, into color or form simply as symbol or allegory. If, instead, one lives into the color one will see how the whole wealth of the color experience pours over one, and that in this living into the color one discovers a whole new world. Whereas allegory merely carries the world as one already knows it even into the color, one discovers a new world if one begins with the experience of color itself. It is a new world which is as creative as the world one has through the senses when one synthesizes outer natural phenomena of nature into abstractions or natural laws.

"I wanted to show you by means of this paraphrase – for anything artistic must be mere paraphrase when it is described verbally – how here in this building we tried not to work anything mysterious into the plastic forms or nuances of color applied by the painter. Instead, what we tried to do was to actually experience the mysteries of these worlds which give us the means of artistic representation." (October 9, 1920)

Sketches for the painting of the Small Cupola

- *Faust*
- *Athena-Apollo*
- *The Egyptian Initiate*
- *Head of the Centaur*
- *The Persian-Germanic and the Slavic Motifs*
- *The Slav with Double, Angel and Centaur*
- *The Representative of Man between Ahriman and Lucifer (The Central Motif)*

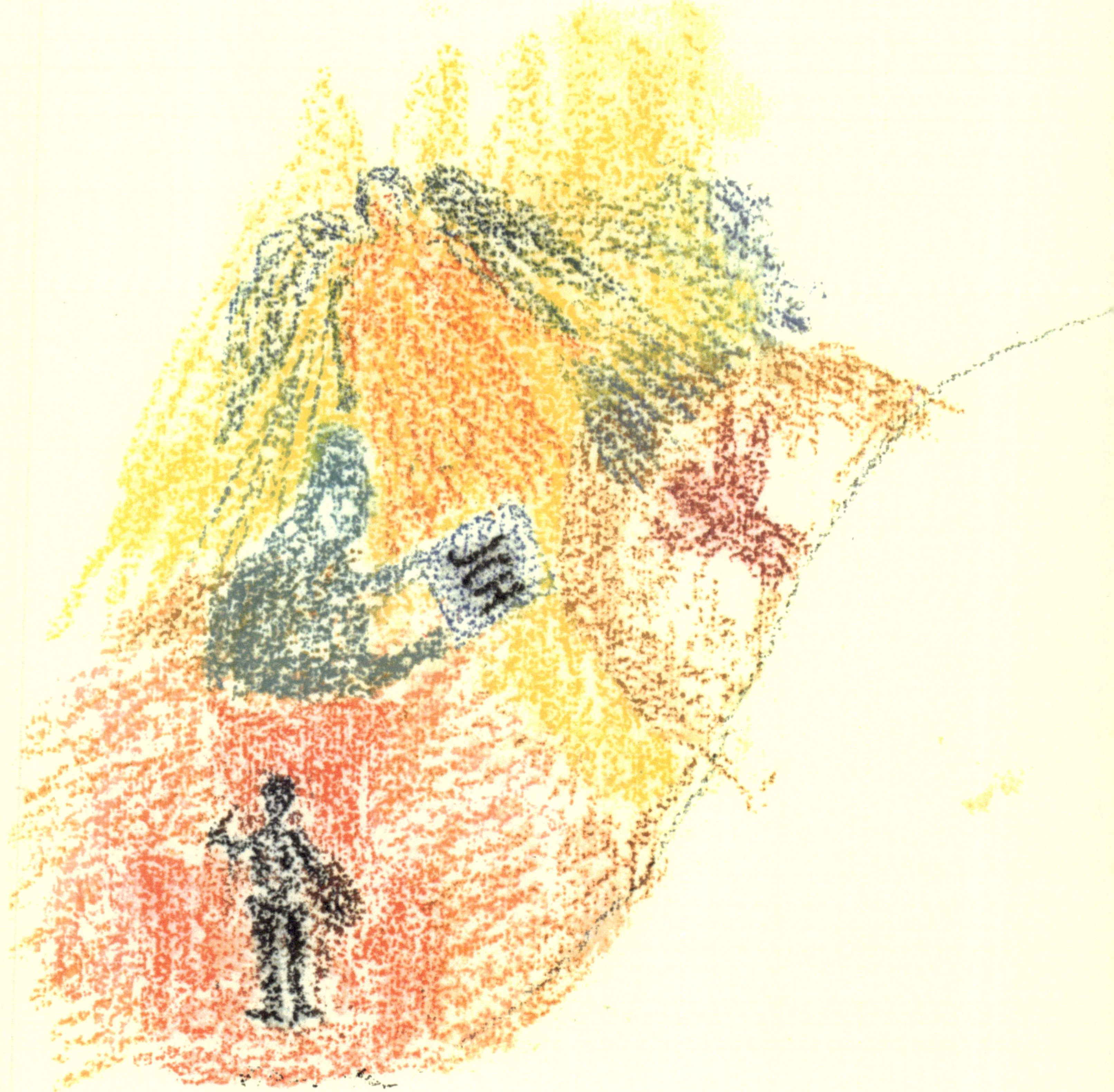

Athena-Apollo

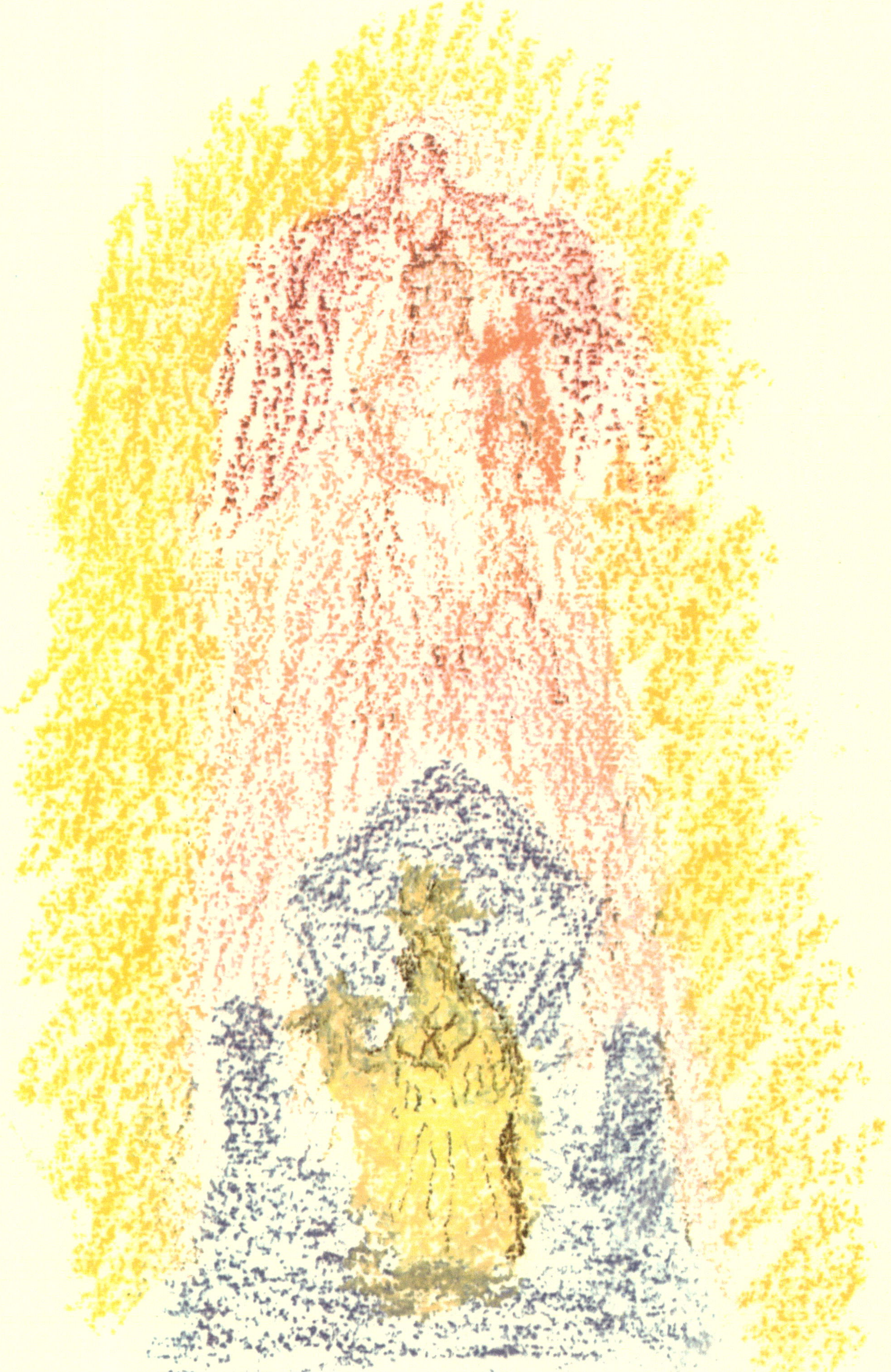

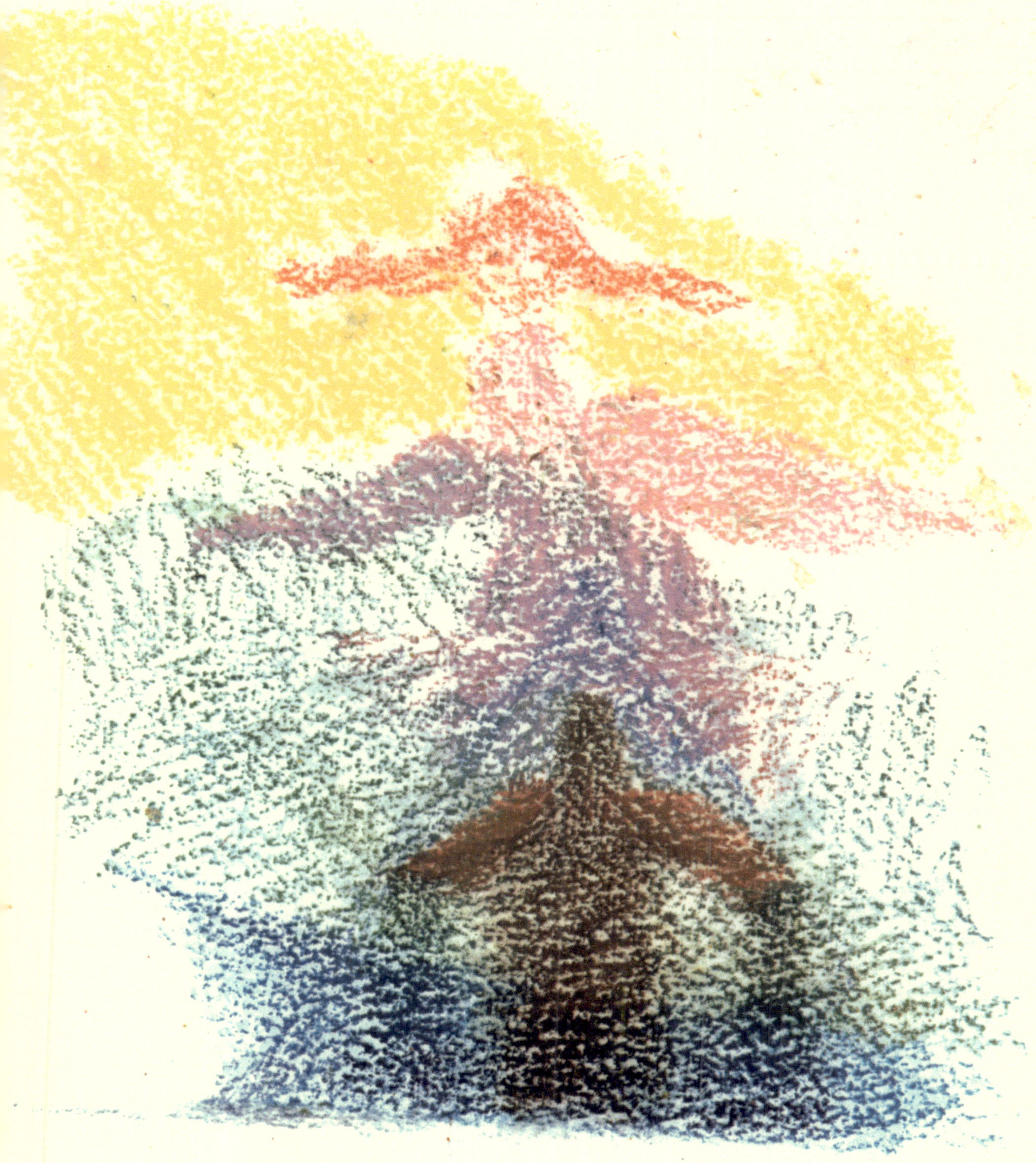

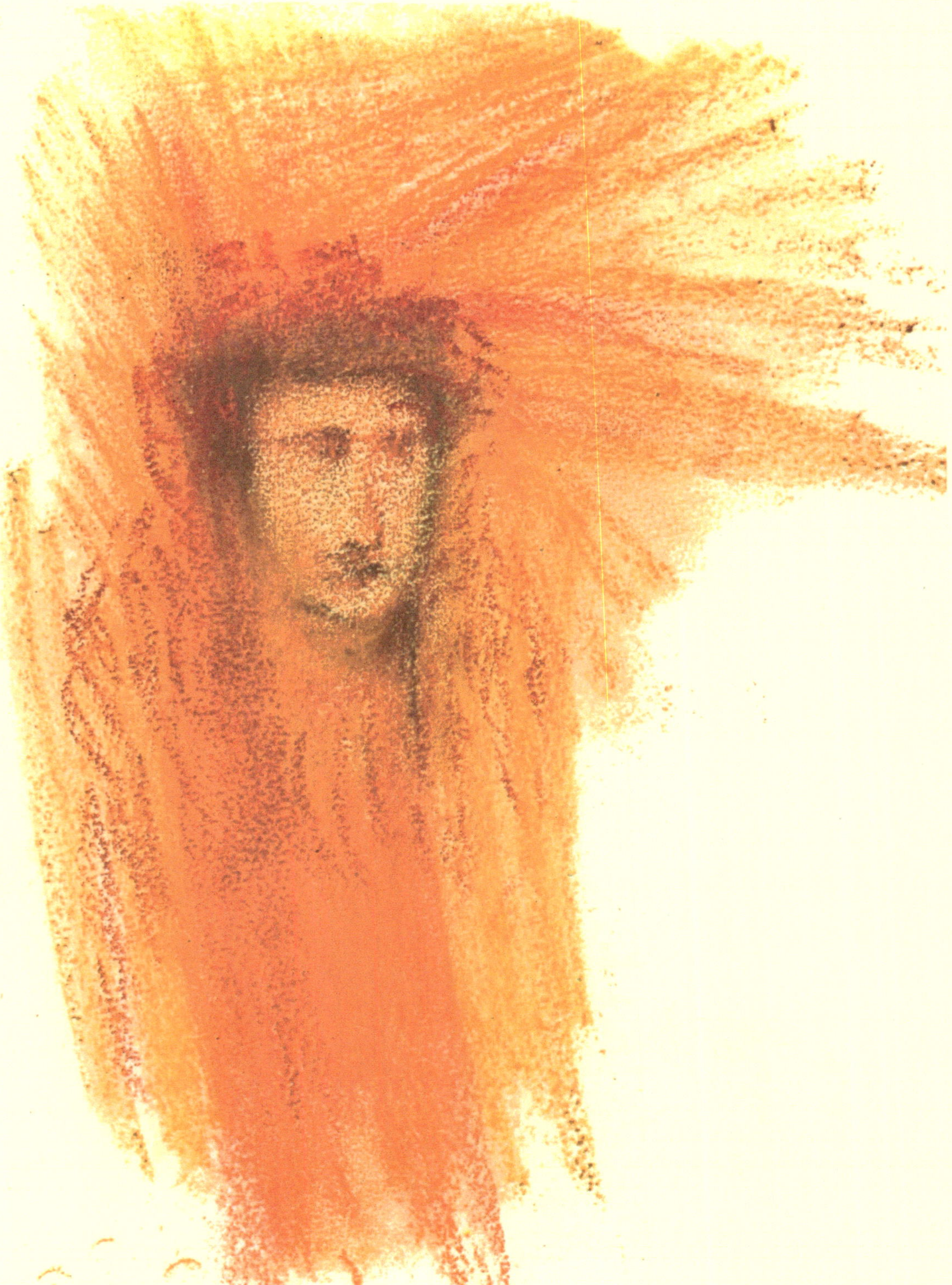

Head of the Centaur

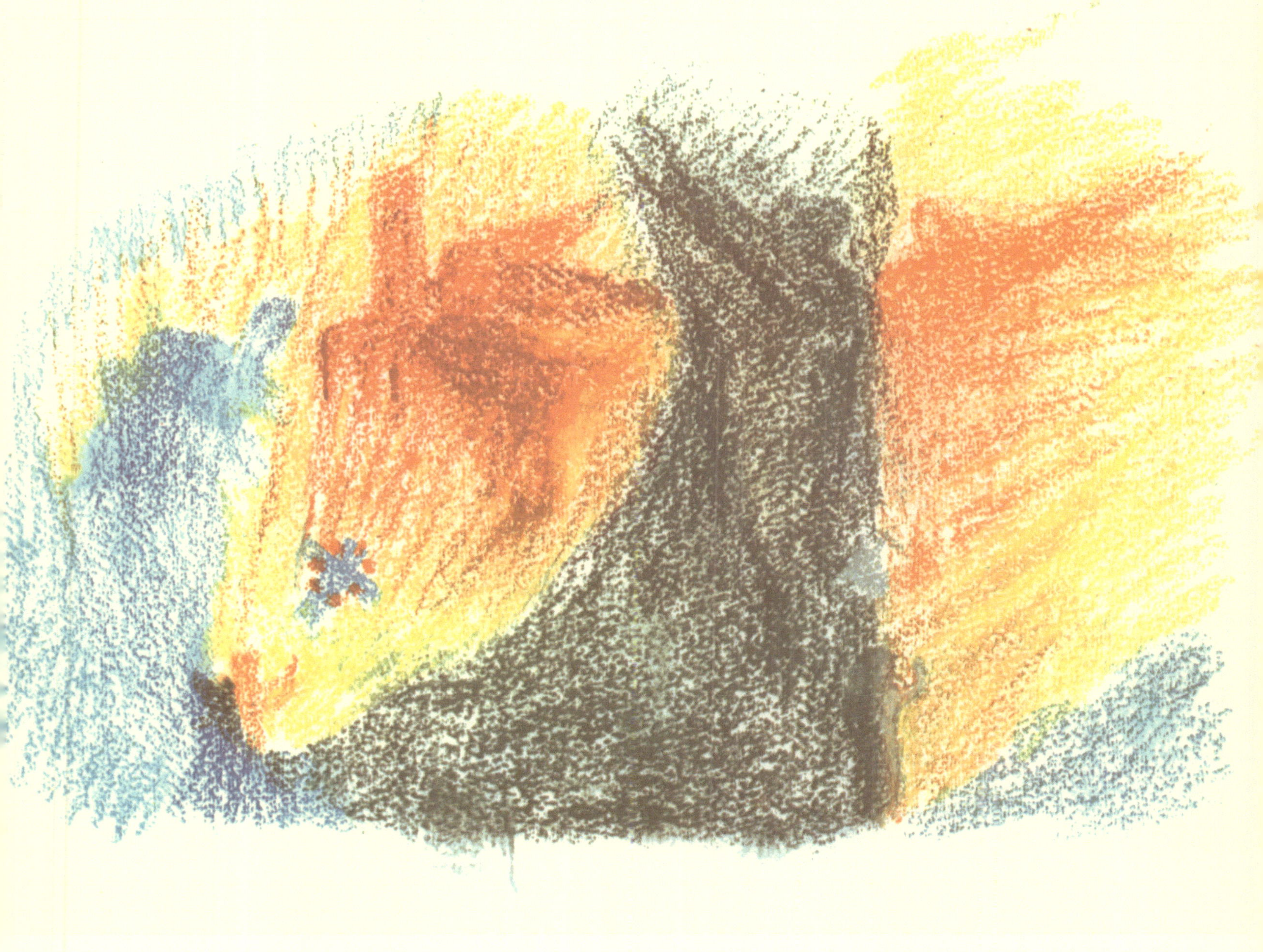

The Persian-Germanic and the Slavic Motifs

The Slav with Double, Angel and Centaur

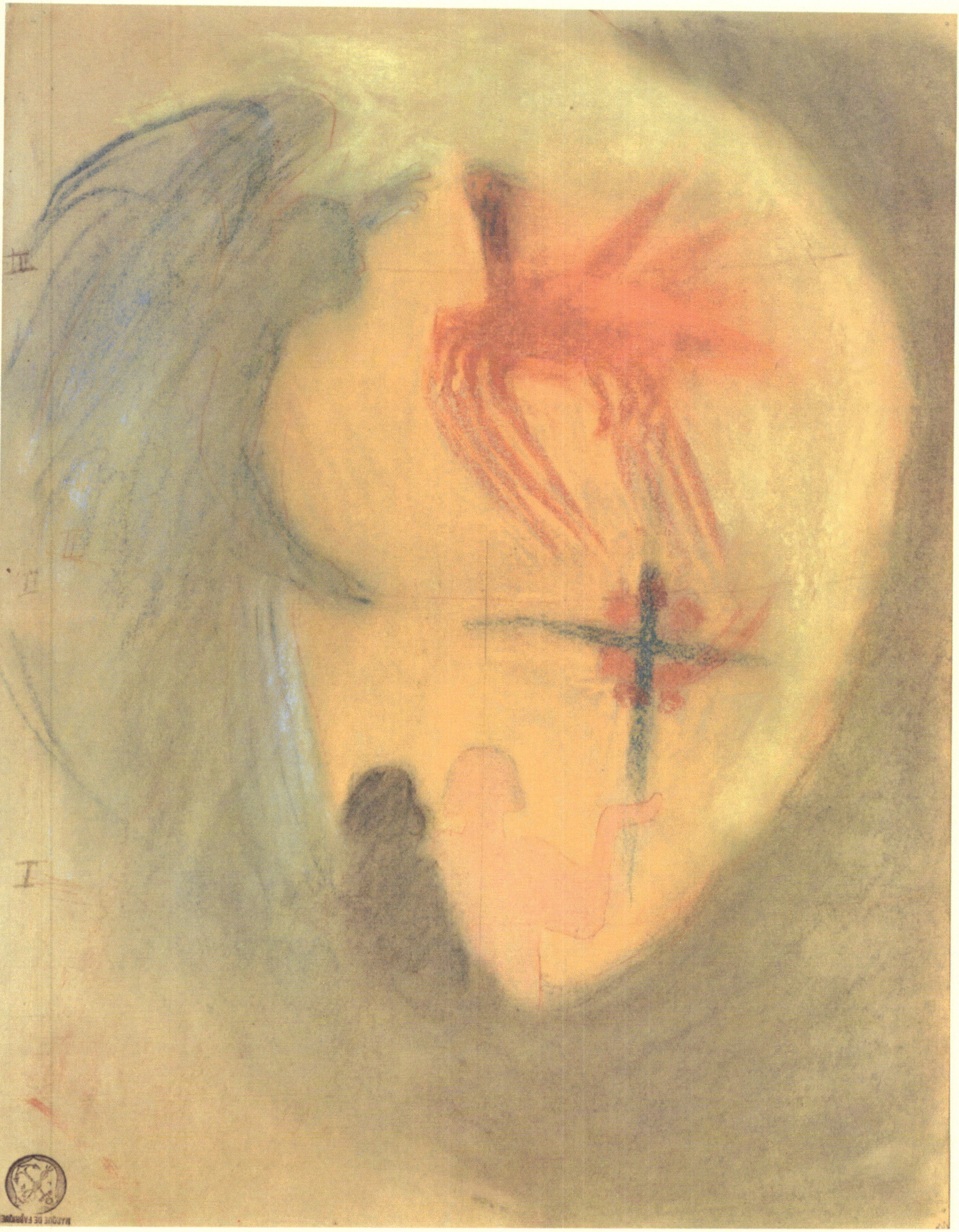

The Representative of Man between Ahriman and Lucifer (The Central Motif)

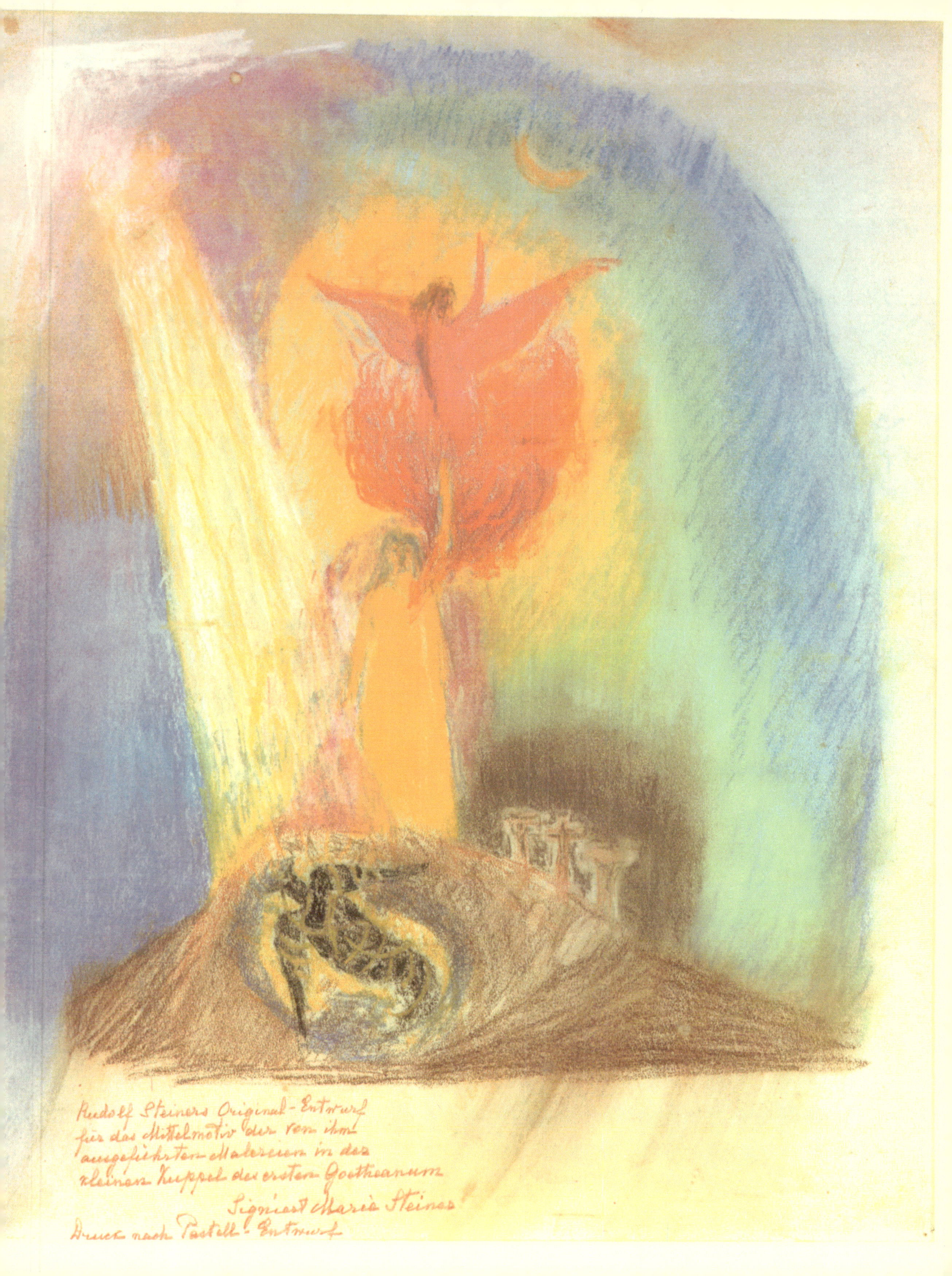
Rudolf Steiners Original-Entwurf
für das Mittelmotiv der von ihm
ausgeführten Malereien in der
kleinen Kuppel des ersten Goetheanum
Signiert Marie Steiner
Druck nach Pastell-Entwurf

THE POSITIONS OF THE MOTIFS IN THE SMALL CUPOLA

The motifs emerge in the color streams of the rainbow in the large cupola, where yellow and blue condense to green. The motifs in the small cupola, on the other hand, are formed through the interweaving nuances of peach-blossom. To the east (in the cupola), in the middle axis, was the central motif of the Representative of Man between Lucifer and Ahriman. The great wooden sculpture was supposed to stand beneath this. The other motifs are grouped symmetrically relative to the central motif in the north and south above the columns.

Above the baldachin in the east: The Central Motif, Man in balance between Lucifer and Ahriman.

Above the first column from the east: Slavic man with the Angel and Centaur.

Above the second column: The Persian – Germanic Initiate with the Child. Above that, Lucifer and Ahriman.

Above the third column: The Egyptian Initiate and his Inspirers.

Above the fourth column: Athena, Apollo, and the Angel-being inspiring Apollo.

Above the fifth column: Faust, Death, the hovering Child facing Faust, and the 'Genius'.

Above the sixth column: The 'Genius' above Faust and the Child project into the area above the sixth column, which is the one next to the stage opening.

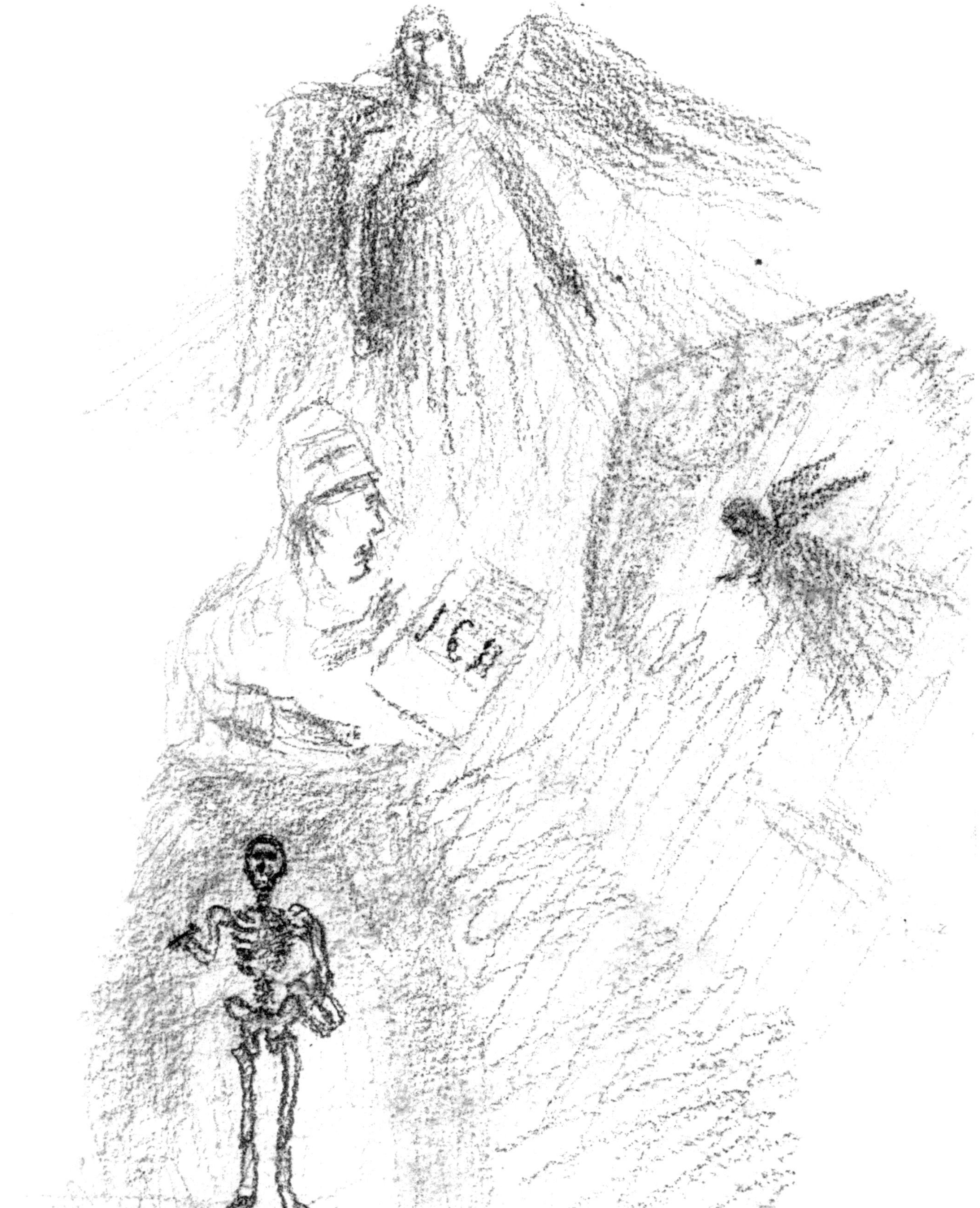

FAUST

"Here you see the searching human being who today feels himself pressed upon by death, death, which always accompanies the most important ideals in the search for knowledge ... ." (January 25, 1920)

Pastel

Among flowing fields of color, blue and black first catch the eye. Yellow spreads down from the top. Overlaid with red, it brings warmth and inwardness; blue, above and within the yellow, brings form. Amidst this simple formation of surfaces and interpenetration of color shines the figure of a winged being, the 'Genius', as Rudolf Steiner called it.
Further down and surrounded by shades of warm red, rose madder forms itself in clearer surfaces. It is confronted by bluish black – black, the 'spiritual image of death' in confrontation with red, the 'lustre of life'.
An area of light is created by a being moving from the side of the stage opening towards the blue. In the sketch, this lighter area is yellowish brown and bluish-red. In the final execution, however, the figure is orange.
The figure of Faust emerges from the center of the blue area. He holds a tablet inscribed in black with the word '*ICH*' (I), the only written word in the Goetheanum building.

Drawing (1914/1915)

The light and dark of the drawing more clearly define the regions, the environment of the single figures. In the lighter area is the seeker for knowledge, the *Ich* before him. The skeleton is drawn in detail.
The winged child, enveloped by light like an angel, floats towards Faust. High above this trinity of Thinker, Child and Death stands the Genius. Besides this there are three further studies to this theme from the year 1917, the time when Rudolf Steiner himself began to paint the cupola. In these, the Genius is shaped out of streams of light and darkness.

Execution

Faust is painted in dark indigo, a color that allows for a cool, inner light but acts as a screen from the outer world. Glowing orange streams toward him; Faust would freeze in the inner coldness of his thought processes were he not irradiated by the child's warmth of heart and light of the future.
"If you look at the small cupola when the light is such that you no longer distinguish the figures from one another but see only the patches of color working on each other in manifold relationship, then you gain a certain impression, the impression of a surface undulating in colors. It is that from which the different forms arise. One who has the capacity to enter into the life of color will find the real human form, actions between human forms, and relationships between human forms arising directly out of the colors. You may sense a need to have an area of blue in an certain spot, to have something orange or red close by; and if you enter into this inwardly, intuitively, then quite involuntarily something like this Faust figure, with the angelic, childlike being hovering before it, will come into being. Gradually you will begin to understand that out of its own nature this blue color forms itself into a kind of configuration reminiscent of the medieval Faust. Everywhere, in the small cupola, you will see that the coloring is the essential element, and that the forms that are in the colors arise out

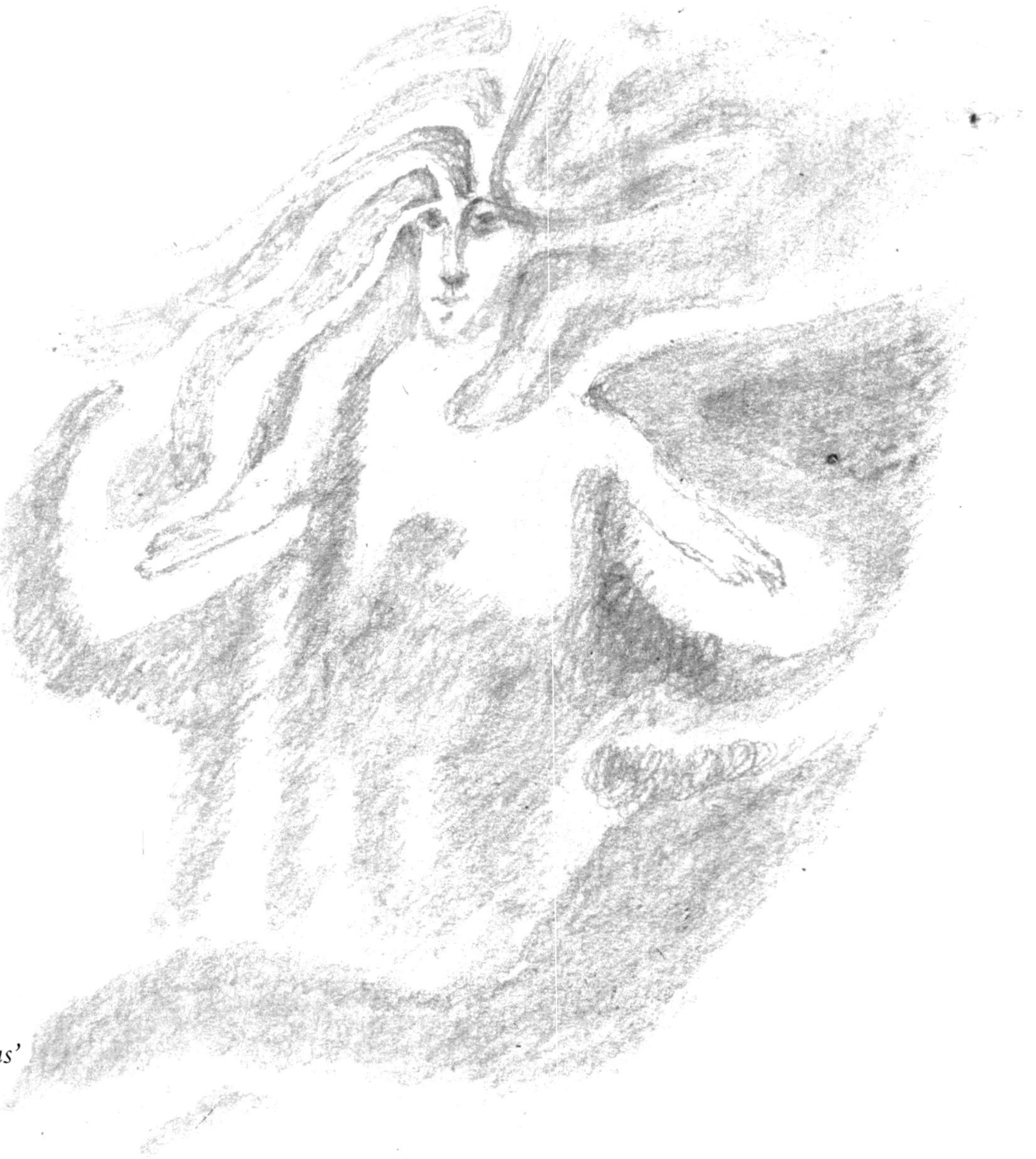

Study of the 'Genius'

of the color. Someone might say, 'But surely, if I want to really experience the individual motifs, I have to first think about them, interpret them.' In a certain sense, he would be right, but only if he also perceives that what has come to life here [in the cupola] is actually a re-experience (*Nacherleben*) of the world of color in the manner just described." (December 30, 1921)

"The main point is that the whole composition of this figure expresses what the spirit of the times brings to light in the searching human being of this particular epoch. You see that expressed, above all, in the eyes, in the mien, in the hand gestures. You see it expressed in the whole gesture of this figure. That we are reminded of Faust is, so to speak, coincidental. This is *the* human being who, in the fifth post-Atlantean epoch, *seeks* in the way man today seeks." (January 25, 1920)

"Here, in the smaller cupola, I was not concerned with drawing some motif or another on the walls. My actual concern was, for example, to have here an area of orange in various shades of orange. The figure of the child emerged out of these color nuances. And here I was concerned that the blue defined itself. That gave me the [Faust figure]. ... Assuredly the form, the substantial elements, have been produced entirely out of the color." (June 29, 1921)

Above the blue and orange, painted in shades of blue and red, is the Genius in an inviting gesture, blessing and directing the child to Faust. Below Faust and opposing the red is Death. In his left hand he holds a book and in his right a pencil, ready to record the deeds and misdeeds of destiny.

"When you see this area of blue here and, next to it, the reddish-orange area, and the black area, *that*, to begin with, is sensed livingly out of the colors. But then the colors gradually come to life and take on forms which later can be interpreted. But, just like one cannot pro-

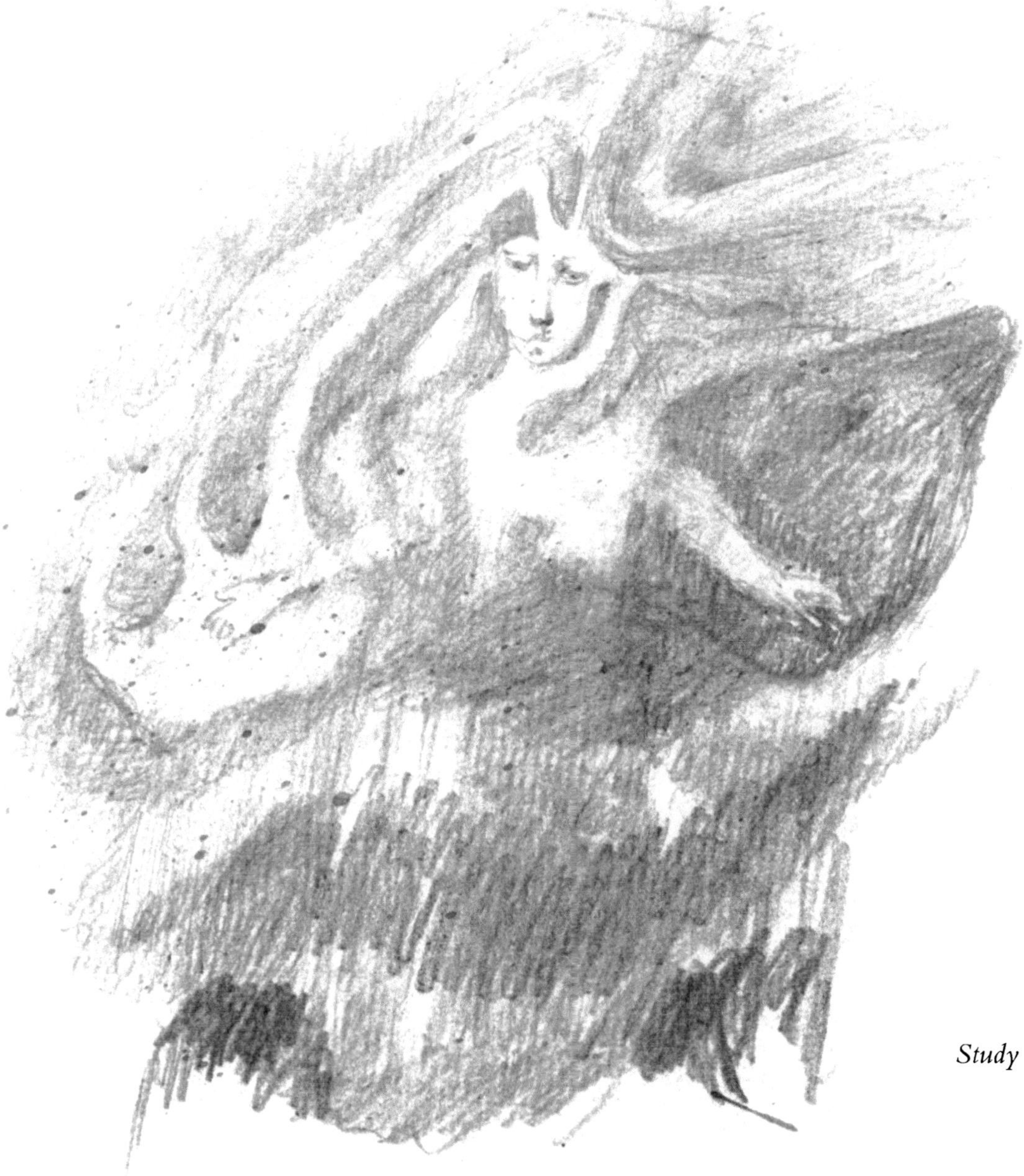

Study of the 'Genius'

duce plants simply with the use of one's intellect, here, too one cannot paint a form that simply has been thought out by the intellect. You must first begin to think when the colors are there; just as the plant has to grow before it can be seen .... *Spiritually* real objects can arise only in the realm of the soul." (August 28, 1921)
To begin with, it seems strange to find one word written within the flowing colors of the cupola, the word *Ich*. "Here you see the only word to be found in the entire building. Nowhere else is there an inscription; everything else is to be worked out in purely artistic forms. But here you meet with the word 'Ich' .... Today, if we contemplate things not merely academically, like little abstractionists, but try to enter with our whole being into the riddles and mysteries of life – and we must do this, if we are to be completely human, to become conscious of our human dignity – then what we know as the laws of nature will penetrate into our souls. They will stand beside the human being who really strives for knowledge. Faust is such a human being. He strives, one might say, out of the mysterious, mystical blue towards the fully-conscious ego, the ego emerging in the word 'I' (*Ich*). In older languages, 'I' was part of the verb form; in our times, it is justified to have it appear for itself." (June 29, 1921)
Faust strives out of blue, the 'lustre of soul'. Red, the 'lustre of life', is confronted by black, the 'spiritual image of death': hard, impenetrable, inexorable and inescapable. On earth, black is the color of mourning; yet, each death is also the gateway to a spiritual event. Just as death holds a special place in modern consciousness, so does the book with the 'black art', the typesetter's cast in which living knowledge is confined, and which must be resuscitated by human thought. Faust, longing to get away from the dismal monuments of his empty, abstract knowledge, feels himself,

"Hemmed in by many a toppling heap
Of books worm-eaten, gray with dust,"

bemoaning that

"Alas! in living nature's stead
Where God his human creature set
In smoke and mould the fleshless dead
And bones of beasts surround me yet."
(Bayard Taylor's Translation)

Just as a skeleton is the remnant of a once living organism, the printed word, accumulated in numerous books, appears like the corpse of once living thought. The art of printing, dating back to the 15th century, allowed the mechanically reproduced word to become ever more the bearer of the human search for knowledge. In earlier times the spoken word had transmitted the immediate soul expression from man to man. With the onset of printing, thought increasingly died into letters which only later become re-infused with life. This process of the death and resurrection of thought is, however, directly connected with man's ego forces. Resurrecting what is dead by means of the individual's spiritual exertions – *that* is one of the most important tasks of the age of the consciousness soul, which began in Faust's time. Thus the 'I' (*Ich*) had to be written down, standing apart, as it were, from the flowing colors of the motif. Rudolf Steiner spoke in a radical way of this "unformed, inartistic, written 'Ich'"[3] that is nonetheless the germinating point of a new development in the history of mankind.

"Intellectualism has developed only since the middle of the 15th century. It has done so by virtue of the fact that our head organs have taken on a configuration which, were it to overtake our organism completely, would lead perpetually to death .... This death process which occurs in the head, and thanks to which we have our intellectual consciousness, is what these colors here, as well as the forms emerging from them, were to bring to expression. This is the only place within the entire building where something appears in writing, and rightly so; for only in this time period has the ego, the ego-thought of man, become so abstract that it can be indicated with mere letters. More and more, ego-thought will be able to be borne only if the ego is in fact filled with the Christ. For this reason, mediaeval mystics such as Johannes Tauler and Meister Eckhardt had the task of developing St. Paul's words in sermons and meditations. As a result, it is fixed for all eternity within the medieval language that developed into modern German in the German speaking regions, that the *ICH** spells out the initial letters of Jesus Christ." (April 5, 1920)

Faust is the central point between child and skeleton, between birth and death. "The sight of this Faust-like figure, with death below him, would be unbearable were it not for the appearance of its opposite, the child flying towards him and the *ICH*." (April 5, 1920)

The whole tragedy of medieval initiation is portrayed in this motif. At this stage in human development, man could gain insight into life only by recognizing the connection between life and death.

"Here you see the searching human being who today feels himself pressed upon by death; death, which always accompanies the most important ideals in the search for knowledge .... There, above the relevant figures, you will generally find their inspirer; however, in the fifth post-Atlantean epoch, it is death itself that inspires – death, approaching man from below." (January 25, 1920)

Death as inspirer? In Greek portrayals, death appears as a youth. The hard, inexorability of death appears as an artistic motif only in the late middle ages: a skeleton with a scythe portrayed in the Dance of Death. Some medieval motifs show skeletons approaching people of all ages and ranks, asking them to dance and then carrying them off. Occasionally death himself, as a skeleton bearing a scythe, comes to collect his victim. *Memento mori*, 'think of death', was a theme of many an medieval religious work, reminding man of the day of reckoning confronting us all. However, the real significance of death as a source of knowledge and as a principle of initiation was to be kept from man until he had reached spiritual maturity in the experience of his ego.

"In the fifth post-Atlantean epoch, initiation wisdom cannot be attained unless accompanied by the full consciousness of the meaning of death, not only in relation to human life, but in relation to the whole world. We are able to think because we bear death processes continually in our heads. If these processes, active in our head at the service of our thinking, were to penetrate our whole organism, we could not live. We would be perpetually dying. We live only because the tendency toward death in our head is balanced by the inclination toward life in the rest of our organism ....

Only when this principle of initiation, the power of death, which is now still in its beginning stage of development, spreads further and further and engenders in mankind of the future the yearning for the compensating spirit – the longing for a youth which is already Jupiter and no longer Earth youth, the youth of the

* *Translator's Note: 'I' is also spelled 'JCH' in German, as in this motif.*

next planetary incarnation of the earth – only then will that which ought to enter into the earthly life of humanity, do so." (January 25, 1920)

The Faust motif builds the transition to the large cupola, relating to the Oedipus motif and the green-yellow mood of the Greek picture. Oedipus, who, because of the loosening of blood ties, has lost atavistic clairvoyance and consequently can no longer understand the oracles, becomes enmeshed in a web of sin spun by Ahriman's influence. Goethe's Faust, who is powerful in thought and living primarily in head forces and has mastered the knowledge of his times, falls into adventures of passion.

"Just like Oedipus had to admit Ahriman into himself in order to confront and conquer the Sphinx, man in the fifth post-Atlantean period must take Lucifer into himself when he faces Ahriman-Mephistopheles; *i. e.*, he must undergo the opposite process from Oedipus .... Now take Faust, with everything his ego has achieved, wanting, so to speak, to cast it all out of his head; as Goethe expresses it, 'I've studied now philosophy and jurisprudence, medicine, and even – alas! – theology/ From end to end with labor keen ...' All this he wants to clear his head of, and he does so by giving himself over to *the* kind of life that is not bound up with the head. He is Oedipus in reverse, receiving Lucifer into himself .... All the misfortunes that befall Oedipus on account of his having to be permeated by Ahriman are of an outer nature. Disaster sets upon his entire generation, not just him himself. And even that disaster befalling himself is indicated externally ....

All events that Faust meets are inner soul experiences, showing something tragic in man's inner life, so that also here Faust represents an Oedipus in reverse. If we contemplate these two figures – or rather, these dual figures of Oedipus and Sphinx, Faust and Mephistopheles – we find placed before us, in a prototypal way, the evolution of the fourth and fifth post-Atlantean epochs." (November 20, 1914)

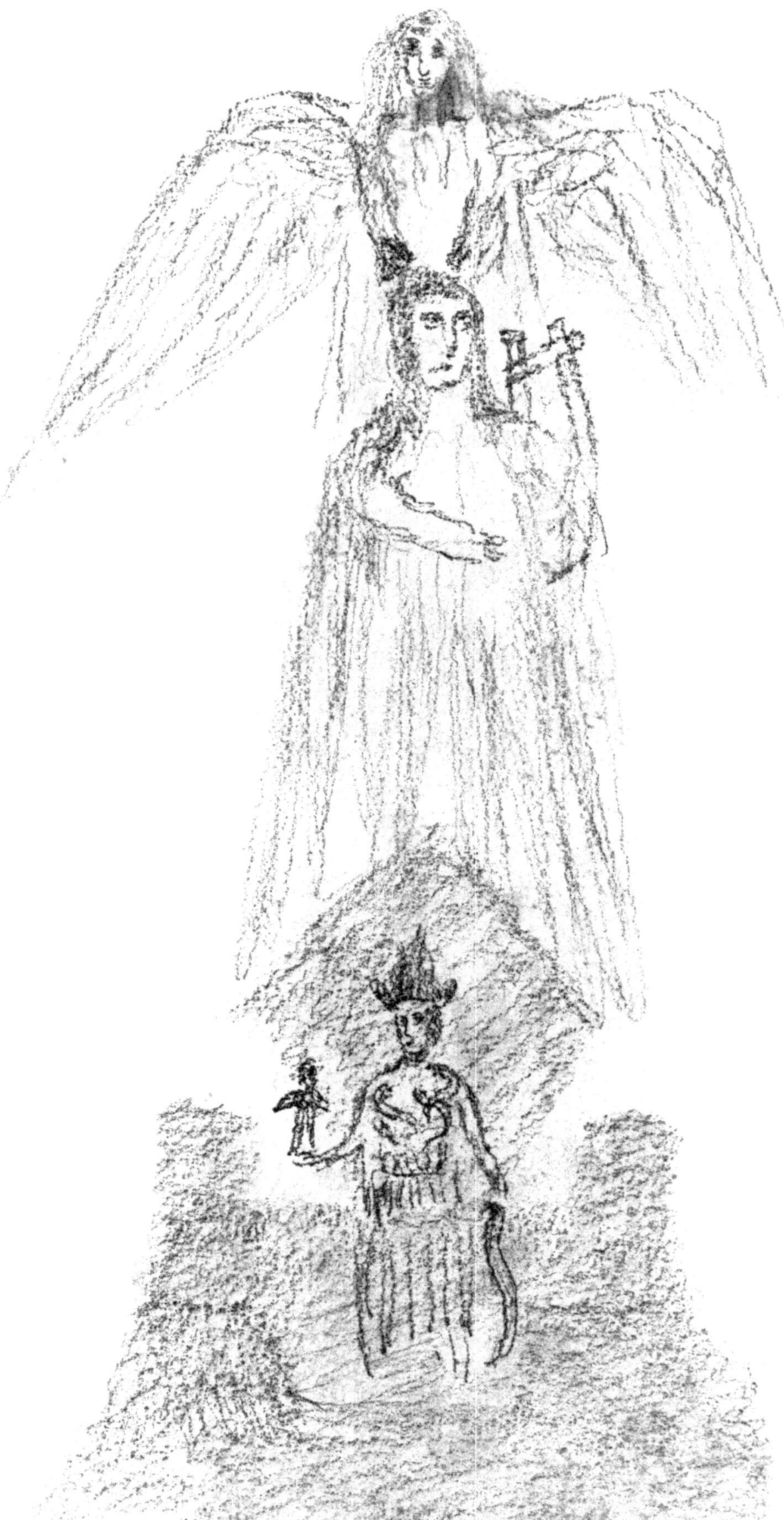

ATHENA/APOLLO

"The light of the spiritual world shining through during the fourth post-Atlantean cultural epoch ... ."
(January 25, 1920)

Pastel Sketch

In yellow, in a world of radiating light, peach-blossom weaves, densifying at the top to carmine red protecting the figure created in the breathing peach-blossom. The red it carries is shaped somewhat like a lyre. Over against the yellow and peach-blossom below stands a ceremonious cobalt blue, its borders more geometrically formed. Yellowish brown, derived from matte yellow penetrating violet, is enthroned in the blue.

Drawings (1914, 1917/18)

Three figures can be recognized within an area of powerful, bright light. The dignified central one with shining eyes and lyre on arm is Apollo. The upper one rises protectively, spreading its wings envelopingly, with arms in an attitude of inspiration. The lower figure with shining helmet, Gorgon on its aegis and Nike in its hand, is reminiscent of Phidias' Pallas Athena. In 1917 Rudolf Steiner added a series of detailed sketches, dramatic line drawings and black-and-white studies attempting in various ways to give expression to the head and face of the divine being above Apollo. These drawings allow one to directly re-experience the way Rudolf Steiner worked as an artist.

Execution

In the final painting, the light yellow surrounding the motif in the pastel sketch has become the image of the god playing the lyre.

"Among the paintings in the small cupola we have here a kind of figure which, ... through its whole forming, through its whole being, portrays the light of the spiritual world *shining into* the human being of the fourth post-Atlantean period as it had to during the fourth post-Atlantean cultural period. Above this figure you will find the inspiring beings." (January 25, 1920)
"Special care was given to this pale yellow out of which it was attempted, purely out of the color, to form this Apollo figure. I tried to impart a certain quality of radiance to this pale yellow through the technical treatment of the color." (June 29, 1921)
To some extent, this treatment is still noticeable in existing photographs.
"Out of its own nature, one was obliged to portray the genius of the sentient and cognitive being as Apollo with the lyre." (June 12, 1920)
The sun god belongs to the world of 'radiating colors', described by Rudolf Steiner in *Theosophy* and 'Lucifer-Gnosis' as the highest and purest region of the auric, soul-spiritual worlds of color:
"For these have a radiating, sparkling, glittering character. They not only light up the space they fill but shine and radiate through it. There is something *active*, inherently mobile in these colors. The others have something inherently at rest, immobile. These, on the other hand, continuously recreate themselves out of themselves."[4]
Above is the inspiring being, "yellow and yellowish white, sunny like an Apollo countenance." (September 7, 1921) Further down is "an Athena-like figure, derived from brownish orange with light yellow. This is the way in which the Greek lived into his knowledge and gen-

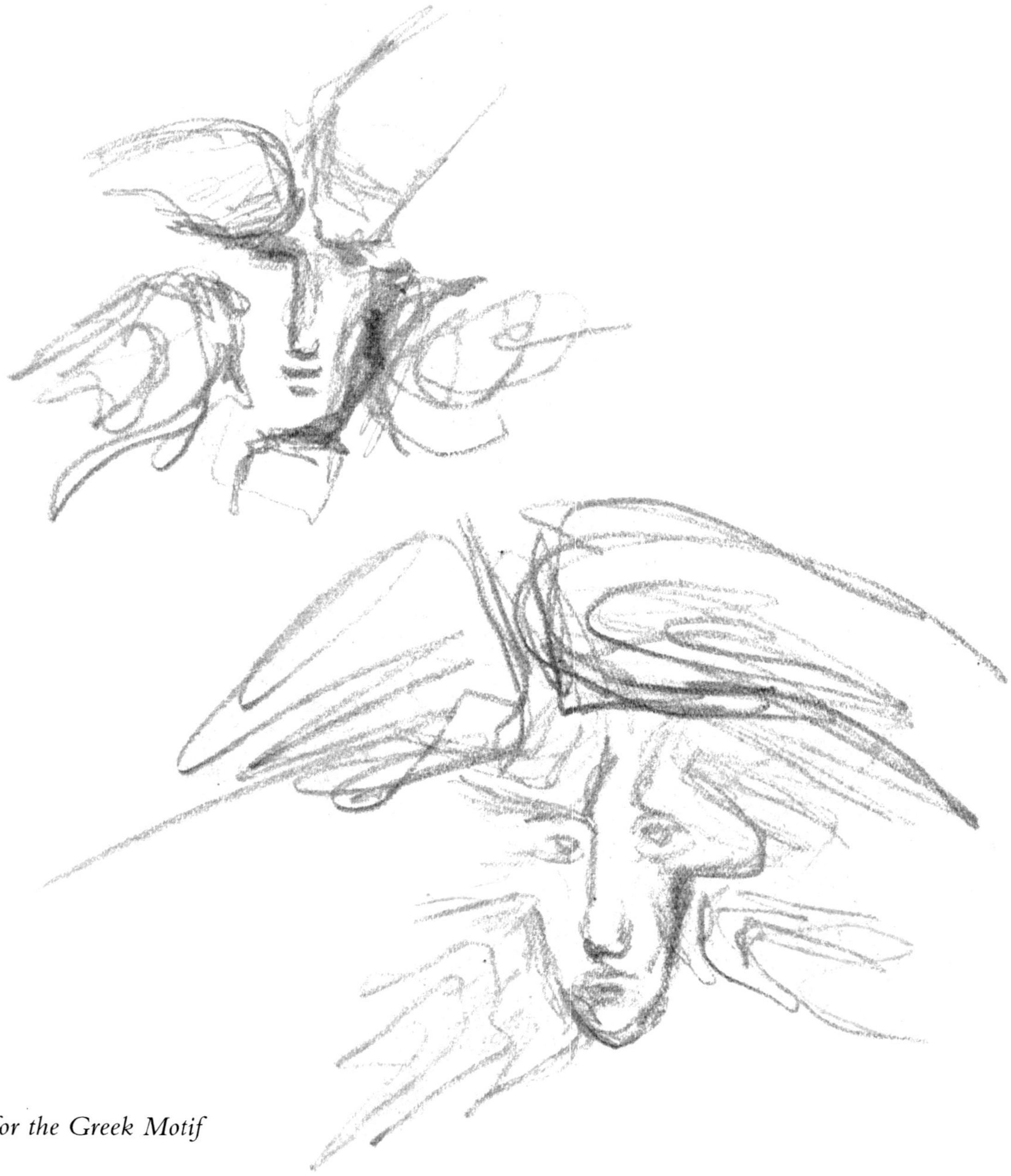

Head Study for the Greek Motif

eral feeling for the world. This figure here is inspired by his angel; it transports us back into the Greek nature." (June 29, 1921)

"These pictures always show, first, the personality to be initiated; above this, the figure which sinks Imaginations into the personality who is to be initiated; and further above, that figure from a higher hierarchical order which brings down the Inspirations." (April 5, 1920)

Out of the brownish yellow to the side, several profiles appear which try to take in what emanates from the Athena figure.

"When one wants to bring such a figure to the surface through the artistic medium of painting, the soul is bare of any conjectures that might lead to the question: 'What does this or that mean?' An inartistic person will go up to these figures and say, 'What do the two or three heads mean there, to the left of the main figure?' That is an inartistic queston, a question which the painter will want to answer least of all because for him who has painted these faces, these forms simply appear within his field of vision. No feeling is aroused within him which would lead to the question, 'What does this mean?' Rather, he senses a necessity from within the creative world forces to surround a figure, that is inspired like this one is, with beings which themselves must be expressed as human figures." (January 25, 1920)

In Athena we are faced with a being who is ever striving to unite energy with intellectual discretion. Under her guidance thinking takes on a pure character, unclouded by passion; it becomes virginal. In Athens, her name is 'Parthenos', the virgin. According to mythology, she was not born of a mother but emerged miraculously from the head of Zeus, her father.

"What did the leaders of the mysteries in ancient Greece mean when they spoke of the virginal Pallas Athena? They meant the wisdom through which man works in a

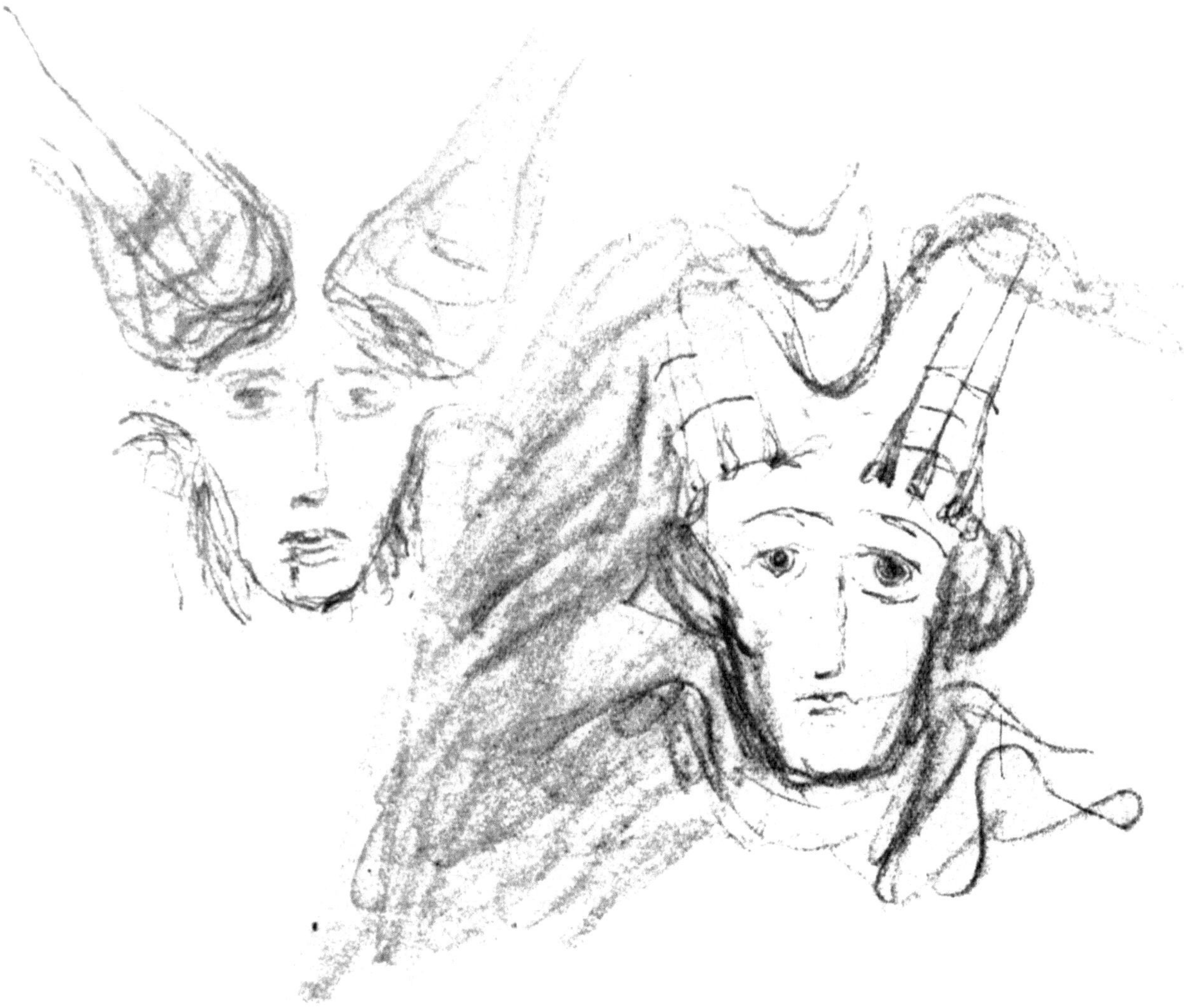

Head Study for the Greek Motif

historical world-context. This wisdom was born in the fourth epoch, into which the Greek culture entered, not out of the world itself, but rather as a reflection of the world; *nota bene*, a reflection of the world or maya. In earlier epochs the priests in the mysteries did not portray wisdom as virginal because in the first, second and third post-Atlantean epochs human wisdom was always fructified by the atavistic faculty of clairvoyance. The possibility first arose in the fourth post-Atlantean epoch also to know something by merely looking upon that which is not impelled by the forces underlying atavistic clairvoyance, by emotions, by passions, by everything that smoulders as fire in the human being, but rather by the virginal reflection of the world, unfructified by atavistic clairvoyance. Thus, the wisdom that is referred to when its representative, Pallas Athena, is presented stems from maya." (December 24, 1917)

Greek mythology speaks of various beings possessing this faculty of thinking not yet possessed by man. Ariadne gives Theseus the ball of yarn so that he might find his way out of the labyrinth; Athena helps the young Perseus avoid looking at the Gorgon Medusa (which would have turned him to stone) by lending him her shield so that he saw the Medusa only in reflection, thus enabling him to decapitate her. Since that time, Athena bears the head of the Gorgon on her breastplate. "The figure of Athena, brownish yellow in color, was also described by Rudolf Steiner as 'Pythia-like'. This points to the working of the female element in Greek spiritual development through which the 'current from the cosmos' was mediated. This includes the forces of the goddess of prudence and wisdom, Athena, who protects heroes, as well as the oracles of the priestess through whom, under the influence of steaming vapors rising from a cleft in the earth at Delphi, the voice of Apollo resounds.

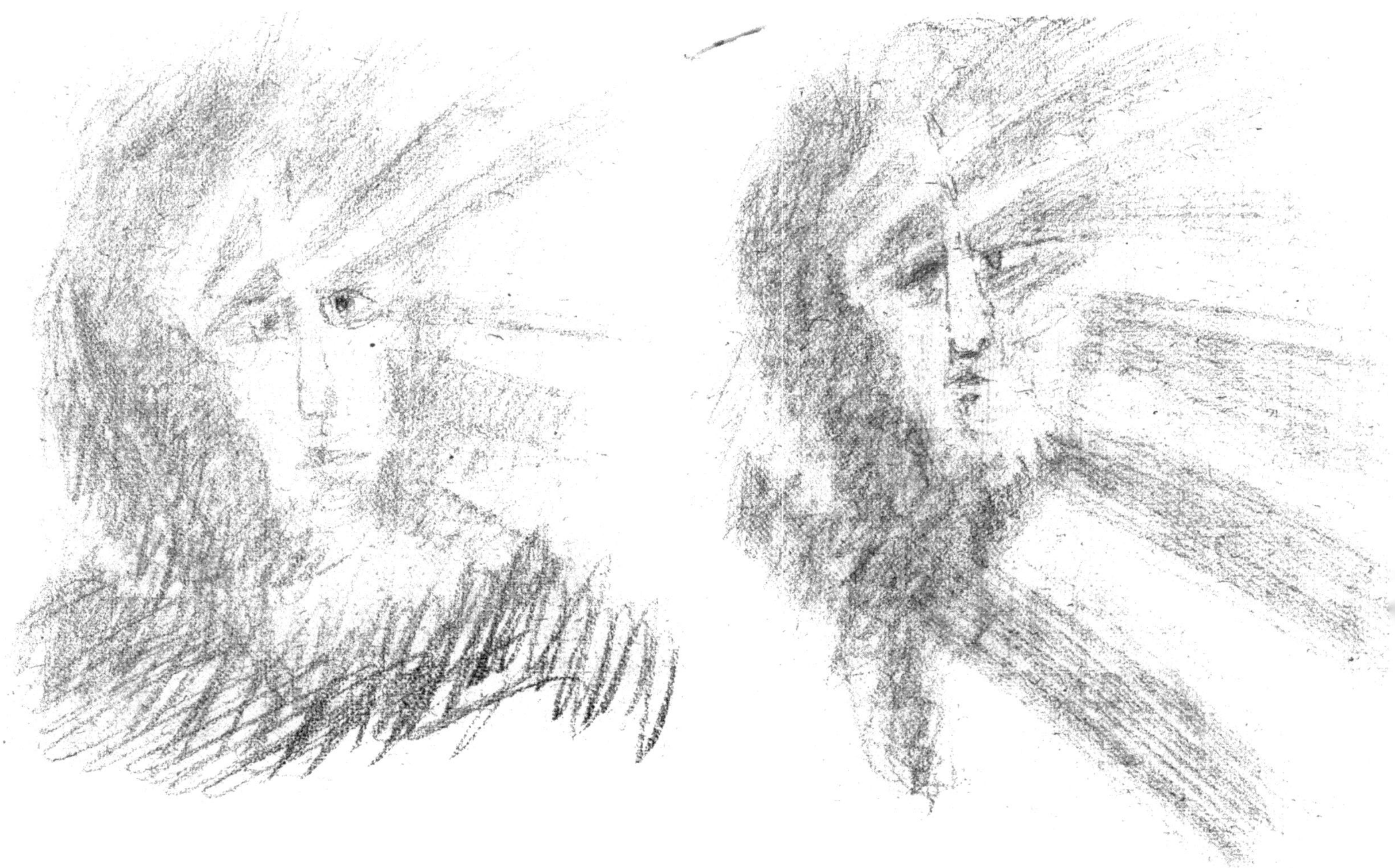

Head Study for the Greek Motif

"Especially at the height of Greek culture, initiation content ordinarily had to be gained by the initiate through female figures who, to a certain degree, switched on the current coming to man from the cosmos ... . In ancient Greece, the Pythia-figures are closely connected with the whole condition of Greek initiation. Thus such things then make their appearance, like [these three] heads, which are worked purely out of the color." (April 5, 1920)

In the large cupola, Oedipus stands in a wide landscape, manly, heroic, holding himself upright between victory and distress. He can solve the riddle of the sphinx but he cannot understand the words of the oracle. The first task could only be solved through the newly gained power of the intellect, but these very powers obscured for mankind everything mysteriously expressed in the oracle. Oedipus, together with the mainstream of Greek culture, had penetrated too deeply into physical corporeality to be able to understand the will of divine providence. From now on the will of the gods would be communicated by the priestesses of the various oracles. Thus in Delphi the wisdom and activity of Athena and the divine oracle worked through the voice of the priestess of Apollo.

"The Greeks, who, in their wonderful mythology, had created something like an after-image of what took place in the spiritual world at the end of the Atlantean period, revered the sun spirit as the harmonizer of thinking, feeling and willing in man. 'Oh sun spirit', those who knew something of this would say to themselves, 'thou hast ensouled thyself in an etheric spirit form. There thou hast harmonized what otherwise would run wildly and uncontrollably through human thinking, feeling and willing, harmonized them upon thy wonderful lyre, upon which thou allowest the tones of the human soul to resound harmoniously!' ... So the Greeks placed the Pythia over such steaming vapors as carry passions from the earth brought into disorder by Ahriman and Lucifer, but Apollo shone over the Pythia, conquered the passions' wildness, and so she became prophetess." (June 1, 1914)

Apollo on the heights of Parnassus, Apollo at the bottom of the Castalian Springs, he is the god of song and the god of purification. He carries the lyre and his lyre-playing is an image of the harmonizing power of his being, which also makes him the god of healing. With the sounds of his lyre he keeps the universe in harmonious motion and fills the earth with the music of the spheres. The plektron with which he strikes his lyre guides the light of the sun from the spiritual world to the earth. Apollo's music brings order into chaos, brings order to the soul forces of man, to thinking, feeling and willing, brings all opposing forces into harmony. As the god of music, he is accompanied by the muses.

"Only we must keep in mind that this, regarding Apollo, is a projection of what happened at the end of the Atlantean period. Something really entered into the human soul from spiritual heights then, something which resounded as a weak echo in the musical arts practiced by the Greeks under the protection of the god Apollo. The Greeks were aware that their music was, so to speak, the earthly reflection of that ancient art which, in order to bring harmony to thinking, feeling and willing, had been practiced in celestial heights by the angelic being permeated by Christ. They did not express it like this; only in their mysteries did they really know what they were dealing with. In the Apollonian mysteries of the Greeks would be said, 'A high, divine being once permeated a being of the hierarchy of Angeloi. That brought harmony to thinking, feeling and willing, and is reflected in the musical arts, especially in the Apollonian arts, that art, for example, which pours out in the music of a stringed instrument'." (December 30, 1913)

The myth of the Hyperborean Apollo hints at the light-nature of this god who, from his ancient home in the north, returns to Greece every spring accompanied by silvery-white swans.[5] According to that legend, Apollo spent the winters with the Hyperboreans. They lived on the other side of the Boreas, of the north wind and northern areas. The Greeks imagined a land of paradisiac beauty and clarity there, a land of eternal light. Pindar said, "No wanderer and no ship can reach it. A holy people live there, knowing neither illness nor old age, neither trouble nor battle.

"What is Apollo, really? Not his shadow-image, such as the Greeks revered, but, what is Apollo, actually? As a super-earthly being he is that being who, from higher regions, poured forces healing to the mind and paralyzing to the ahrimanic and luciferic powers. This caused such an interaction in the human body of brain, breath, and lungs with larynx and heart as came to expression in the projection of this interaction into song. For the correct interaction among brain and breathing, and speech organs and heart, is the bodily expression for the proper interaction of thinking, feeling and willing. The Healer, the super-earthly Healer, is Apollo. We have seen his three stages of development, and the Healer underlying Apollo is born on earth and the people call him Jesus, which, translated into our language, means, 'the Healer through God'. It is the Jesus child of the Nathan line, the Healer through God, Jehoshua Jesus." (December 30, 1913)

Rudolf Steiner wanted to portray this comprehensive Apollo figure in a fifth *Mystery Drama*. The performance was planned for the summer of 1914, but was prevented by the outbreak of war.

"The new drama, the not-yet-written drama – how often my thoughts return to it! The action was to take place at the Castalian Springs, in the Temple of Delphi. Greece was to live again in its genesis within the mysteries, through which it rose to greatness. The land of Greece – light and clear, but also deep, dark and mysterious – striving upwards from the lower realms, from the realms of the Mothers, the chthonic divinities, to the sun, to Helios, to Phoebus Apollo, and through these, to Christ – shaped into words by one who knows."[6]

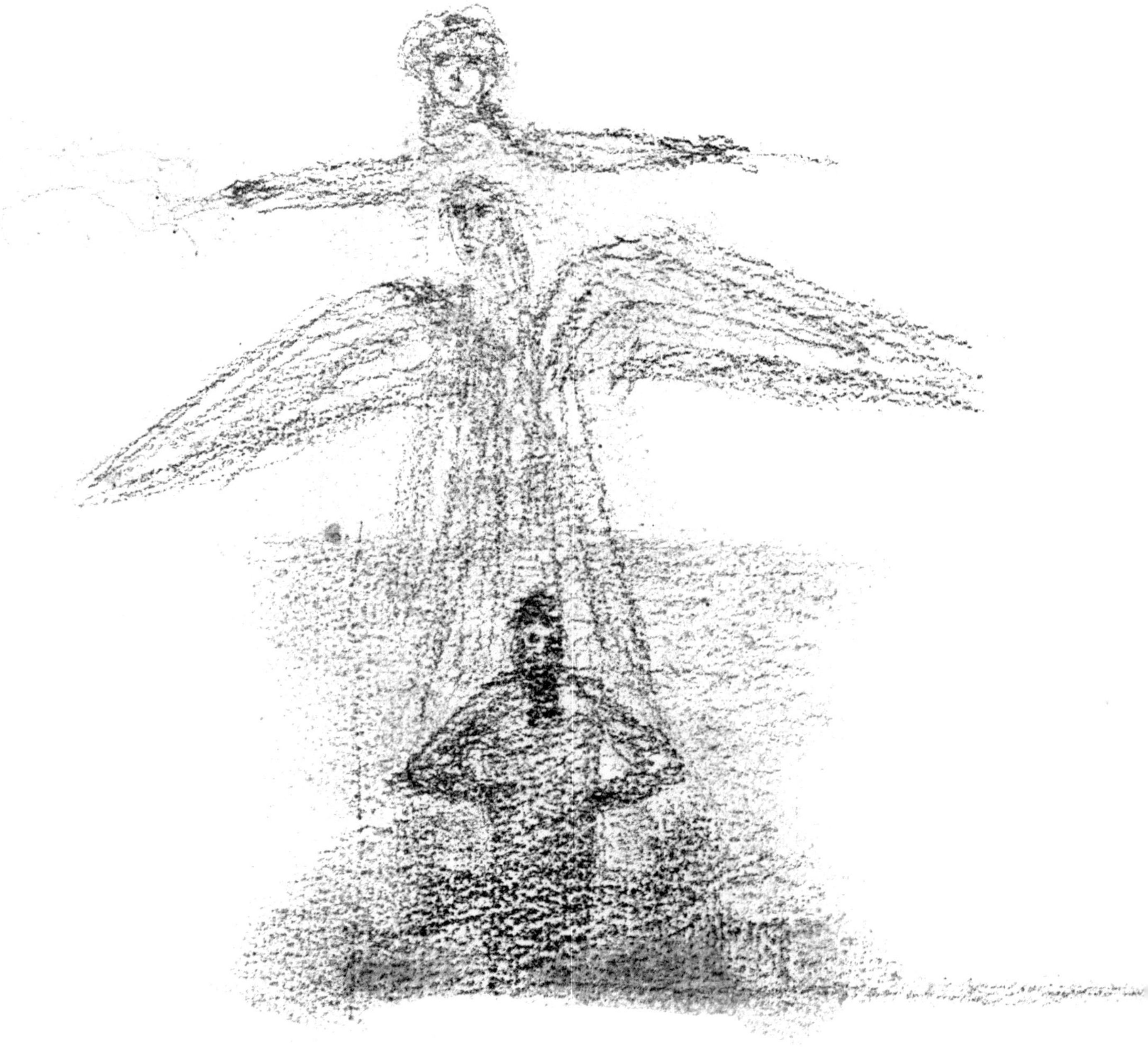

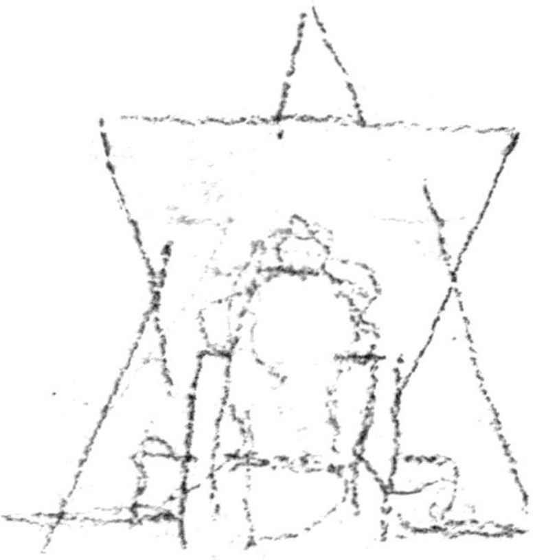

THE EGYPTIAN INITIATE

"The Egyptian *knower*, which is to say, the image for that ancient time opposite to our own in which Faust is striving for knowledge." (June 29, 1921)

Pastel Sketch

The colored background is dark blue below, going over into dull bluish green, with yellow above. A pervasive blue, applied now more lightly, then more strongly, creates a feeling of self-containment. Brownish red with reddish violet and blue produce a dignified brownish violet. Streaming violet-rose spreads itself out above, inclining gently downwards. In the heights, a fiery red shines within the yellow. Whereas the picture of Faust is built of the triad of blue-orange-black, the foundation for the motif of the Egyptian initiate results from yellow streaming in from above and blue supporting below, wherein penetrate very dense brownish red, floating violet-rose and light red. This color environment encloses its own space in inner experience.

Drawing

The posture of the Egyptian is calm, firm, and strictly symmetrical. His ceremonial beard indicates priestly dignity.[7] Above him rises a delicate figure with somewhat feminine features, her sorrowful contenance surrounded by a halo of light, her wide fanning wings in breath-like motion. Still higher, a youthful-appearing being with a joyful look opens arms widely. The drawing includes a sketch of the throne-pediment of the column, designed to harmonize with the painted motif. The Egyptian sits upon the throne made of two interpenetrating triangles, held simultaneously within the forces of light and space. These triangles form the same sign encountered by Faust in the book of Nostradamus as the sign of the macrocosm.[8]

Execution

"Here you see two figures which inspire the knowing, world-feeling Egyptian initiate. He [the middle figure] is a somewhat darker color – brownish red, I would say – as is the Egyptian initiate below him." (June 29, 1921) "Of the two figures above, the lower one is the one which sends the Imaginations down into the Egyptian initiate below, while the other is the one which allows the Inspirations to flow down into him." (January 25, 1920)

The painting was executed by Margarita Woloschin, with Rudolf Steiner going over it only slightly to work its colors together with those of the other motifs. The inspiring beings, in comparison with the original sketch, have been done very freely. Their influence appears to flow from top right to bottom left.

Upon measuring the figures in the cupola in the proportions indicated, Woloschin found that they would encroach on neighboring motifs. "When I mentioned this embarrassment to Dr. Steiner, he said, 'Don't worry. In the spiritual world, objects are not placed side by side; they interpenetrate. In art, too, the figures can weave in and out of one another. The colors should be transparent, should have depth'."

"Once – probably to encourage me – Dr. Steiner praised my Egyptian, throned larger-than-life in his seat. I asked him what in particular he found good about it. He pointed to part of the mouth which I had painted in certain transparent, mosaic-like colors. Colored surfaces, painted next to and over one another, should create the form, which should arise out of the inner gesture of color."[9]

The Egyptian itself is reminiscent of images of the

Pharaohs, which were virtually unchanged in position and gesture through thousands of years, as if created for all eternity. Seated on a throne, arms crossed or placed on the thighs, looking into the far distance and listening to the inspiration of the gods, they have overcome the transitory and purely personal: they have been lifted above individual existence and become 'Osiris'.

"[The Pharaoh] had to be brought so far that he could say to himself, 'If I want to rule over my people I have to sacrifice a part of my spirituality; I have to extinguish part of my astral body, part of my etheric body. The Osiris and the Isis principles must become active in me. I myself must desire nothing. When I say something, Osiris must speak; when I do something, Osiris must act; when I move my hand, Isis and Osiris must work through it. I must exemplify Horus, the son of Isis and Osiris'." (September 14, 1908)

A similar theme is touched upon in the Egyptian scene of the fourth *Mystery Play* in a dramatic confrontation of characters. The neophyte is initiated into the elements. The confusion created by his giving expression to subjective feelings rather than describing perceptions gained from spiritual sight during the sacred ceremony becomes particularly tragic because he had been chosen to be advisor to the Pharaoh whose duty as rightful heir to the throne was to receive cosmic wisdom and conduct social matters according to divine council.

"The part which the Pharaoh gave up, which he sacrificed, was the very part which gave him power. For justified power is not gained by raising the individual personality as a personality; justified power arises through receiving into oneself what transcends the limits of the personality: a higher spiritual power." (September 14, 1908)

In the well-known, monumental sculpture of Chefren, Horus, the falcon-god, is depicted towering over the pyramid-builder's head with outspread wings, showering him with inspiration. In later times, Horus was revered as a divine child, an aspect brought to mind in the cupola here in a fiery, active element of red in the yellow.

In the large cupola, the Egyptian looks upon the pyramid, sphinx and mummy as great riddles, as if from outside; in the small cupola, on the other hand, the initiate, in seclusion, gazing inwardly in the posture of meditation is prepared to hear divine inspiration.

How can we experience today what lived in the ancient Egyptian's soul as he raised his inner vision to Isis and Osiris?

"If we look into ourselves, making use thereby of the sensations, the feelings, of the ancient Egyptian, we say to ourselves that to begin with, we have within ourselves active thinking. ... Now, how thinking relates to thoughts, perceiving to perceptions, how activity stands in relation to what results from activity and finally appears before us, thus Osiris relates to Isis .... The supersensible power that one senses as Osiris can be thought of in sensory images as what emanates from the sun as sunlight, permeating space with the weaving and quickening, active power of light. And in what can be sensed as Isis can be seen what comes to us as reflected, thrown-back sunlight from the moon, which of itself is dark – like the soul, when active thinking does not fall into it – and waits for the light of the sun in order to reflect it back, like the soul waits for the Osiris-Power in order to reflect it back as Isis-Power." (February 16, 1911)

The stellar script speaks of this accord between Isis and Osiris in the passage of sun and moon through the heav-

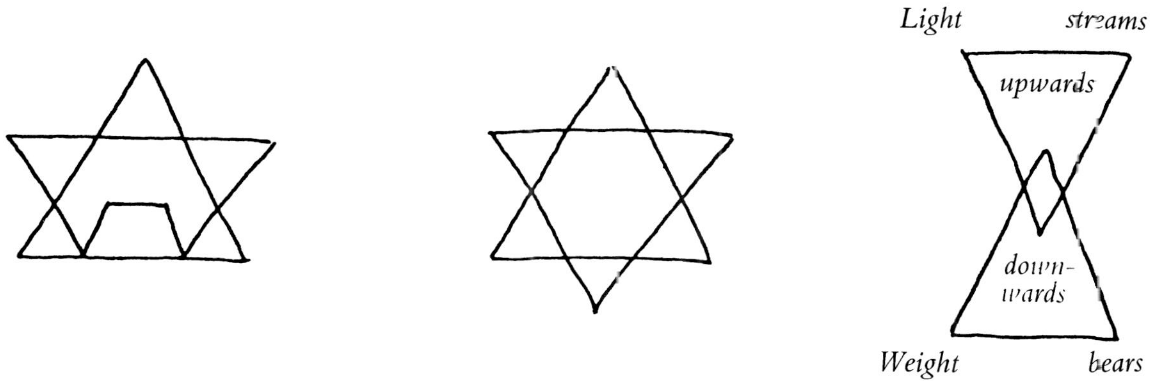

Indication by Rudolf Steiner

ens; it also speaks of the other spiritual powers which reveal themselves through the relationships of the stars, particularly the zodiac, and of the planets.

"Hermes brought the stellar script down in mathematics and geometry, teaching the Egyptians to find in the stars what happens on earth .... When Sirius, the Dog-Star, became visible in Cancer, they knew that soon the sun would enter that sign whose rays come down and conjure forth, so to speak, what the Nile brings to the earth with its floods. Thus they knew that Sirius is the watch guard; he announces what we must expect. That was part of their cosmic stellar timepiece. And for the ability to farm the land properly and manage what was necessary for the outer life, they looked up gratefully to the Dog-Star. And they looked further up to where the movements of the stars express the universal clock, as they had been taught in ancient ages past.

"In such or similar situations, the Egyptians consulted the stellar script. They saw in Thoth (or Hermes) that being who, according to ancient tradition, had set down the very earliest records of cosmic wisdom and, in accordance with inspirations received from the stellar script, formed the physical alphabet, taught man farming, geometry, surveying – in short, taught everything man needs for physical life. But all of physical life is naught but the body of a spiritual life; spiritual life is connected with the entire universe, and out of *this* Hermes was inspired." (February 16, 1911)

The myth of Isis and Osiris is an expression of the feelings of the ancient Egyptian, who felt himself to be the bearer of a higher being hidden within himself. The myth takes place within himself. The Osiris nature "becomes imprisoned in something formed like a coffin for the spiritual part of man. In this coffin, invisible to the outer world, the Osiris part of man disappears. However, something mysterious in the conceptual world of the ancient Egyptian remains there, the mysterious Isis nature. She remains in order to attain again – indeed, by way of penetration of the intellectual forces – to that from which man has originated. Thus something in hidden human depths strives to restore Osiris to life. The power of Isis in man's soul is to gradually lead him out of his present state towards Osiris. And it is this Isis-Power which enables man – of course, not to separate himself from physical-sensory nature while he is physical man – but enables the human being, although remaining outer and physical and standing fully in the outer, physical world, nevertheless inwardly evermore to look up to a higher ego which, in the view of all the great thinkers, lies deeply hidden behind all human powers. It is this human being – not the outer, physical man, but the one spurred on to rise to spiritual light, ever driven on by the Isis-Powers – who appears as the earthly son of he who did not come out into the earthy worlds but rather remained hidden in the spiritual world: Osiris. This invisible human being, the one striving for his higher self, was felt by the Egyptian soul to be Horus, the posthumous son of Osiris." (February 16, 1911)

Osiris, conquered by the forces of Typhon, can be reached only in two ways: through the portal of death and through the portal which leads to initiation. In the following description, Rudolf Steiner attempts to arouse an experience of the origins of what is clothed in the Isis and Osiris legends. This origin lies in genuine spiritual perceptions of initiates who passed on their experiences in the pictorial imagery of Egyptian mythology.

Rudolf Steiner describes how the neophyte in ancient Egyptian mysteries was transported into the spiritual world through initiation, his vision guided "into a world of spiritual facts and spiritual beings" until he had an experience that made him feel he was at the end, on the far bank, had come to the farthest point into a completely different region than any he had ever been in before. Earlier he had been together with those beings who work upon his physical and etheric bodies. Now he treaded upon the "holiest places" where he felt united "with the being who works upon that in [him] which goes from one incarnation to another", working upon his astral body. He felt himself completely bound together with this being, not at all outside of it, but within this being. And out of this he received this impression: "Within this being lie the forces that bear the soul from one incarnation to another, lie the forces, as well, that enlighten the soul between death and a new birth. All of that is contained therein. But when there pulses towards you, like spiritual, cosmic warmth, a force which indeed does bear the soul from death to new birth; when there penetrates toward you like spiritual light that which enlightens the soul between death and new birth; and when you feel how this warmth and this light stream out from this being with whom you are united there, you really are, then, in a very special situation. You have had to drink of the waters of Lethe, have had to forget... your intellectuality, for this could only deceive you here, and you have not yet gained anything new. In feeling the cosmic warmth that bears the soul to new birth, you stand within the sea of forces that enlighten the soul from death until new birth. Thus you feel the power and light emanating from this being. You look upon this being in such a way as if you could do naught but ask of it, 'Who are you? For only you can tell me who you are, and only then can I know what bears me in my innermost human being from death to new birth. Only then, when you tell me, can I know what the innermost being of my human nature is!' But silent, speechless remains this being with whom one feels so intimately bound. One feels the most profound depths lie within it, bound with oneself in one's own deepest being. The urge arises for self-knowledge, to know what one is – yet silent and speechless remains the being." (February 5, 1913)

There, on the far bank of spiritual life, the neophyte was united with a being he could not understand intellectually and which itself had to give birth to the answer concerning who it was. But it remained silent. Long did the striving neophyte have to wait, long did his soul have to carry the longing for an answer to that question, "Who are you?" And in the depths of his longing a power was developed that, as time went on, led to the great riddle's solution, and he said to himself:

"That is Isis! That is the speechless, silent goddess whose countenance cannot be revealed to one who sees only with mortal eyes, whose countenance can be revealed only to those who have worked their way to the banks [of the spiritual region] just described, so that they can look with those eyes that proceed from incarnation to incarnation and are no longer mortal. For mortal eyes sheathe this figure of Isis with an impenetrable veil!" (February 5, 1913)

It was Isis who, out of the depths of longing, bore out of herself another being. Who was this being born out of Isis?

"He took his birth to be what can be designated as 'the sounding forth through all space of that which is the Music of the Spheres', together with what is called the Cosmic Word, the creative Cosmic Word that permeates all space and pours into the beings everything that must be poured into them, like the soul must then be poured into the physical and etheric bodies when it has passed through life between death and new birth.... And this 'Cosmic Word' is, to begin with, the Appearance of Osiris." (February 5, 1913)

Thus the initiate had before him, on the one side, Isis; on the other, the being to whom she had given birth – the Appearance of Osiris.

" 'Isis in the company of Osiris' is how it appears to immediate perception, for it was believed in the most ancient Egyptian initiation that Osiris was at once son and spouse of Isis. And that was the crux of the older Egyptian initiation, that the neophyte, through this initiation, experienced the secrets of that soul existence which remains bound to man even when he passes through the time that lies between death and new birth. It was possible, through the connection with Osiris, for him to know himself as man in its deeper meaning." (February 6, 1913)

A statue of Isis in the temple at Sais bears the inscription, "I am the All; I am the past, present and future. No mortal has yet lifted my veil."

"When the Egyptian let these words work upon him, he also thought at the same time that Isis was once united with Osiris when Osiris still wandered over the earth. Profane people conceived this in legendary fashion. In the mysteries, the priests spoke of the ancient Osiris time as that era when clairvoyance united man with the surrounding spirit of nature." (January 6, 1918)

In later times, Egyptian initiation took a tragic turn. Clothed in the fashion of legends, this change found the following expression: Osiris, torn from Isis, was taken to Asia. Isis, sorrowing, looks in vain for her spouse and son. "Let us inscribe once more before our souls what the initiate of later times experienced. Then, too, he could be led through the universal expanse to the shore of existence; he could experience all the beings that build up the physical and etheric bodies of man; he could tread upon the shore of existence and come into view of the speechless, silent Isis and perceive in her the existence of the warmth being that contains the forces that lead man over from death to a new birth. He could then also come to know the light that enlightens the soul between death and a new birth, and the yearning arose, to hear the Cosmic Word and Universal Harmony. Yearning lived in the soul when the soul united itself with the silent, speechless goddess, Isis. But – the goddess remained silent and speechless!" (February 5, 1913)

Osiris was taken from Isis at a certain point in time, a turning point in Egyptian spiritual life. Egypt's great mission had been fulfilled. Now, another people were to step forward who were to bring about the appearance of God in the "I Am".

"This was the point in time in which Moses lived, for Egypt's karma was fulfilled in that Moses was not only initiated into the secrets of the Egyptian mysteries, but he also took them with him. When he led his people out of Egypt, he took with him that part of the Egyptian initiation which added to the sorrowing Isis, as she later became, the Osiris initiation. The transition from Egyptian culture to the culture of the Old Testament came about in this way. Yes, Moses had carried away the secret of Osiris, the secret of the Cosmic Word! And had he not left behind the helpless Isis, then that could not have sounded for him in the way that it must have sounded – as he had to understand it for his people – the great, significant word, 'I am the I AM, *ehyeh asher ehyeh*'. Thus the Egyptian mysteries were carried over to the ancient Hebrew mysteries." (February 5, 1913)

And so the Egyptian initiate experienced in a way the death of a god. That god who once revealed himself in the spiritual world gradually disappeared from spiritual view.

"What was significant and peculiar about Egyptian initiation in later times is that one actually arose into the spiritual world to find not joy and bliss, but to take part in the gradual dying away of a god who was once present in these higher regions as Cosmic Word and Cosmic Tone ... ."

What disappeared from Egyptian spiritual life, what had been carried off by the Hebrew people, emerged again in the Middle Ages, but in a new form.

"How did that which had been submerged in ancient Egypt re-emerge? It re-emerged in visible form as that sacred chalice which then came to be known as the 'Holy Grail' .... And in the emergence of the Holy Grail one can sense what had been submerged in ancient Egypt. In the emergence of the Holy Grail, we have before us everything that constitutes a post-Christian renewal of the ancient mysteries." (February 6, 1913)

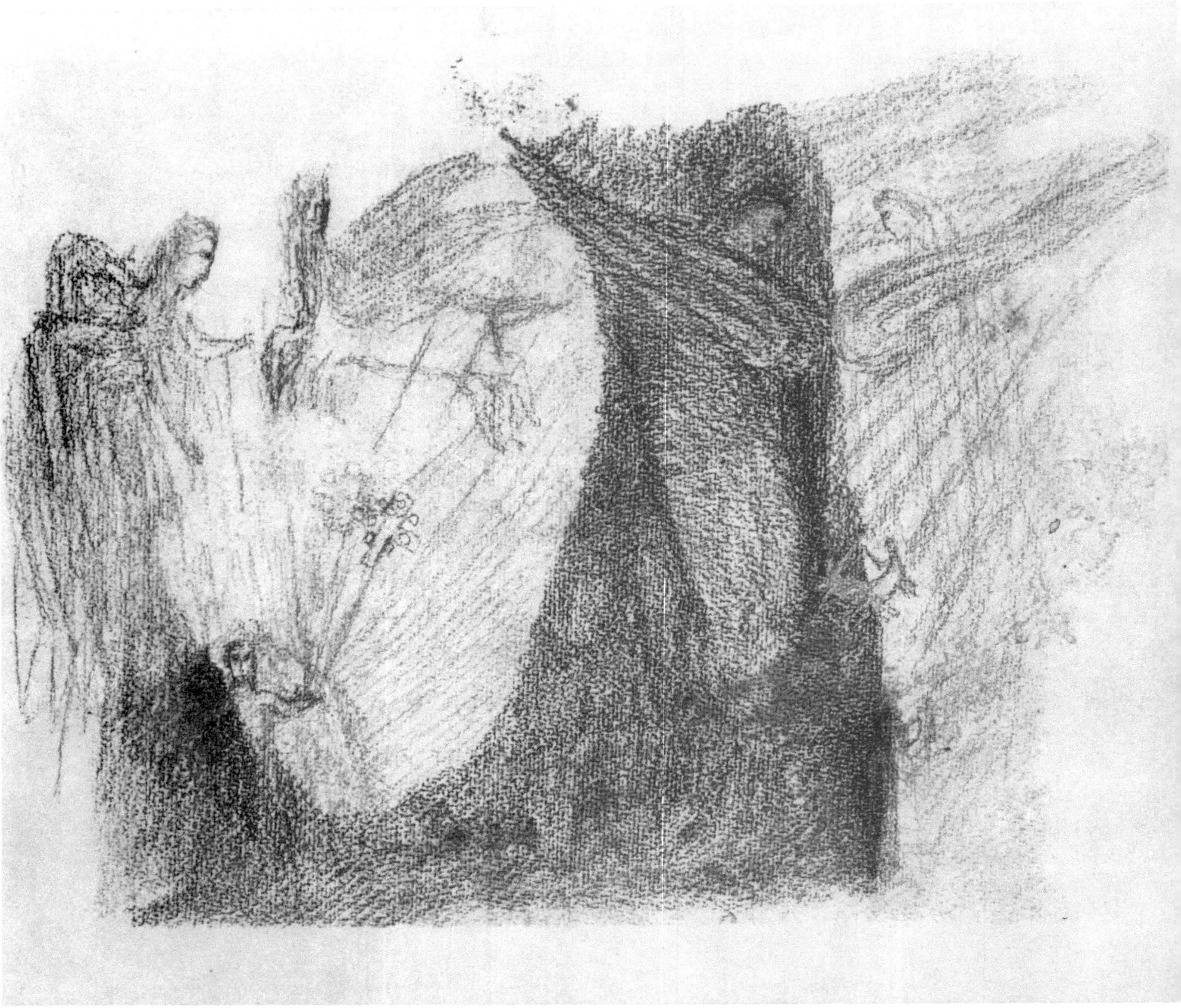

THE PERSIAN/GERMANIC AND THE SLAV MOTIFS

Pastel Sketch

The motifs of the Persian-Germanic and Slav were sketched together on one sheet of paper. The color background is the same for both, indicative of how the motifs live and weave into one another.

Here we find an area of light, in an encompassing blue. Where the blue thickens, it crystallizes into a hard black, rising steeply like a mountainous formation. Reddishness moves towards it, powerful and yet lighter than the stormy, churning red on the other side of the mountain. Red and black meet, appearing like winged beings: light and dark, the archetypal opponents in Persian culture. On the other side, the blue of the Slav motif speaks gently to the yellow, within which an intense, powerful red suggests something cosmically animal. A reddish speck indicates a human shape with upraised arm. Blue, floating in yellow, forms a cross surrounded by red – the rose cross – providing the fulcrum of balance.

Drawing

Whereas the pastel is an elementary, artistic intuition sketched 'out of deep color depth of space',* the play of light and dark in the drawing provides answers to questions regarding the thematic content. Here, too, the black mountains are salient. The black of the figure appears more differentiated and bears masculine traits. To the side, rising light shapes a luciferic being; radiating light creates a floating winged effect. Its countenance bears feminine traits, the profile fine and head modestly lowered. Here stand masculine and feminine opposite each other. Under these, two little centaurs appear. Below, half in darkness and half in light, stands the Germanic Man, who has to live in this duality and who carries the child. Out of the red a winged being has taken shape, a centaur of the air. Where there was mild blue on the pastel an angel appears here, its noble demeanor and bearing expressing both admonishment and blessing. Next to the Slav is his shadow, its arm raised toward the floating rose-cross in a gesture more like receiving than carrying. The rose-cross, its shape faintly repeated, radiates a light that touches and binds man, angel, and centaur in future promise.

The mountainous black, so salient in this picture of Germanic Man and Slavic Man, is also significant in relation to and within the sequence of the culture motifs in that it separates past and future, making space for a new, self-proclaiming event at whose center shines forth the image of the risen Christ.

---

* *"aus Farbendunkels Raumestiefe"*

THE PERSIAN/GERMANIC INITIATE

"The Germanic initiate, the Germanic knower, caught in the tragedy that the duality – the luciferic and ahrimanic – works especially strongly in him." (June 29, 1921)

Drawings

Several detail studies elucidate the pastel sketch. The figure of the initiate appears noble, dignified and calm. The movement of the arm carrying the child is intimated in just a few strokes of the pencil. Lucifer is surrounded by currents that indicate a relationship between larynx and forehead, similar to the way Rudolf Steiner carved the same figure in his wooden sculpture of the 'Group'. A small centaur exhibits his contradictory nature in a grotesque characterization of the animal that borders on caricature: small, hard hooves and a large head with crooked, crossed eyes within a contorted countenance.

Execution

"Thus the actual development of mankind has been painted in this small cupola from the perspective of the soul, although not chronologically, as you will see shortly, but *inwardly*. For now we are returning not only to approximately the earlier, second post-Atlantean cultural epoch; rather, we are going back, as well, to the Persian principle of initiation which, however, continues to develop – what was the original Persian principle of initiation, but, which is also the Germanic principle of initiation. Thus, moving on to the next picture, we have the Germanic principle of initiation. Basically, this Germanic-Persian principle of initiation is founded upon dualism; and everything depends upon the insight that all initiation within the cultural stream that began in the original Persian cultural period and continued into the Goethean cultural epoch – which, geographically, extends from central Asia over the Black Sea, northwards over the Black Sea, to Europe – this initiation stream must indeed seek its salvation in the precise knowledge of how the human being stands within the quest for balance between Lucifer, whom you see here on the right, and Ahriman, whom you see here on the left. *That* is the important thing – to realize that this cultural stream must gain all its strength by finding a state of balance between the ahrimanic and the luciferic.

"And an attempt was made precisely in this figure, inspired by the ahrimanic-luciferic itself, by that which asserts itself here to the right as the subhuman luciferic, and, to the left, as the ahrimanic, to show in the bearing and entire physiognomy that spirituality which must flow directly to man from a real grasp of this duality, this ahrimanic-luciferic duality, in which man must seek equilibrium.

"This child that you see here, in a way carried by the initiate, is also there for a good reason. For man could not bear what comes to him through being inspired by this dual principle – it would kill him, inwardly – had he not this rejuvenating, childlike force constantly before his gaze. When you see this in the cupola, you will notice that very strong efforts have been made to gain what is intended here directly out of the color. Also the effort has been made to derive the contrast between the luciferic and the ahrimanic from the colors. One must not only keep looking for meanings, but seek the essential through artistic feeling." (January 25, 1920)

In the cupola, Lucifer is no longer borne by wide, light-woven wings, as in the pastel. Streams of yellow and red play about the head, rise high up and spread out above it: reddish yellow, "worked out from yellow, worked out from yellow into lightness". (June 29, 1921)

Ahriman is in yellowish brown. In this motif "the most important thing is to make that duality in the world, the light luciferic and dark ahrimanic, visible in its whole impact upon the world." (April 5, 1920)

"The real nature of a human being standing before us cannot be grasped all at once, not even with all possible powers of cognition. He bears within him both contrasting polarities: one which continually pushes him towards a fanciful, false mysticism and to false theories, ever driving him towards the unreal, unfounded, nebulous, i. e., the luciferic; and one which makes a philistine of him, that inclines the spirit in him to gravity or weight, i. e., the ahrimanic, painted here with its shadow." (June 29, 1921)

"These are not two Ahrimans, but Ahriman and his shadow. As a matter of fact, Ahriman does not move about without constantly taking his shadow along. Ahriman himself would be a far too stiffening, dessicating principle were he to appear here, for example, fully elaborated. One feels a need to include his shadow, which somewhat lessens his rigidity. When you study the colors in the small cupola, you will see that the attempt has been made to bring that ahrimanic-rigidifying to expression through the properties of dark brownish-grayish colors. The attempt was made to work everything out of color." (January 25, 1920)

To the right is Lucifer. "That is just he who represents us [as we would be] if we had but a heart and no mind – the luciferic figure: fanciful, mystical, theosophical, [everything] that wants to go above and beyond man." (February 28, 1921)

"You will understand the ahrimanic and luciferic completely only if you view them in their relationship to each other. If you look only at Ahriman or only at Lucifer, you will not really understand either, [but you will do so] only when you have the two next to each other because Ahriman and Lucifer work in the cosmos in such a way that the effects of one are taken up by the other, made use of by the other, and vice versa. Thus, actually, even their [painted] shapes can be properly understood only if one grasps them in their living relationship." (January 25, 1920)

Two profiles confront each other: one is elongated, rising and expanding to the world of light; the other, dark, looks pinched and pressed together. "Consequently, where the Germanic element and its inherent dualism should be portrayed, this collision of brown/blackishness against reddish/yellowness also comes to view: the reddish/yellowishness of revelation, the brownish/blackishness of reason." (October 23, 1920)

"If you notice, for example, how the forward-thrusting effects of Lucifer's forehead here actually result in Ahriman's forehead being taken away or, otherwise put, hardening towards the *back* of the forehead, then you see as well such interplay as is present in nature's organizing forces." (April 5, 1920)

This "interplay" can be sensed in every detail, comparing, for example, the big, dreamy, desirous eye of Lucifer with the narrow, derisive look of Ahriman.

Further below stands "that human being who experiences the duality so exactly, thanks to these two contoured forces, polar and opposed to each other, and is able to bear it only if the child is set next to him: the man of the present, in his split nature." (February 28, 1921)

The Initiate is painted in yellowish brown, the child in clear yellow.

"He holds the child, radiant next to his somewhat gloomy figure, here on his arm .... [He is] the type of man such as those men of knowledge who lived in ancient times in the entire geographical area west of Persia and north of the Black Sea, and lives on in the Germanic nature in central Europe. Here is the child, [standing] on the arm of the aging person who harbors the thought, the memory, of the youth within himself. The split in his nature, the dualistic element which expresses itself particularly in the Germanic nature, is revealed to the eye of knowledge as the confrontation of opposing powers – the luciferic, ... the ahrimanic." (September 7, 1921)

Just as Faust finds a counterbalance to death (the skeleton) in the innocent child who still lives wholly in the spirit, the child here enables the Germanic person to bear the inner discord of luciferic/ahrimanic inspiration.

Between the inspiring opposing powers above and the seer below, two small, centaur-like figures are imbedded in reddish and brownish fields. "Dualism is portrayed here in a way that does not yet attain complete penetration of the figures, resulting in a physiology that descends even into the animal realm."[10] (September 7, 1921) One, in red, belongs more to the light; the other, in blue, adheres more to the realm of darkness.

"See how Ahriman corresponds to a kind of centaur-figure, how Lucifer also corresponds to a kind of centaur-figure, how the two are bound together, how they want to come apart but cannot, how they mutually complement each other even in their colors." (April 5, 1920)

In contrast to the noble expressions of the Initiate and the child, the two little centaurs depict distortion and imbalance in the face of luciferic/ahrimanic inspiration.

"Sometimes, when one works for months on end on

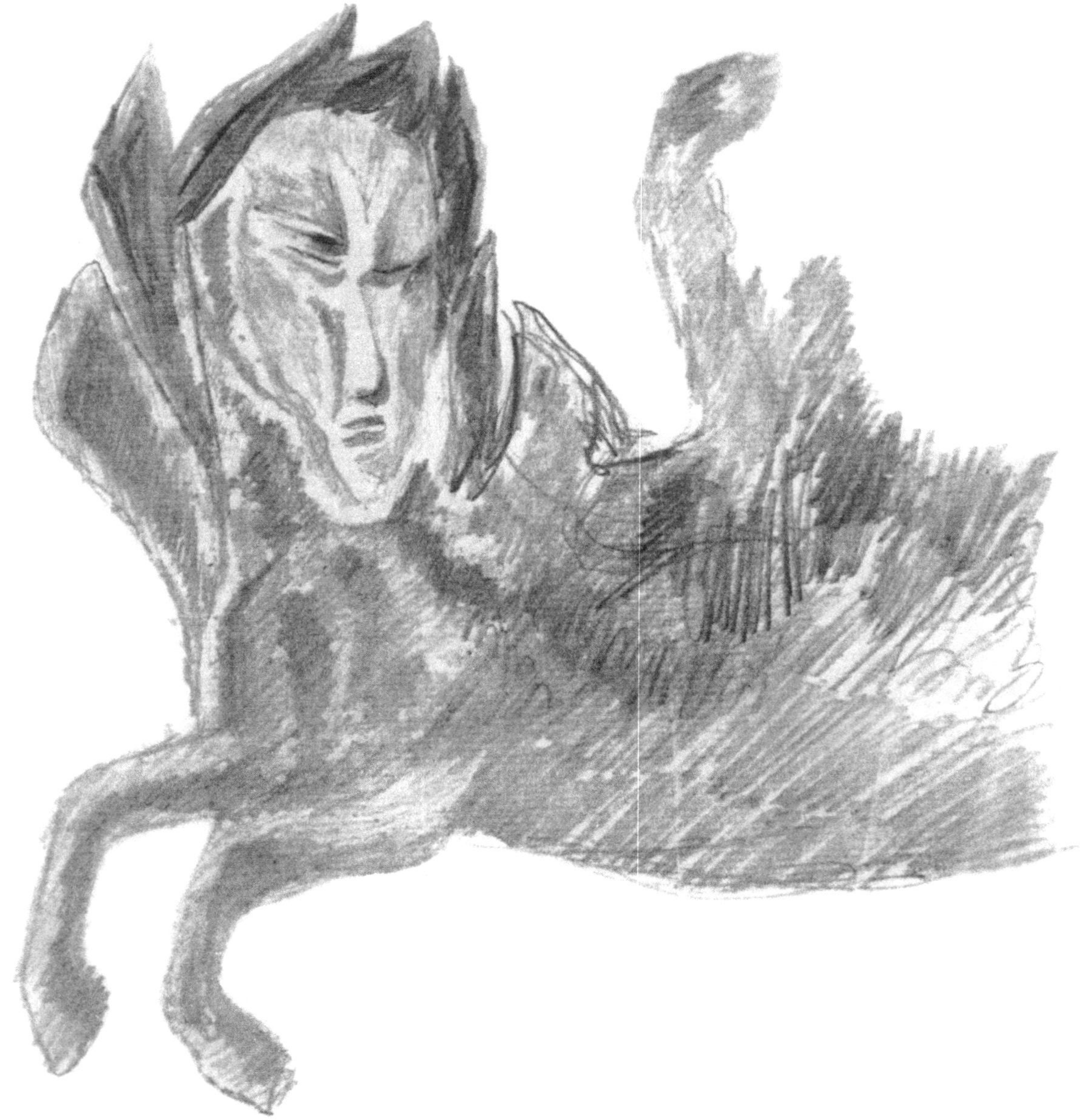

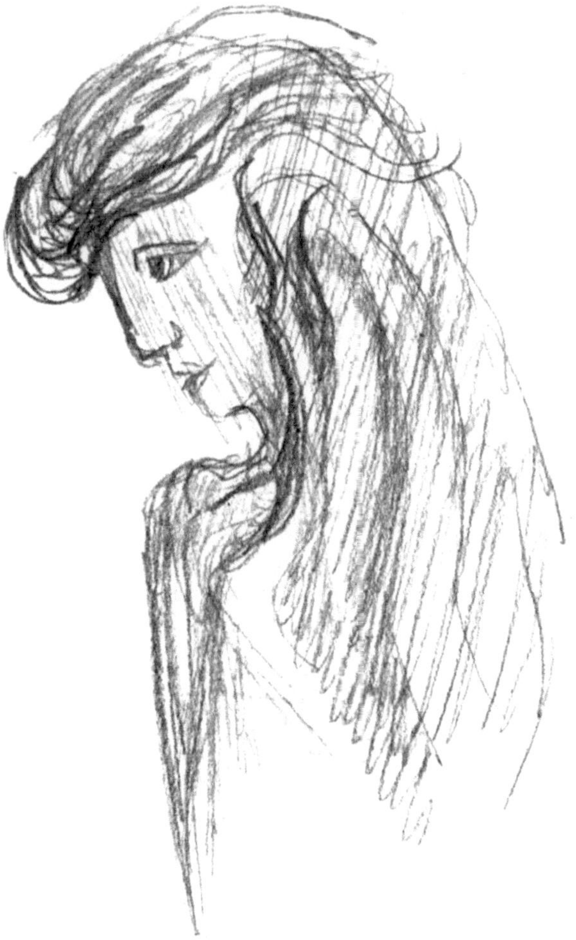

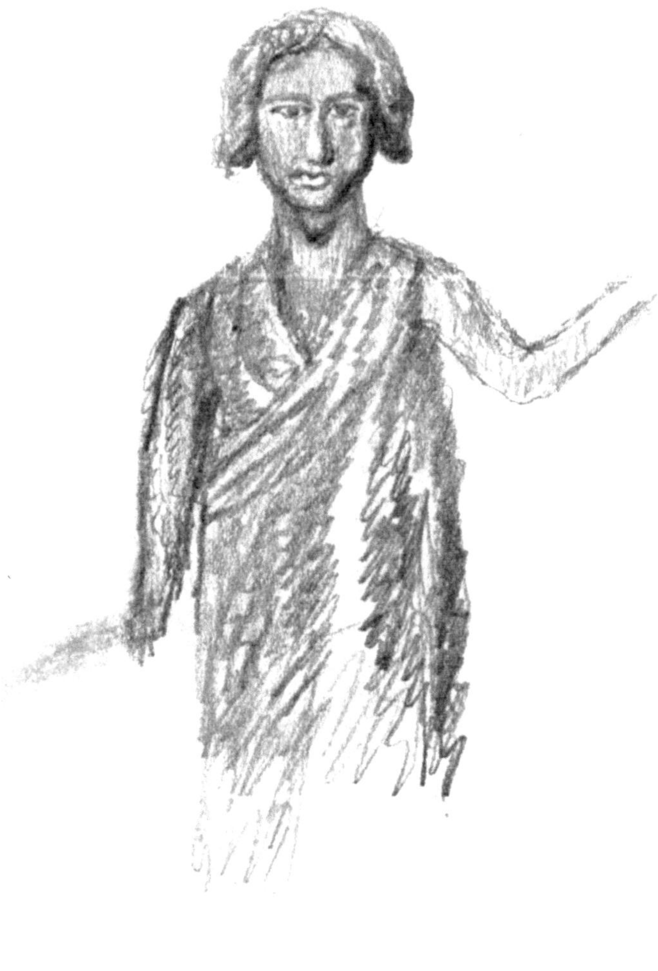

something like this, one just feels 'bugged'. And when I was working on these figures that abound with ineptitude and ugliness, this bug got into me to portray them just like Mr. and Mrs. [Woodrow] Wilson. That was just like a bug!"*[11] (June 2, 1920)

"And under these is the Persian-Germanic Initiate, bearing the child lightly upon his hand, suggesting how man must accept the future and find hope for the future by seeing through dualism." (September 7, 1921)

In order to stand up inwardly to these dualistic forces and, confronting them, preserve one's own self, one needs certain qualities which are also characteristic of the folk-temperament qualities sought in the portrayal of the Germanic Initiate.

"In this face and with the appropriate color, I had hoped ... to express what more or less *can* be expressed in a figure that remains under the influence of this dual principle. One needs inner firmness and, at the same time, imperturbability of temperament or character, plus the joyous inclination towards the childlike and youthful, in order to *bear* everything that one experiences under the real inspiring influence of the dualistic principle." (January 25, 1920)

The Persian motif in the large cupola leads back into the history of the evolution of mankind. That experience is intensified in the Persian/Germanic motif of the small cupola where the drama in individual souls and the battle between light and darkness are depicted.

"I have tried to make visible here how one would inwardly experience that civilization ... which, far back in ancient times during the Persian-Zarathustrian culture, viewed the world as a dual, split world in which light and darkness cast their influence; how this view of the world was transposed from Asia to central Europe; and how it still comes to expression in Goetheanism ... . For the essence of our Germanic-German culture is that we constantly experience that opposition between light and darkness, already brought to expression in the ancient Zarathustrian culture, which cleaves our souls so deeply when we sense on the one hand something that, like light, wants to rise above and beyond ourselves, and, on the other hand, something which, like gravity or weight, wants to draw us down into the earth." (June 12, 1920)

Goethe involved himself deeply in the study of the confrontation of light and darkness. In *West-East Divan*, he made a study of the nature of Persian culture, which is very apparent for instance in his poem 'The Legacy of Ancient Persian Faith' and accompanying reflections in prose. But his interest was kindled even more by his study of color. The first time he looked through a prism, he recognized that color actually arises only where light and darkness meet. This genuine intuition, grasped at the very first glance, grew into a body of manifold experiments and studies, scientifically worked out and verified, that later found publication in his *Theory of Colors*[3]. Whereas science popularly speaks of color as arising from light, Goethe spoke of color born of the confrontation between light and darkness.

This experience is a foundation for the art of painting. In painting, one experiences "not just the inwardness of the soul, but the inwardness of the things themselves – how they work within the laws governing the space of light and darkness, which contain that mystery of color to which Goethe tried to give theoretical expression in his *Theory of Colors.* Therein lies also the possibility of painting or portraying spiritual mysteries. Indeed, this possibility still remains in the evolution of mankind: to paint the Mysteries of the Spirit out of the inner nature of the colors in relation to one another and out of the inner nature of light and dark." (January 17, 1917)

«Da hat man da auch manchmal seine Mucken . . . . So ist mir die Mucke gekommen . . . . Das war etwas wie eine Mucke!»

SLAVIC MAN

This motif depicts "what will arise when dualism will have so evolved that man will sense himself as a double nature, a higher and lower man; when he will feel that he has his shadow within himself but as a shadow which he digests soul-spiritually." (June 12, 1920)

Pastel Sketch

The man bearing the cross of roses – blue wreathed with red – stands within peach-blossom with his shadow next to him in grey. Above him are the blue angel, in a gesture of benediction, and the fiery, strongly-modelled centaur of the air. (Compare the pastel and pencil sketch on page 153.) This sketch is on yellow paper, enhancing and harmonizing the basic yellow moon.

Detail Study of the Head of the Centaur (Pastel Sketch)

Blue's inherent formative forces pierce the warm tones of red and yellow creating the expression of the face.

Execution

Here the roses which wind around the blue cross in the pastel sketch have become stars. Above them is the centaur in yellow and red. Above the man is an angel-like flower in blue. As we approach the eastern middle-point (of the small cupola), we find this double figure. It is that nature which will emerge from the chaotic Russian nature. Indeed, the Russian soul contains, so to speak, the preparation for the soul-configuration of the future, even though it must plow its way through the most varied chaotic conditions. There man is still at a stage where, basically, he constantly has a second 'man' tagging alongside him. This is entirely apparent to clairvoyant vision. Actually, every Russian has his own shadow which he has always by his side. That leads then to apprehending something like an inspiration out of the dim nature of the soul, as has been attempted here in the blue angel, orange on the other side, and the centaur-like figure above. That relationship which the Russian soul as a kind of future soul has to nature, to the world, is captured there." (December 30, 1921)

Olga Kosticheff[12], a Russian doctor present during the construction of the Goetheanum, recounted how Rudolf Steiner painted the blue angel. She watched closely how everything emerged out of layer upon layer of liquid color, transparent and overlapping, gradually forming wings and the gesture of arms. Last of all appeared the face. That is, the configuration "of an angel-like being born entirely out of the color of clouds" came as a result of the process and was not the starting point. (January 25, 1920)

"For this reason we have here this characteristic angelic being, painted entirely in blue, formed out of the various nuances of blue. Above this is a kind of centaur, a kind of air-centaur." (June 29, 1921)

"Now you have to imagine that the inspiring being here is more spiritual than the former one was; consequently, this angel-like figure, emerging completely out of the blue ... (and) this centaur are essential to the inspiring being. You see, this inspiration leads simultaneously to the starry realms. One recognises man in his relationship to what is non-earthy in the cosmos. But the inspiring entity itself can no longer be grasped as something similar to man. If one tries to give it shape, one comes to beings no longer similar to man, but who possess certain traits of form, character and temperament, which although reminiscent of man, are no longer human." (January 25, 1920)

The picture of the centaur – half man, half horse – frequently appears in mythology. In Greek tradition he retained forces stemming from ancient clairvoyance and, therefore, connected with the animal side of man. Cheiron, the wise, was one of these. As the 'noble pedagogue' he initiated Achilles, Hercules and Aesculapius, sons of the gods, into the strength of courage, the knowledge of plants and the wisdom of the stars.

"Here, at the top, you see a figure reminiscent of the animal: the animal as though transported into the world of stars, having become etheric and bearing within itself the forces of initiation of this future time when these forces ... more ahrimanic in character, will be balanced by the superhuman, the angelic element approaching from the side .... It is something that is etheric-animal and etheric-superhuman. It is the working together of the mysteries that live in one or the other of these figures that will bring about initiation in the coming epoch." (April 5, 1920)

"Above the Russian (you see) ... the inspiring stars, and above that a kind of cloud which takes on the shape of the centaur, which, making its way through the stars, stimulates from the cosmos, the soul-spiritual forces present in embryo in the Russian of this time." (September 7, 1921)

"In future, when man will have reached maturity, this figure will be placed next to the angel as the real inspirer, but today he is still by nature a centaur. Here this centaur with the starry heavens in between correctly senses the evolution in the spirit which hovers between the angelic and animal. Man stands, so to speak, between the animal which has taken on human form in his instincts and passions, and the angelic in which the ahrimanic element gains access to the spirit, thereby attaining cosmic significance." (February 28, 1921)

This man, bearing the rose-cross, stands in peach-blossom; his shadow is somewhat darker: grey, turning to violet.

"We tried to show here an initiate, i. e., a man receptive to spiritual revelation, in the coming sixth post-Atlantean cultural epoch. (This receptivity is already present as a prelude to future events.) A portrayal of such an initiate could only be achieved purely out of the color. To do this we had to represent not a Russian of the present time, but something that can be perceived in him. Strictly speaking every Russian is always accompanied by his shadow. He always has a second man and this has been expressed here." (January 25, 1920)

"Whoever sees a Russian actually always sees two: the Russian who dreams, who actually always floats about three feet above the ground, and then also his shadow." (June 29, 1921)

The Russian motif was entrusted to Margarita Woloshina. When she asked Rudolf Steiner how to portray the face, he answered: "Not sentimental or tormented but optimistic and strong."[13]

Germanic man experiences the duality of Lucifer and Ahriman, active within him. The Russian, however, experiences a second man beside him, a dark, passionate shadow of his higher striving. "There (we see) is not merely, as in Central Europe, a split human being bearing Lucifer and Ahriman, the dreamy and the materialistic, within him. There (we see) a human being who has a second human being like a shadow next to him. In future man will have to incorporate his shadow; only then will he truly become a man of the future." (February 28, 1921)

Man's experience with his shadow holds possiblities for the future but it is also fraught with dangers known to the Russian. It is apparent in works such as Dostoyevsky's novel, *The Double*. In this novel the main character, a minor civil servant, sees himself sitting at his desk, walking along the road, or in company with other people. This repeated experience, always new and different, causes insecurity and illness and finally leads to mental derangement. What is the origin of this shadowy double in man?

"There are always things in man's soul which, so to speak, he does not fully control but for which he has a special affection. In such things of this nature with which man has a peculiar inner connection, Ahriman is particularly active. There are areas in man's soul which can be, in a way, detached from the whole of the human soul. Since man has not complete control over these areas, Ahriman takes hold of them .... In actual fact, we have within us all manner of thoughts that can take on human forms. When man confronts these thoughts as living thought-beings, when Ahriman has the chance to make such parts of the human soul independent, to give them human forms, when man thus becomes familiar with the elemental world; then, in this independent part of his being he meets the double. The double is always a part of the human soul, given human shape by Ahriman." (August 30, 1913)

In scene 5 of *The Soul's Probation*, Johannes Thomasius is dismayed by the passions embodied in his Doppelganger which he had not recognized before because he had not wanted to admit to them.

> Oh, what great guilt I heaped upon myself
> That I must now behold,
> A lustful caricature of my love
> Which I regard as sacred ....

The double reminds him of his responsibility to redeem him.

I must not ever leave you.
You will in future often find me at your side;
I shall not go from you until you find the power
Of that which you are to become.
(*The Soul's Probation*, Scene 5)

In Slavic regions, a people is being prepared, 'the actual Christ-people' who will develop the strength to purify the emotions and through their love for the earth will overcome the double nature.

"The mystery of Russian geography lies in the fact that what the Russian takes from the earth first of all is the sunlight reflected from it. The Russian really always takes into himself the light received by the earth from the cosmos; he loves his earth, but he loves it for the reason that it is a reflection of the heavens ... . But that part of the earth that the Russian loves, which permeates him, causes certain weaknesses in him. Above all, however, it enables him to overcome the Dopppelganger. ... For this reason, it will be his task to provide the most important impulses when the time comes in which this Doppelganger-nature will have to come to an end." (November 16, 1917)

In Soloviev's philosophy and in his conception of the Christ-principle, we have the seed of what will come to fruition in the sixth post-Atlantean period:

"Essential to the Christ-concept is an understanding of what happened to the man Jesus of Nazareth who was endowed with all the necessary qualities when the Christ entered into him. Here we have two natures in one being – this must be well understood – although on a higher level they unite again. You cannot fully comprehend Christ if you do not understand this duality. But this can only be achieved by a philosophical understanding which intuits that the time will come when man will enter a culture where his consciousness soul will be such that the spirit self can enter into so that in the sixth cultural epoch man will experience himself as a duality, with his higher nature restraining the lower one ... .

"Let us remind ourselves how in the Indian culture the ether body was developed, in the Persian culture, the sentient body; in the Egyptian/Chaldean culture, the sentient soul; in the Greco-Roman culture, the intellectual soul; and, in our own culture (not yet concluded), the consciousness soul is developing. This will be followed by the spirit self entering through the consciousness soul so that the spirit self shines through the consciousness soul, which must gradually be prepared for the task of the sixth cultural epoch. This culture – most eminently a receptive culture for it must devotedly await the permeation of the consciousness soul by the spirit self – is being prepared by the peoples of Western Asia and by the Slavic peoples of Eastern Europe." (June 16, 1910)

In the large cupola, the Indian, stars shining out of the red above him, listens in devotion to the revelations of the holy Rishis. In a gesture expressing both receiving and carrying, the Slav bears the blue cross, the roses of which have been transformed into stars. The primeval words of the Brahmin, heard by the Indians, speak in a different way to the Slavic man bearing the cross.

SOUTH AND NORTH SIDE

"Here we have passed the center. Looking east to the left we have the same centaur you see there on the right. This angel is symmetrical to the one just seen, but here he is in yellow-orange. Below it you would now find the Russian with his double, but symmetrical to what was shown before." (June 29, 1921)

During the painting of the northern part of the small cupola, Rudolf Steiner mentioned that the southern part was to be carried out in complementary colors. He himself began this by painting the angels blue on the south side and orange on the north side. Assya Turgeniev reports, "It was a great surprise to see the blue angel of Russian culture transformed on the north side into the complementary color orange. A group of artists had helped to erase, with a few exceptions, what had already been painted and now began to transmit Rudolf Steiner's paintings from the southern part of the cupola symmetrically to the north. But they lacked the courage to transpose the motifs into their complementary colors; the task was difficult enough as it was."[15]

Opinions differed as to what was meant by Rudolf Steiner's indication to paint the north side in complementary colors. According to van Bemmelen, it meant extreme opposites such as *blue* and red;[16] according to Assya Turgeniev, true complementaries, i. e., *green* and red. For the artists engaged in this work the task was so new and unusual that they did not take it up but merely made a mirror-image copy in the same colors.

The task had been set. What was its significance? Julius Hebing[17] suggests a simple exercise to demonstrate the etheric forces at work in the interplay of complementary colors. Paint an area of strong red, for example, and next to it one in the complementary green as an after-image as it arises before your eye, and from this, again the complementary color, repeating the process until the phenomenon becomes lighter, recedes, and finally vanishes. This provides an immediate experience of the etheric interchange in the eye.

When teachers from the Waldorf schools visited Dornach, Rudolf Steiner often drew attention to the nature of color as revealed by the blue and orange angels. "Working in the way in which we have here with a few friends in the small cupola, you come to a living relationship with color. When painting blue, for instance, you discover that characterizing anything connected with inwardness is in the nature of blue itself. Let us say, with an angel who is moving out of his inwardness, you will feel a quite spontaneous urge to use blue because the blue hues, this light and dark quality, call forth in the soul the feeling of a movement that emanates from the soul realm. The yellow/red evokes in the soul a feeling of something radiant revealing itself to the outer world. So when something appears aggressive, admonishing, when the angel wants to communicate something to us, wants to speak to us from afar, this will be expressed in tones of yellow and red." (August 23, 1919)

The significance of the cupola paintings lies in the "aura-like illumination shining from within," which can also be experienced in complementary after-image. "If we look at a human face, we should imagine it 'in reverse'; the concave parts as convex, dark hair as light, light as dark, etc. But we should also convert the facial coloring, not only dark to light but each area of color into its complementary shade, e. g., a red patch into green, etc. If we fully enter into this experience the color will reveal something of the character of the person concerned. A pale green, already thought of as a complementary color, would signify that the person cannot get away from things closely connected with the physical body. A dark green indicates spiritual striving, and blue an intense striving for the spirit. We begin to see through these colors as though transparent; they are the colors of the ether body. This will only work if experienced inwardly. In this way we shall be able to recognize the true character of a person better than by any other means. The most our intellect can do is to realize that the outer world is maya; in the reverse image, however, we see it in its true form. Here, at this point, the intellect is compelled to stop or it will become confused and lose the firm ground on which it stands. Our thoughts are a reflection of the world. Imagine a mirror and an object reflected in it; if we place another mirror opposite the first mirror, we shall see a reflection of the reflection that is by degrees becoming blurred in the distance. This is what would happen with us if we were to start fantasizing and drawing conclusions in the attempt to find something *new* instead of contemplating what is hidden behind the sense perceptible. The one leads us into confusion; we must rather experience these things much more with our *feelings*." (October 14, 1911)[18]

Here Rudolf Steiner speaks of the fact that by searching for the shade of green complementary to the individual incarnadine color, hidden character traits may be found. So the obvious question arises: Are there hidden qualities in the beings portrayed in the cupola which could not be expressed in one picture alone, 'hidden qualities' of the gods, Apollo for instance, different aspects, as mythology presents them in their many facets?

The correlation of the colors in the south and north sides points to a higher unity. Looking at the motifs we might ask: Where does the purely complementary effect come to expression; where is a more polarized effect justified; and where does the original color assert itself? No unequivocal conclusions can be drawn from sketches or photographs since the final version often was quite different from the pastel sketches, and particulars given in slide lectures also vary. So some things must be left to artistic perception and consideration. Just as questions arise about the interplay and effect of the complementary colors, so they also arise with regard to the mirror-image representations of the same motifs. In the small building in Malsch and in the hall in Stuttgart the apocalyptic seals were placed symmetrically. (See chapter on 'Precursors') St. John's apocalyptic vision, which was sealed up in these images, came to life again in the cupola paintings in the first Goetheanum. The symmetrical mirror-image arrangement continued to be effective although in a different form.

"The most important thing for modern man to realize is that everything contained in the word 'I' or 'I am', in everything he has in his consciousness when he perceives himself inwardly within his soul, he sees only a mirror-image, a mirror-image encompassing all the concepts connected with and worked on by this ego ... . What really underlies this rift between man's will and his ideas, between the two poles of the life of ideas, which has become a mirror-image, and the life of the will, which has been pushed down into the unconscious and is passed in sleep? What is the real cause of this rift? The cause is the impulse for freedom, working its way up in human evolution, in the historical development of mankind." (December 28, 1918)

An Attempt at a Complementation of the North Side in Both Form and Color

With regard to the motifs in the small cupola, the question remains as to what influence the use of the complementary colors has had on the forms. If we follow the inner life of the color, expression and form make a new and different statement and bring out another side of the original motif than previously noticed.

If you try to imagine very naturally and carefully the north side in complementary colors starting with the south side and without feeling obliged to make a 'reconstruction', you will discover that through the interplay of the complementary colors new sides of the same being will be revealed.

Slavic Man: Both the orange and the blue angel in the south were painted by Rudolf Steiner. An attempt at carrying this motif further might lead to something like the following:

The delicate violet background brings about a mood of inwardness and piety. The centaur, soaring upward in colors of violet and blue/green, expresses more strongly his relationship to the constellation of Sagittarius than does the one in yellow/red. Does this lead us into the world of imagery of the nordic sagas? Is it reminiscent of Wotan's winged eight-legged steed racing through the air?

The cross now shines in golden orange. The stars, in a light tourmaline green against a violet background, no longer shine but take their place in the circle in quiet strength. Man, in a dull green gown, the lighter-colored double beside him, carries cross and stars into the future.

The Persian-Germanic Initiate: Here Lucifer appears in severe violet and blue/green, proud and arrogant; Ahriman in blue/back and whitish-grey, 'the cold, cosmic light'. The child is in pale violet and peach-blossom and the initiate in a serious, dignified indigo blue.

The Egyptian Initiate: At the top the basic violet gives way to green/blue. Is the floating green/blue Horus, the divine child? Isis appears in yellow going towards green, the color of moonlight. With a gesture of benediction she inspires the initiate, here in blue surrounded by warm colors: orange, vermilion and dark red. Surprisingly, these colors are frequently used in Egyptian art.

Athene-Apollo, the Greek Motif: Here the shining yellow of the sun god in the south becomes a solemn carmine/violet; in the north the brown of the throne becomes a dull indigo. The carmine red of the inspiring being at the top shines in tones of greenish yellow through grey/violet. In form and gesture, Apollo becomes serious and admonishing in this wintery northern representation. Especially with regard to Apollo, we can feel that we get a complete picture only through the two complementary portrayals: the one in the south (summer, God of the muses, Lord of the Castalian Spring) and the one in the north (winter, the nordic mysteries of Hyperborea).

The Faust Motif: Triumphant in his search for knowledge, Faust stands upright in tones of yellow and orange, reminiscent of Rudolf Steiner's eurythmy figure for knowledge, the colors of which are white, yellow and orange.[19] The child floating towards him is pale blue.

Black and White Photos

- *View into the Small Cupola*
- *Detail of Faust*
- *The Genius above Faust*
- *The Child Surging towards Faust*
- *Apollo and Inspirer*
- *Athena*
- *Two Inspiring Beings from the Egyptian Motif*
- *The Egyptian Initiate*
- *Lucifer and Ahriman and the Persian-Germanic Initiate*
- *Detail of the Persian-Germanic Initiate with the Child and two Centaurs*
- *The Blue Angel of the Slavic Motif (south side)*
- *Slavic Man with Double and Centaur (south side)*
- *The Orange Angel of the Slavic Motif (north side)*
- *The Representative of Man between Lucifer and Ahriman (north is to the left of the viewer, south to the right)*
- *Ahriman (from the central motif)*
- *Lucifer (from the central motif)*
- *Partial View of the Painting in the Small Cupola (towards the east)*
- *Partial View of the Painting in the Small Cupola (towards the south)*

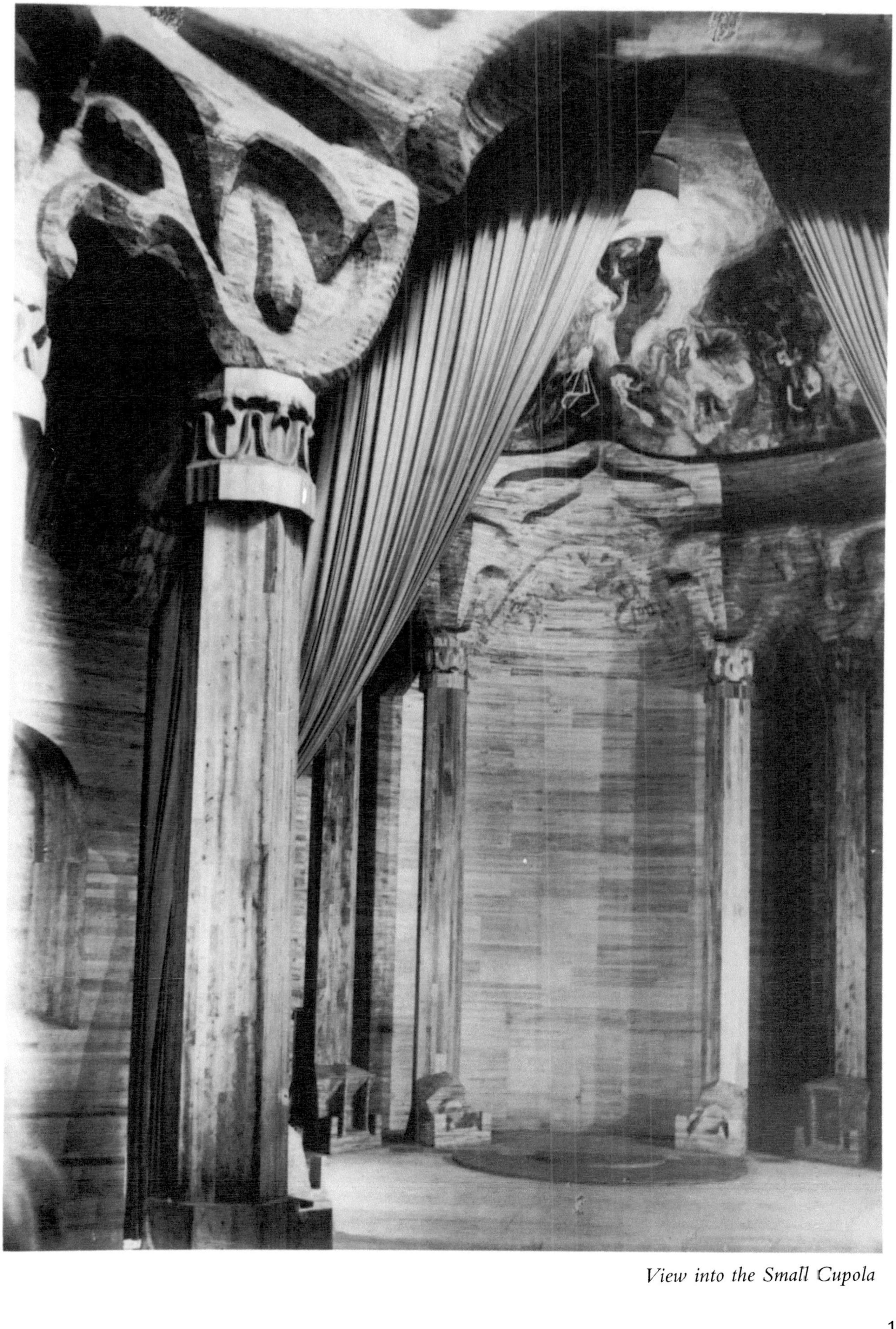

View into the Small Cupola

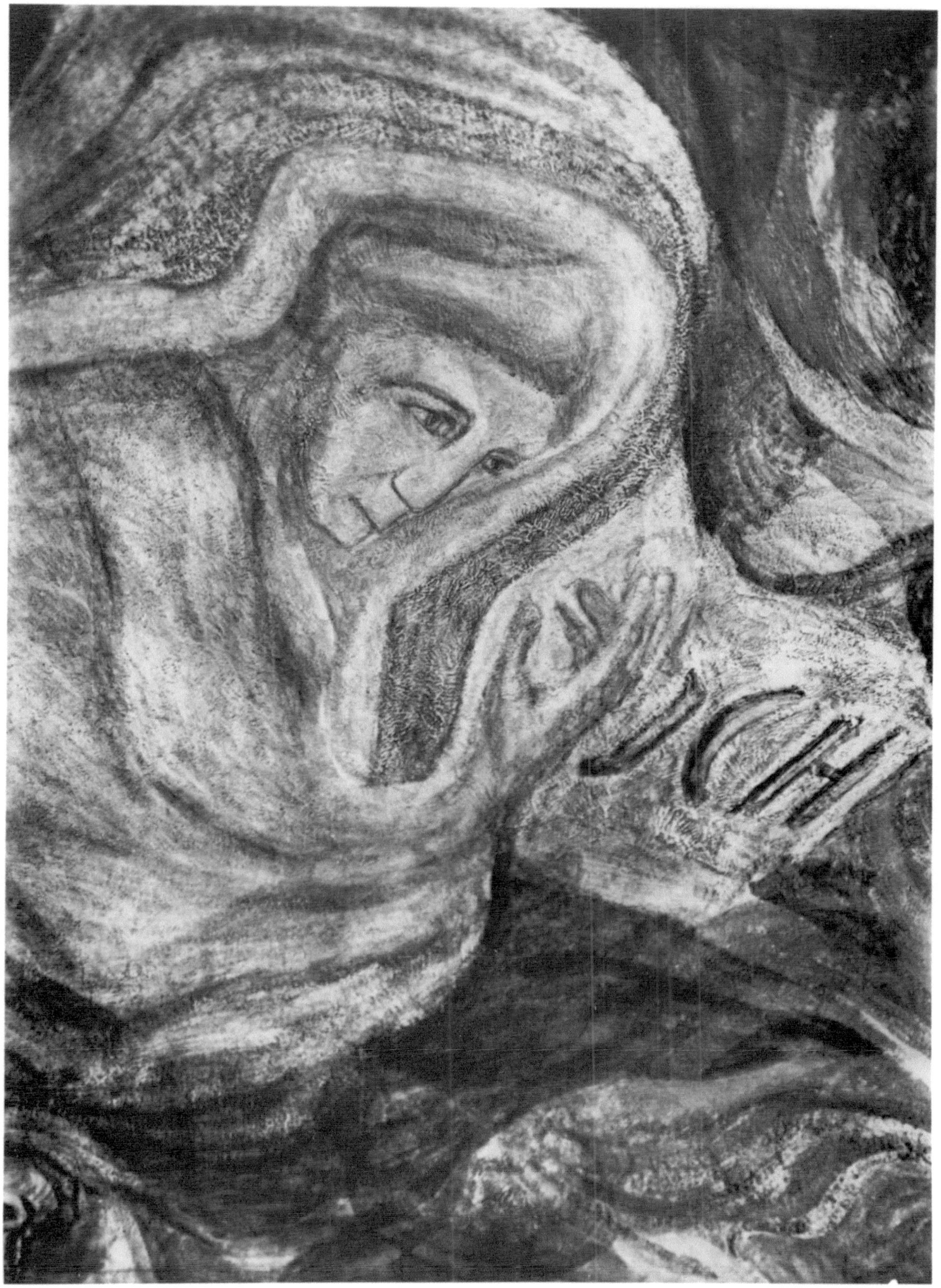

Detail of Faust

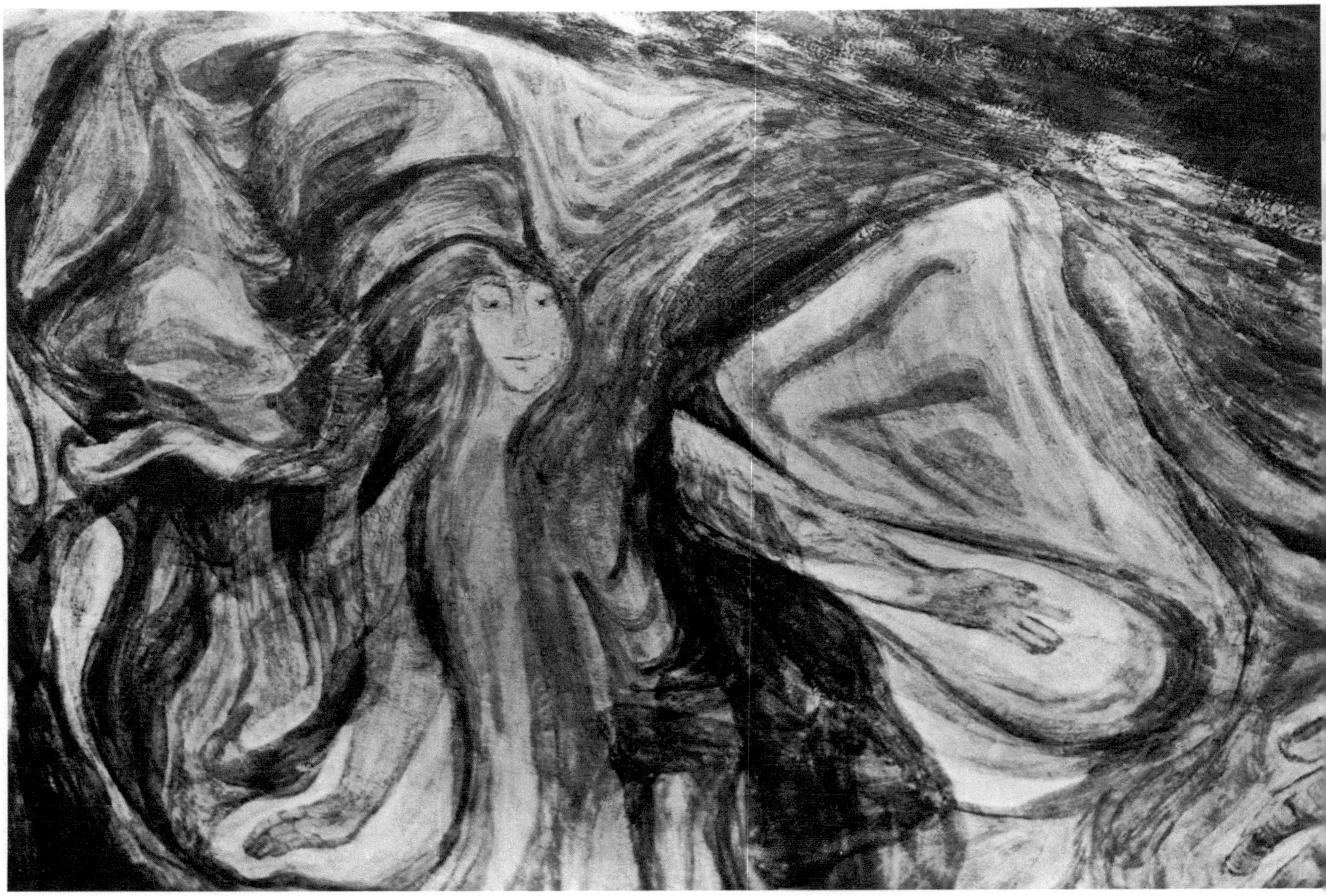

The Genius above Faust

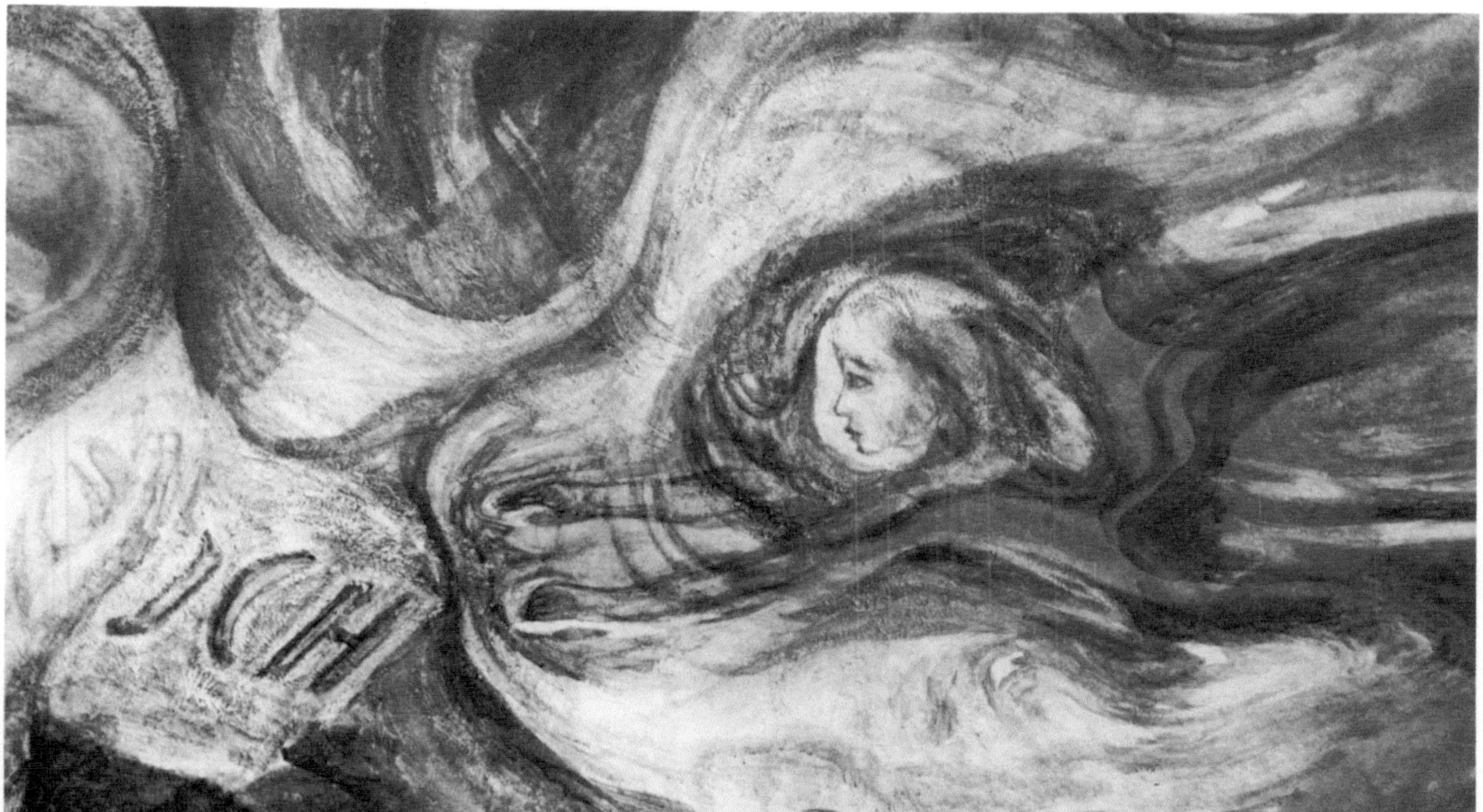

The Child Surging towards Faust

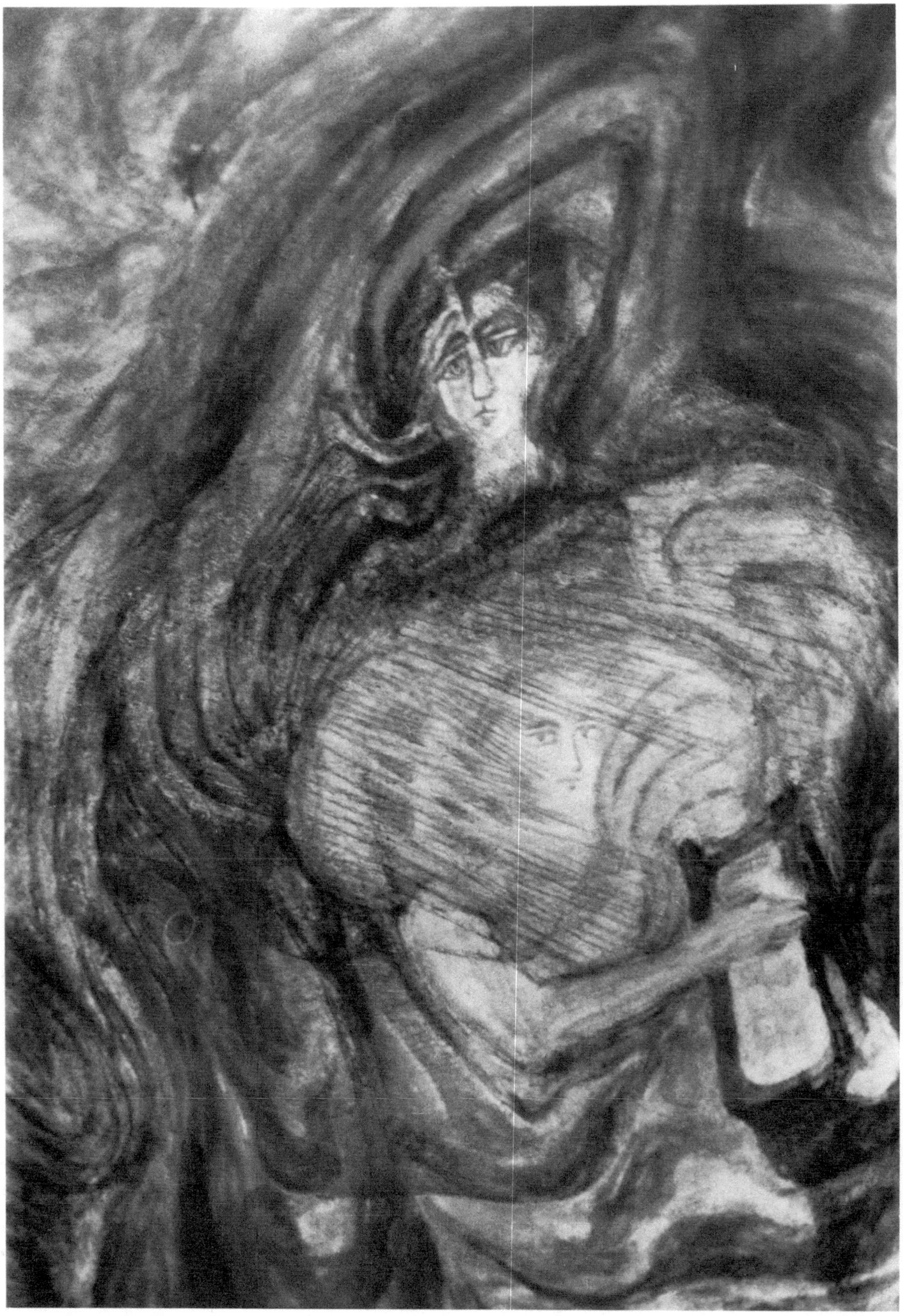

Apollo and Inspirer

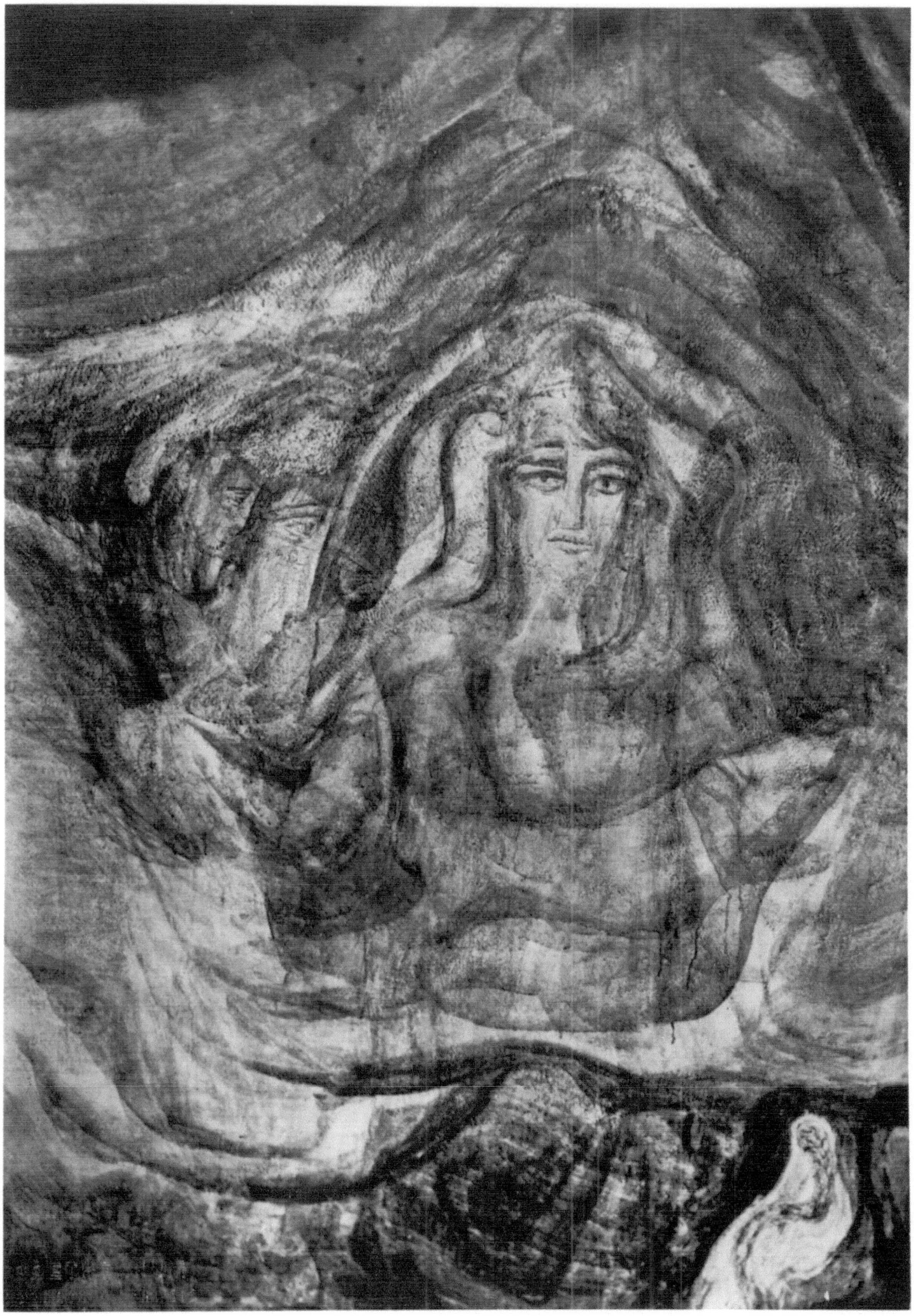

Athena

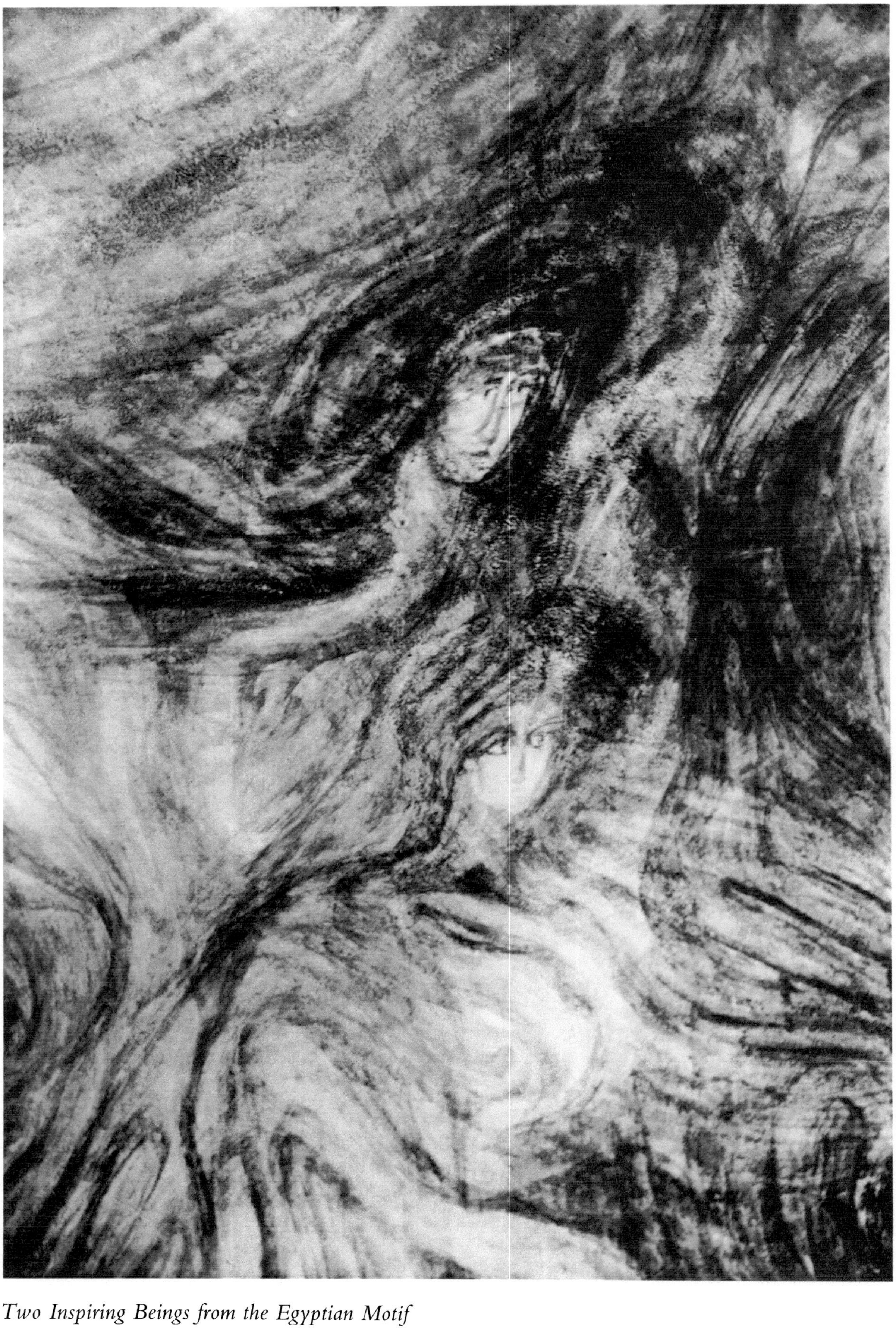

Two Inspiring Beings from the Egyptian Motif

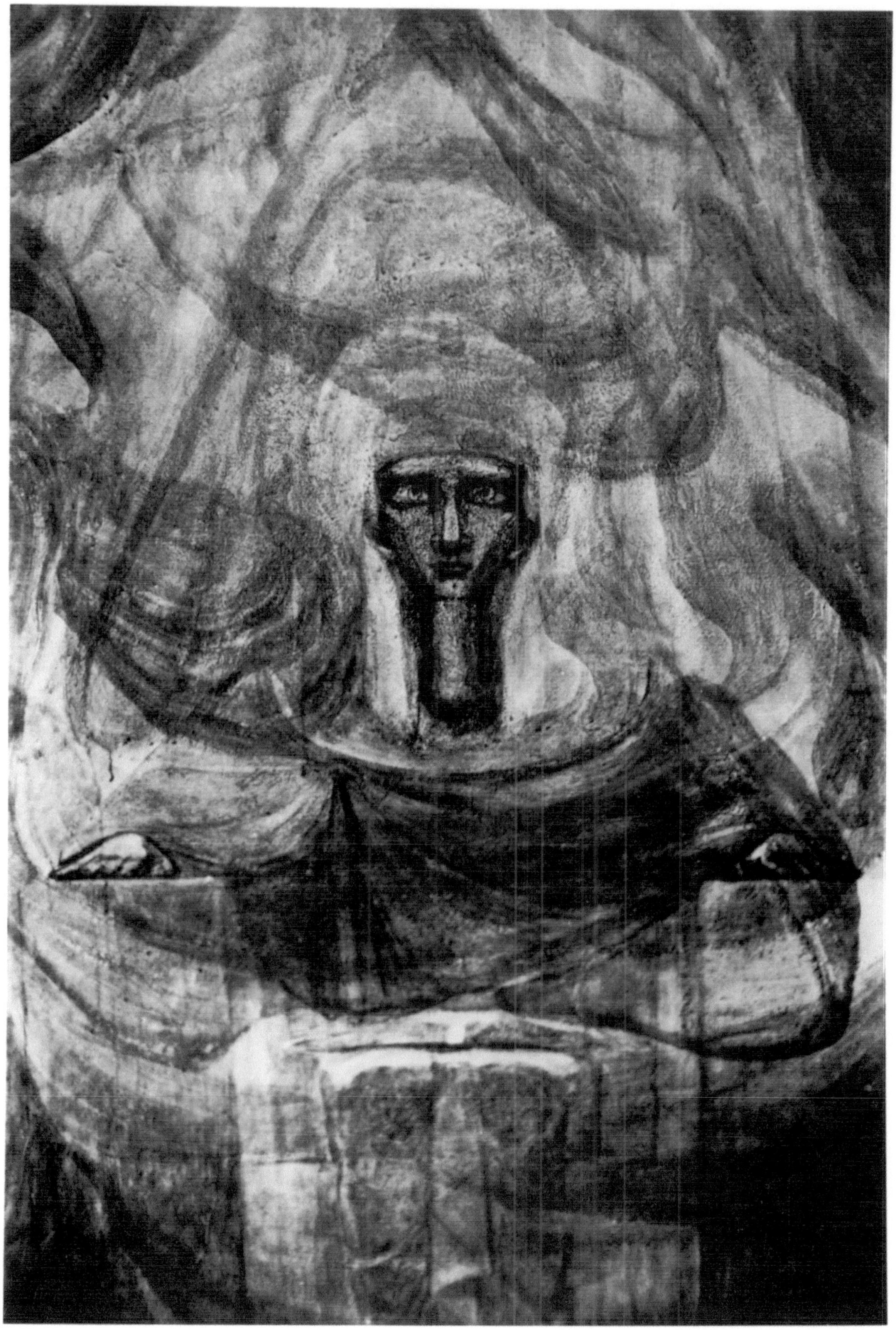

The Egyptian Initiate

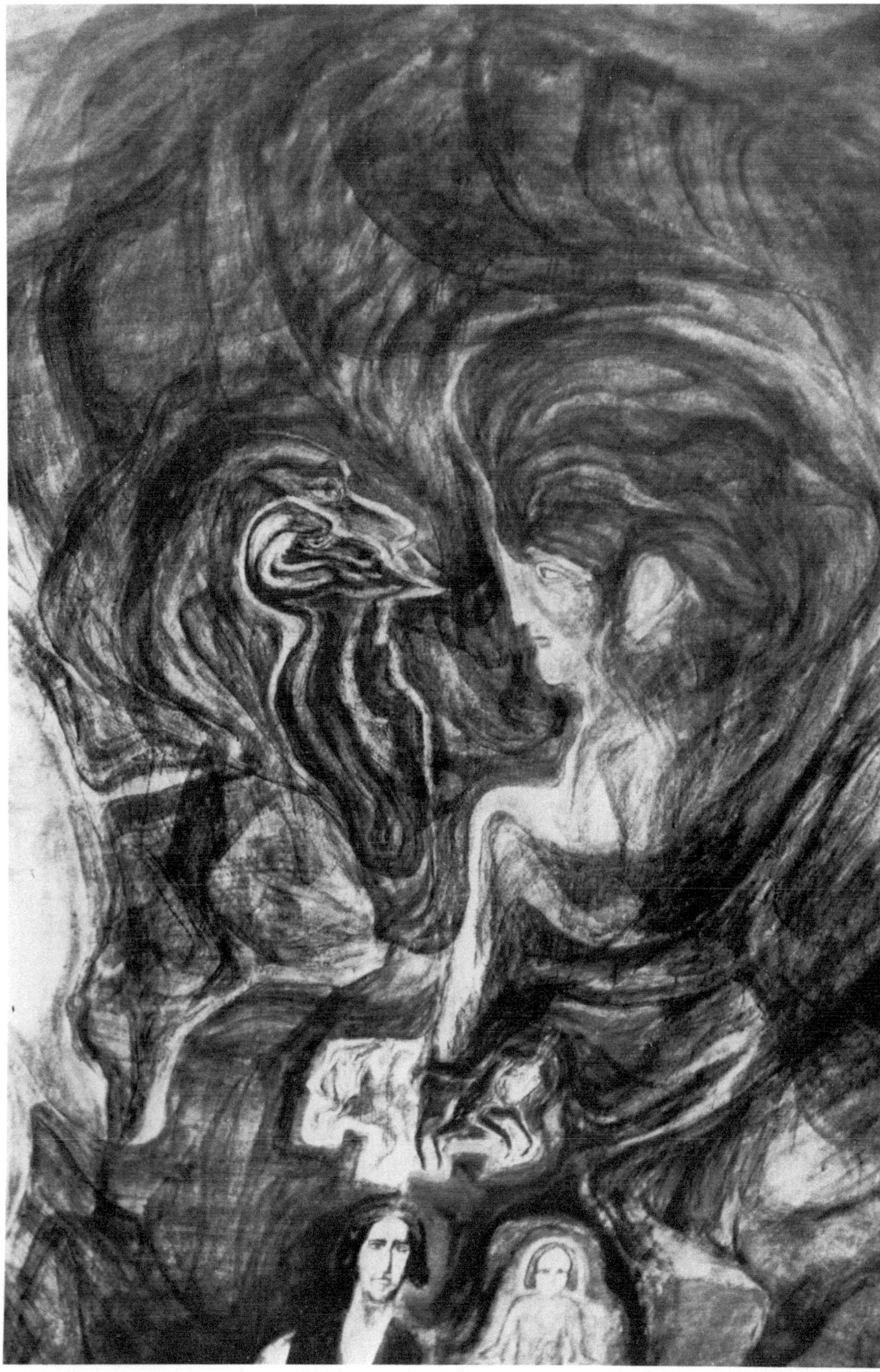

Lucifer and Ahriman and the Persian-Germanic Initiate

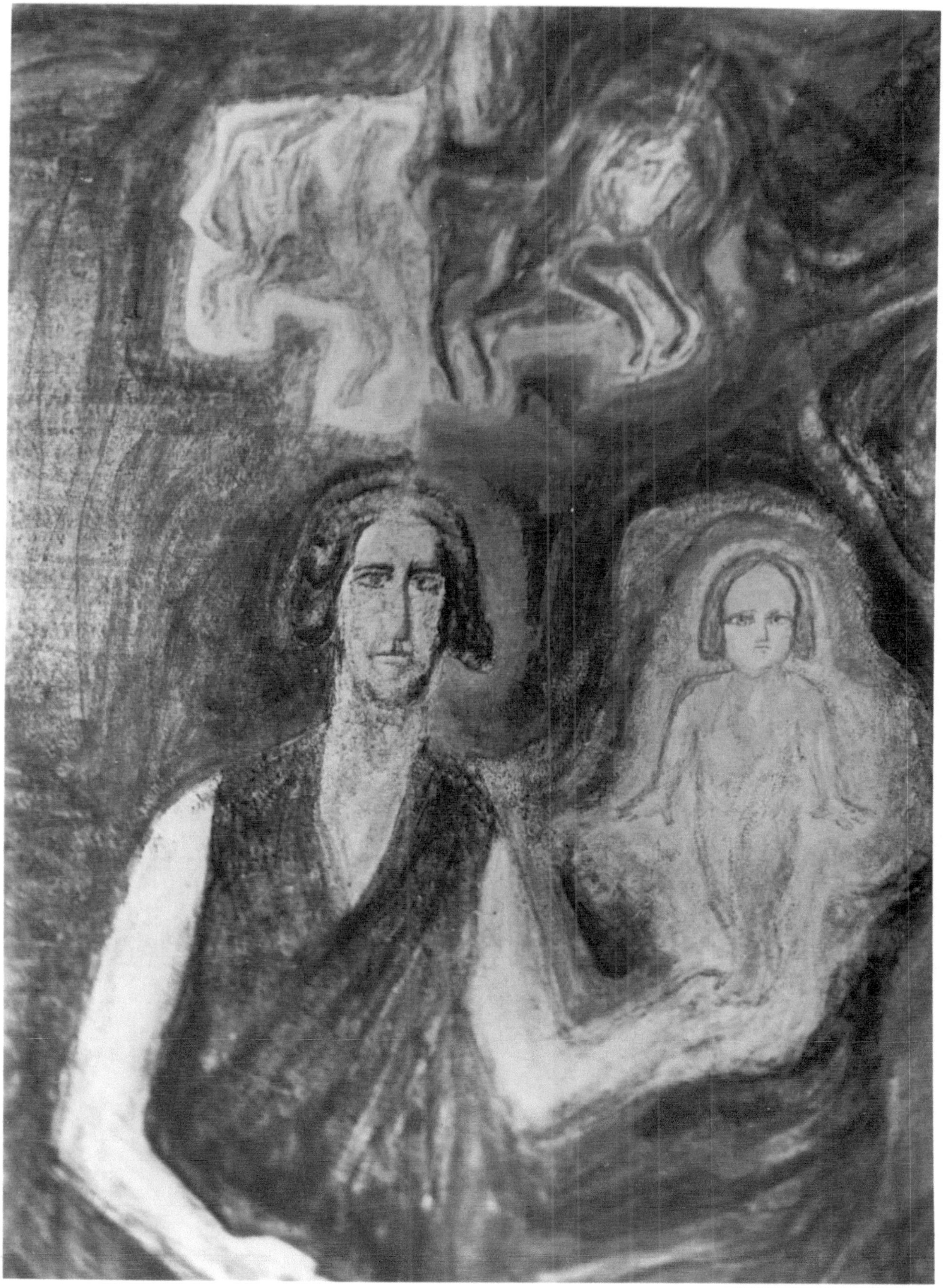

Detail of the Persian-Germanic Initiate with the Child and two Centaurs

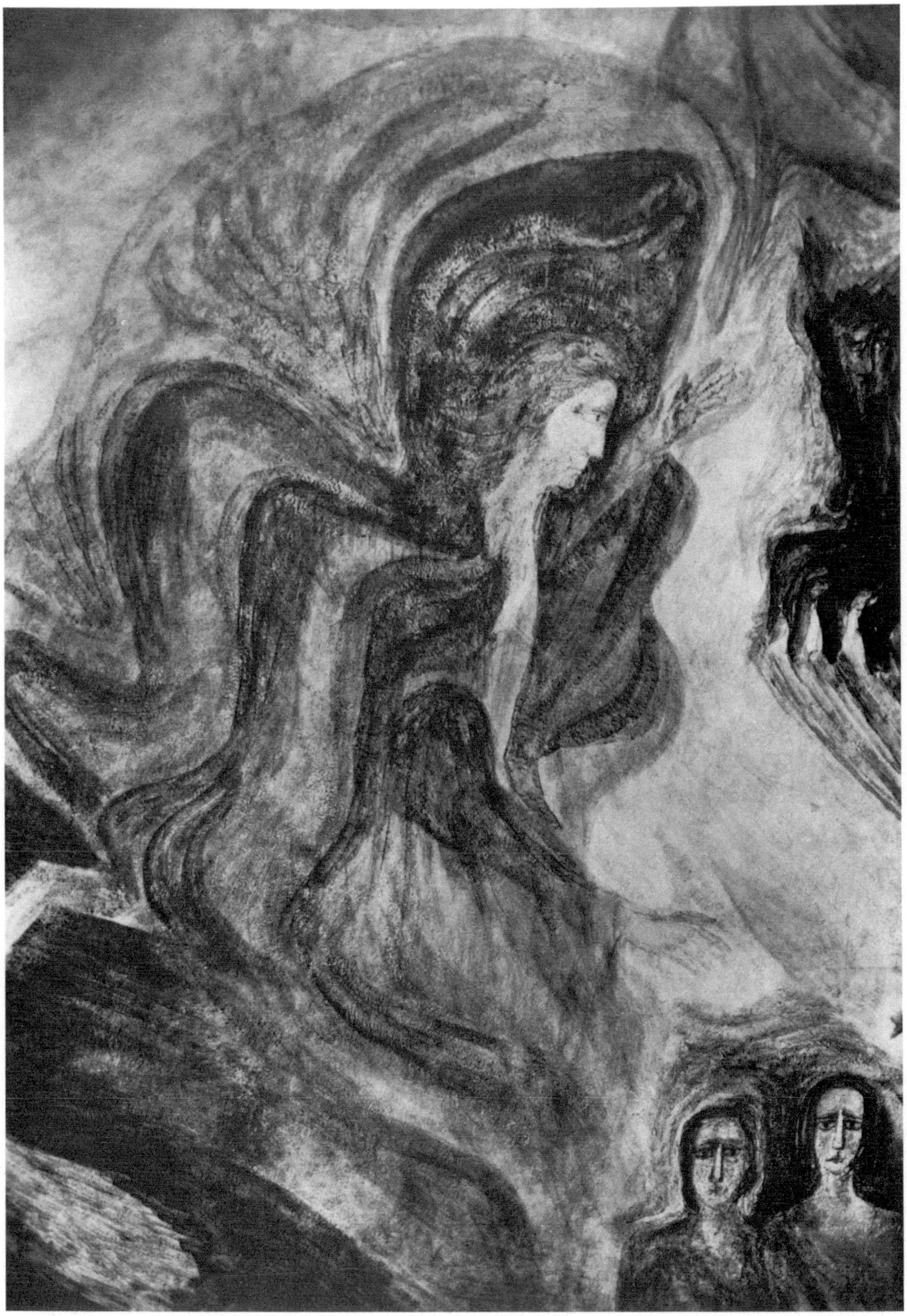

The Blue Angel of the Slavic Motif (south side)

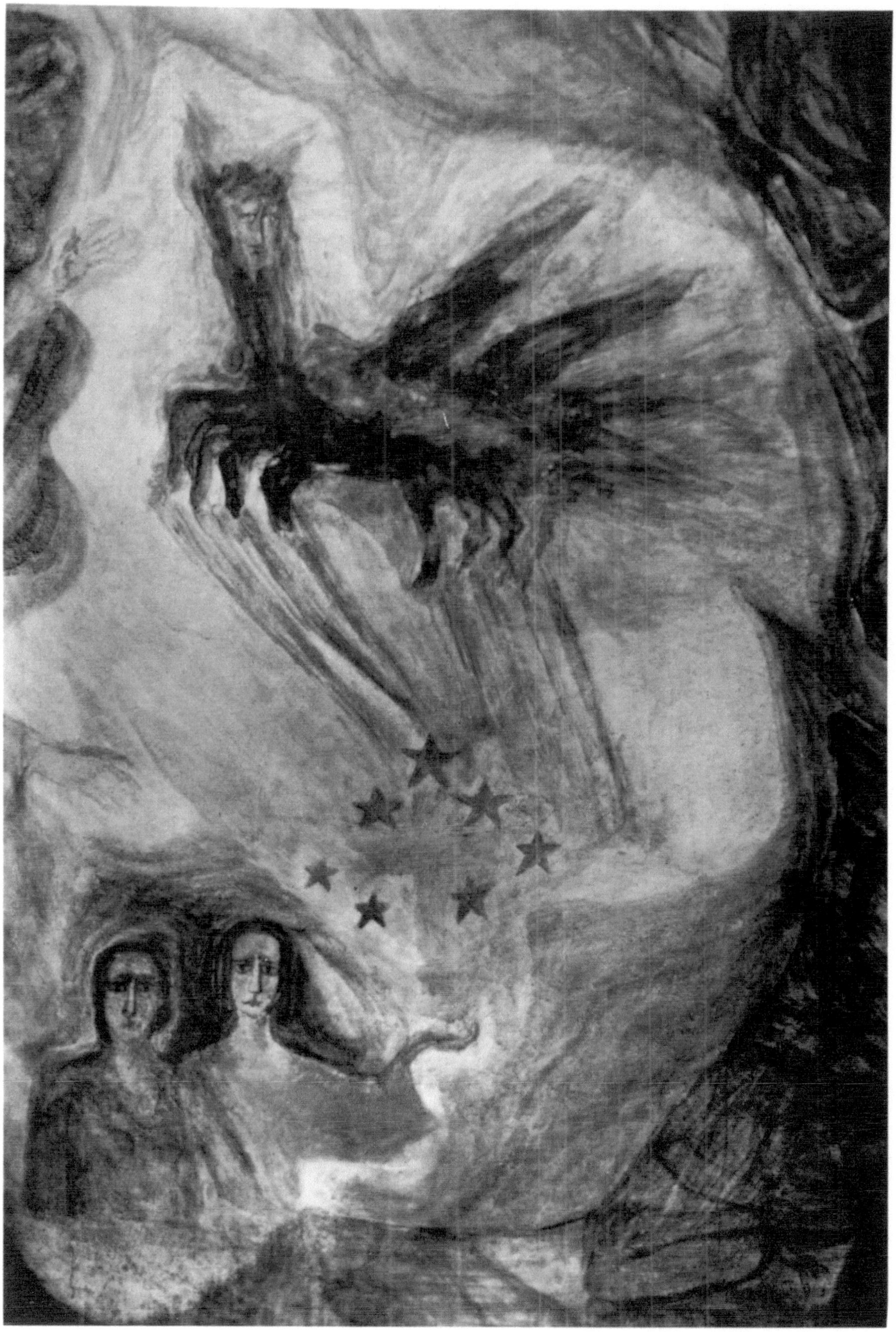

Slavic Man with Double and Centaur (south side)

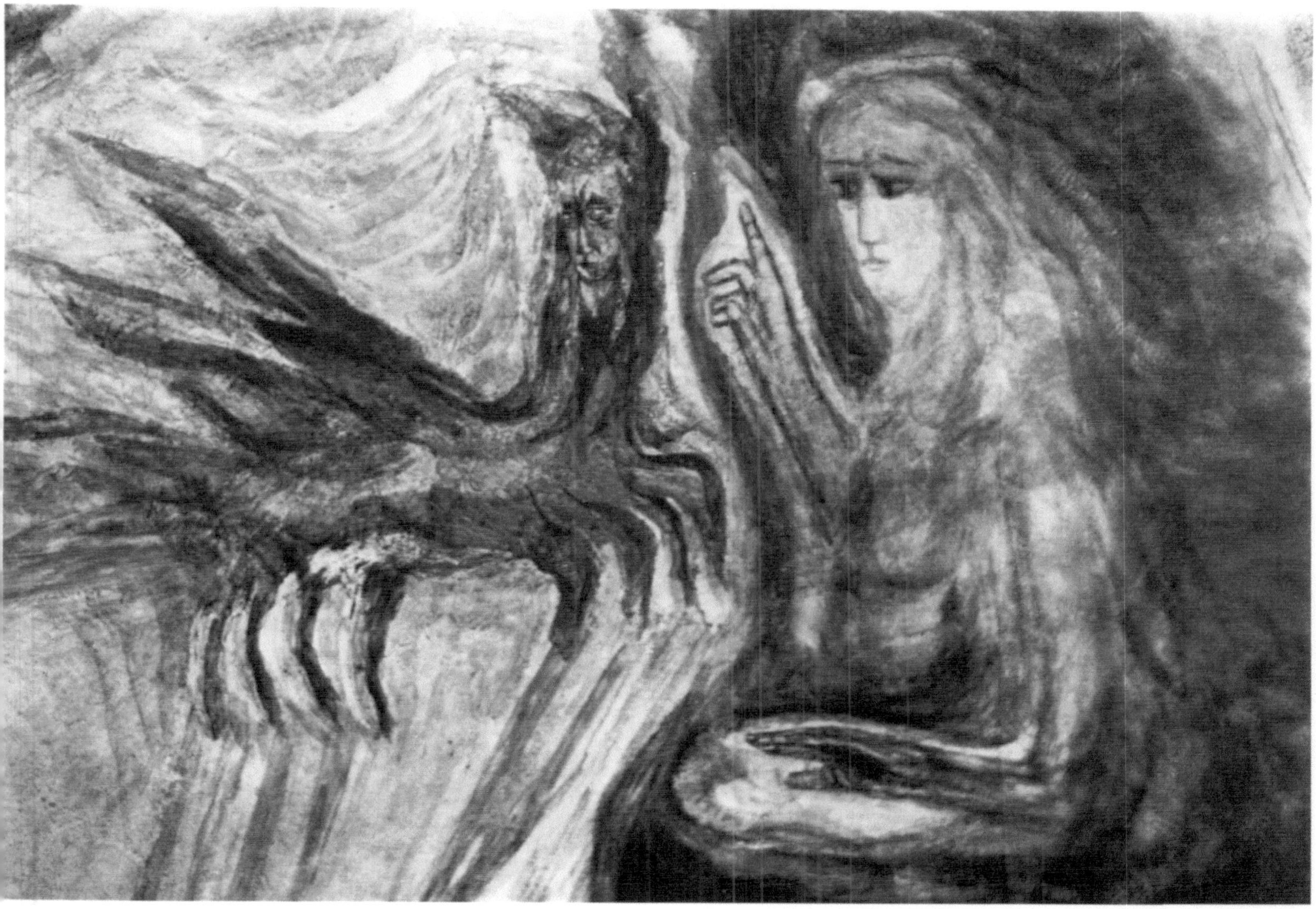

The Orange Angel of the Slavic Motif (north side)

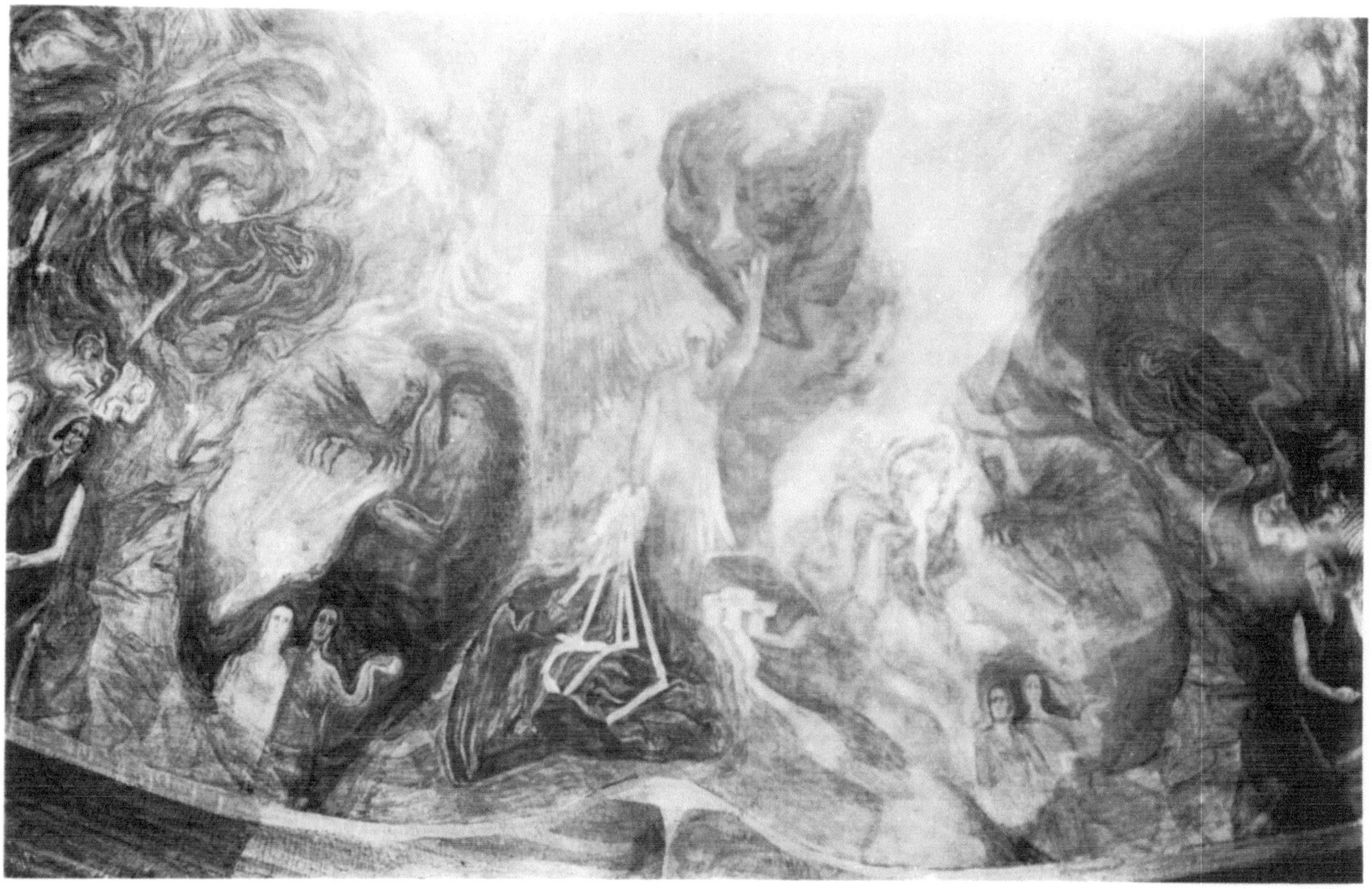

The Representative of Man between Lucifer and Ahriman (north is to the left of the viewer, south to the right)

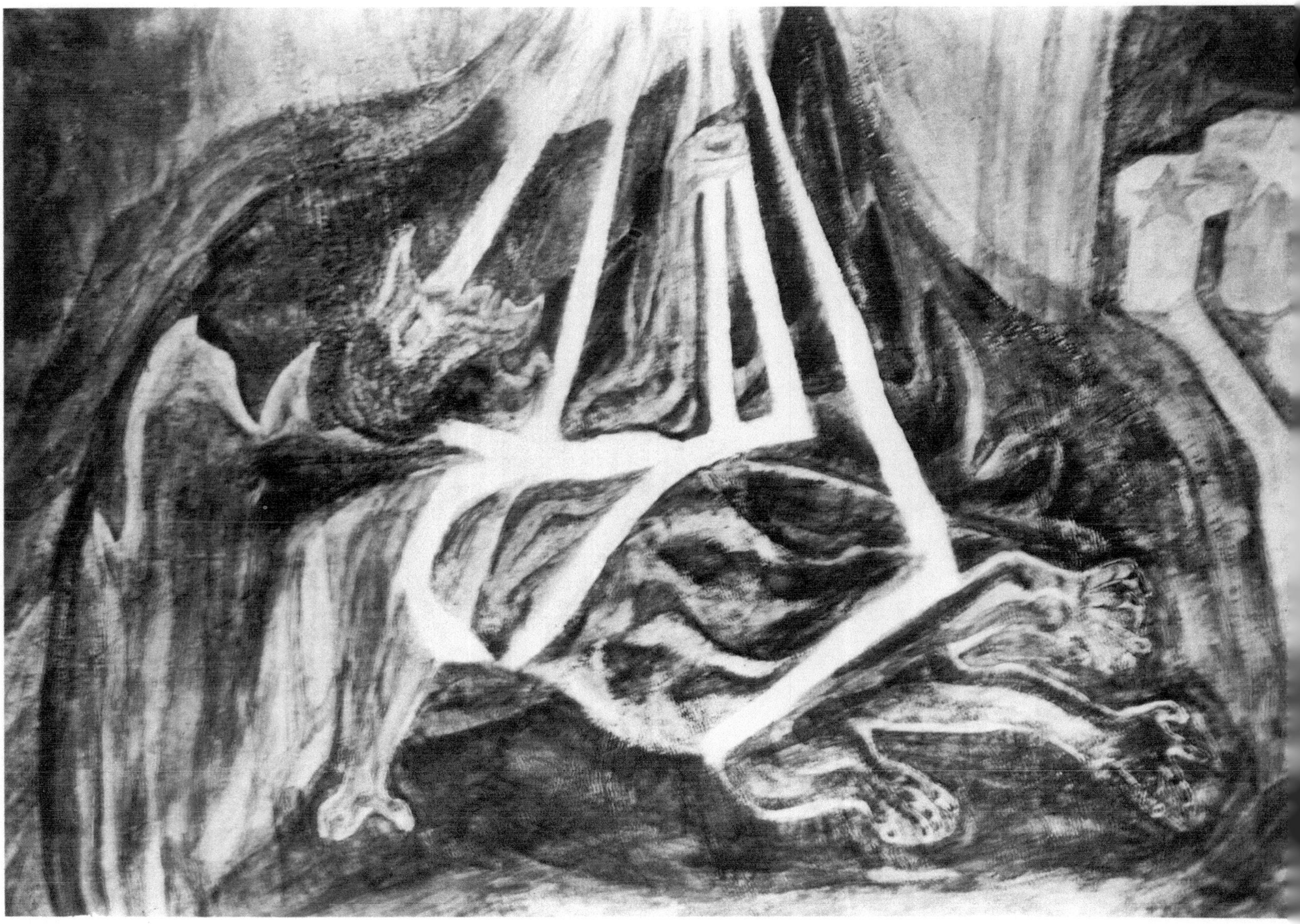

Ahriman (from the central motif)

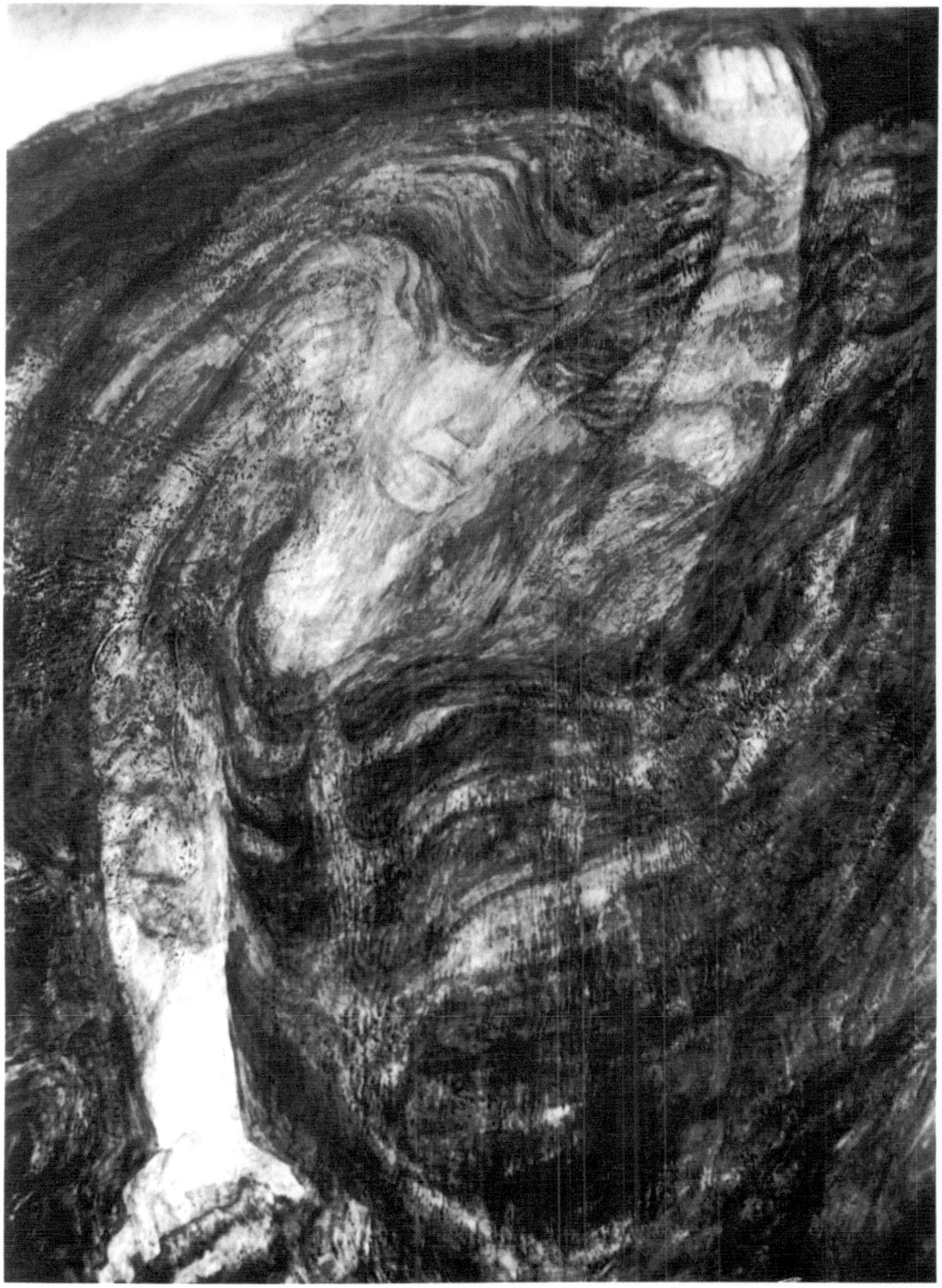

Lucifer (from the central motif)

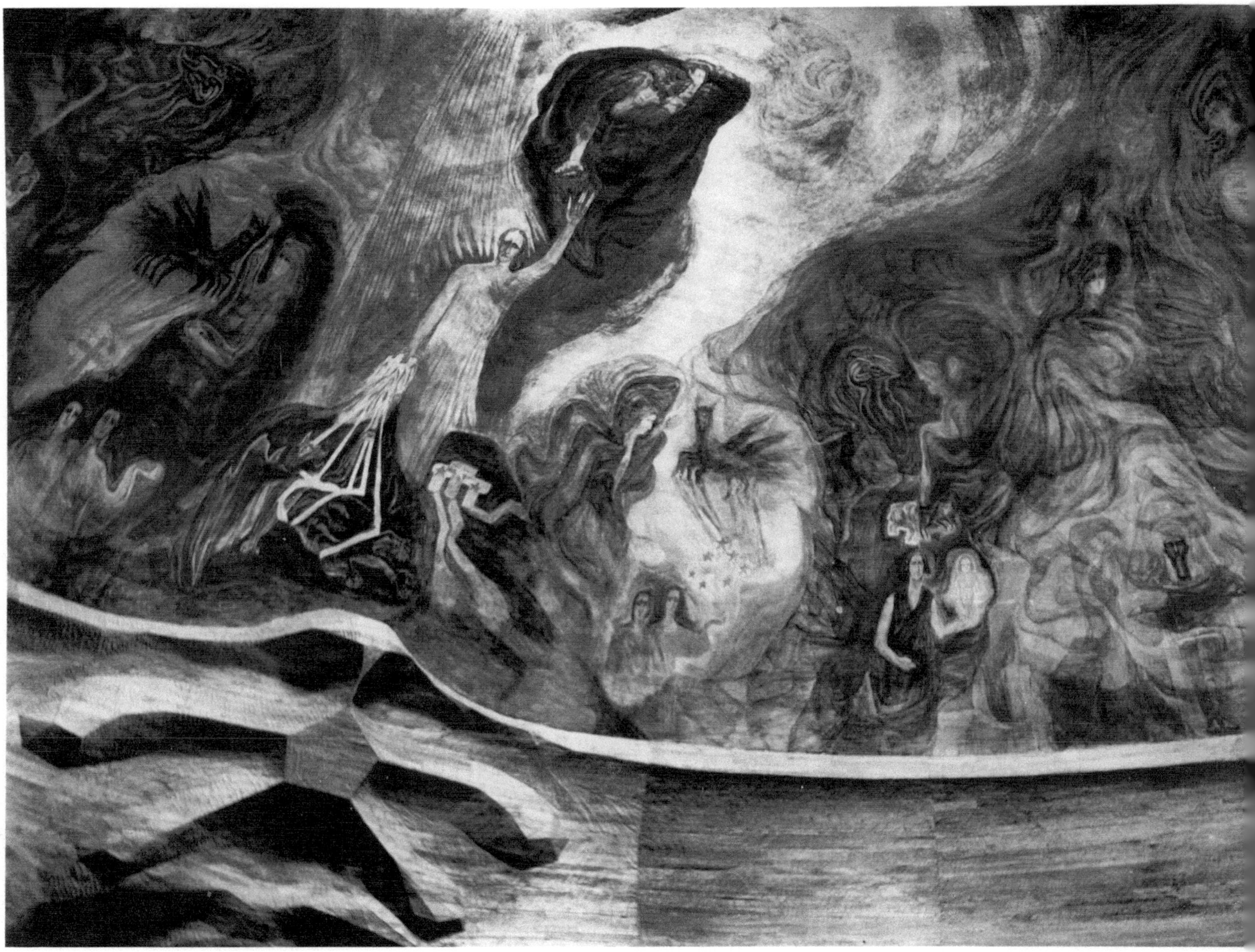

Partial View of the Painting in the Small Cupola (towards the east)

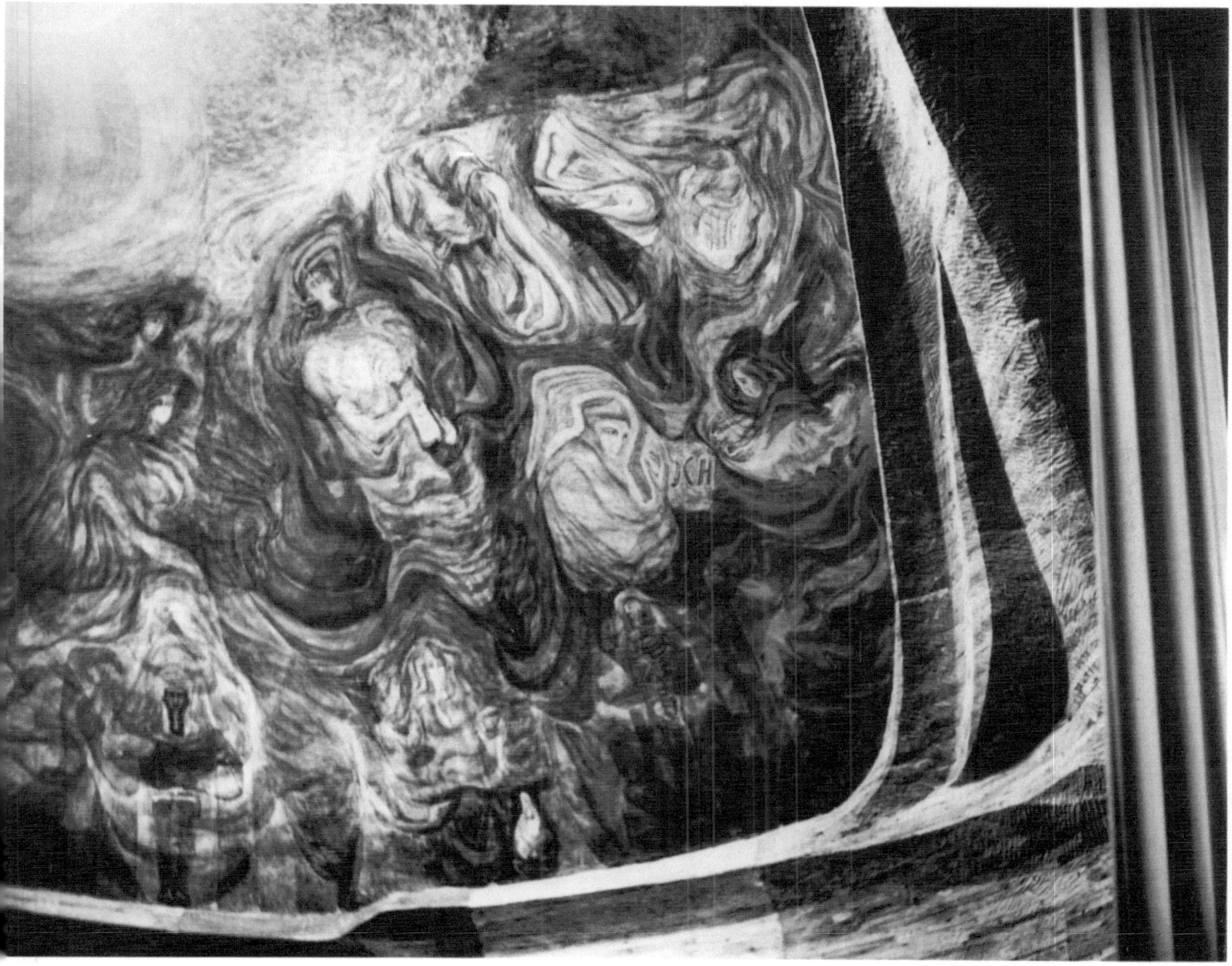

Partial View of the Painting in the Small Cupola (towards the south)

Color Photos

- *The Faust Motif*
- *The Greek and Egyptian Motifs*
- *The Persian-Germanic and Slavic Motifs*
- *The Central Motif with Blue Angel on the right and Orange Angel on the left, both with Centaur*

The color photos reproduced here of parts of the small cupola are 'Urachromes' made by Emil Berger, Solothurn in 1920. This was a time when color photography was in its very beginnings. They give only a vague indication of the color values. But, because they show the conception and handling of the surfaces, it seems justified to publish them here, in spite of their obvious shortcomings.

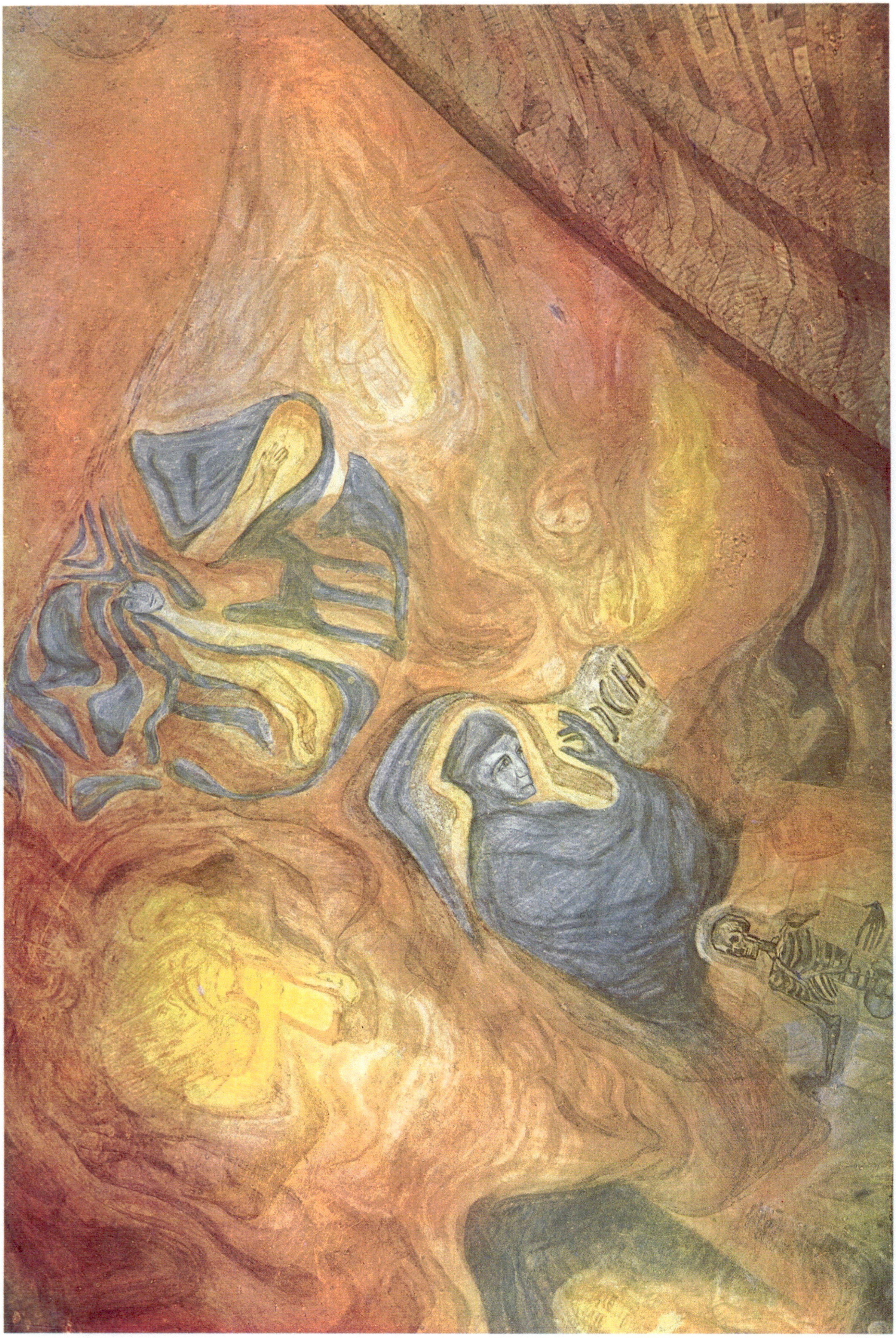

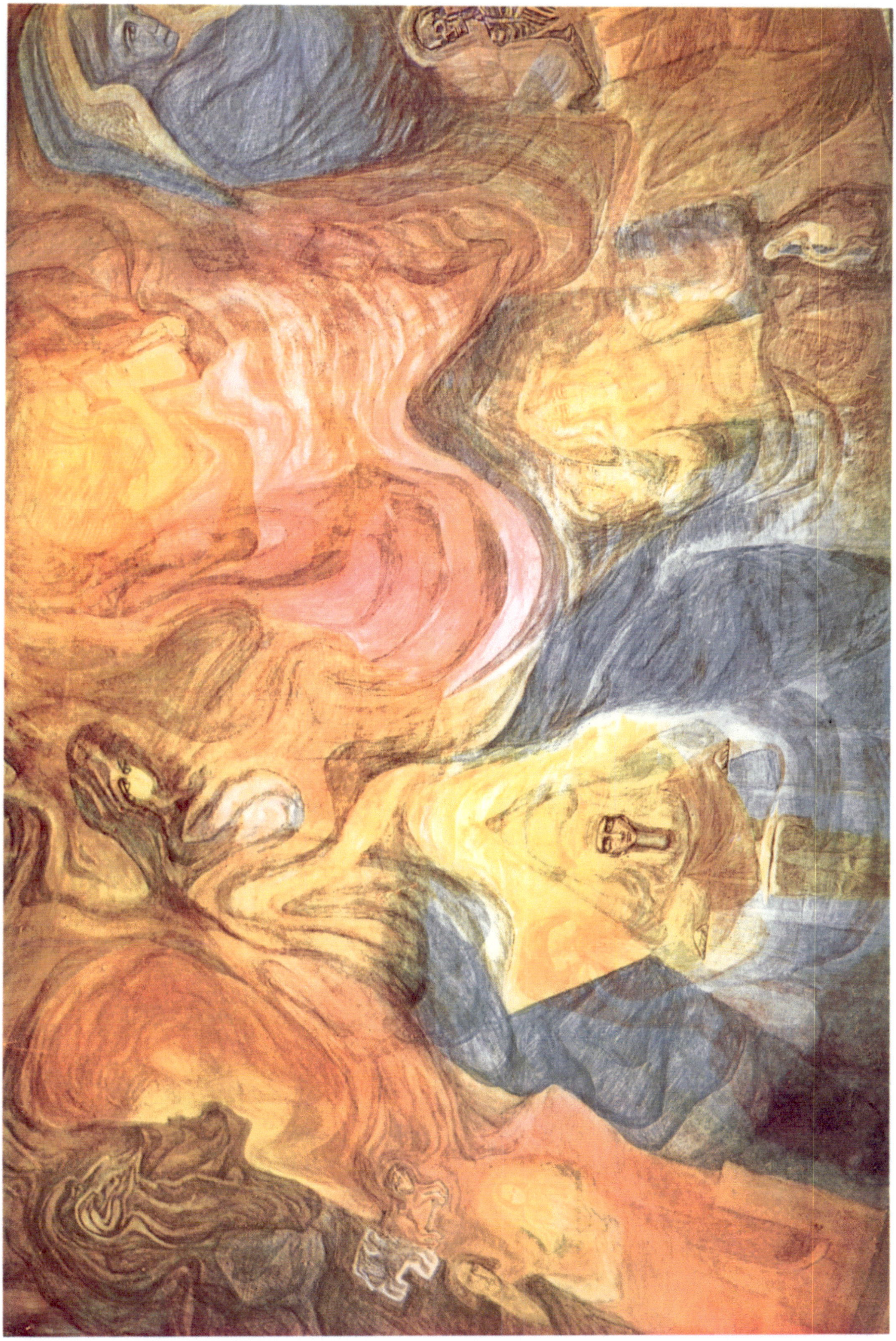

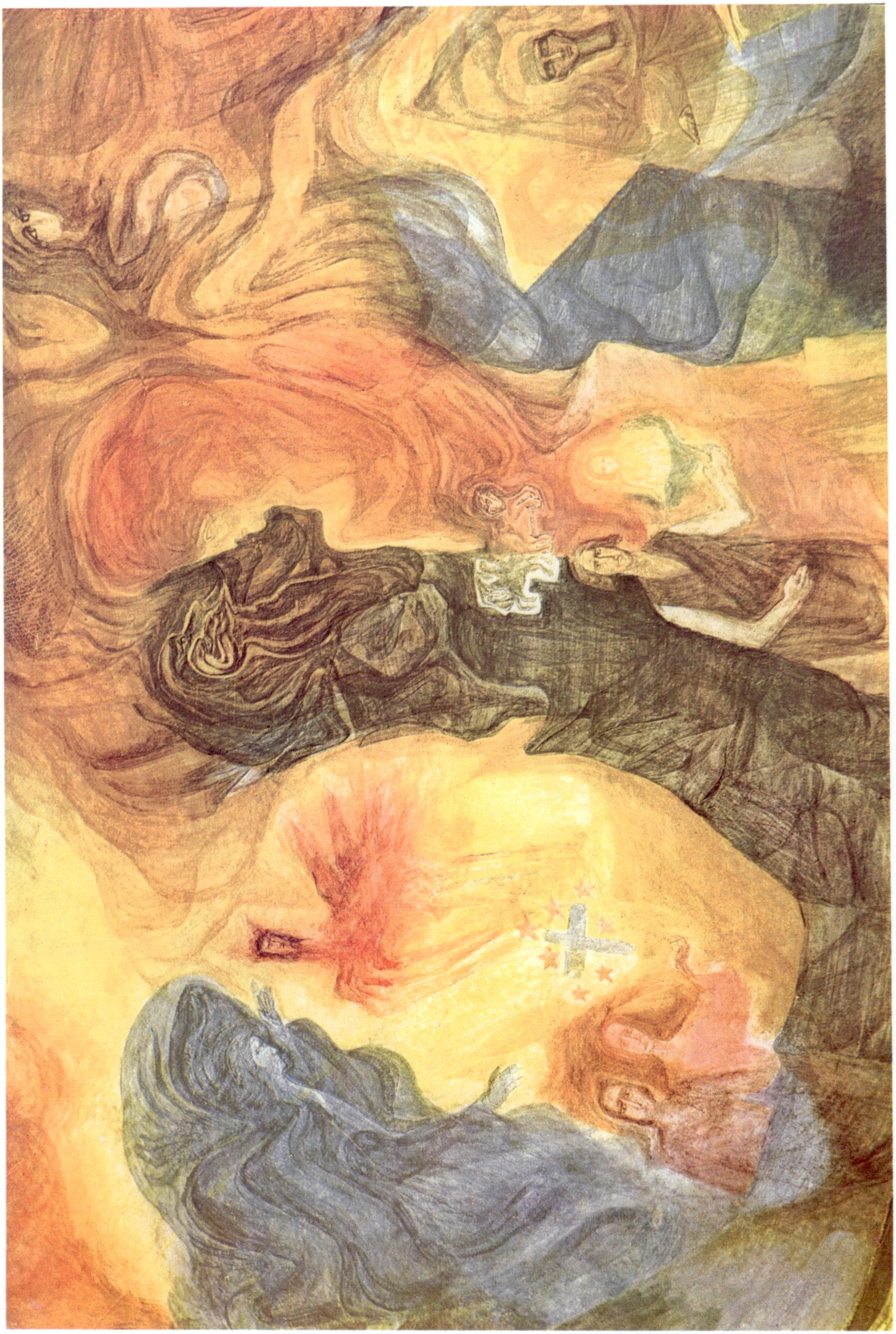

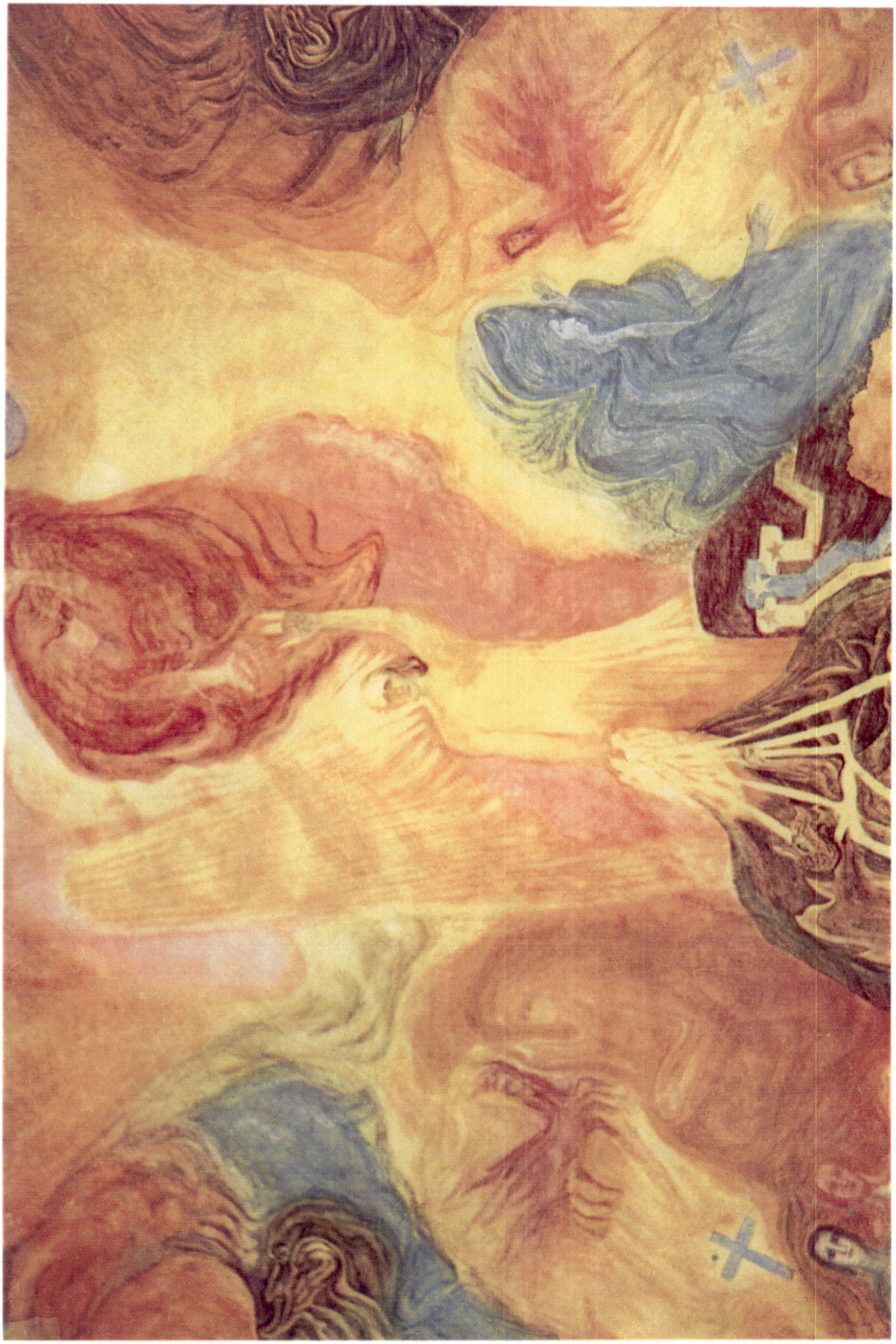

THE CENTRAL MOTIF – CHRIST BETWEEN LUCIFER AND AHRIMAN

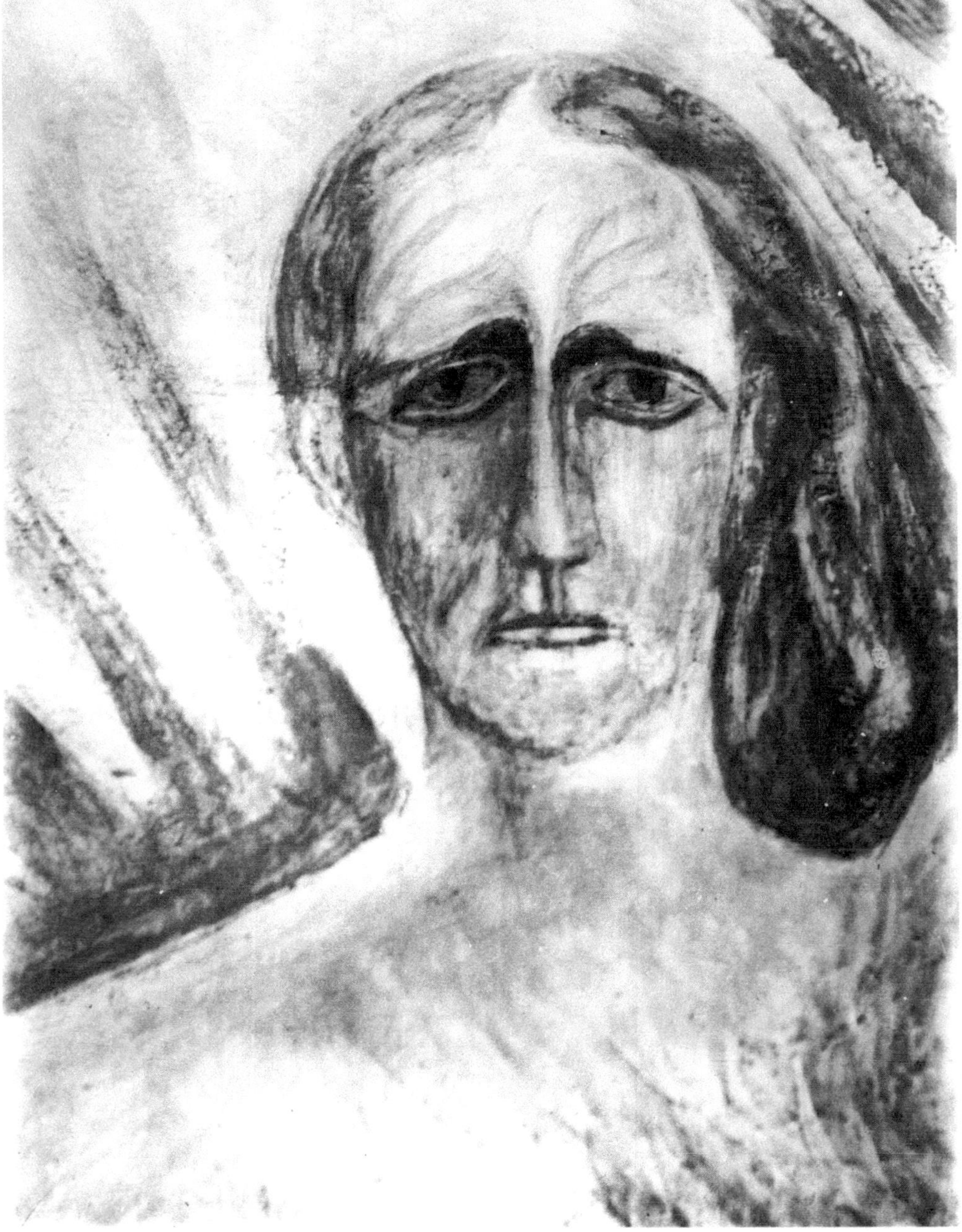

THE CENTRAL PAINTED MOTIF

"In this central figure, I was actually trying to portray Love, both in painting and in sculpture. One should be able to experience this artistically: here is the form in which the Divine appeared on earth. One should sense this from the form, from the contours, from the surfaces, and here in the color itself." (June 12, 1920)

The architrave to the east of the small cupola is a metamorphosis of the powerful motif at the entrance in the west and of the free-swinging forms of the proscenium arch. In the shades of sunny ash wood, it seemed to blossom out like a star. Above it the image of the Resurrected One rose in radiant colors, painted by the hand of Rudolf Steiner. The other painted motifs harmonized with this and formed with it an integral whole, curving from the stage opening around to the east. To the south of this mid-point was the blue angel 'born out of the cloud color'; to the north, the admonishing angel in orange. The black chain of mountains dividing it from the past gives way to light from the future.

Pastel Sketch (see page 155)

The central figure is in a warm yellow surrounded by peach-blossom tones. Above him is the Light-bearer, radiant in red, soaring flame-like and bold and arching his wings regally. To his right and below him in blackish-brown is the dragon-like form of the dark spirit of denial, wound round by yellow rays that seem to chain him. This is how the human being stands between these counter-powers, creating the balance with an ego-gesture directed equally toward the heavenly and the earthly poles. The vertical figure has a powerful effect, much as in the small model. To the left side of the picture and below is a heavy dark brown, like a wall against which the crosses stand in a dull earthy color. Over Lucifer's hand, raised in pride, hovers the sickle moon in an Easter green. From the right and above stream the forces of light and life in peach-blossom tones.

With the simplest of artistic means, active colors contrasted to cool browns, and yet supported by them, a language is achieved that affects us like a revelation. From the pastel sketch stream the magic and freshness of a first conception for a mighty work.

Execution

Robed in flowing yellow as if descending from the heights of heaven, the central figure shines into the space around him. If the motifs of the large cupola tended toward the light, toward yellow, the '*lustre* of spirit', so here the *lustre* becomes *image*, the radiant garb of the loftiest spirit. His left hand is lifted to Lucifer; the fiery rays from his right hand descend into Ahriman's sphere. Lucifer is painted entirely in reds: fanatical, mystical, fiery, passionate, "all that causes a man to constantly consume himself inwardly, that sets him afire with joy, pleasure, greed and lust." (April 5, 1920) Lucifer "is fashioned in particular from the color red, from red and yellow. I wanted to define this only out of the colors, so that the whole, if one wanted to say, luciferic experience, is one of red-yellow, arising out of that burning, phosphorescent color; it expresses everything that inspires a man to expand out beyond his own head." (April 5, 1920)

Ahriman is "in yellow-brown, tending more to brown, in places drawn down into blue-back." (June 29, 1921) This dragon-like being is contoured more sharply; the bat wings are larger and sharper than in the sketch, the limbs formless and shrivelled, and the forehead receding as a man would appear were he nothing but intellect.

In the pastel, Lucifer appears as the proud, soaring light-bearer. In the final version he is, to be sure, surrounded

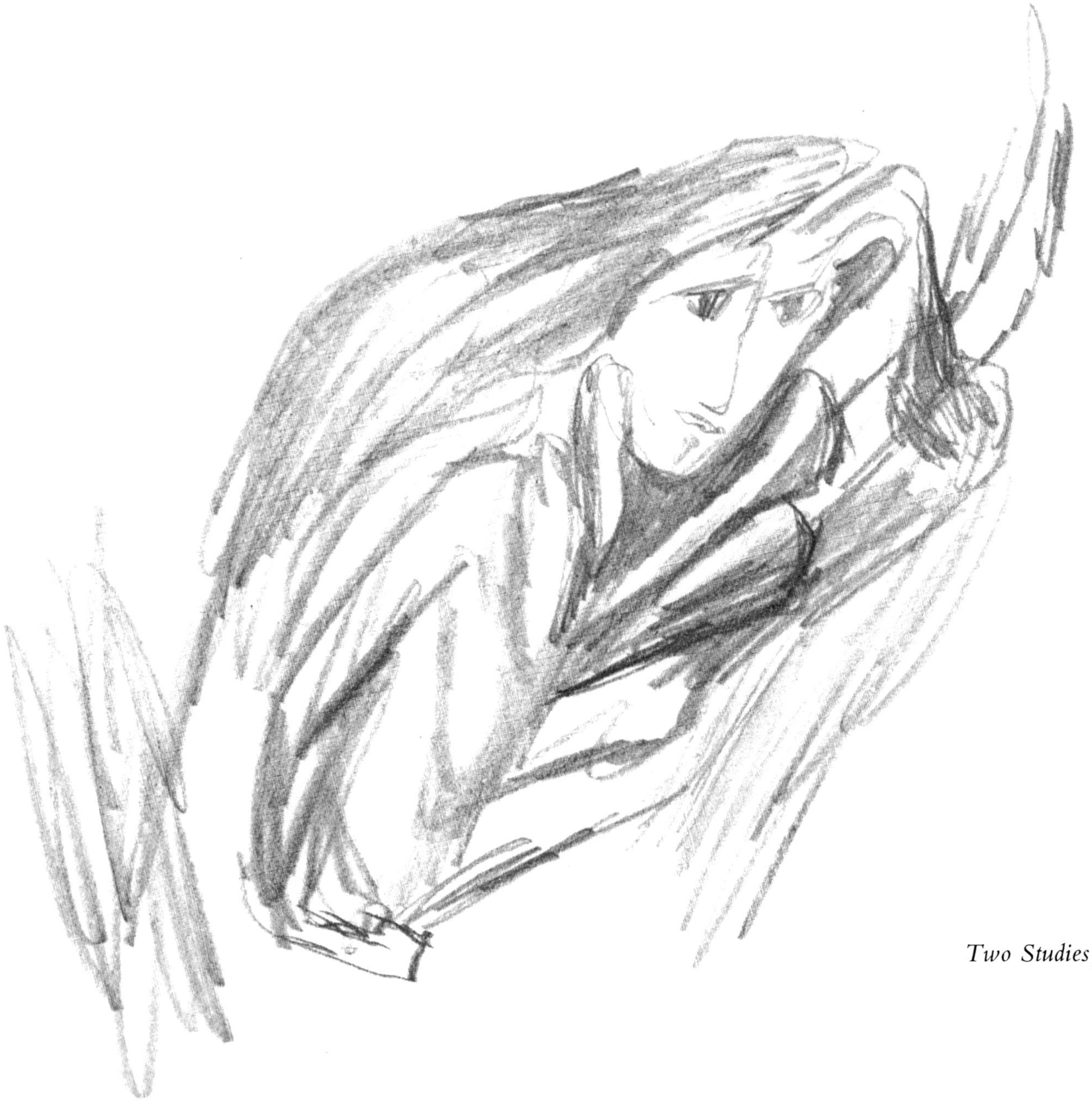

Two Studies for Lucifer

by a red that flares mightily upward, yet these flames are collapsing inwardly and the upstretched hand contracts convulsively in its fall. The countenance betrays the tragedy for which there is no solace: to be banned from the power of Love because he has exiled himself from the purest Love that streams out from the manly form.
"There should be nothing aggressive in this, when the figure of Lucifer is painted above, poetically depicted as he then plunges and is shattered, not because he is assailed by the Christ, but because his luciferic being cannot endure the proximity of embodied Love. And if Ahriman down below, the representative of the ossifying principle, suffers torment – this being who concentrates in himself all that would fetter mankind to the earth and never let him free again from its surface – it is not because bolts of lightning have been cast at him by the Christ figure, but because to a degree through its own soul disposition the ahrimanic being draws forth lightning from this personified Love for his own torment." (June 12, 1920)
"The ahrimanic, caught here by rays of fiery light ... is everything that presses man down to the earth, is earth's gravitation in man, even as the luciferic is that through which man yearns to abandon the earth. The ahrimanic: what is inwardly exhausted, in deep inward suffering; the luciferic: what leads man to bewilderment, illusion, hallucination. With Ahriman everything is bony, everything hardens ... and becomes inwardly frozen in pain, enduring, endless pain, whenever the fiery rays light upon his coldness." (April 5, 1920)
"From a physiological standpoint, man is not the creature of uncomplicated physical growth so often pictured by a trivializing science. The human being always has a tendency on the one hand to sclerosis, on the other

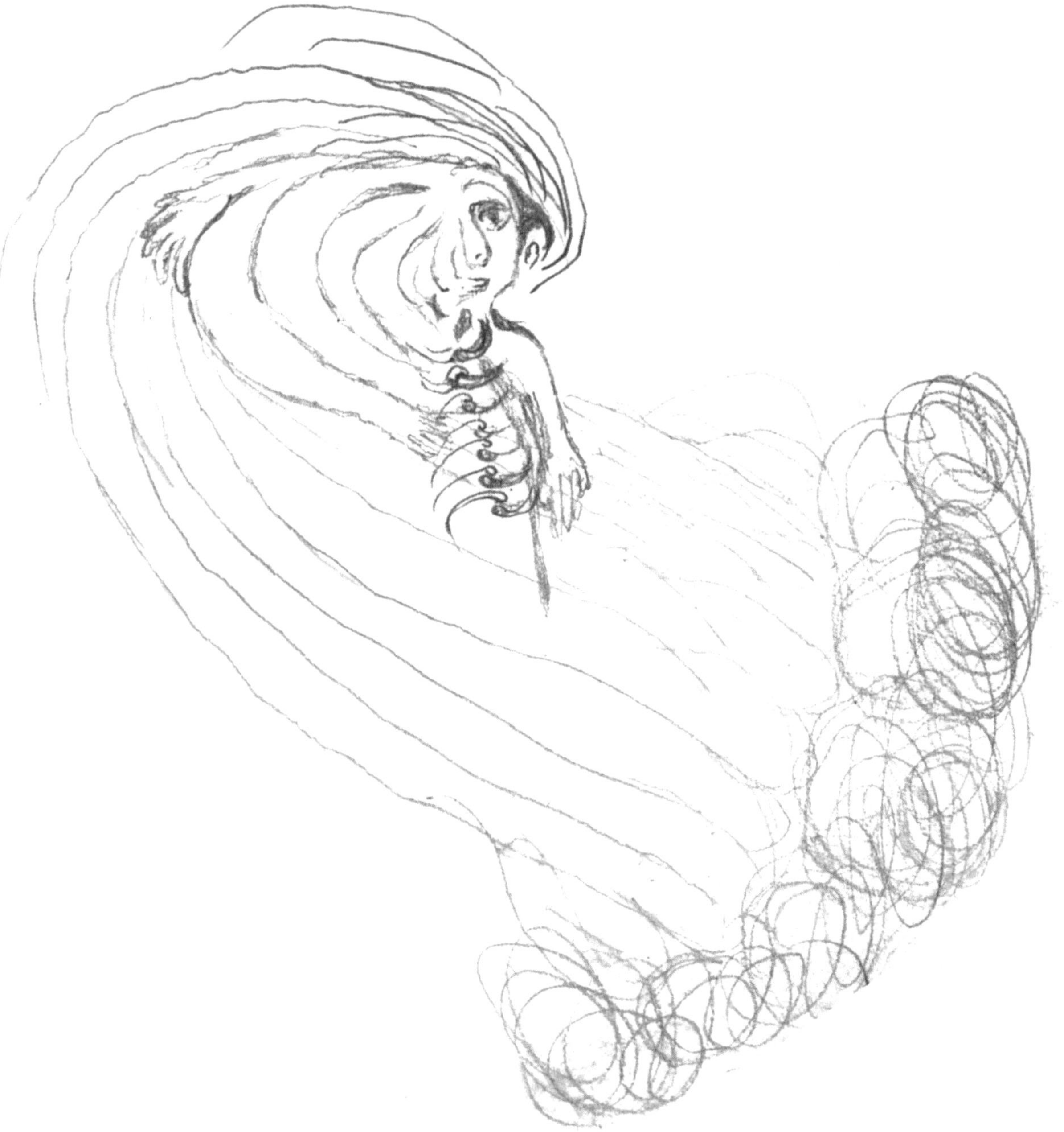

hand, to softening, to mucosity. The softening tendency, which is what would ensue if the blood gained the upper hand, derives from Lucifer. Insofar as fevered states become the dominant formative principle in human physiology, the luciferic is prevailing. Then the human form takes on the shape of that being more and more. In fact, human beings had that shape during the ancient Moon period. We could also say, that if the growth principle predominant in the heart and lungs were the only one, the human being would assume this form. A physiological state of balance is achieved between what rises in the blood and what produces sclerosis only through the fact that the contrary ahrimanic pole opposes it." (January 25, 1920)

The effects of the sun and moon are more fully and forcefully executed in the painting than in the sketch. The lunar world seems to hover and create space. From the solar heights, forces of light and life press into the depths of the earth, as if obedient to the gesturing hand of the central figure. Between sun and moon is the radiant figure of the Risen One. The Easter event rays forth as a cosmic, not an earthly, happening, for it is the constellation of sun and moon that determines the Easter festival. The experience of Easter calls upon the soul to open itself to the language of the stars.

The crucified figures, more sensed than seen in the brown of the sketch, are stars in the finished painting, the central one shining brighter than those to the left and right. From the crosses, painted as broad surfaces, stream gentle tones of red and blue, brightening the dullness of the earth. Pain and torment have been overcome in this resurrection picture and transformed to starlight. The peach-blossom color streaming from the crosses transmutes the earth, endowing it with new etheric life. In the gentlest, simplest manner, the colors hint at the mysteries of the blood and of the transformation of the earth.

"Just as the continuous transformation of the blood into etheric substance takes place in the region of the heart, a similar process takes place in the macrocosm. We understand this if we turn our gaze to the Mystery of Golgotha, to that moment when the blood of Christ-Jesus flowed from His wounds ... . This flowing out and streaming into the earth gave to the earth a substance which united with the earth in an event of the greatest significance for all time to come, an event that could only happen once." (May 26, 1908)

"In the moment when blood flows from the wounds of the Redeemer, the aura of the earth takes on a new form. An entirely new energy enters in, an energy that is an impulse of the greatest import for earth evolution, for which all that we have seen previously was mere preparation." (June 23, 1908)

"Through the event on Golgotha, what had streamed to it before from outside, the power of the Logos, was now taken up into the spiritual being of the earth. What was it that lived in the earth before? It was the force which had rayed down on it from the sun. What lives since then in the earth? The Logos Himself, who has (through Golgotha) become the spirit of the earth.

"As true as it is that your soul-spirit lives in your body, it is just as true that the soul-spiritual being of the earth lives in its physical body which you walk about upon, made up of the stones, the plants and the animals. And this soul-spiritual element, this earth-spirit, is the Christ. *Christ is the spirit of the earth.*" (May 26, 1908)

"Christ had descended from still greater heights to the sun, where Zarathustra beheld Him. His force then passed over into the beams of the sun, and there He was beheld by the Egyptian initiates. Then, His force lived in the sphere surrounding the earth, where the Greek initiates could see Him.

"In our time He should be seen as He once wandered among men as a Being with an earthly body; He should now be seen in the form proper to the Resurrected One, to Him who is within the earth, who has beheld the secret of the earth and can now gradually let this secret flow over into human evolution." (April 24, 1922)

In Berlin in 1909 Rudolf Steiner had already spoken of the task of creating a new picture of the Christ, in connection with Raphael's *School of Athens* and the *Disputa.*

"If we look at the *Disputa* with spiritual vision, we see in the center the Father-God, the Divine-Son or Christ, and below them the Dove of the Spirit ... . You will often come upon this image: the Christ issuing from a shape like a bird, as though being born from a winged being; for the entire mystery of the Christ, that descent from higher worlds, was once experienced as a freeing from nature which was pictured as a higher, yet spatial, world; hence, the wresting free from the shape of a bird, the Christ being born from the bird. Let us place this image before our souls and in its light study the *Disputa.* Here we also find a winged creature – the Dove of the Spirit. Oh, this Dove of Spirit which stands, so to speak, as a great riddle-symbol among all the Christian symbol contains much significance. The painter of the future will have this task: to paint what is born out of this Dove of Spirit, which itself is a passing symbol that will be replaced in the Trinity by something else .... Therefore, it seems good to me that just these two pictures stand before our eyes because they point prophetically to a third picture. It is a pre-Christian view that comes to expression in the first picture; what has transpired through the Christ is expressed in the figure-world of the second picture. What is to come about through the Spirit, the emissary of the Christ, who will appear unveiled – this is to be expressed in the picture that can stand before the soul of each and every anthroposophist as a grand ideal." (May 5, 1909)

Three years later (in a lecture on May 8, 1912) the capacities and experiences of wonder and awe, the feelings of sympathy and love and responsiveness to conscience are described as the way to find the Christ again in our time and to picture Him according to His true nature.

In Berlin on May 14, 1912, the task of creating a picture of the Christ through spiritual vision was gone into in greater detail. "Every picture of the Christ should in reality partake of the ideal of the Christ-form. And the feeling that strives towards such an ideal is this: one tries to realize something that is still in process insofar as the feeling must arise ever more and more that if you wish to picture the Christ, you should not rely on what is already there. Instead, you should let everything that a spiritual immersion in the spiritual evolution of the world can give you through the three essential impulses of wonder, sympathy and conscience gather force and work within you and permeate you inwardly."

Toward Christmas 1914, when the framework for the first Goetheanum was already in place, Rudolf Steiner produced the pastel sketch for the central motif of the small cupola, 'The Representative of Mankind between Lucifer and Ahriman'. He thereby brought the new Christ message to expression for the first time in color.

Arhild Rosenkrantz, the one first assigned to execute this motif, reports a conversation with Rudolf Steiner. "When he spoke of this new representation, which would be necessary for mankind in the future, he rose from his chair, stretching his left arm over his head and directing his right arm downward, and said, 'You must think of the central Christ figure emerging from the yellow color. Over his head in gradations of red and carmine, Lucifer, seeking to free himself from bonds to the earth; beneath him in orange tones earth-bound Ahriman'."

He translated this imaginative description at once, slightly altered, into a sketch, which was then to be copied at the eastern end of the small cupola. On the same day he explained the composition of the carved group, which he executed with the help of Edith Maryon. He made a further drawing for one of the windows, where the overcoming of Ahriman and Lucifer is depicted.

"It was as if the imagination of the central fact of Christendom and of the mystery of human life stood before him, as soon as the Goetheanum had reached the stage where this crowning motif could be incorporated. Here one was confronted by genuine inspiration, for he seemed to conceive in a single moment a composition containing a complete world-view."[1]

The Easter evening scene from Goethe's *Faust*, in which the words 'Christ is arisen' resound, was performed in eurythmy for the first time at Easter 1915. On this occasion Rudolf Steiner pointed out that the creation of a true picture of the Christ is a task belonging to the future. "And imagine that a painter in our day, furnished with all the means of the art of painting, were to let the symbol of the Mystery of Golgotha work upon him and wished through his art to answer the question. 'What is it that appears to me when I begin with the symbol of Christ-Jesus lying in the grave and then, with what I have gained from this, I look into my own depths? What appears to me? It is the Christ in his Jupiter-splendor – in his future splendor – fettering Ahriman in the sub-earthly with bands of light, so that he cannot lay hold on man, and overcoming Lucifer, so that he cannot draw the human soul along his path.'" (April 4, 1915)

Somewhat later – in 1918 or 1919 – Rudolf Steiner himself painted the image of the Risen One among the motifs of the small cupola. He commented on this in some of his lantern-slide lectures. "Just as I am convinced that the common image of a bearded Christ which we usually see first appeared in the 5th or 6th century, I am also convinced that the figure represented here is a true picture of Him who at the beginning of our time period wandered through Palestine as Christ-Jesus. ... This head, as it appears to me from spirit vision – insofar as one can give it a form – holds the true features of Him who lived as the Christ in Palestine when Christianity began." (June 12, 1920)

"We must try to view the Christ as spiritual scientists. And as far as I believe I am able to represent such a vision, naturally after everything that one can only see preserved in the Akashic Record has been transformed to the spiritual, this figure is that of Him who actually wandered through Palestine at the beginning of the new age. Yet this should not be understood in the sense of a portrait study, but rather it could be felt that the Representative of Man relates in such a way to history. Everything must proceed from a sense for the artistic." (April 5, 1920)

"I make no demand that it be believed on my authority that this is the true image of the Christ. Yet this is how I see it, and this I affirm out of deepest inwardness to be the Christ-figure." (February 28, 1921)

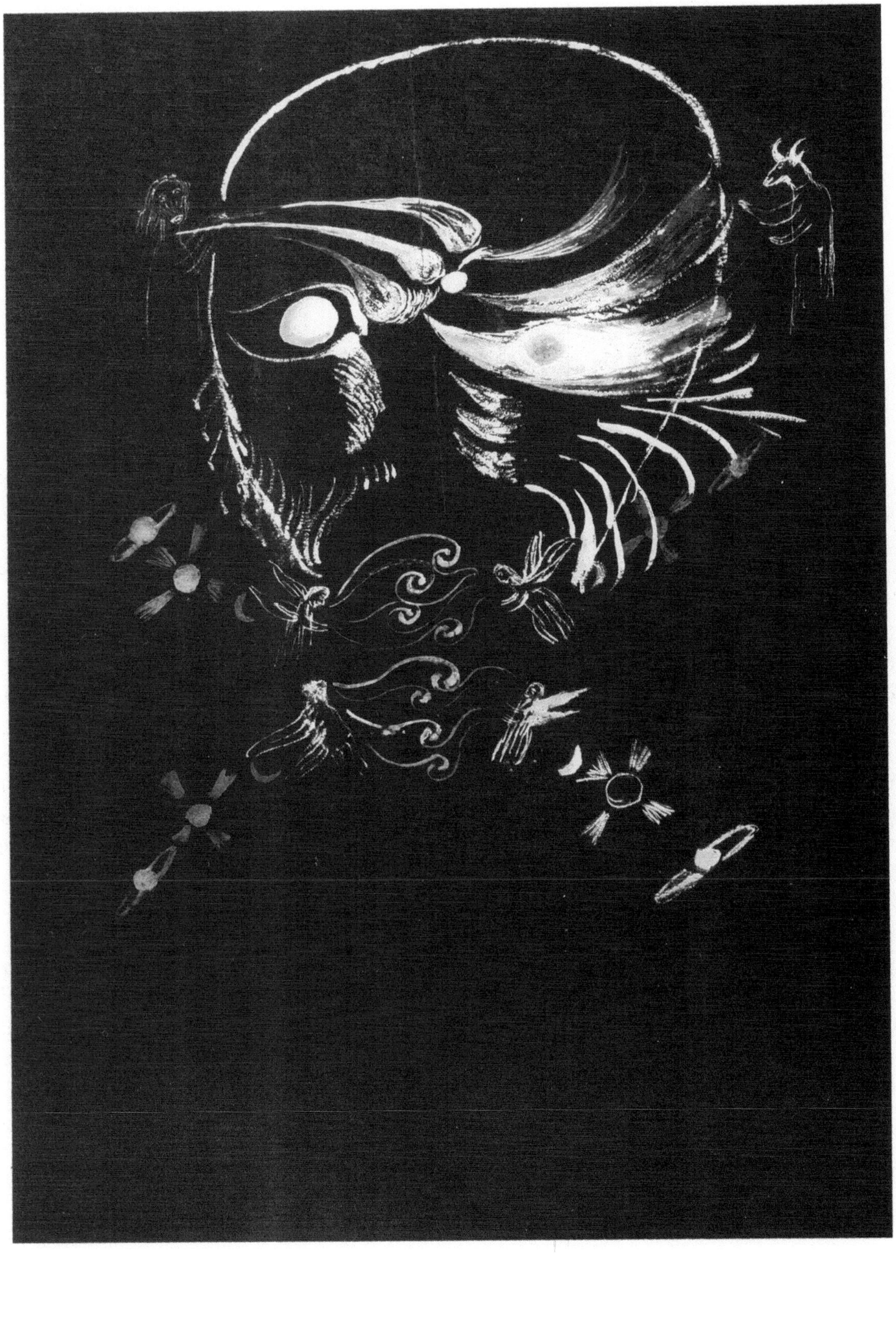

Ink Drawing of the Red Window (white on blue)

THE WINDOWS OF COLORED GLASS

"You will find etched on the glass panels much of the content of spiritual science, always as seen imaginatively: the nature of the dreaming or waking human being, various secrets of creation, etc., all not in symbols, but as it is seen. The intention is artistic, but is completed only when the sun shines through them." (July 3, 1918)

The picture of the Risen One was painted at the eastern end of the small cupola. To the west, outside the doorway to the large cupola room, the glowing red of the western window forced one to pause and reflect. For this window and for those of the large hall, Rudolf Steiner created a new window art in a single color in which the images appear when the sun shines through the light and dark shadings of the etched glass.

"The panes of glass are not all of one color, but one color is always followed by another. Thus when one enters the hall, one experiences a interplay of various colors from the different windows. The whole space is then illumined through and through by a color-symphony." (February 28, 1921)

The shades of color changed with the movements of the sun through the course of a day and year, and according to the more northerly or southerly position of the windows. Assja Turgeniev pictures the impression: "On entering the hall, one was each time astounded afresh at the play of colors in light and in shadow, in a space that, in its proportions, appeared so balanced, harmonious, and alive with the cupola resting lightly on the columns, and the ever-unfolding, living forms of the capitals and architraves in between .... Out of the passageway around the hall, overshadowed by the vault of the architraves, poured concentrated jewel-like color from the windows. The colored beams were mirrored on the flat planes of the columns; they tinted the carved forms of the pedestals and spilled out into the hall like colored waves, meeting and neutralizing one another in the center into a soft, warm light. All the more intense and varied was the play of complementary colors in the shadows, a gleaming interplay, forever changing with the shifting sun. Every human face was transfigured to a painting, taking on fresh nuances with each movement. Within the darkened curvature of the stage surged the reflected beams from the hall in an endless wealth of delicate shades of color .... .

"Everything in the Goetheanum was in shifting movement, and this included the color effects from the windows. Here, the rainbow colors had not been frozen into glass, but rather the onlooker perceived their life and being as the deeds and sufferings of light.

"The beholder of these etched windows was offered the unified effect of a single color differentiated only through the nuances of light that created the picture. The experience of color was a way into the picture, and the picture in turn was a way for his soul to expand and take on form."[2]

This path began in the glowing red of the triptych at the entrance in the west and led on through the hall toward the stage in green, blue, violet and peach-blossom.

We must once again sense our way toward the spiritual and soul qualities in the living colors, which Rudolf Steiner made use of here. "If we look in particular through a glowing red, we come into touch with beings within the natural kingdoms of a most peculiar kind. If a glowing red becomes a window through which we may look into the kingdoms of nature clairvoyantly, we then encounter beings whose work provides the most salutary forces for the future of our existence on earth. Where they are present in the kingdoms of nature, inner human forces arise by which a man becomes ever more chaste in his blood; that is to say, in his life of passion. When we look into nature in this way, we behold them, and they admonish us in our subconscious; they do the most to rouse us to make headway in the purifying of our passions." (Evening of October 15, 1911)

"If we identify ourselves with green and move through the world within this green color ... and now try to put everything else aside ... viewing the green as the surface of a colored sea into which we plunge, if we try to live into the world in this way, then we sense that what we are in this incarnation is strengthened inwardly. We experience a leaning toward inner health, but also a stimulation of the egoistic forces within us." (January 1, 1915)

"Were we to repeat this with a surface of blue, we would sense the need to go on through the world with blue, overcoming the egoism in us, becoming, as it were, macrocosmic, learning devotion, ... We would feel blessed by divine compassion, passing through the world in this way." (January 1, 1915)

"Assume that a human soul is looking at nothing save the blue of heaven. Then a certain moment arrives when the blue of heaven comes to an end, when we see blue no more, when there is nothing more we could describe as blue, using any human language. However, if we concentrate on our own soul at the moment when blue ceases to be blue for us, then we will note a peculiar soul-mood, as though when the blue vanishes , an infinity opens before us into which a particular soul-mood, a peculiar feeling, a precise soul sensation pours – into the emptiness that arises where blue had been. If we would give a name to this soul sensation, to what wills to pour forth into the endless distance, then we have a word for this. Our soul feels *pious*, feels piety in beholding this infinity, is surrendered to piety." (April 3, 1912)

"In perceiving the blue of the heavens, we are perceiving the ether around us. To begin with, we are looking *through* the ether. It allows this at first, but then makes itself perceptible as the blue of the sky. The existence of this heavenly blue is described rightly for our human perception when we say: to be sure the ether is imperceptible, but it rises to perceptibility because of its grand significance in the universe, by proclaming itself, revealing itself in the blue of heaven ... but here we already enter the domain of the supersensible." (June 4, 1924)

The blue in the second pair of windows deepens to violet in the succeeding pair, to the night-time threshold of death and birth. This reaches its greatest intensity in the peach-blossom of the final pair of triptychs. "We then enter the spiritual world. This is the color that descends as far as the surface of the body, the color that lifts the human being above material things and leads him on into the spiritual." (May 7, 1921)

Just as the colors intensify and take on a more inward quality, the sequence of pictured motifs shows a similar progression. Rudolf Steiner called this "a path into the spiritual world".[3]

THE MOTIFS OF THE WINDOWS

Anteroom (west window):

The Revelation of the Divine is viewed through red.

Large Cupola:

In green, Ahriman's influence in the cosmos is seen in the north and Lucifer's pain and striving in the south.

In blue, the threefold sun and the harmony of the spheres is seen in the north and in the south the influence of the zodiac on the human form.

In violet, death is depicted in the north and birth in the south.

In peach-blossom the power of love redeems Lucifer and Ahriman in the north; in the south, the working of the stars and the building.

The following reproductions are etchings made by Assja Turgeniev after Rudolf Steiner's sketches for the windows.

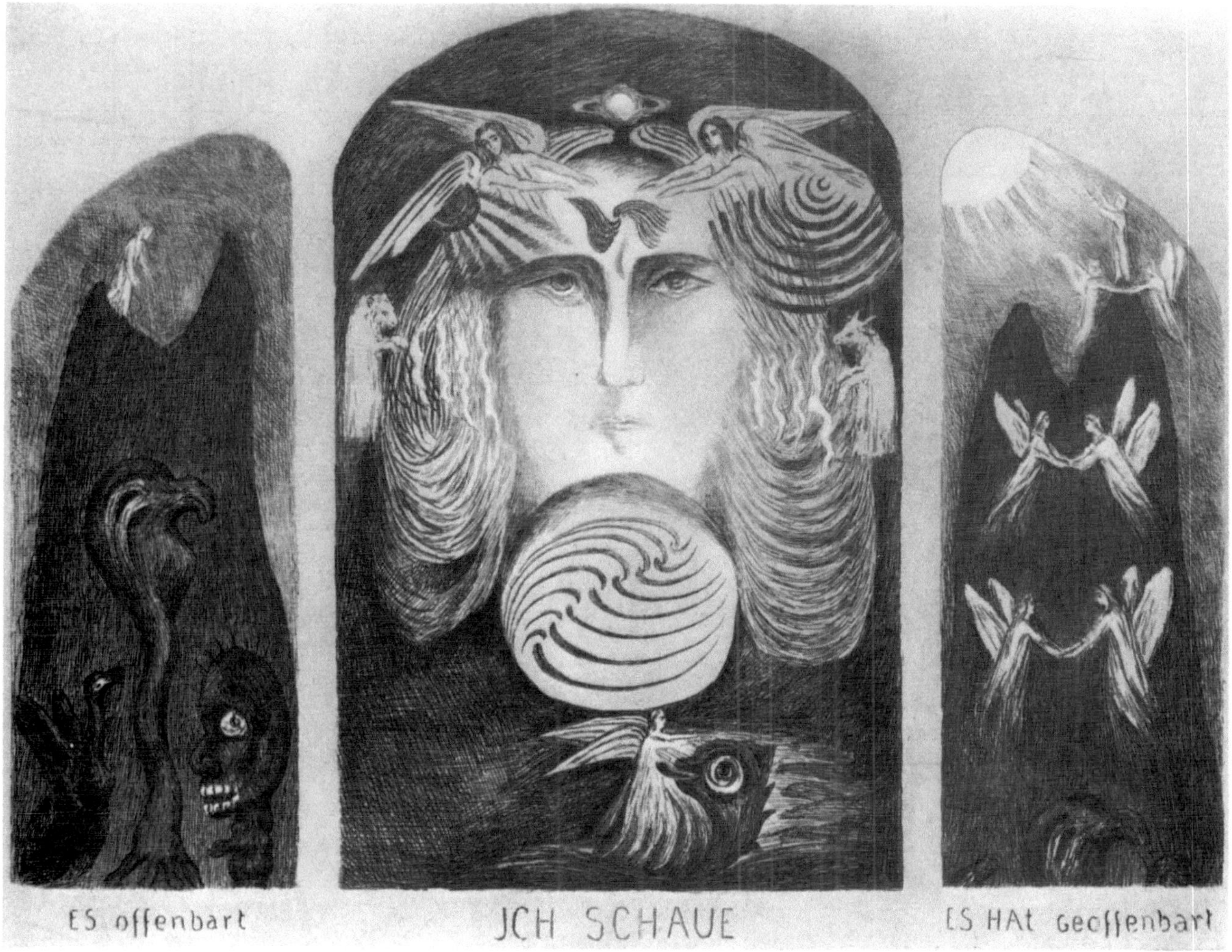

It reveals | I behold | It has revealed

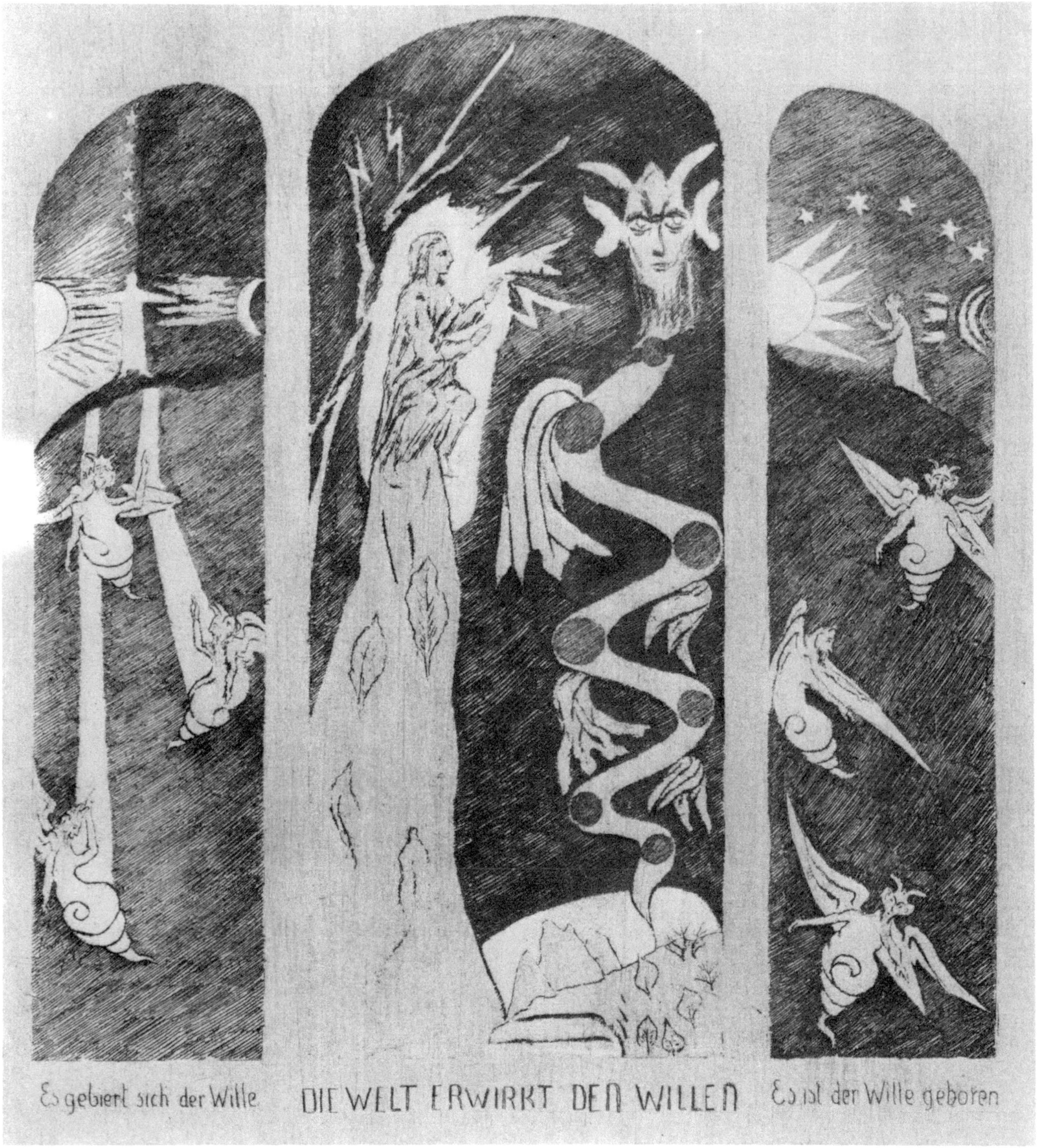

The will gives birth to itself | The world forges the will | The will is born

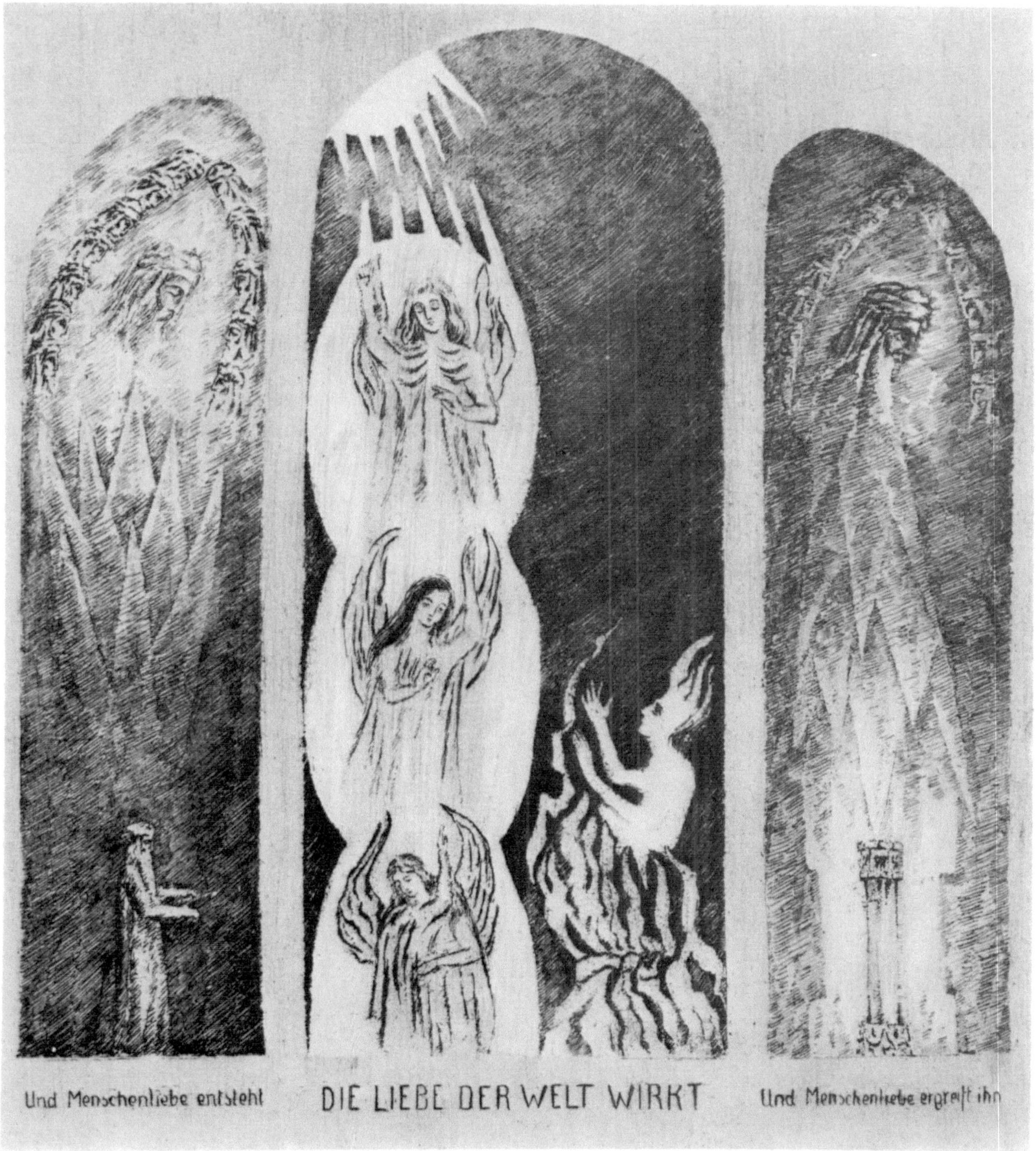

And human love arises The love of the world works And human love takes holds of him

The Green Window in the South

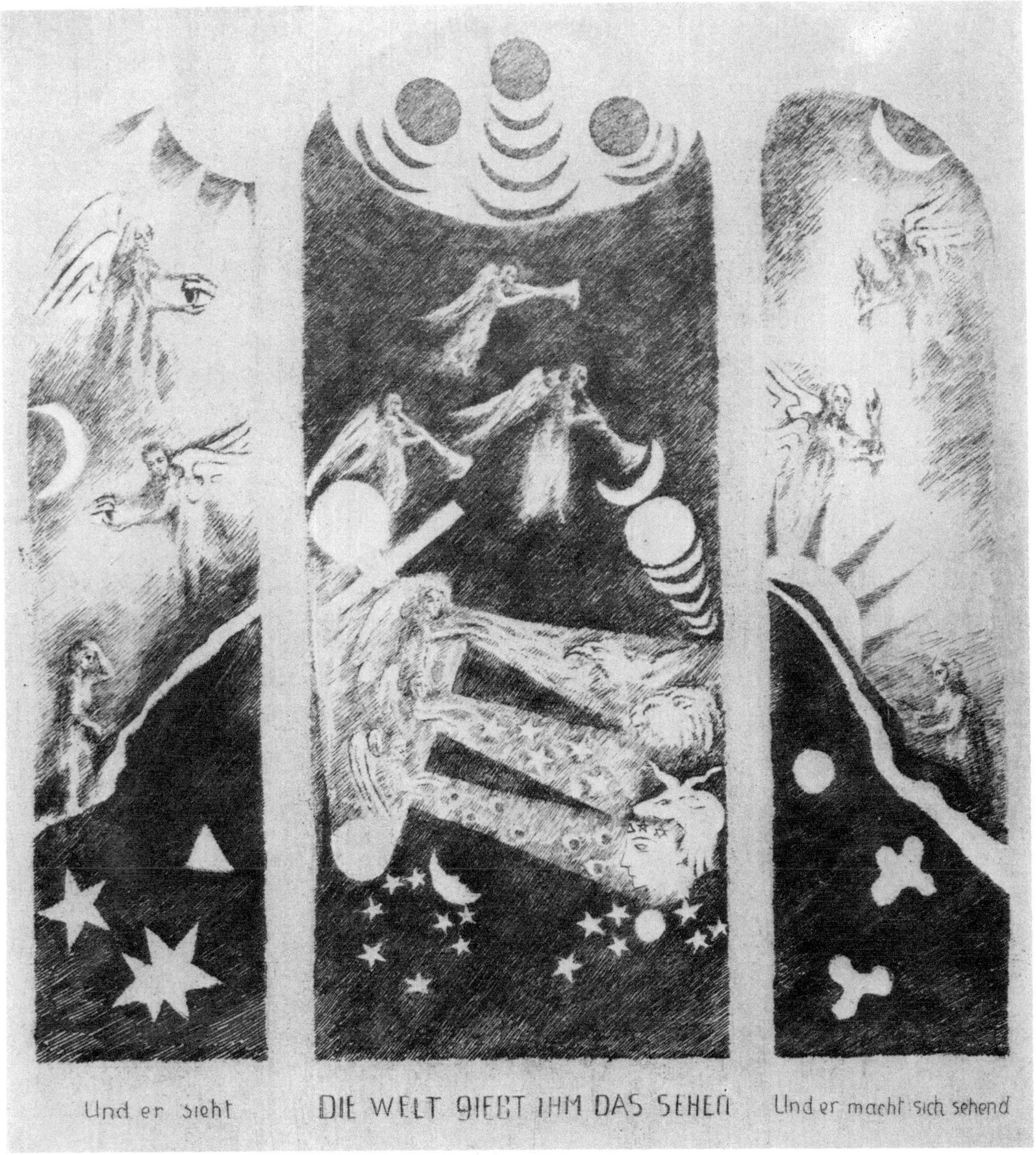

And he sees

The world gives him the power of seeing

And he develops seeing

The Blue Window in the North

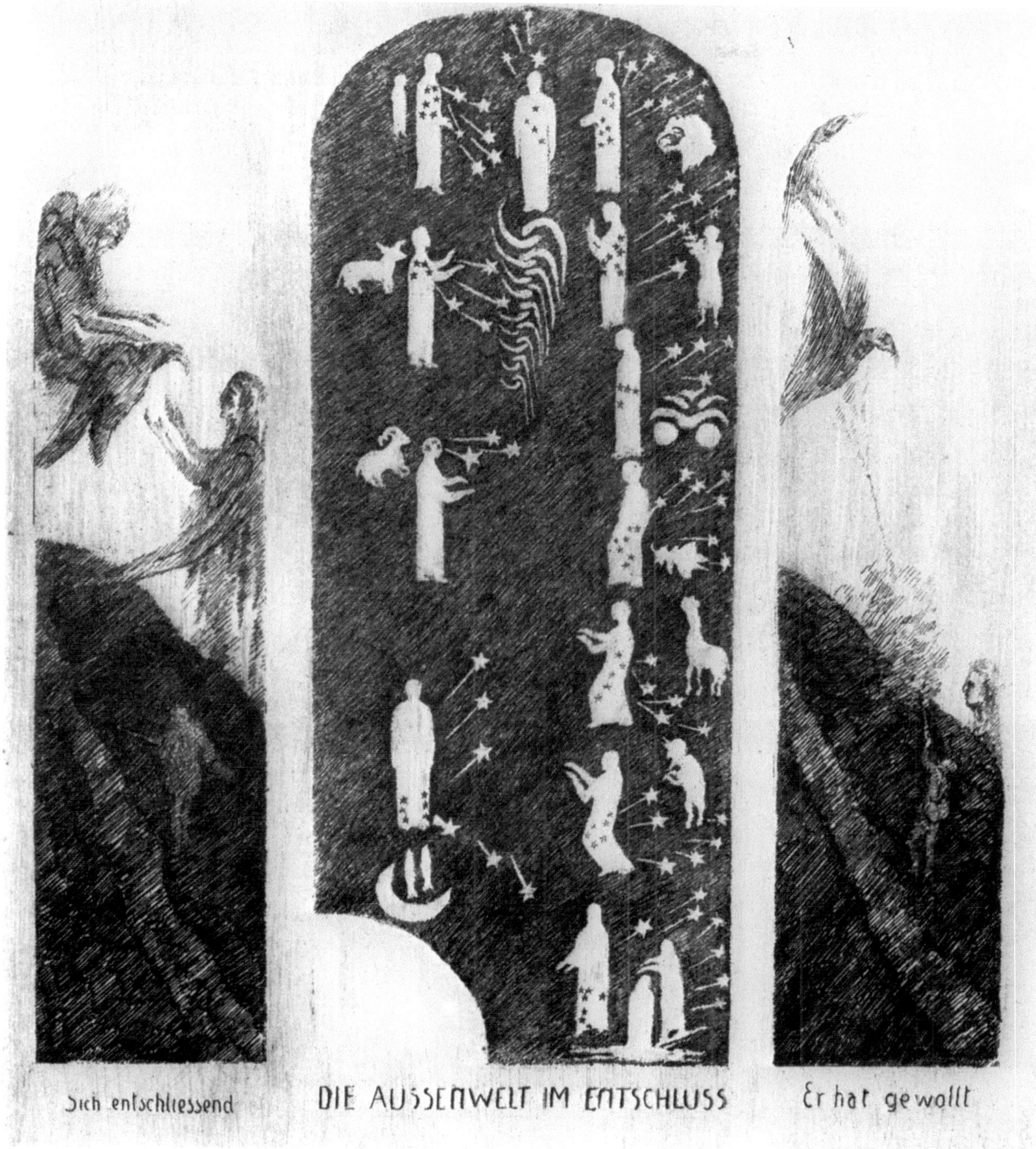

Deciding

The outer world deciding

He has wanted

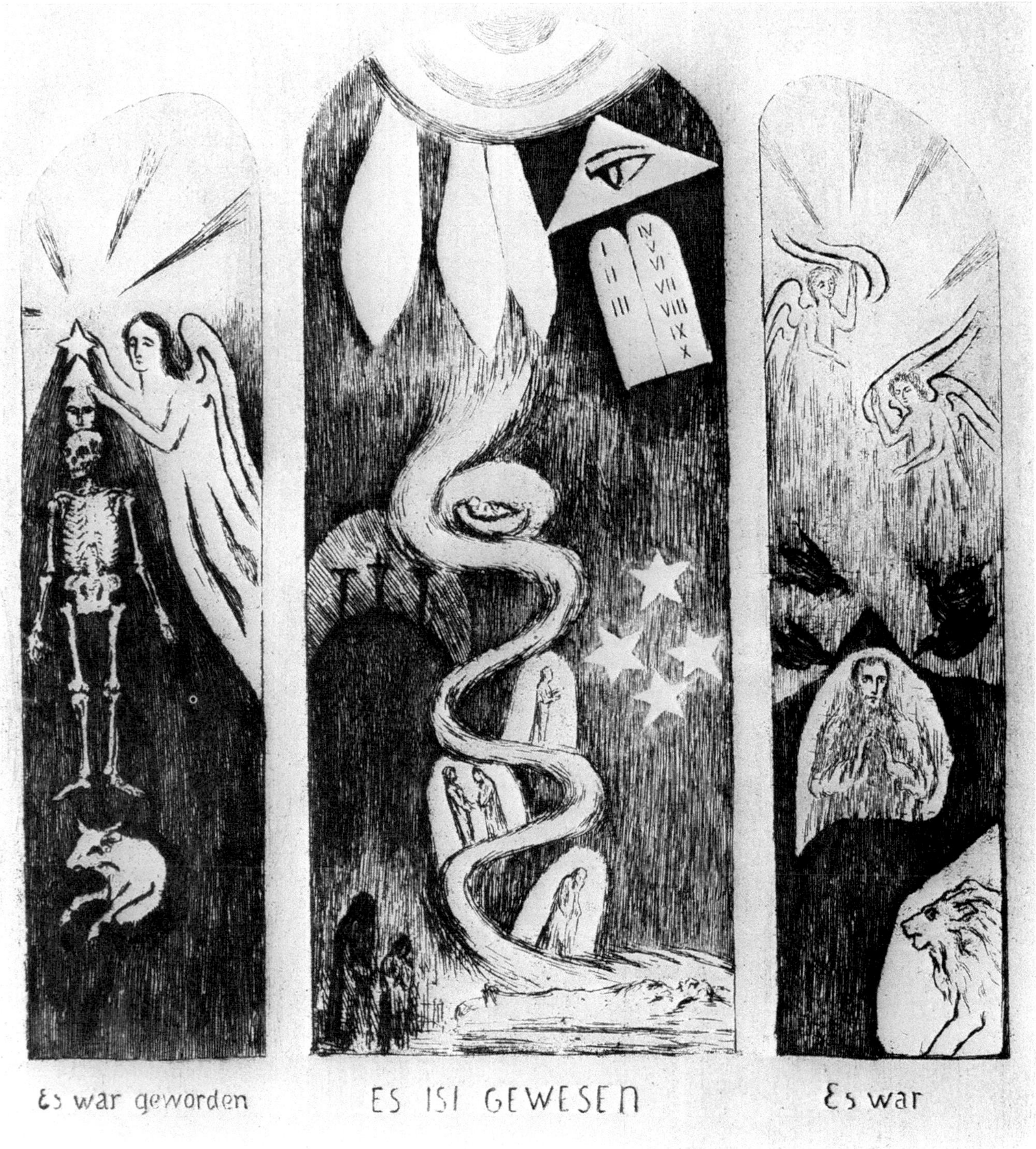

It had become

It has been

It was

The Violet Window in the North

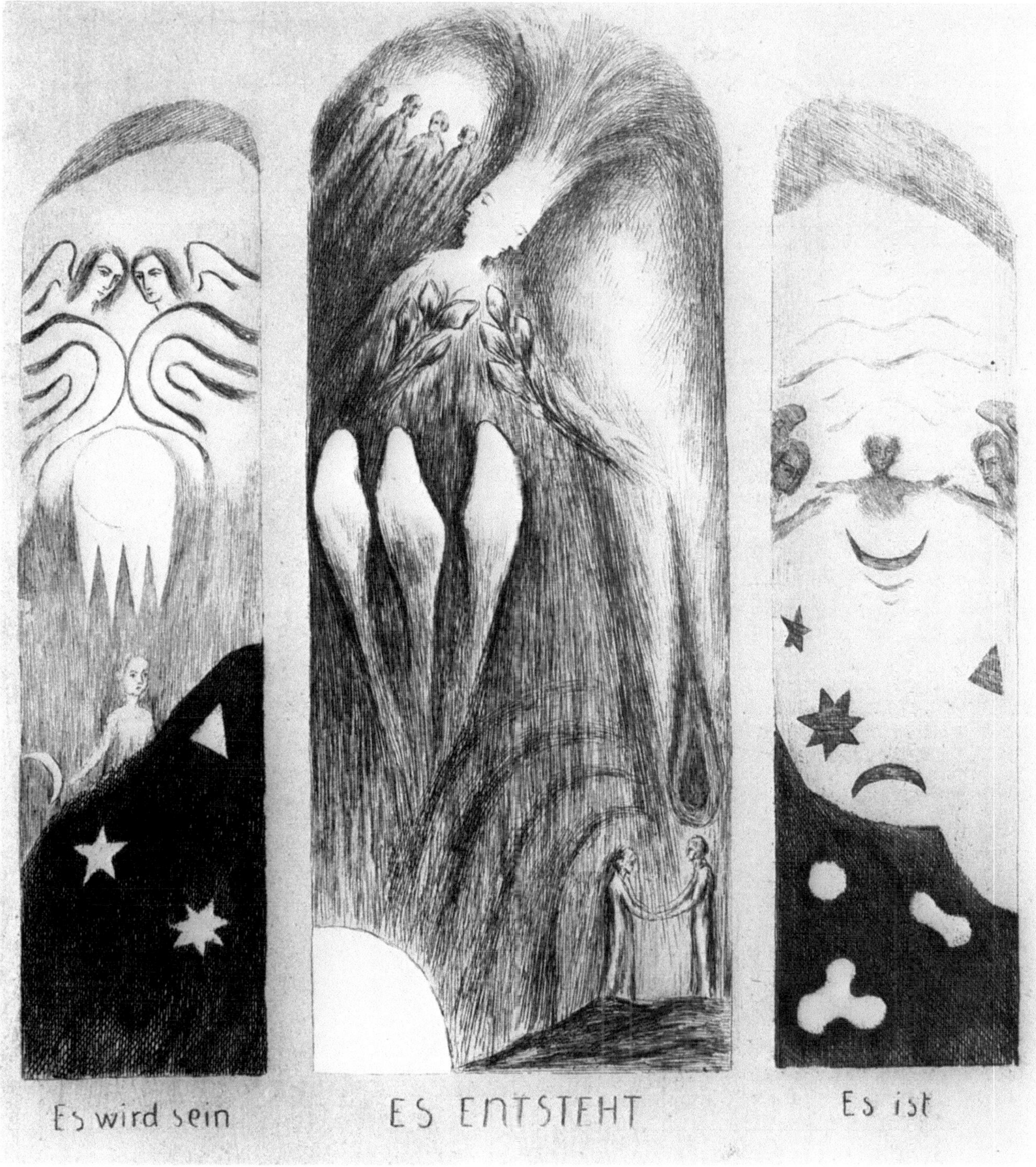

It will be   It arises   It is

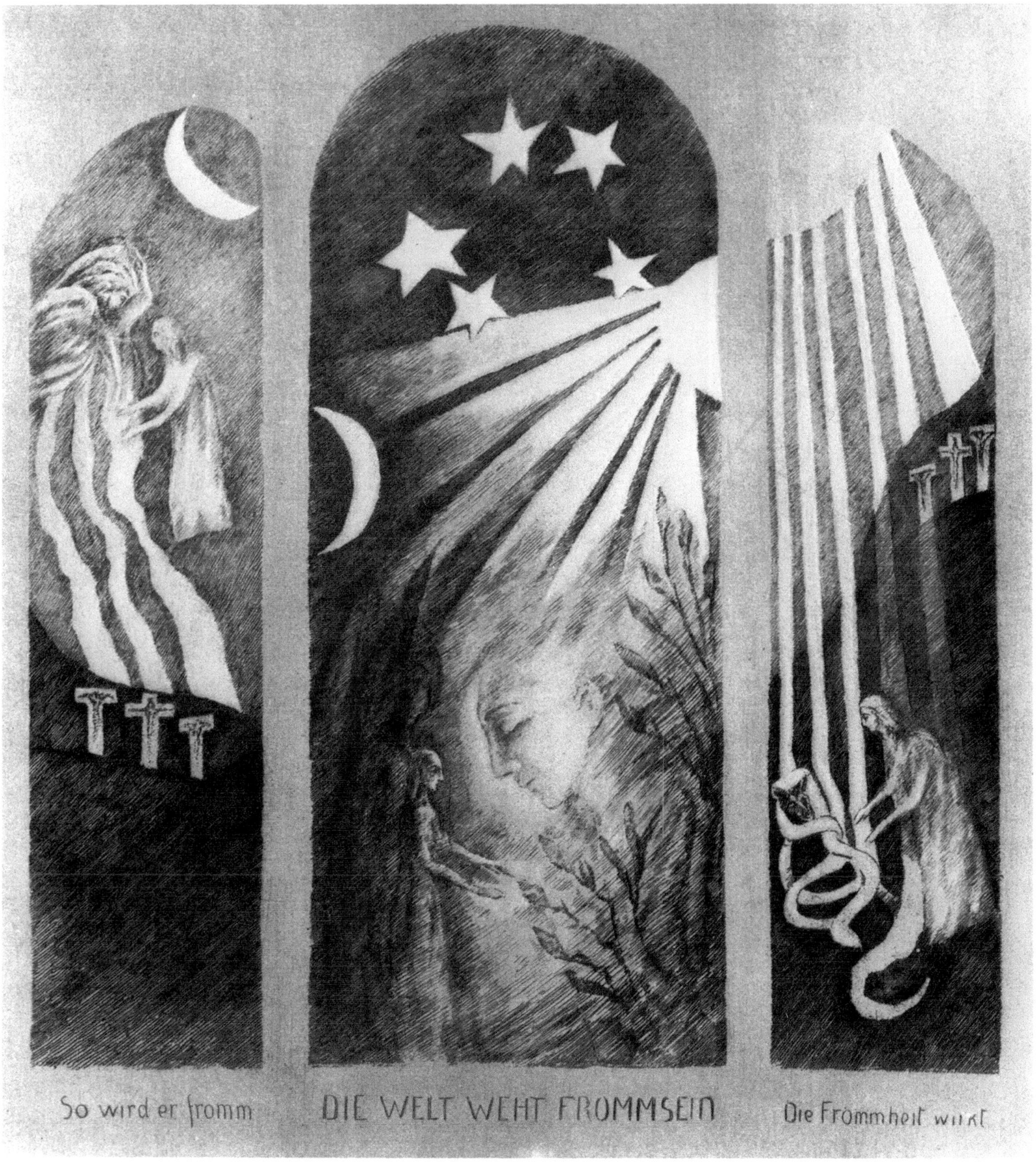

So he becomes reverent

The world wafts reverence

Reverence takes effect

The Peach-Blossom Window in the North

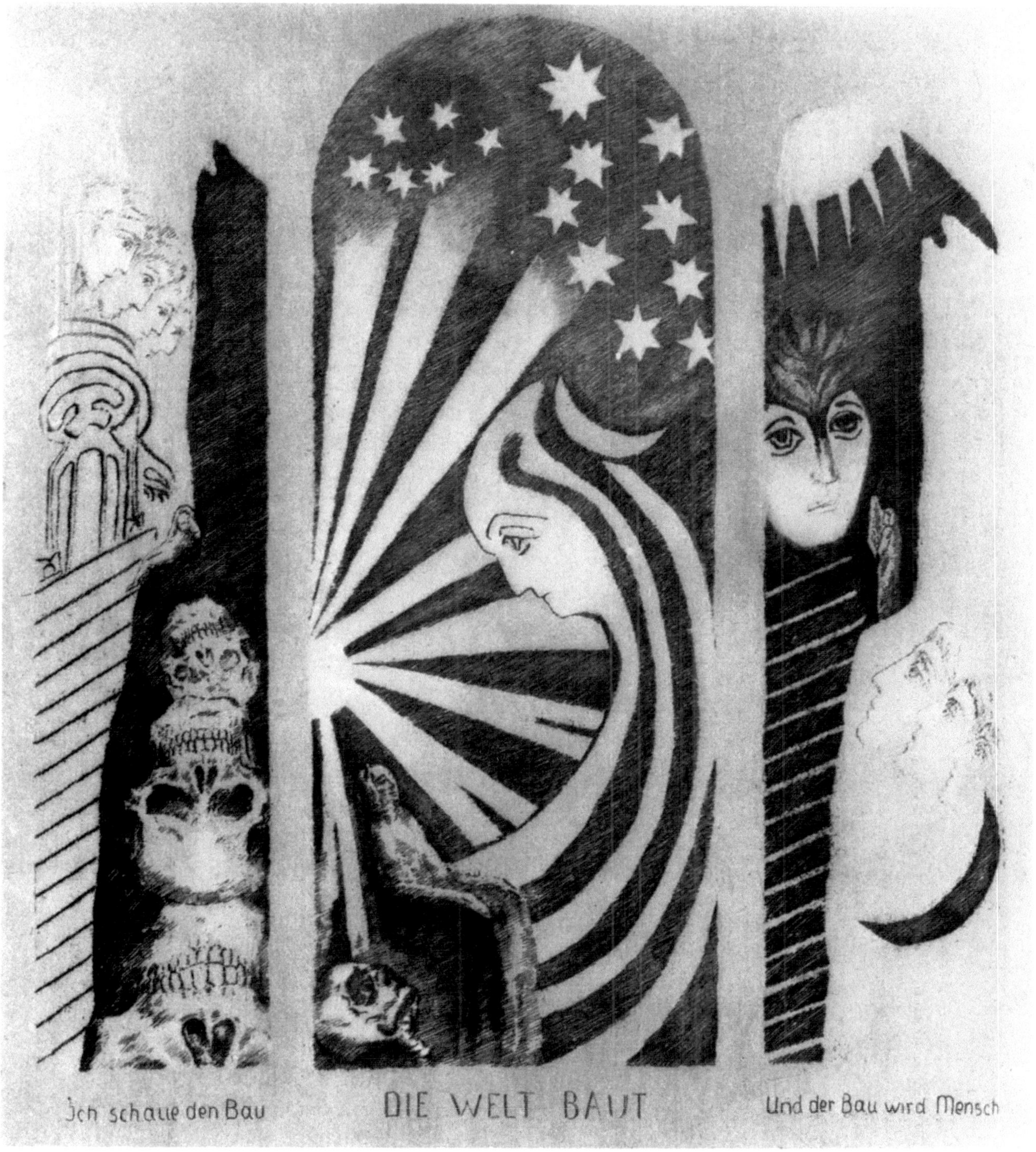

I behold the building

The world builds

And the building becomes man

The Peach-Blossom Window in the South

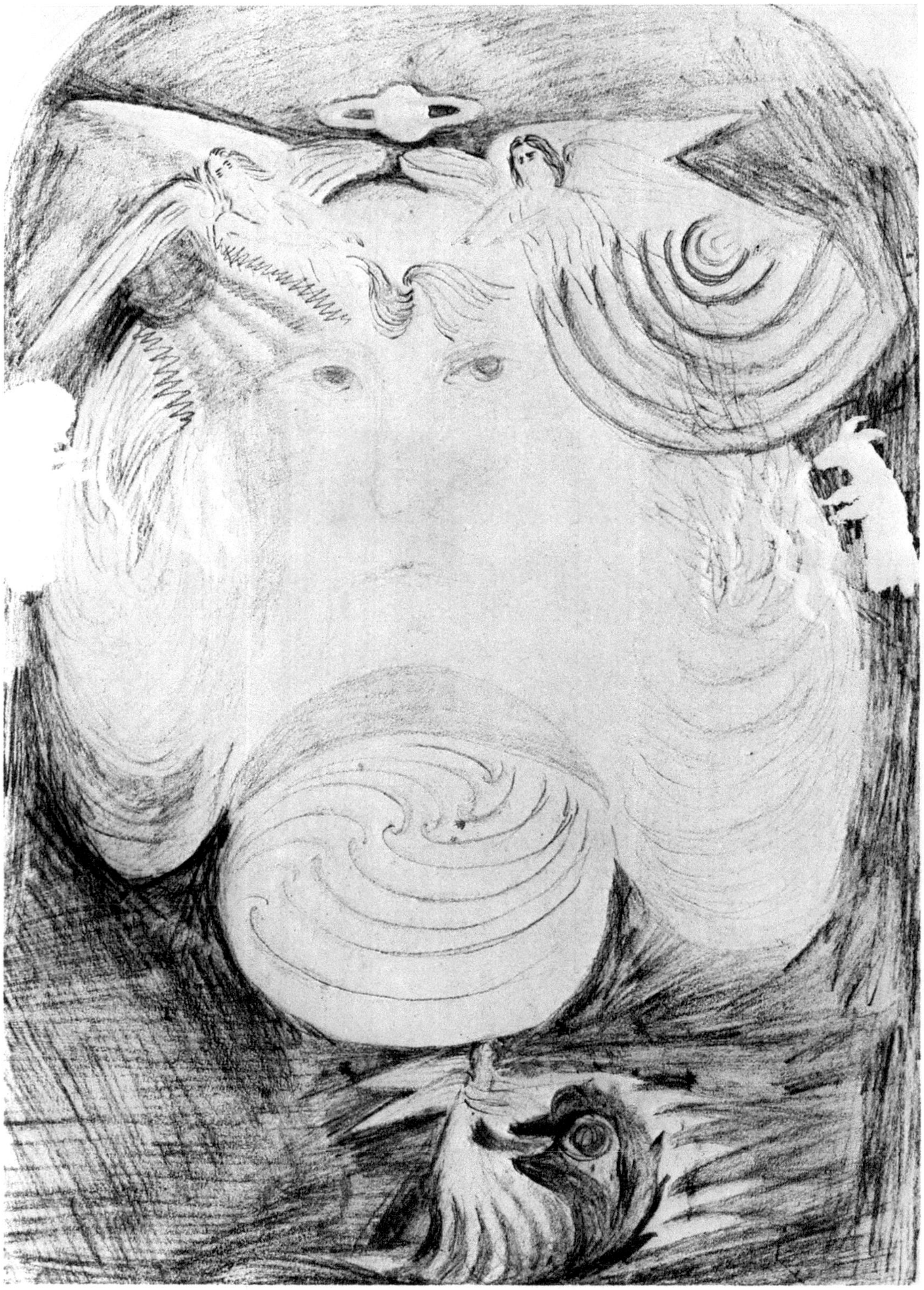

Sketch of the Middle Panel of the Red Window

THE WINDOW MOTIFS

The Red Window in the West

From the center of this threefold picture, a great countenance shines forth out of the red contemplating the divine revelation. The ringed planet is lofty and distant, as though sending its influence from the far-off past. From the sun proceed rays, from the moon wave-like movements. Angels, with broad pinions, waken the power of vision in the triad of Saturn, sun and moon. Beneath the weaving of sun and moon are the lion and bull, whispering the secrets of the universe to the soul in streaming light and pulsing sound.

"Into the ear of man, to the left and right, the secrets of the universe are actually being whispered. Thus we can say, the bull is speaking into his left ear, the lion into his right ear. If we want to represent something like this as a motif and (put it) into words, we can give no more content to our words than is in the picture already. Thus when we take in such a picture, we see there is nothing one-sided about it: lion to the right, bull to the left. It must certainly be clear to us that we only understand such a picture, if we are living inside the world-view from which it proceeds. If a person does not stand within a living Christian experience, he will not be able to respond with understanding when confronted by such a symbolic statement. The artist experiences a great deal when he lives his way into such a vision. But such an experience may not be passed on as abstract thought; otherwise, it begins at once to fade." (August 28, 1921)

We see a spiralling form on the forehead and a second form, covering a broader expanse, in the region of the larynx. What in ancient art took its form out of a dynamic geometry – say in the volutes of a Greek column or in the sixteen-petalled rose-window of a cathedral – this works here as a pure, etherically breathing shape, as a spiritual organ. "The larynx (here reveals) clearly the organ for etheric formative forces." (August 28, 1921)

In the lower darkness, the bright figure of Michael battles the dark dragon. He fights without casting his eyes upon him. Were he to behold him, it would imply recognition, and this would already be too much. The rhythmic arrangement of light and darkness on the surface of the plane accords with the movement of the "formative organ for the etheric".

On the left-hand panel, a bright human figure is descending into a mountain ravine, out of whose depths rise three grotesque shapes. The one to the right has a massive head, with a glassy eye, dangerous protruding teeth and a stunted body; next to it, another figure with a bird's head and a vulture's beak twists upward, serpent-like; the third has a small head, its body succumbing to weight, with a feeble indication of wings. When Rudolf Steiner was asked whether we could assume these shapes to be distortions of thinking, feeling and willing, he brushed this aside with the remark, "See that you make no abstract scheme of this; otherwise, you block your access to these things. These creatures are realities, not abstract thoughts."[4]

In the panel to the right, the grotesquely distorted bestial shapes are sinking into the abyss, while angels waft the human soul to the mountain peak and to the sun whose light is streaming over the whole.

As an approach to his artistic work method, it is interesting to study the sketches Rudolf Steiner made prior to the execution of this window: a pencil drawing (picture opposite), and probably preceding this a sketch with white india ink on a blue background (see p. 226) which reflects still more directly the process of vision in connection with forces from Saturn, sun, and moon.[5]

In executing the copper etchings of the window motifs, Assja Turgeniev had the benefit of the personal advice of Rudolf Steiner. She writes concerning these sketches, "Dashed off, almost childishly inept, and yet, the closer one studied them, the more grand and unapproachable they became, and the more one became aware of one's own inadequacy in facing these sketches. After many years, when working on the windows for the second Goetheanum, I was forced to experience still more concretely how I could discover something new in a sketch day after day for months. I had to review my work continually, without being able to come nearer to the original."[6]

Two pen drawings portray the distorted bestial shapes and indicate the angelic beings who guide the human being to the summit and to the sun.

When Assya Turgeniev lay the sequence of etchings before Rudolf Steiner, he wrote beneath each sheet a threefold mantric text, which was then incorporated into the etchings.[7] These are the same texts that were already noted on Steiner's motif-sketches, doubtless of an earlier date.

The Green Window in the North

Center: A man seated on a pinnacle of rock, enveloped by flashes of lightning. Opposite him Ahriman, grand in expression as a hierarchic being. Beneath him, as though withering, fading, the resounding planets: Saturn, Jupiter, Mars, sun, Venus, Mercury, moon, earth.

Left: Held and upborne from all sides as though harnessed in a universal force-field stands a man, whose arms are stretched out horizontally between sun and moon, controlled from above by the vertical stance of the planets, while screw-like, snail-like beings of will with their pointed wings send up rays from the depths.

Rudolf Steiner wrote next to this sketch:

> "And the spirit of gravity
> gathered all contradiction.
> And this became
> resistance
> in the will of man."

Right: Man turns to the sun. The planets form a gentle, protective bow and bestow their forces without dominating. The ahrimanic beings active on the left pane have withdrawn and no longer influence the human will.

The Green Window in the South

Center: The right side of this pane remains dark. The opposite side is subdivided into a three-tiered space of light, while the sun beams down from above.

In the darkness below, a fire blazes. Arms stretch outward; a face in profile with a crown of flames gazes upward toward the sun.

In the light-space are hierarchical beings, each in his own sphere of light. The lowest repulses the forking flames with a strong gesture; the middle figure creates the balance with a receptive gesture and one of blessing; the upper figure closest to the sun points the way into the heights.

Left: Below, a priest-like figure moves with dignity; above it is a face in profile, with closed eyes as though asleep. Around it is a bright circle of twelve faces that seem to be guiding and protecting it. Light strives upward from below in the form of separated raying planes.

Right: The human contenance has awakened, the eyes are opened wide; he is beholding. The twelve faces appear shadowy, as though quietly withdrawing. In the bright radiance streaming from above stands the Mercury column, to which correspond the 'pillar words': FROM THE I. Impelled and driven by the ego, evolution may now proceed.

Rudolf Steiner wrote on this sketch:

> "And the light
> of spirits
> became the light
> of man."

In the green window to the north speaks Ahriman; to the south is Lucifer and the human being wrapped in luciferic flames.

> "Both of these powers stand before the world
> of soul:
> the one lives as the tempter deep within;
> the other dims the eyes
> when they turn to view the outer world."[8]

This pair of green windows, showing the influence of Ahriman and Lucifer in man, met us first as we entered the hall. They could be experienced as the soul's ordeal, similar to what the Egyptian had to face in the stare of the sphinx before he set foot into the temple.

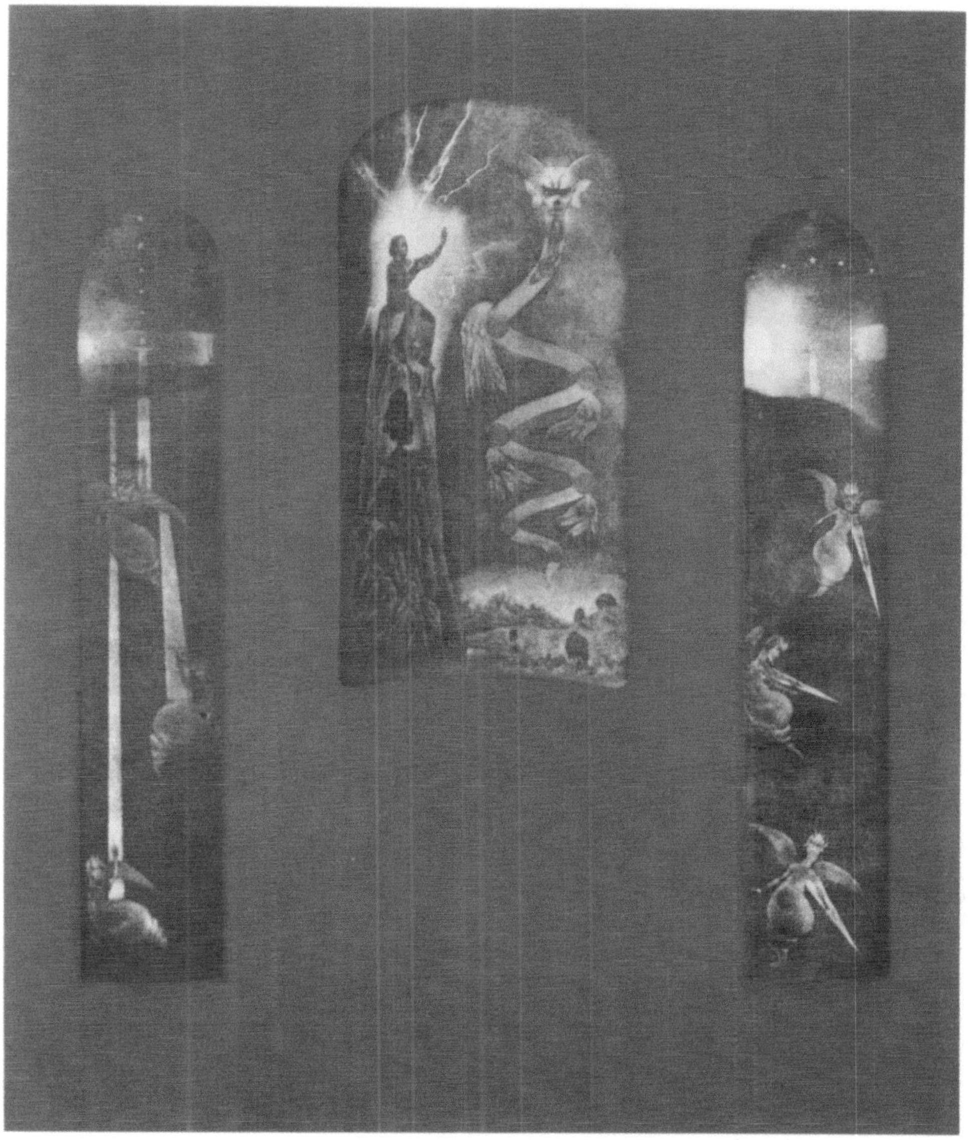

The Green Window in the North (from an old color slide as is the illustration on p. 245)

The Blue Window in the North

In the central pane, a threefold sun sounds forth a rhythmic influence from the heights.
On the pane to the left, the sun streams from above, with a waxing moon below it. The right hand pane shows the waning moon above and underneath it the rising sun, toward which the man has turned himself. This cosmic script establishes the wealth of imaginations that arise here.
Beneath the sun in the central pane, angels blow their trumpets and the spheric harmonies resound. Winged soul beings, born of the light, send out moving streams of light and radiance. The first figure sends its influence to the eagle and lion; light from the second has a stellar quality, directed to the lion and bull; from the third a lunar weaving bears light to the bull and the archetype of man. Farther below, groups of stars arrange themselves around the sun and the moon, whose profile looks to the scene above.
On the left hand pane, angels are bearing great eyes, that is, the power of vision in the outer world, to the man climbing upward in the light. In the pane to the right, angels are bearing forearms to the man striving toward the rising sun, that is, the possibility for action, for touching, for coming to grips with the outer world.
Triangle, pentagon and heptagon below on the left hand pane, have become organic living forms when they reappear on the right.

The Blue Window in the South

The blue window in the south shows twelve human figures, formed and impelled by influences from the stars. Next to them, like hieroglyphs, we see animal forms indicating the zodiac.

The form of man, born out of the cosmos through the mediation of the stars, has been described by Rudolf Steiner in a new way. "Divine-spiritual beings stand opposite one another in the universe. The visual expression of this confrontation is the contour of the starry heavens. Their will it was to create man as the totality of what they are, in a single, unified form. The universal goal of their choir-like collaboration is to bring the human form into being .... The human being is the ideal and goal of divinity."[9]

This picture gives us the task of learning to read the instreaming stellar influences on the human form. The forces in the head are related to Aries; the influence of Taurus is expressed in the larynx and in the sense of words; the symmetry of left and right has to do with Gemini; the encompassing gesture of the rib-cage with Cancer; the heart with Leo; the solar-plexus with Virgo; the capacity for balance with Libra; the sexual organs with Scorpio; the thighs, knees, calves and feet with Sagittarius, Capricorn, Aquarius and Pisces. Cancer is emphasized in this circle of twelve by the nine-times repeated double spiral; Aquarius is distinguished as the sign of the Baptism and Pisces by the sickle moon with a pair of fishes.

The Cancer spirals – an enigmatic sign! It can be compared with the sixteen-leaved spiral in the red window, as well as with the drawing by Imme von Eckardstein in the 1912–13 *Soul Calendar*[10] which brought the midsummer mood of Cancer to light. In the accompanying text, a spiritual 'ventral grating' (*Vordergrat*) is mentioned. When spiritual forces unfold in the course of inner development, this is called 'Vordergrat'. It is a question whether these double spirals, repeated nine times in the vertical, are to be understood in this sense.

Hermannn Beckh relates the sign of Cancer to the words of John the Baptist, "He must wax, but I must wane", the expression of an end and a new beginning. He also indicates that this sign is a picture of the material that carries within it the seed of transformation, from the simplest change to the loftiest and most spiritual transubstantiation.[11]

In Aquarius, he who is to be baptized bows in humility before the one destined to baptize.

The figure attached to Pisces stands upright over the cup of the moon, gazing into the future. A world cycle is completed. "The loss be gain for you," says the final or moon line from the Pisces verse of Rudolf Steiner's *Twelve Moods of the Zodiac.*

The hunting motif appears on the left and right panes – a motif of will in action.

Left: A winged figure with earnest mien holds a bird out to a second winged figure whose arms are outstretched to receive it. In the darkness below steals the hunter with his gun.

Right: The bullet flies and kills. The two winged figures have withdrawn. The thrust of will – for will is in the shot – alters the world. The deed transforms life.

"You find there in the blue window to the left a man who plans to shoot a flying bird. In the right pane, you find that he has pulled the trigger. The bird in the left picture is in a sphere of light. Around the man, you find various figures who live perceptibly in an astral body, at first when he is about to shoot, then after he has shot. This is a reality, albeit one taken from a secular setting."[12] (August 28, 1921)

If will works into the thinking, then thinking takes on life, becomes creative. Thus we see 'thinking' on the sketch for the northern window and 'willing' on the sketch for the south window. The northern window offers an abundance of imaginative motifs taken from the life of the cosmos. The southern window is a revelation of the cosmic twelve-hood and of the will forces active in the hidden depths of man.

The Violet Window in the North

In the center: A man, lying in his coffin and mourned over by his family, is engrossed in the panorama of his past life. He surveys a long and winding path, sees himself successively as an old man, then in the meeting with another ego, then as a youth and finally as a child in the cradle. The path moves past three crosses on the left and four stars on the right. In the heights, one finds the eye of God and the Mosaic tables of the law.

"When the human being has passed through the gates of death and has lived through the period of time in which he can look back on his previous life, has lived through the time up to the point he lays aside his etheric body when he moves on into Kamaloka, then he steps before two figures .... Two figures stand before him after death. One of them is Moses – and a person knows quite well that he stands before Moses – who holds up before him the tablets of the law. In the Middle Ages, this was called

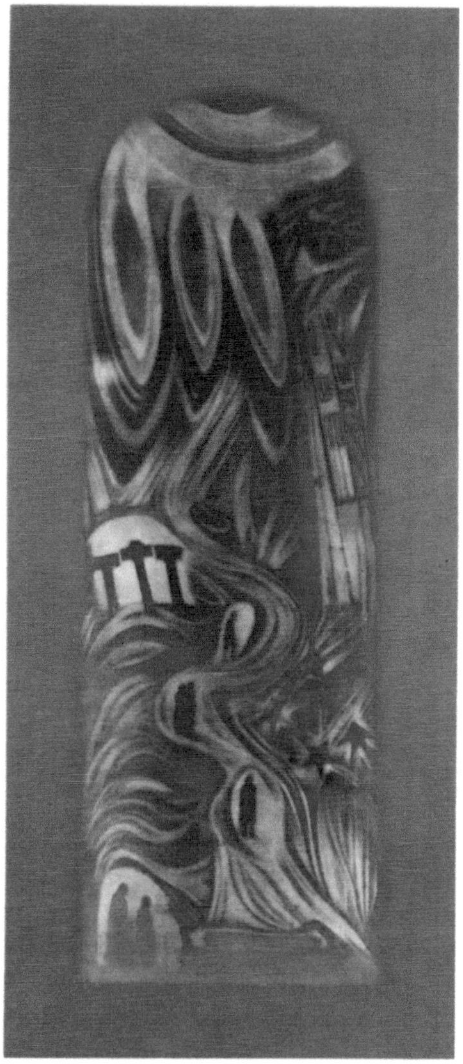

'Moses of the severe law', and a person had in his soul a compelling consciousness of the degree to which he had deviated from the law, even in the most hidden recesses of his soul. This other figure is called 'the cherub with the flaming sword', he judges this deviation .... What a person encounters in these two figures, Moses of the severe law and the cherub with the sword of fire, establishes to a certain degree the karmic account." (December 2, 1911)
Left: Led by its genius or angel, the entelechy in the form of a star abandons the skeleton. The bull, an image for the forces of earth and gravity, is left behind in the depths. The path into the spiritual world may now be entered on, whether during sleep or in the life between death and rebirth.
"I fall asleep. Until I waken, my soul will be in the spiritual world. There it will encounter the essential power who guides my earthly life, a being present in the spiritual world, who hovers above my head. There it will confront its genius. And when I shall awaken, I shall have had this meeting with my genius. The wings of my genius will have beaten upon my soul." (February 20, 1917)
Right: Deep in the earth, surrounded by his own inner light, fed and informed by ravens, a figure reminiscent of Barbarossa wakes. He waits out the time for fresh deeds, which the angels in the light-filled heights point out to him. In the depths, corresponding to the picture of the bull, we see the lion, the beast of sun-like courage, facing the light.

The Violet Window in the South

Center: A Janus head can be seen above, one face turned backward to its companions in the spiritual world, the other gazing downward to the couple who as parents are prepared to receive the soul. Arms with a plant-like gesture lower the seed of individuality from heavenly realms down through a fourfold gateway to the parents on earth.
Left: The sun, enveloped by weaving etheric shapes, sends its beams down upon the child. At his side stands the waxing moon. Angels gaze downward upon the infant soul entering an earthly environment. From below the formative forces shed their crystalline influence as triangle, pentagon and heptagon.
Right: From the moon-sphere, borne by undulating, weaving moonlight, released by the angels, hovers the child, the soul striving toward incarnation. In the earth-darkness the sharp-edged crystalline forms have softened to the seed-shapes of organic life.
The message of the violet window in the north has to do with the experience of death and the anticipation of rebirth. In the southern window, we see the path of the soul from the community of spirit-companions to the parents waiting on the earth.

The Peach-Blossom Window in the North

In the organic sequence of windows, the peach-blossom color of the last two tryptichs is an intensification – from the red of the ante-chamber in the west, through the green, blue and violet of the hall to peach-blossom. In its position due north, this window receives little light in the course of the day or the year. This external fact lends it a veiled, mysterious quality.

The northern peach-blossom window introduces the motif of redemption. In the central pane, the human being is gazed upon by his higher nature out of the vegetative-etheric world. The waxing moon receives the light of the sun, bringing forth and enlivening the plant world. Above them, radiant and large, stand the five planets.

An angel with lifted wings accompanies the soul toward the light, to the sun-spirit, inclining to him from cosmic heights. The tender, intimate encounter takes place in the purity and innocence of the plant world, in the midst of sun-drenched, sprouting life.

In the left pane, the waning moon stands high over Lucifer. Light proceeding from the moon and from the Light-bearer touches the earth where three crosses stand. Leaving the crosses behind him, the spirit-form steps into the lofty cloud-realm of Lucifer. Darkness weaves into the all-too-brilliant light, so that color may arise.

On the pane to the right, the darkness, rising well beyond the middle of the picture, is penetrated by mighty solar forces. Their rays press deep into Ahriman's dark kingdom. The fetters seem still tighter, more tragically knotted than in the painted version. The redeeming Love bends over the one who is exiled to the depths of earth. Ahriman's redemption rays forth from the peach-blossom light.

"The good would not be so great a good, if it could not grow greater through the overcoming of evil. Love would not have such great power were it not forced to become such a force as is able to overcome even the ugliness on the countenance of evil men." (June 25, 1908)

In the Manichaean legend, it is told how the first man is sent down from the realms of light "to mingle with the realm of darkness and through death to overcome what should not be, overcoming it from within.

"The profound thought here is this: the kingdom of darkness shall be overcome by the kingdom of light, not by punishment but by mildness, not by resisting the evil but by mingling with it, in order to redeem evil as such. Insofar as a part of the light has entered into evil, evil itself will be overcome." (November 11, 1904)

"If we bring a comprehension of the Christ, of a new spiritual life, if once again we bring imagination, inspiration and intuition into what has become mere knowledge of the outer world, then we redeem the being of Ahriman." The battle for the spirit is the task of the present fifth post-Atlantean age. The transformation of evil beacons to us as the task and goal of the future sixth age.

The Peach-Blossom Window in the South

Center: A man sits in an austere mediative mood and posture; near him, underneath, is a skull. The sun sends powerful rays through the darkness behind and over him. Are these an imagination of the constructive forces of the sun, active in nature and in human life, as these were revered in the northern mysteries, a prescient vision of the sun at midnight?

The soul is engrossed in inner spirit-perception. Its higher being, earnest yet loving, inclines toward it, enveloping it with streaming light. The head of this being opens into a vessel, like a moon-chalice, that receives the influences from the stars and ushers the soul into their light.

Left: A rock wall towers in the darkness within which we see a heap of skulls. On the steep declivity, a figure rests or sleeps. Vertically striving, harmoniously rounded forms meet and grow together to become the picture of an organic, living building. Countenances woven of light hover over the building, gazing at the sleeper or dreamer, who is given over to the force of gravity.

Right: The rock wall has now grown bright. Faces in profile, light-engendered, gaze up at the wakened man, who has risen out of gravity and holds a lyre in his arm like the bard Orpheus whose music tamed the passions and moved stones to utterance. His glance is directed toward a god-like countenance with great eyes and a radiant forehead from which light is weaving and streaming into the solar regions in the heights.

"You will see in the left pane how something is emerging which is similar to the western entrance to the [first Goetheanum] building. On the pane to the right, you see something like a head. On the left a man is sitting on the edge of a cliff, looking at the building; on the right he is looking toward the head. This has no speculative-mystical significance. This building could not otherwise have arisen, save through the fact that one experienced the human head shape in it in a veiled way. The contours of the building are given to our preception, on the one hand, out of an organic force; on the other hand, out of the form of the human head. Thus the man sitting on the cliff-ledge beholds the building in metamorphosis, here as a human head, there as its outer manifestation. With this – if I may be allowed to say so – a motif is given which merges with an inner experience." (August 28, 1921)

On the original sketches for these side-panel motifs Rudolf Steiner wrote:

"The threshold veils itself.
The threshold manifests itself."

Summary

In the green *south* window, higher beings lovingly point out the sun path to the sufferer in flames. This reveals to the man who is already on his way, to the active striver, the picture of his higher ego, strengthening him to act out of the 'I'.

In the blue *north* window, love sounds through the universe as the mystery of the threefold sun. It brings spheric harmonies to audibility and summons the soul-forces to endow man with the capacities to see and create.

In the violet *south* window, love directs the view into the realms of beginnings and becomings, out of which the child seeks the path to earth, finding there the hearts who will take it in and guide it into earthly existence.

The message of the peach-blossom *north* window is devotion and surrender to the spirit of the sun, which is inclining to the human soul. The loftiest power of love lives in the radiant figure who seeks out the powers of resistance in their own realms in order to redeem them.

Associated with the motif of the green *north* window are weight, contradiction, will, resistance – the words written on the sketch to characterize Ahriman. A man whose will is dependent on sun, moon and planets, who is under the influence of ahrimanic will-beings in the depths, frees himself and turns to the sun by his own resolve.

In the blue *south* window, will speaks a different language. On the two side panes, it is the will of the hunter that changes the world. The words "the outer world in resolve" belong to the central pane. Will becomes shaping power, the moulding of the human form out of universal forces.

In the violet *north* window, the shaping activity has come to an end; the body is laid aside. Now the inexorable tablets of the law come into their own. The deceased surveys his life back to the cradle. He abandons the dead form as a star and anticipates a future life.

From the peach-blossom light of the final southern window, a sense for the midnight sun of the will awakens in the meditant. He beholds the sickle moon as a holy vessel bearing light from the stars.

The man reclining at the edge of the dark cliff senses the forces striving for a new architecture. Lifting himself out of gravity, taking the lyre in hand, whose ordering spheric tones transform death into etheric life, he beholds the fashioning and creating forces as a divine countenance. "And the building becomes man."

THE WINDOWS IN RELATION TO THE PAINTED MOTIFS IN THE SMALLER CUPOLA

The axis of the Goetheanum runs from the red window in the west to the central motif in the east. The battle of Michael with the dragon frees the way to the One who bestows forces with which we may stand firm in our battle with opposing powers. The building's axis is the path from Michael to Christ.

"If with most inward, heart-warmed feeling we can penetrate into what Michael and his host signify, what their deeds and their mission among us consist of, then we shall arrive at this: that our human bond with divine-spiritual beings remains intact as it was in the beginning. Then we may understand how to cultivate the language of the Christ concerning the cosmos. For to understand Michael in our time means to find the way to the Logos, which lived as the Christ among men on earth.

Michael-Christ will be the word that gives us our bearings in future, as we set out between the luciferic and ahrimanic powers on a path that is true to the cosmic plan and on which we may arrive at our earthly goal."[13]

The path from Michael to Christ in the first Goetheanum was accompanied by an interplay between window motifs and the motifs painted over the pillars of the smaller cupola. The question arises: Is it possible to find a relation, an inner connection, between them? Carl Kemper is surely the first to pursue this thought. A drawing of the building's ground-plan shows diagonal lines drawn from the pillars of the smaller cupola to the windows in the large cupola. Following the hint, we actually come upon relationships that are not derived simply from the artistic concept of the whole. (For the color indications on the north side of the cupola, we refer to the study of complementaries of page 187.)

The Slavic Man (south side)
The Green Window (in the north)

The Slav – painted in peach-blossom on a yellow ground and framed by the blue of the angel and the red of the centaur – gains the capacity to overcome his double nature through the cross which is garlanded with stars. His mission is yet to unfold in the future; he seems therefore to provide an answer to the question raised by the window motif; namely, how does a man wrest himself free from determination by the universe and the ahrimanic beings of will? The answer is given insofar as the Slav, through the power and proximity of the central figure, is bearing roses into the future, transformed into stars.

The Slavic Man (north side)
The Green Window (in the south)

In the attempt to find a complementing counter-color, a more contained color appears on the north side. The pious, inward mood of the pale violet background is united with the gold-orange of the cross and its light green stars. Out of this mood, we can derive its relationship to the window motif. "The love of the world takes effect." The mysterious twelvehood of the faces wakens and accompanies the ego of man. Again, the Slavic man acts "out of the I" under the transmuted sign of death, now a vessel of light. A path toward the redemption of Lucifer is thus indicated.

The Persian-Germanic Initiate (south side)
The Blue Window (in the north)

The blue window in the north speaks of the threefold sun calling spheric harmonies forth into audibility. It was Zarathustra who indicated the spiritual activity of the sun, its "resonant influence on life", and he taught the polarity of light and darkness. This opposition determines the dramatic collision of brown-black and red in the Lucifer and Ahriman of the Persian-Germanic motif. Amidst this contention, the human being bears the child, to whom belongs the light of the future.

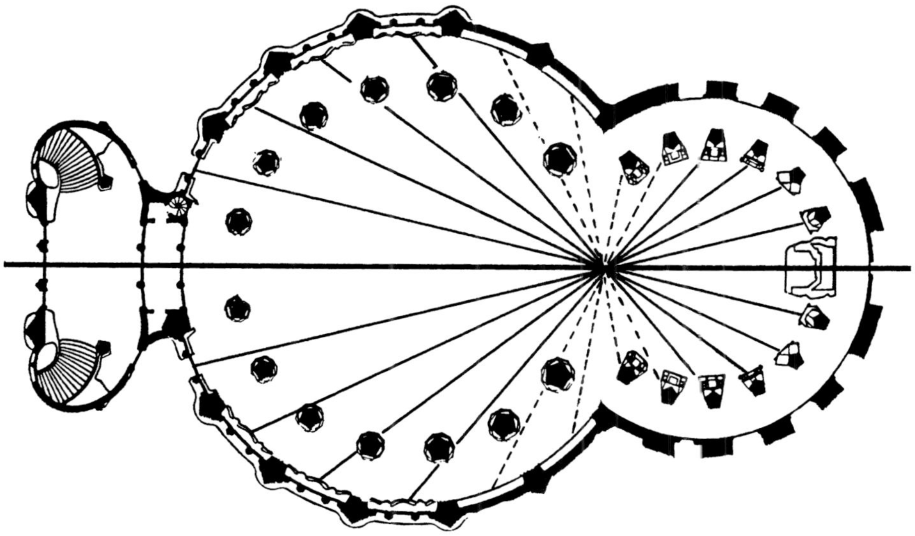

The Persian-Germanic Initiate (north side)
The Blue Window (in the south)

The meeting between Ahriman and Lucifer on the north side is characterized in subdued colors: violet-blue-green confronts blue-black-grey. The Zarathustra-initiate can endure this encounter not only through the forces of the child (the colors pale-violet and peach-blossom dominate), but also through the wider cosmic relation to the zodiac depicted on the blue window. The progression through time of the Spirit of Light, according to Zarathustra, was "the expression of the spiritual activity of Ormuzd"[14] the path of Ormuzd through *Zaruana akarana* or the zodiac. Here the cosmic path of the sun is given a Christian turn. The hunting motif, picturing a willful intrusion into the outer world, also points to Zarathustra.

The Egyptian Initiate (south side)
The Violet Window (in the north)

According to the Egyptian view, an initiate is on the way to becoming a 'son of Osiris' or even an 'Osiris'. He strives to stand before his 'father' who can be reached only beyond the threshold of death or of initiation. In death or in initiation, he arrives at a survey back over his life, as pictured in the Egyptian *Book of the Dead.* This motif leads over to the northern window, where the deceased man is being mourned by his family, and the stages of the life behind him are indicated by a winding path.

The Egyptian Initiate (north side)
The Violet Window (in the south)

This window illuminates the mystery of birth. The child's path out of heavenly spheres onto the earth reminds us of the story of Horus, the divine child, who was also acquainted with the sphere of the moon, from which (in the right pane) the child is approaching the earth. The rays (in the left pane), guiding the child downward from a sun-orb swathed in etheric forces, is reminiscent of Egyptian representations of the sun.

Athena-Apollo (south side)
Peach-Blossom Window (in the north)

Here it is the colors that establish a connection between the motifs. Apollo, the radiant sun-god, bestower of the forces of light and form, appears in glowing gold, surrounded by a reddish-carmine that condenses to carmine-violet above. This harmonizes with the picture of the sun-spirit inclining from the heights, shown in peach-blossom in the north window.

Athena-Apollo (north side)
Peach-Blossom Window (in the south)

Now in its related complementary color, the northern relation of Apollo has become more earnest, severe. His mission lies in the music bestowed on Greek culture through Orpheus. This we can perceive in the upright figure holding a lyre on his arm in the right-hand pane. The stones, set into resonant motion by his song, now form the temple according to musical law.[15]

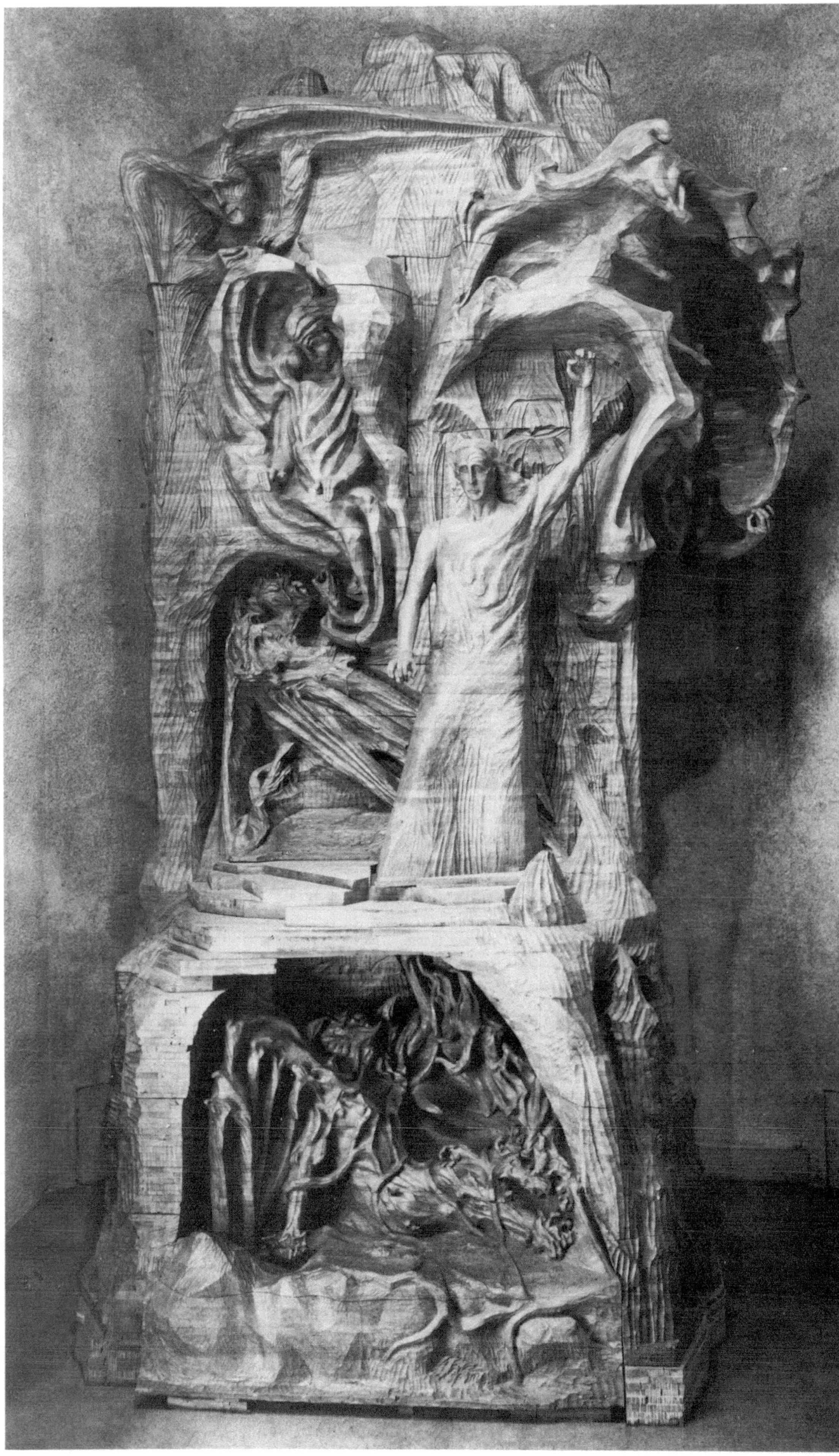

THE CENTRAL MOTIF IN THE CARVED STATUE

The massive wooden 'Group' sculpture was to have stood in the small cupola of the first Goetheanum between two pillars of ashwood, on which would have rested the architrave, also of ash. Above this was the painted figure of the Risen One. As the statue was still in Rudolf Steiner's workshop-atelier, it was preserved from the holocaust on the Sylvester evening of 1922–23. Since 1932 it has been on view in a room specially built for it in the second Goetheanum.

The statue's dimensions and grandeur speak directly to the beholder. His eye moves over many form elements: the boldly soaring, the tragically collapsing and the harmoniously balancing. Rounding, swelling, expanding shapes stream about a countenance that breathes and relishes its own beauty. This is Lucifer, the light-bringer. Below him, the forms take on quite another character: wings sharply folded, a craggy profile with receding forehead, features distorted by the pain of a hard, icy intellect. This is Ahriman, the lord of the powers of death. The figure between, moving with upright step and quiet inner force, with its left arm uplifted, its right directed to the depths, reveals in this gesture a bridge between heaven and earth "in a god-imbued inner reconciliation of being."

Above the raised arm of this figure, we see a toppling Lucifer, tragic beyond words. Broken are the mighty pinions formed for proud flight, cramped the hands, with an expression of terror, of deadly fear and despair as he plunges to the depths. Below in his cavern is Ahriman with his strange bat-like wings, seeking to raise himself but in vain, trying to burrow into the earth, to brace himself, yet forging the while his own fetters. His cramped, sclerotic hand, no longer able to grasp anything, is heartrending.

"In his passage through time, he wants to vanquish space; he is wrapped in darkness, into which he sends the beams of his own light. The more he is able to realize his own ends, the deeper the frost grows about him. He is a world unto himself, withdrawn into his own being, affirming himself only by denying the world. He moves as if uncanny forces from unlit hollows in the earth accompanied him.[16]

"The Christ, however, stands in the midst, as the one who introduces the Parsifal element into modern times, who causes others to overcome themselves not through power, but through his very existence: he does not overcome them but they overcome themselves." (May 18, 1915)

This sculpture serves as a new, comprehensive proclamation of the Christ, as does the painting. Here, too, Rudolf Steiner intended, as he so often said with emphasis, to find a spiritually "correct" expression for the figure of the Christ.

"The essential thing is to experience what lies in this figure as such. It will then be a matter of course for you to find your way from what is artistic in this figure to the Christ Himself. In other words, if you can sense what lies in this figure, you can discover the Christ as the Being at the center of all earth-evolution. The Christ can be discovered today as a purely spiritual experience." (January 25, 1920)

Much that is helpful for an understanding of this work can be gained by a study of the successive models,[17] and furthermore, they grant insights into the working methods of Rudolf Steiner and Edith Maryon, the English sculptress who collaborated with him from the beginning.[18]

The first of Rudolf Steiner's models, about a foot high,

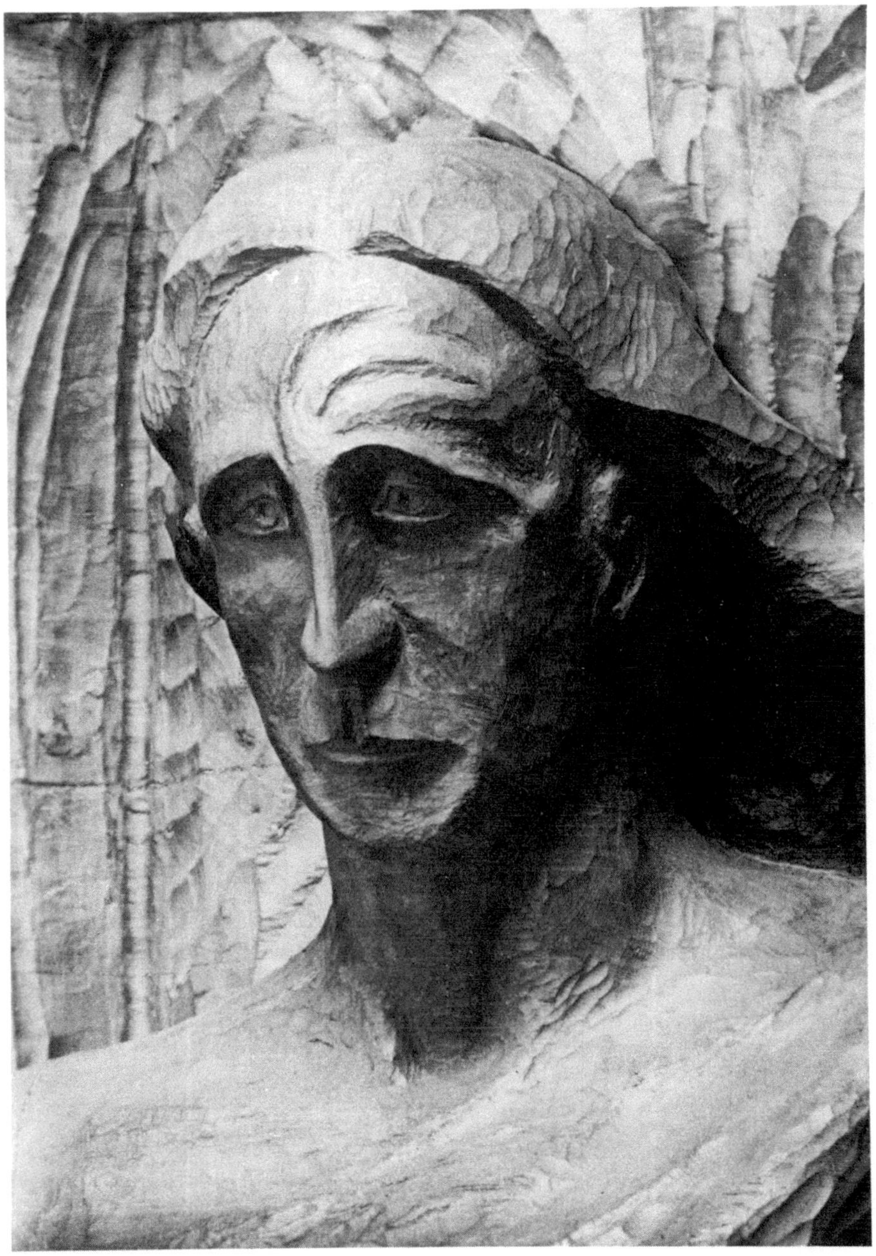

Head in the Wood Sculpture

came about in the autumn of 1914. It contained already the tension between the central figure, a toppling Lucifer, and Ahriman in his cavern. It reveals a power that works directly as mystery art. One could think of Cycladean idols, although the immediacy of early Greek art does not affect us in the way it would if it belonged to our time. Rudolf Steiner attempted to develop these forms further in studies of the individual figures. Hermann Ranzenberger reports concerning the origin of a model of the Ahriman head, "In those winter days of 1915, when Rudolf Steiner was occupied with work on this 'Group', he one morning brought with him a small object wrapped in cloth as he came from his house and passed the Goetheanum building on his way to the sculpture studio. Meeting the writer right in front of the Goetheanum, he spontaneously held this object out to him, removed its covering and, pointing to the wax model of a head, said without even taking the time to wish the writer good morning, 'Look now, this comes completely from the soul, completely from the soul', repeating several times, 'completely from the soul'. It was a study for the head of Ahriman!

Rudolf Steiner had doubtless modelled this study during the night, or at least shortly before, for something of the magic of a freshly conceived sketch hung over it. One might be permitted to say, you sensed his joy at this successful work of art – outwardly so small but tremendous in import."[19]

Here, too, it was a matter of a representation that was spiritually "correct". This went so far that later on, as he modelled the full scale head, he spoke of Ahriman 'sitting as model'. "This is spiritually true, 'according to the model', true to nature artistically. Ahriman had to 'sit' for me." (July 3, 1918)

By Easter 1915, a two-meter-high model of the whole composition was ready. In order to carry out the carving of the 28-foot statue itself, it was necessary to build an atelier with corresponding dimensions. The individual figures were now modelled in their full size. These models, still in existence today, are expressive to the strongest possible degree: Lucifer in his beauty and tragedy and the fettered Ahriman, he who forged his own fetters. The central figure impressed the painters most deeply. (cf. p. 31)[20]

In the course of the work on the 'Group', it was noticed that a balance had not been achieved. To the left and above something seemed to be missing. To arrive at balance, a rock-like shape was added, from which a winged face with asymmetrical features emerged. "It was not just a matter of adding a clump of rock, but of following the sculptural thought a step farther. Thus arose this elemental being, to a certain extent growing out of the rock." (July 3, 1918) "... This being up there, we have been so bold as to portray quite asymmetrically, since it appears in a place where a symmetrical form would contradict the whole composition." (August 20, 1920)

The single figures are not 'shoved together' as is often the case with multiple-figured sculptures, even those of artistic merit. The entire group is elicited from the play of forces within a given relationship.

What is new in this composition derives from the fact that the forces of Lucifer and Ahriman appear in man, become visible exerting their diverse influences on man and are then brought into balance within him. It had been planned to carve the 'Group' in variously colored woods, but these, because of the war, were not obtainable. The extensive carving was therefore done wholly in warm, sturdy elmwood. "To incorporate a story, an action, an event in any other substance than wood would have been impossible. ... It seems to be a fact that all *antique* motifs can be brought to expression better in stone or metal, whereas all *Christian* motifs – and our motif is Christian in the most eminent sense – are better in wood." (August 3, 1918)

"Naturally, what has been created here is imperfect. But it is so, that every beginning must be imperfect. ... For me it is a fact that the Christ who wandered through Palestine wore the features you see on the wooden figure." (January 25, 1920)

When questioned by Friedrich Rittelmeyer, who was often in the atelier, Rudolf Steiner gave further hints about the appearance of the historic Christ. " 'Is it really possible that simply by meditating on the words of Christ one is able to say something about the appearance of the Christ?' 'How do you think he looked, then?' was the quiet reply. ... 'I find the type anything but Semitic, Doctor,' I said. 'Yet,' came the answer, 'the parts around the mouth and chin are Semitic; it is the upper part that is Aryan.' 'Then it is true what Chamberlain and others claim, that there are Aryan elements in the Christ?' 'Certainly, both are there.' What Steiner explained in lectures, that in the distant past two streams of humanity had been sent out, the one within the more Aryan peoples (who were to seek the divine mainly as revealed in the external world), the other in the more southerly, Semitic tribes (oriented to the divine revelation within), and eventually both streams were joined in Christianity, is reflected impressively in this head."[21]

The eurythmist Asta Blumfeld told this from personal

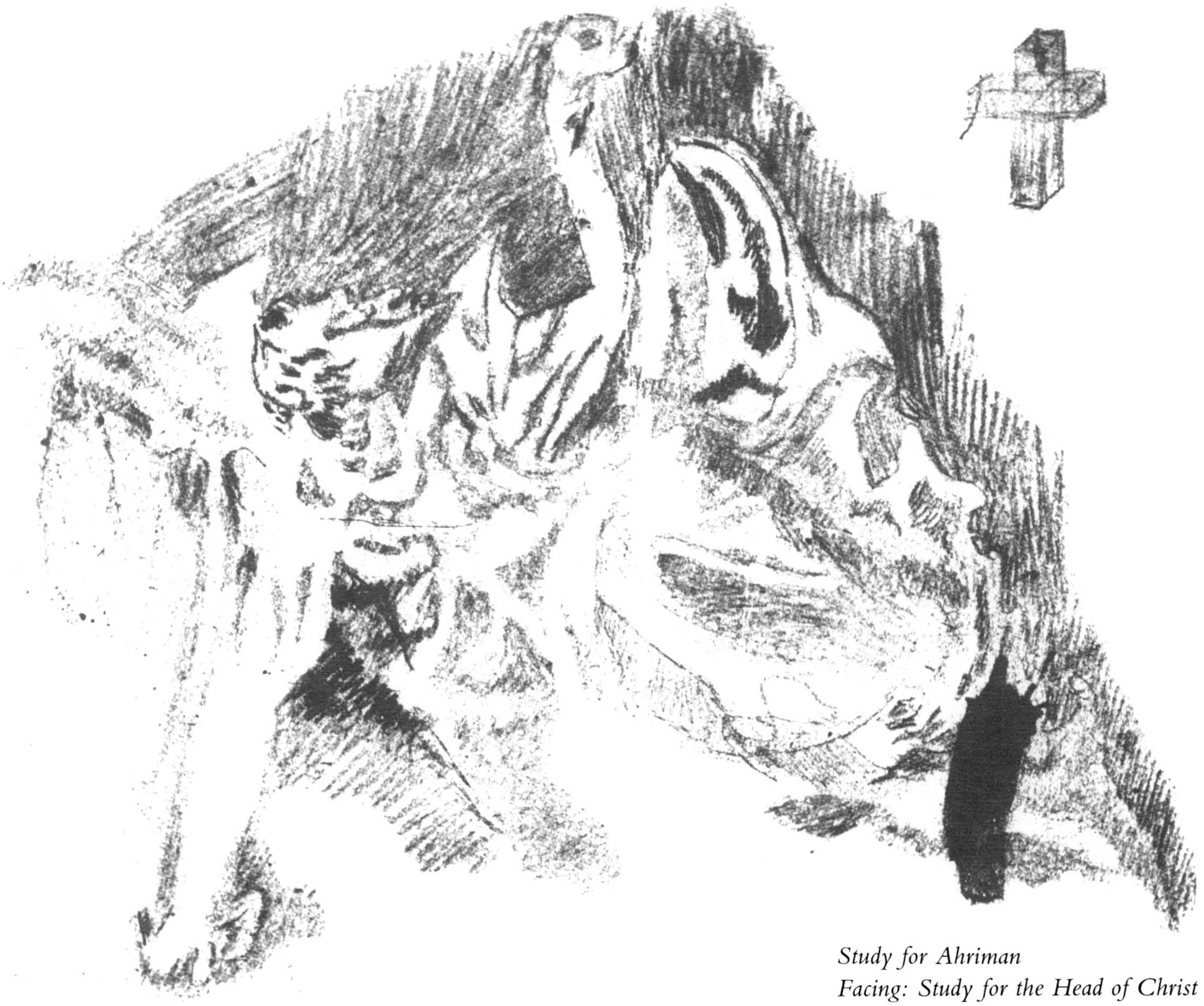

Study for Ahriman
Facing: Study for the Head of Christ

experience. "We came into the atelier where the Christ statue stood. The middle figure was already, as far as concerns the head, just as it is to be seen today. I can still hear Rudolf Steiner, after saying some things I regret I cannot recall, answer a question. I can still hear his penetrating, resonant but quiet voice, which notwithstanding struck me to the core, 'Yes, he really looked like this.' And then repeating, 'He really looked like this'."[22]

"If one were to try some time, after long absorption in the spiritual-scientific idea of the Christ, to bring it into a picture, one would come to a figure in which one would recognize something in the face toward which all of art could exert itself, yes, must and will exert itself. Something in this countenance, solely in the face, will speak of the victory of forces over all other forces of the human form. If men were able to fashion an eye that lived and streamed out pure compassion; a mouth not designed for eating but for uttering true words that express conscience residing in the human tongue; if a forehead could be fashioned, not lofty and fair but beautiful in bringing to clear expression what is contracted in front to that which we call the 'lotus flower' between the eyes – once all this were fashioned, we would discover why the prophet says, 'He is without form and fairness.'

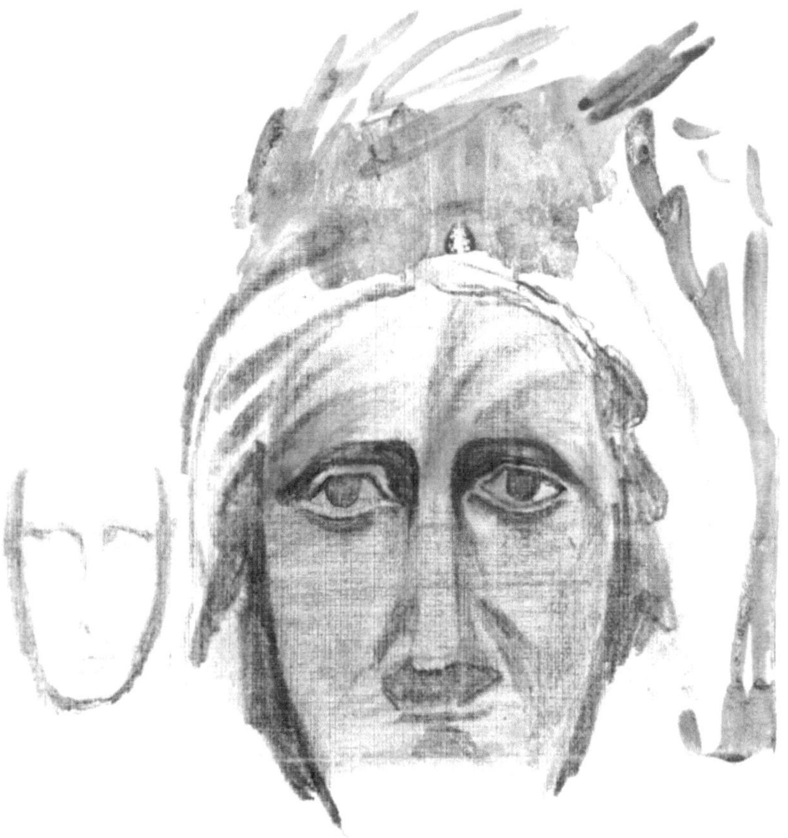

This does not mean beauty, but rather that which will triumph over decay: the figure of Christ, where all is compassion, all is love, all is submission to conscience." (May 8, 1912)

The Christ figure was never completed. Rudolf Steiner was working on it up to the last phase of his life. The experience that wakens in the soul when beholding the central figure and its facial expression – "Not I, but the Christ in me" – leads us on to grasp the pronouncement that the Christ is to become the Lord of Karma, as is pictured in the lectures on the Gospel of St. John.

"The Christ says, 'The deepest secret of my being is the *I AM*.' The true, eternal power of the *I AM*, or of the I that has power to penetrate the other members, must flow into man. It lives within the earth-spirit. Let us hold this before us in full earnestness, in complete earnestness, that the Christ-will is to mediate the true possession of the 'I' for every man, to waken the God in every man, to kindle step by step the Lord and King in every man. What follows? No less a fact than that the Christ expresses in the highest sense the idea of karma, the law of karma. Then at last will we understand the karma idea fully; then will we understand it in this Christian sense." (May 26, 1908)

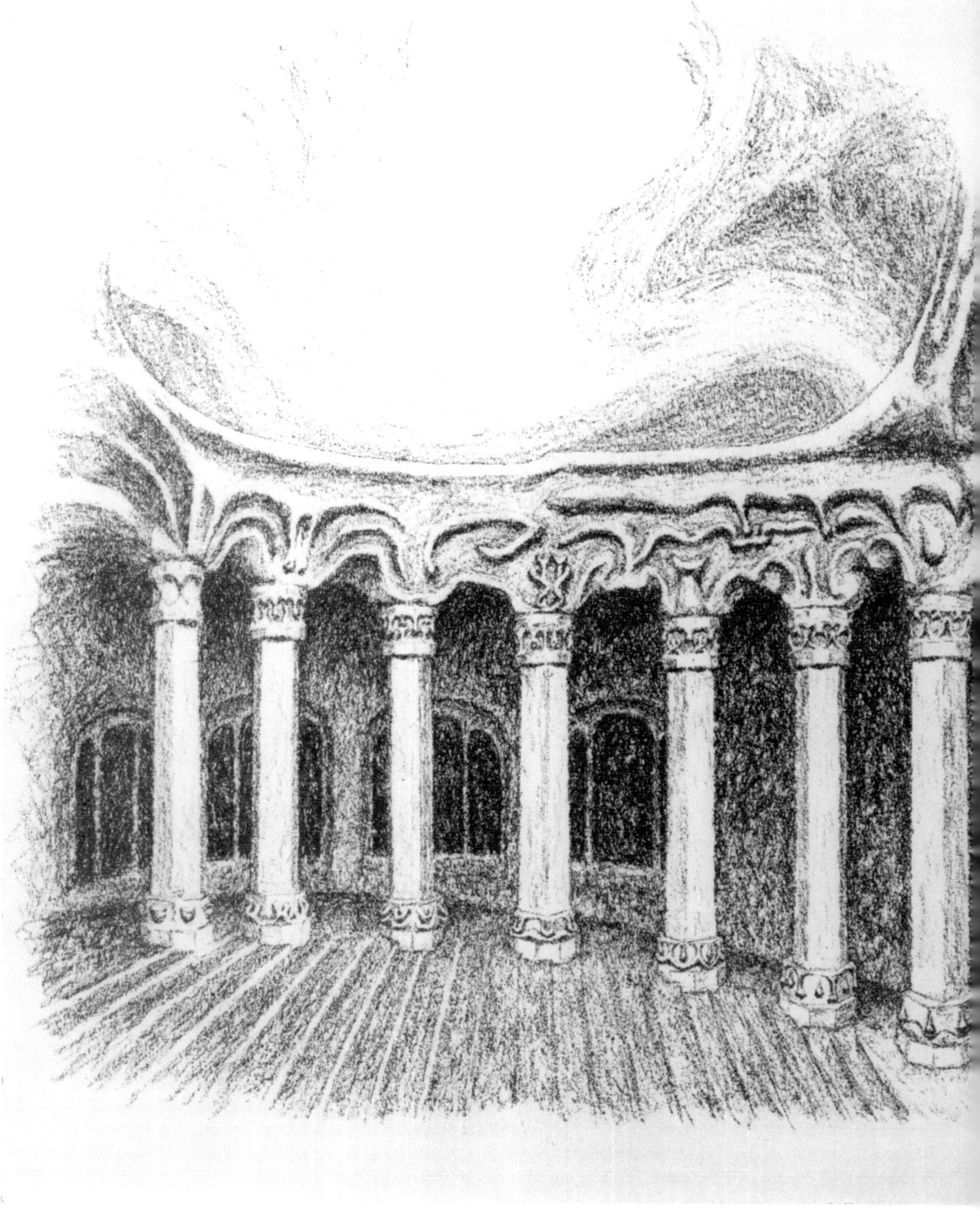

Drawing by Heinrich Eckinger

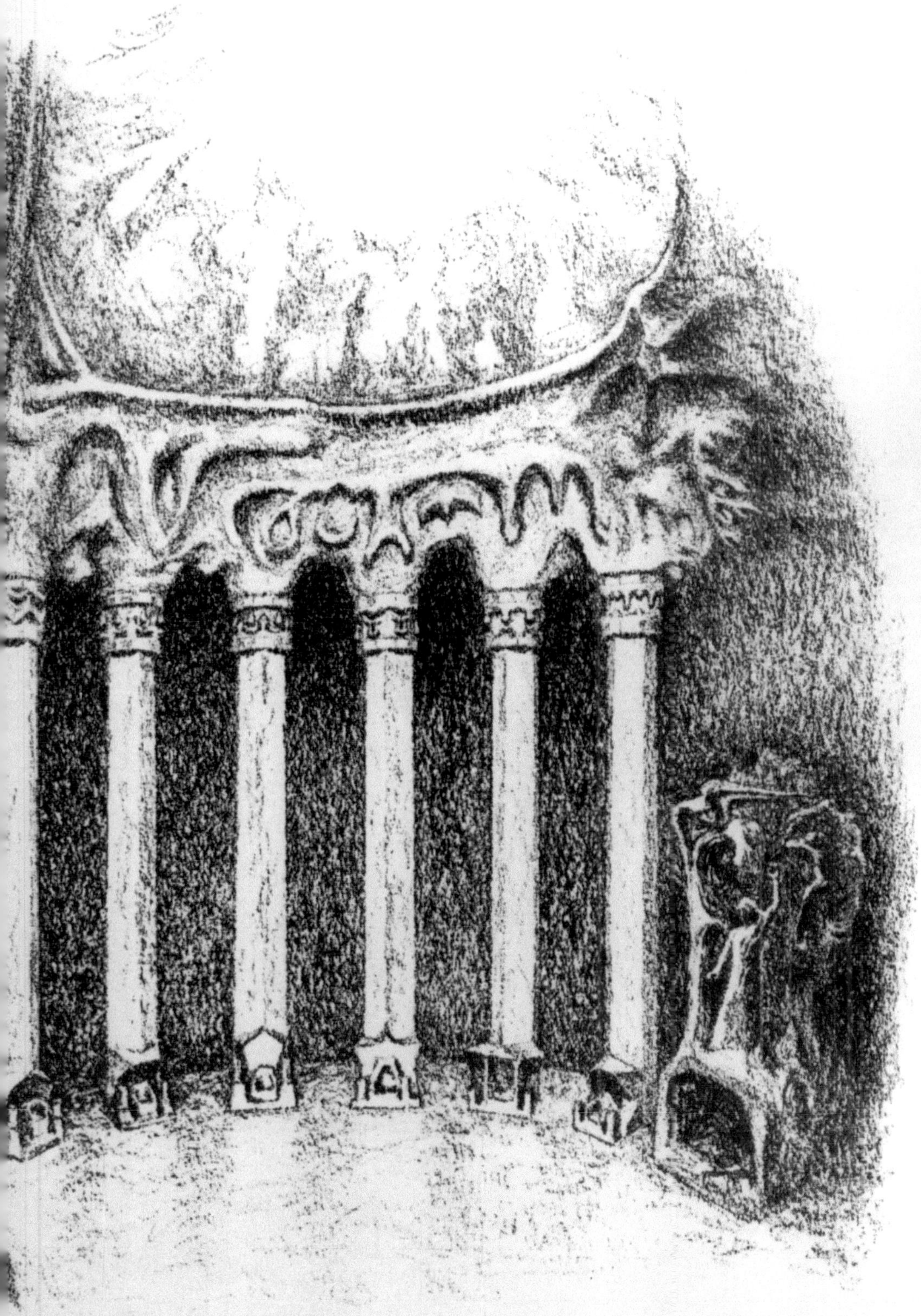

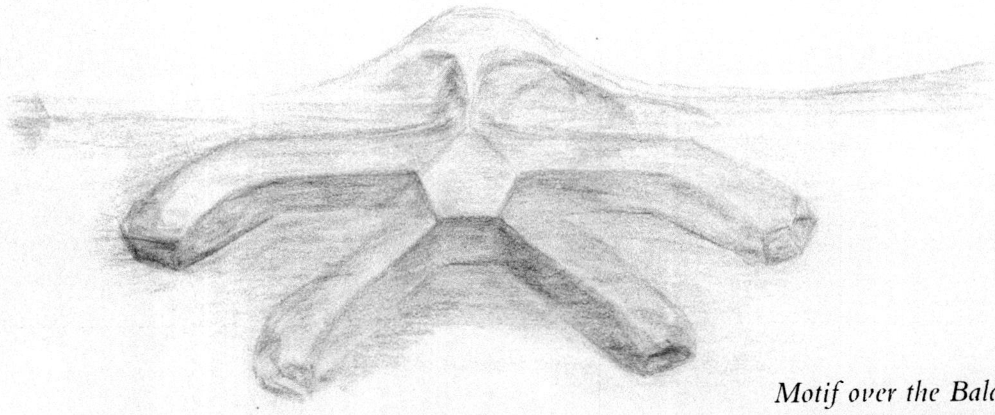

Motif over the Baldachin
Motiv über dem «Baldachin»

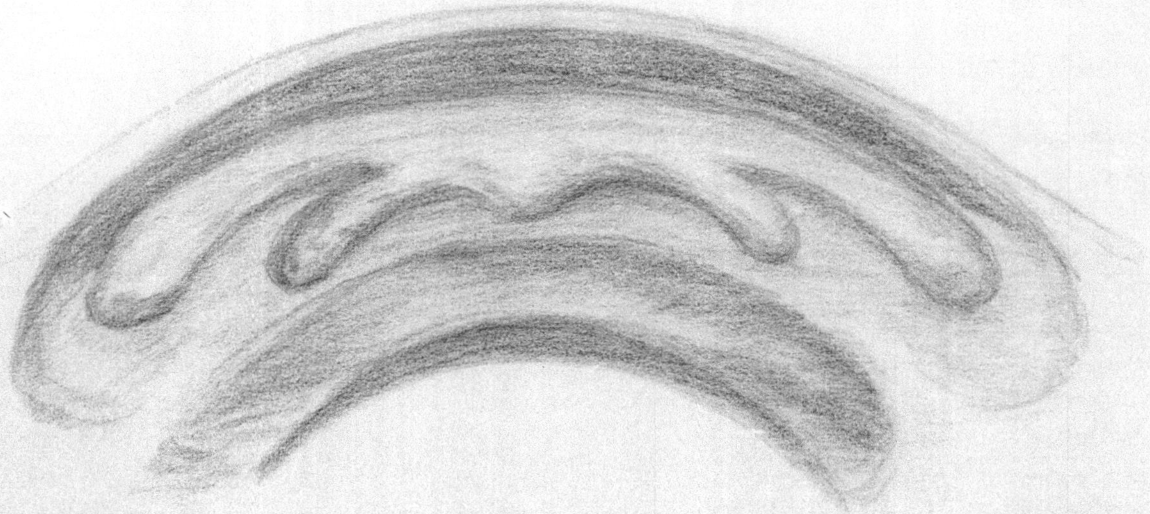

Stage Arch
Bühnenbogen

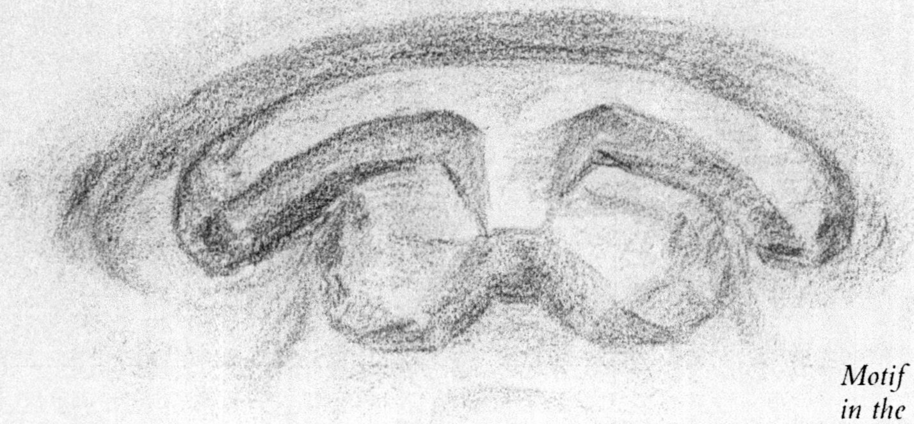

Motif over the Entrance in the West
Eingangsmotiv im Westen

Drawings by Daffi Niederhäuser

THE BASIC ARCHITECTURAL PHENOMENON

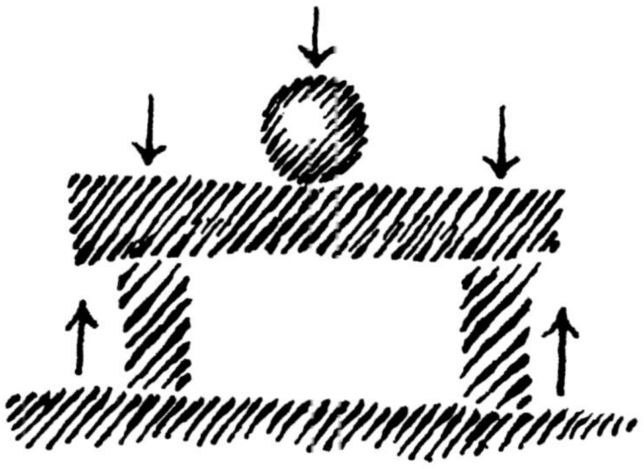

Weight (Ahrimanic)

Balance (Divine)

Support (Luciferic)

We see clearly from the red-chalk drawing by Heinrich Eckinger (p. 256) where the 'Group' statue was to be placed. It was to stand at the east wall of the smaller cupola, beneath a baldachin comprising all the form elements of the architraves, at the midpoint of the twelve columns – an archetypal expression of the twelve and the thirteenth. The picture of the Risen One in glowing colors would have soared above the statue.

"It is as though everything otherwise to be found in the cupola or in the whole of the building is concentrated and synthesized in this 'Group' in the east, in this Christ-like figure between Lucifer above and Ahriman (who will have his consummation in the cavern-group at the bottom). Here we have really the entire mystery of man: Christ, Lucifer, man, Ahriman; and through it a continuation of the architectural conceptions that occur in different stages of metamorphosis from ancient Greek times through the Gothic up to our own time The Greek temple was nothing but a dwelling for a god; it had no significance save in enclosing the divinity. We cannot consider these architectural forms as anything but the house of a god. The medieval Gothic cathedral only had meaning when filled by the congregation; otherwise, it was a forsaken place. The nature of its walls betray the fact that its significance lies in the presence of a congregation. Here, the inside of this building should make manifest to men what a man is: a being who has to establish his balance between the luciferic and the ahrimanic." (April 5, 1920)

The idea of the tension between Lucifer and Ahriman and the balancing force of the central figure was carried over by Rudolf Steiner into the field of architecture. He saw it in the trichotomy of support, weight, and the balance established between them. He called this the "basic phenomenon in architecture". This principle can be recognized and appreciated in each of the sculptural elements of the first Goetheanum. It undergoes metamorphosis according to the particular situation or the place it appears – massive and powerful in the motif over the western entrance, more modest as it is modified for the entrances in the north and south or for the forms surrounding the windows. Also related to these forms, but brought to greater differentiation and flowering, are the sculptural elements in the arch over the stage opening and in the baldachin of the small cupola.

Rudolf Steiner helped us experience these force-relationships by using a simple example. (cf. diagram above).

"We do not want to look at this merely, but to feel that the cross-beam must have a certain thickness; otherwise it would be crushed by the weight. The supports or columns must have a certain mass or else they would collapse. With the sphere on top we must experience pressure, with the columns their lift, with the cross-beam its balance. Our experience is architectural only when we climb inside what is bearing down as weight, inside what is giving support, inside what is providing the balance between weight and support ... .

"Here we feel a supporting, upward-striving luciferic element, here a weighing, downward-pressing ahrimanic element, and here a balancing between the luciferic and ahrimanic – a divine element. So are we enlivened, even through lifeless nature, by Lucifer and Ahriman and by Him who rules over them, forever working the balance between the two.

"When we learn to sense the luciferic, the ahrimanic and the divine in architecture in this way, we shall feel gripped inwardly by architecture and become aware how a richer sensing of the world pulls the soul out into things, as it were, conducts the soul out into the world. Through this we shall gradually gain awareness that we as souls are not only within the skin of our bodies but belong to the cosmos." (January 2, 1915)

We can observe how the forces of weight and support are brought into an organic balance in the column that supports the stairway and in the sculptural motif at the foot of the staircase. Rudolf Steiner comments on this. "When it was time to work out this form, I said to myself, 'Whoever goes up these stairs needs something or other to hold onto that will indicate to him the inner stance he should have while ascending them.' And now look at these three forms that stand at right angles to one another in the three dimensions of space. But it is not enough that you merely observe these beings in their perpendicularity to one another with the eye; you must grasp as well how these forms overhang, that they thrust outward, bear down, *weigh down in overhanging.* If you sense this whole form through and through, then it will express for you the frame of mind one could consider desirable in a person going up these stairs. Whoever climbs them should have the premonition that in this Goetheanum building he will find something that gives him firmness, assurance and strength for living ... .

"Here we have one of these curves (*Bogenrichtungen*) that can only be understood in the context of organic architecture. Stand in the building here and look in this direction, feeling the building around you. That is to say, sense how a person enters or exits here, how he climbs the stairs and approaches the main mass of the building. Then you will sense that this energetic curve must be just as it is. Moreover, you will sense what is meant by such a shape as this, where the attempt is made to convert purely columnar or pillar-like forms into organic

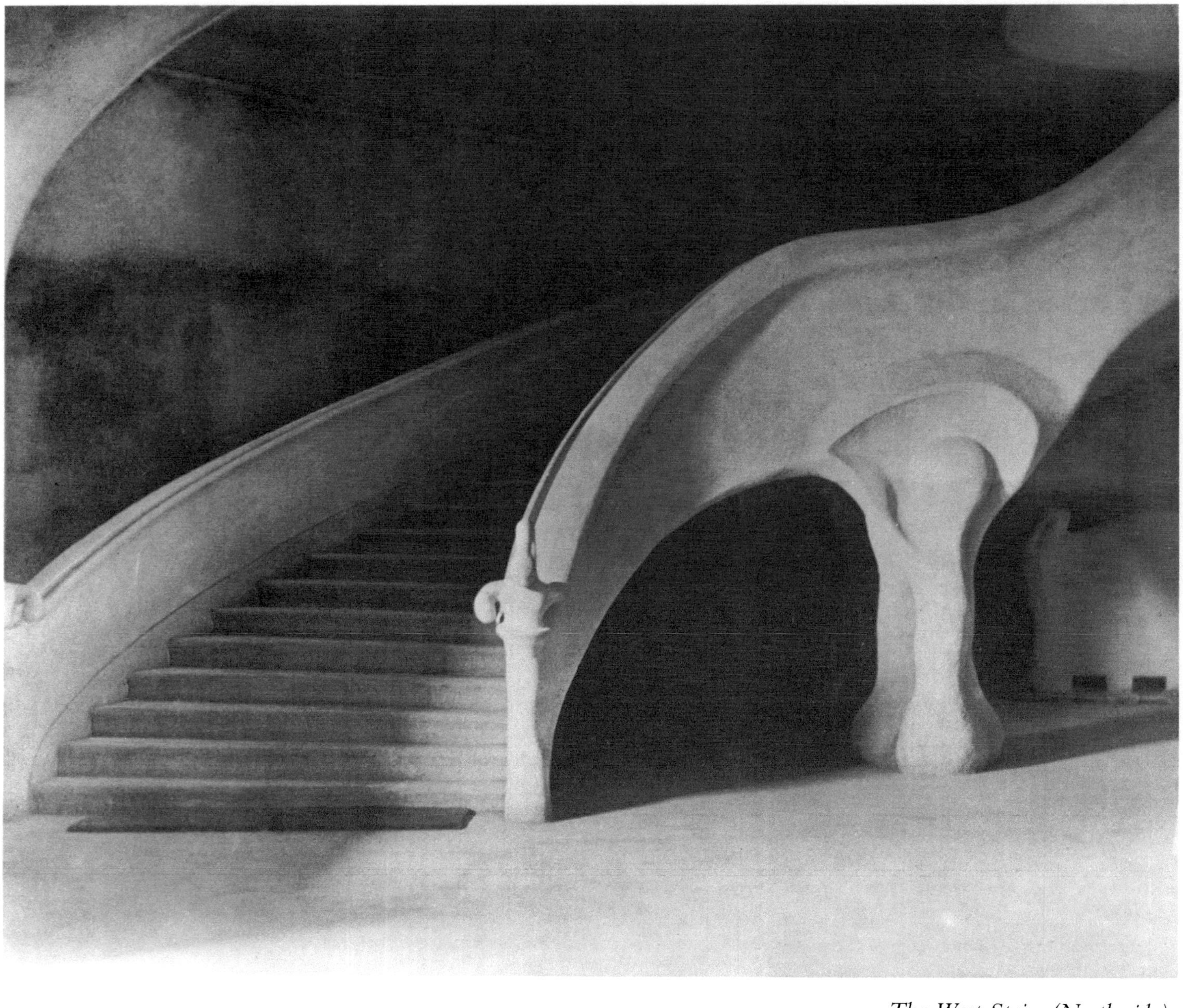

The West Stairs (North side)

shapes. Nothing more lies behind this than the form impression you have when feeling your way through something that has a weight-bearing or supportive function – then this form is inevitable. Whoever is reminded of an elephant's or a horse's foot here is free to be reminded of it, but he is merely demonstrating that he is beginning from an imitative and not an artistic point of view. The point is to sense how something must be supported here, and how what supports it grows out into these forms, changes direction then into these other forms, and braces itself further with this arching line in a contrary direction. This is not to imitate but to sense the forces at work within it that give or bear the weight, and to place at their disposal forms capable of giving or supporting weight.

"In ordinary notions of building we experience only the geometric and mechanical dynamics of weight and counter-thrust. Here, however, every surface and line should give expression to the fact that a building can, to a certain degree, contain the beginnings of a sense for what is alive." (January 23, 1920)

What comes to meet us in this way as a basic phenomenon in architecture can be followed out into many details, of which a few will be taken up here.

The motif on the newel-post of the stairway in the west invites and helps one to ascend. It furnishes support and balance in the three spatial dimensions left.

The side panels of the windows incline toward each other in a brotherly fashion, so that light, speaking through this threefold window, may reveal the stages of an inner path.(1)

The ground plan has been characterized as "a path from the lower to the higher ego." (cf. June 28, 1914 and Carl Kemper in *Der Bau.*) I experience my ego (my 'I') as a point. The periphery – the cupolas – offers help in finding and holding on to myself as an ego.(2)

The elevation(3) expresses the attainment of uprightness, an experience in feeling; the enclosing gesture of the cupolas is an experience in thinking; whereas to step along the building's axis has a relation to the will, a will that moves on to the central motif of the wooden sculpture and the picture painted above it. (cf. p. 36) Floor plan and elevation correspond inwardly to the trinity that upholds the world.

A similar lawfulness can be read in the sculptured forms of the columns, particularly in the large cupola. The pedestal motifs are reminiscent in a way of stages in plant metamorphosis: seeding, sprouting, unfolding, pausing, blossoming, fruiting and forming new seed.

The motifs in the capitals point to more comprehensive lawfulness and this becomes clear in the change of direction between the fourth capital (where the forces work from above downward) and the fifth (where the impulse speaks upward from below). The capitals move from the simple mirroring planes of the first or Saturn capital: '*the it*', to the budding life of the second or sun capital: '*toward it*' and the moon capital: '*in it*', on to the fourth, which reaches a certain completion in '*the I*'. The 'I', a gift from the cosmos, unfolds its powers and becomes capable of acting: '*from the I*'. It works out of my inmost being: '*out of me*' and unites itself with its spiritual origin: '*I into it*'.

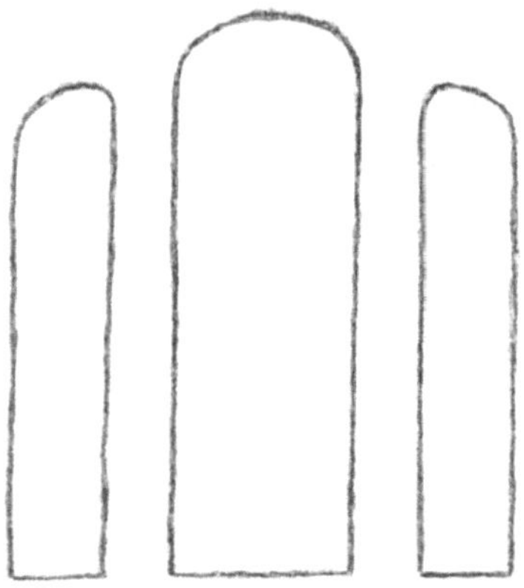

1

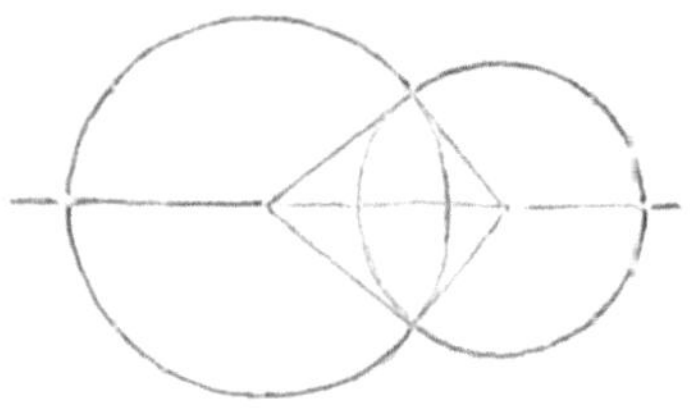

2

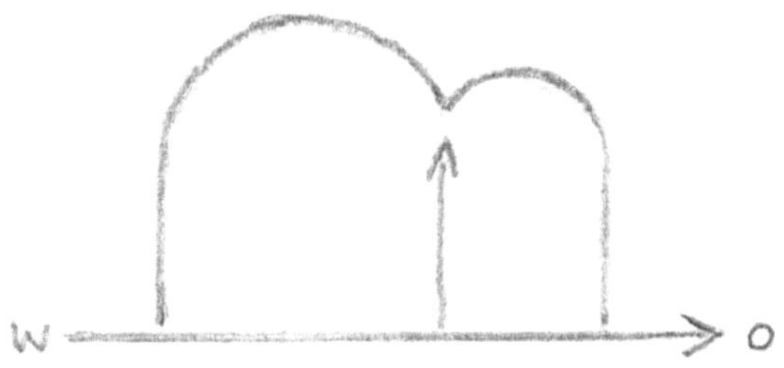

3

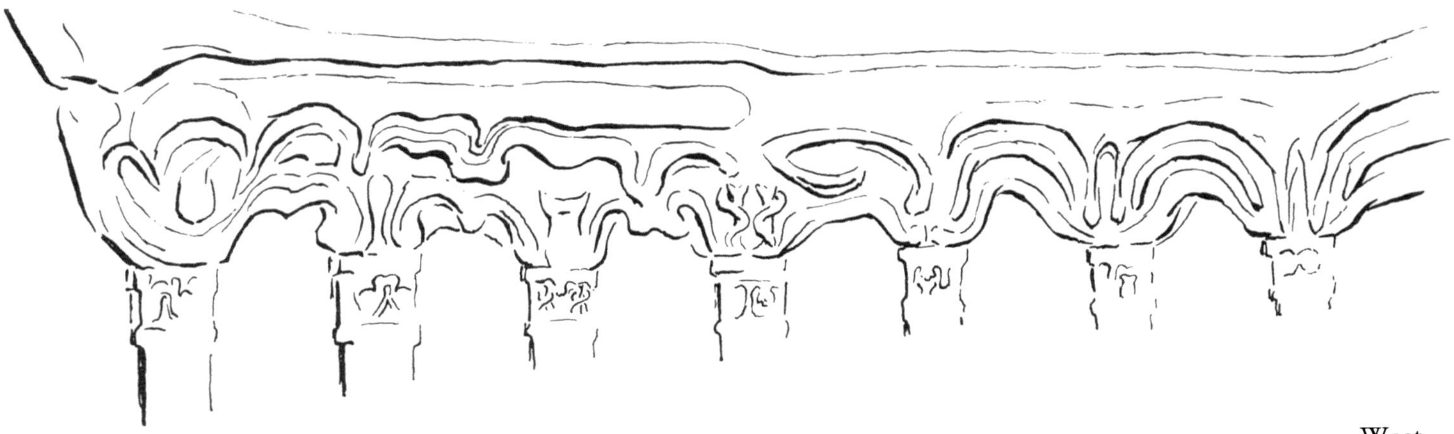

Ost east West

Drawing by Assya Turgenieff

This evolution in seven stages, given in the forms of the seven capitals, can also be grasped musically. Rudolf Steiner spoke of the "invisible music of our columns" and often employed musical terms to characterize the singular qualities of these motifs.

"The attempt is made to bring architectural forms into a musical flow. A musical soul-mood can be produced by the sense one can have of concord between the columns and what is related to them. We sense an invisible music as the soul of our columns, of our architecture and of the sculptured forms that belong to them. Something of the nature of the soul lives in them."

"It depends upon movement, the moving, the activity that forms itself, but rhythmically forms itself, experiences itself in melodies – that is to say, it has to do with time."

Karl von Baltz has taken up this idea.[23] "Music finds its home not in the tones but 'between the tones' (Gustav Mahler). This implies at the same time that it never stands still, rather manifests in movement. However, this is inaudible, purely spiritual, a continual striving. May the diagram that follows be kept in motion by the reader!

It is not tones that are meant in any case, rather *intervals* with their force of striving, their tendency to evolve. The first intervals: prime, second, third, fourth, seem to give us something enclosed in themselves. The fourth and fifth (Mars–Mercury) are the two intervals belonging to the earth. The intervals from prime to fourth can be compared with breathing in and the fifth to seventh with breathing out.

The columns of the first Goetheanum were not only given these signs (Saturn to Venus) but also words:

♄ Prime .... the it
☉ Second .... toward it
☽ Third .... in it
♂ Fourth .... the I
☿ Fifth .... from the I
♃ Sixth .... out of me
♀ Seventh .... I into it

Whoever experiences these pillar sayings inwardly as differentiated forces allows the tones and the forms of the pillars to vibrate together. The seven intervals secure the creative life. Movement, relatedness, and striving toward the other live at each stage. This would be the aspect of 'creating out of the I'."

Another possible approach to these columns and the intervals between them is by way of the gestures given for intervals in tone eurythmy, here described by Elisabeth Day-Bleiker.[24] "The intervals of music become visible here as movement and gesture. The 'invisible music' in the pillar-motifs and the coming to visibility of the intervals through the gestures of tone eurythmy correspond inwardly to one another.

The prime rests as a seed, sheltered within the mystery of the octave space, closed within itself, sounding in itself. The second wrests itself free from this seed-state with the strength of inner questioning. Manifold life is released from unity. It pulsates in quickening tremors and throbbings. The form that appears is almost the same as that of the prime, only it appears changed and amplified through the enlivening.

The third blossoms in harmonious resonance within me. 'That which we bring about in the third, we bring about

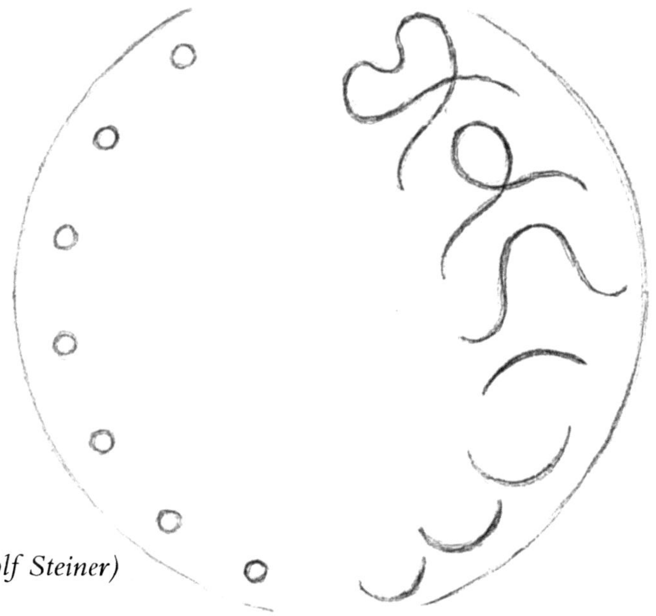

Interval Forms for Tone Eurythmy (after the indications of Rudolf Steiner)

within ourselves.' It shapes for itself a similar form, an expansive gentle wave, and the inwardness appears again altered.

The human being takes hold of himself in the fourth. He concentrates his force in himself becoming smaller than he is. 'One changes oneself into a pleasant dwarf.' That is, the unfolding tones are dammed up. This form concludes the development of the lower tetrachord. It strengthens the experience within itself. Then, how can the evolution proceed if it already appears at an end? 'Every development happens in leaps.' This leap, however, must happen between the fourth and the fifth.

The lower tetrachord rests in the enveloping octave space like a seed in the womb of the earth. The octave allows the prime to sound out of its profound cosmic slumber, the seventh allows the second to arise, and a heaven-bound sixth releases the third into the cosmic dream. Only in the fourth do the forces of the lower tetrachord awaken to themselves. This awakening, then intensified, is lifted up in the fourth; the curious timbre of the raised fourth or tritonus (for example, C–F) appears. The whole of the ego's mighty tension is at work here. It breaks through the preceding forms and opens itself to the new space of the upper tetrachord – a leap into infinity.

The tonal consciousness becomes larger. The onward-flooding forces of the octave take hold. They fashion for themselves the fifth, create the sixth and experience themselves in the seventh. 'The fifth is – man himself.' The arms now encircle a space filled by man himself. The feet move through the form, at first dipping into the past through memory but only to create its bond to the future. We begin to feel our way into a mighty vibration that affects the peripheral organs and even the skin.

As a blossom opens to the light, the sixth opens to its new environment. It breathes in the sounding light around it, a sounding blossom. An interchange takes place: in blooming, in breathing. Form takes wing. The crossing of streams within the form manifests a brotherly exchange – the first time this occurs.

In the seventh we abandon ourselves, consumed in spirit-fire, striving to merge with our surroundings. Even the skin, which in the fifth had offered protection for our humanness, now becomes an obstacle. 'It falls away from his body in shreds, like from the flayed Marsyas.' A trembling in swiftest vibration ensues. The form becomes rhythmic in the repeated striving for the octave.

Then at last the octave arrives, uniting with the whole of evolution. 'It sinks into the base tone ...' revealing that the scale is man himself. 'In the octave man has refound himself on a higher plane.' The octave conceals the twelve within it. It called the fifth, sixth and seventh into existence, and now it has its turn, drawing into itself each preceding stage."

Likewise, the entire building resounds from the prime to the octave and back to the prime again. The fourth column betrays a certain isolation in the same way as the musical fourth. And the more energetic tonal movement, intensifying from the fifth into the sixth and seventh is consonant with the fifth, sixth and seventh columns.

"I was surprised to notice, when I arrived at the seventh column, that the relief of the first column – were one to turn it inside out like a glove – would fit precisely into the hollows of the last column. This is also the case with the second and sixth columns and with the third and fifth, with the fourth column standing between. This was not a sort of abstract mystical principle of sevenfoldness that was there from the beginning; yet, as the musical scale is a sevenfold being, so here the columns had to be developed in such a way that a kind of octave in the feeling for form found fulfillment in a sevenfold sequence. For the eighth would have been the octave; here it had to transmute into that other sphere of feeling we encounter in the small cupola, which contains something that meets this evolution with a receptive gesture." (October 16, 1920)

The incision, the change of direction from a downward to an upward dynamic between the fourth and fifth columns, is significant in the sequence of seven. It is a transformation; an inversion takes place in the non-spatial. Metamorphosis in its highest form is a passage through the spiritual. This principle holds at the last for the transmutation of forces that are active in the human form from one earth-life to the next.

"This evolution, which ... is demonstrated in our organism, is divided in two parts in that everything belonging to the upper part of man is a metamorphosis of the lower man in his previous earth life. There is a period between death and rebirth when a total inversion takes place, when what had been inwardly is given an outward direction .... You see, people say that a proof of repeated earth-lives is needed today. Well, we have first to develop a method for finding this proof. Whoever can observe the human head in the right way, whoever has a sense for this kind of observation, will arrive at an understanding of this metamorphosis of the lower man into the human head. But he will not be able to understand this without taking account of the intermediate stage of life between death and a new birth." (April 25, 1920)

It is this transformation that is to be seen in the mural 'The Circle of Twelve – the O', painted in the large cupola above the stage opening.

Thus, both the carved forms and the painted motifs of this building lead us on to confront the greatest of riddles – that of human destiny – and to a sense for what Rudolf Steiner expressed in the words: "In the Goetheanum were forms that would awaken a perception of karma."

"An architecture suited to the man of today, that would catch his eye in the right manner and gradually bring his naturalistic way of viewing things, which conceals and obscures karma, into an intuitive contemplation – this was present in a particular form (in the first Goetheanum). Within these forms an anthroposophical content could be expressed and wrestled with; this is what provided inner vision. Among all the other things that have already been brought out, it was the Goetheanum, this building, together with the way anthroposophy would have more and more been produced in it, that was a training in karmic vision. Such an education of the organ for karma must find its place in modern civilization." (April 17, 1924)

The Goetheanum was built to house the *Mystery Dramas*, and the smaller cupola was to serve as a stage. The drama of karmic events between various persons was to have unfolded on a stage which was itself a picture of the spiritual guidance of mankind. The audience would have been surrounded by colors and forms which encompassed change and metamorphosis, reincarnation and karma.

The forms of the large cupola, kindling insight into karma, lead on into the smaller cupola, to Him who will be recognized in increasing measure, from the twentieth century onwards, as the 'Lord of Karma'.

In this way the men of our time are to learn that the Christ will reveal himself supersensibly more and more and will increasingly weave the threads of karma into earthly matters. They will come to recognize in this spiritual power the destiny that the Greeks could not yet recognize, a destiny that is to lead men to live out their karma in their following incarnation in the most appropriate way. When they experience their destiny through succeeding incarnations, men will look up to the Christ as to a judge, as the Lord of Karma. They will then relate themselves to their destiny, will be encouraged to deepen their souls until they are able to say: this destiny has not been appointed me by some impersonal force, but by something to which I feel an affinity in my inmost being. I relish my karma because it is making of me a better and better person. Thus do we learn to love karma, and this then is the impulse by which we come to know the Christ. Men first learned to love their karma through the Mystery of Golgotha. But this will go on and on, until men learn that the earth would never have reached its goal under the influence of Lucifer alone, that human evolution without the Christ must end in corruption." (April 17, 1912)

In the first Goetheanum the sculpting of the 'Group' statue and of the columns and architraves was conceived of as a whole.

"By this means the admonition 'Know Thyself' should,

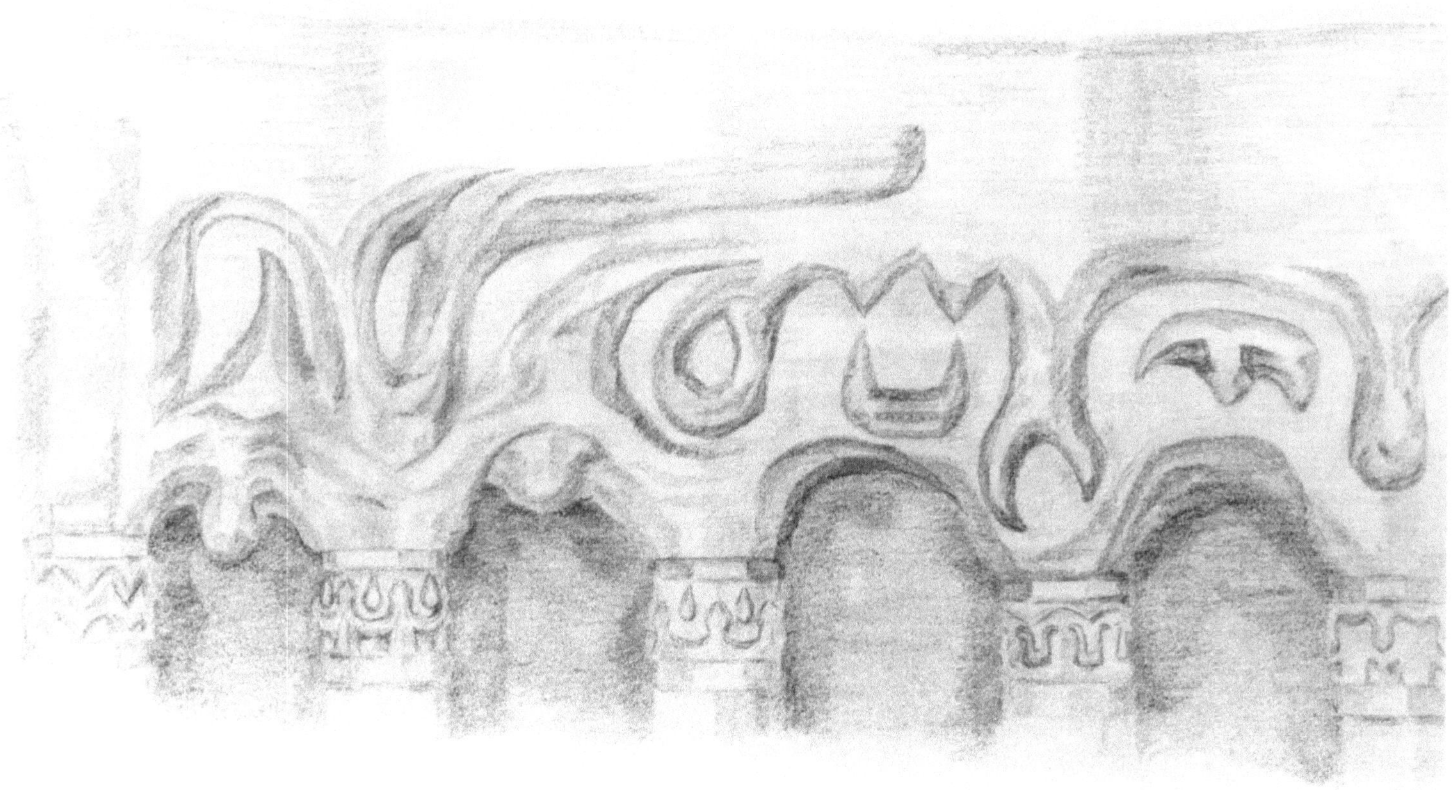

Architrave and Column Capitals in the Small Cupola (North side) Drawing by Daffi Niederhäuser

so to speak, resound through hall and audience in the form of pictures and sculpture, not in abstract forms but expressing that trinity of which I have often spoken, which I am convinced will be the trinity of human culture in future times. And thus this figure in wood must be set up not at the building's center, but as its central figure." (June 12, 1920)

THE GOETHEANUM AND THE GRAIL

"To the degree that mankind is able to absorb knowledge of the Grail in the course of its development, the impulse given through the Christ-event can become ever more meaningful. The inner side of Christian evolution will complement the outer more and more. What can be revealed about the higher worlds in relation to the mystery of the Christ through imagination, inspiration, and intuition will more and more permeate human thinking, feeling, and willing. The 'hidden knowledge of the Grail' will be unveiled. It will increasingly pervade every expression of human life as by an inner power."[25]

The cultivation of an inner dimension, implied by the Christ-principle, became the architectural principle of the Goetheanum. This was anticipated by Goethe in that unusual building inspected by Wilhelm Meister in the 'Pedagogical Province'. Here there are two galleries, richly decked with murals of the great events in Old and New Testament history. In the first gallery, Wilhelm could see the history of the Israelite people up to the destruction of the temple in Jerusalem. When he enquired after the 'Divine Man, who was still teaching until shortly before the latter event', he was led into the second gallery, "where Wilhelm at once recognized pictures from the second Holy Book. They seemed to be carried out by another hand than had painted the first. All was milder – figures, movements, surroundings, light and coloration. 'You see here,' said his guide after they had passed by one of these pictures, 'neither actions nor situations, but rather miracles and parables. This is a new world, new and different in its externals from the old, and with an inwardness that was entirely lacking there'."

Still a third gallery is hinted at – 'the shrine of suffering' – in which the Passion of Christ is expressed. This is opened only once a year, and thus constitutes the most intimate stage on the indicated path from without to within. The essential nature of Christianity is shown in its relation to this path. It is not given to a single people, as for example the religion of Jehovah was given to the Hebrews. "What the individual encounters inwardly belongs to the second religion, the religion of the Wise Men. Such was the religion which Christ taught and lived as long as he moved about on earth."

Rudolf Steiner shows the relationship of this significant Goethean view to the Grail tradition. "The Grail-stream takes this form: whoever would visit the temple of the Grail must travel impenetrable paths, sixty leagues long; the temple lies completely hidden; one learns nothing there unless one asks. In short, the prevailing spirit of the Grail creates a bond between what is most intimate in the human soul (where the consciousness soul awakes) and the spiritual worlds ... .

"Goethe lived in this spirit of the Grail even if its strength lay in the deeper forces of his consciousness. If you look for this quality of the Grail, you will find it everywhere. In a certain regard, Goethe did not stand alone but joined with what had preceded him ... . That which led him to distinguish three stages – that of a folk-religion; that of a religion of the wise, introduced to the individual in the second chamber; and the most intimate religion of all, containing the mystery of death and resurrection, which speaks to the soul in the third chamber – that which led him to lift the religious active in the sense world up to the spiritual heights is the spirit of the Grail." (November 3, 1918)

The Spiritual Temple of the Grail

Around the turn of the 12th century, the well-known Grail epics of Robert de Boron, Chretien de Troyes, Wolfram von Eschenbach and Albrecht von Scharffenberg appeared and were then disseminated by the courtly minnesingers and troubadours among the nobility of Europe.[26] Prior to this, said Rudolf Steiner, the Grail mysteries were known only to a few of the 'wise' in Europe, in whom "arose ... the significant imagination: something was present in the bread of the Last Supper that synthesized forces streaming from the outer cosmos down to the earth, permeating it and conjuring forth from it the plant world. What is entrusted to the earth from the cosmos and then springs forth from the earth again is combined and synthesized into bread and builds up the human body.

"Still something else emerged from the mist, if I may so term it, that had gathered over the old traditions; something else passed over to these European sages which had its origin in the Orient, to be sure, but now, emerging from the mist, was understood by certain individuals. That was the other mystery, taking its place alongside that of the bread – the mystery of the holy vessel in which Joseph of Arimathea gathered the drops of blood trickling down from Christ-Jesus. This was the other side of the mystery.

"If the bread is comprised of everything that constitutes an extract of man's nature and being, then in bread and blood (for which wine should be only the outer symbol) these European sages saw something more. They had developed themselves in secret mystery places and surpassed by far the mass of the population, who were able to take in no more than the events in Palestine, or if they did approach learning only found their way into the abstract fantasy world of Arabism. But these individuals – who distinguished themselves through something that was like the ripest, the over-ripe, fruit of oriental wisdom and at the same time the ripe fruit of European perception and feeling – developed what they termed the mystery of the Grail. But, they said, what this mystery of the Grail is, is not to be found on the earth." (April 16, 1921)

Where then is this secret to be discovered? This became the central theme of the great Grail epics. The various poets give emphasis to virtues, qualities, attitudes of soul, contents of consciousness. The Grail had its origin in Paradise, according to Wolfram von Eschenbach. Robert de Boron says that it was carried down to earth by angels and handed over with its power of resurrection to a descendent of the ancient Hebrew stream who understood the mystery of the bread and was the first to cultivate the mystery of the blood. When this man, Joseph of Arimathea, lay in prison, wrapped in darkness and sentenced to die, the Risen One himself brought him the Grail.

"This vessel, into which you let flow my blood, catching it as it left my body, shall be called the cup. The tablet that is to lie upon it shall represent the stone that lay over me when you placed me in the grave. This you should call to mind all your days. These things are the sign by which men shall remember you. All those who shall behold your cup shall belong to my company. They shall receive fullness of heart and joy for all eternity."[27]

A bond with the divine is suggested in this way, a bond which could never have occurred in this way before the Mystery of Golgotha because it takes place in the depths of the human soul. Here begins a new and ascending evolution for mankind. The Grail, as it descends gradually from Paradise to earthly humanity, gives men the power and shows them the path by which they can elevate themselves again to Paradise.

Two great imaginations from these epics might be considered in this connection: first, the Round Table with its circle of knights presided over by King Arthur and Queen Guinevere. This was fashioned by Merlin in preparation for the fulfillment of the mystery of the Grail. This first imagination suggests the zodiac surrounding the sun and moon, or the twelve tribes of Israel gathered around the ark of the covenant.

The second imagination is that of Parsifal who gives birth to capacities and virtues in himself in order to ensure that his pilgrimage to the Grail will be crowned with success. This imagery portrays a yearning and a seeking for the Holy Grail proceeding from the most precious, intimate need of the human soul.

A hunger for the divine lay at the heart of the religious mood in medieval times. People felt deserted by the gods, Rudolf Steiner relates. The gods were distant from them. By comparison, the Greeks felt the gods quite near, wandering about among them as their companions; for example, Athene with Odysseus on his long adventures. Thus, the Greeks built their temples as houses for their gods; not so the men of the Middle Ages. It was not the gods who came inside their religious structures, but the people in search of the divine.

"Thus the mood of soul among men became one of yearning, and they built on this yearning, believing they would be happier in their search if gathered together as a community. They were convinced that what they recognized as the divine-spiritual was not something that guided human affairs directly, but rather veiled itself in the hidden depths. If one wanted to express what he yearned for and sought, he could do so only by referring to the mysterious. The expression of this complex mood of soul is the temple, or in this case the cathedral, which finds its truest, most typical form in the Gothic." (December 13, 1919)

A clear expression of the medieval soul-mood is to be found in the architectural imagination of the grand temple of the Grail, evoked by Albrecht von Scharffenberg in his *Younger Titurel.* Titurel is the one who received the charge to build the Grail Temple. He fashioned its foundation out of onyx. But he did not know how he was to erect the temple. He pondered long over this, until all at once he discovered the entire plan for the temple sketched in the veins of onyx on the floor. Thus the temple's dimensions were given by the creator God himself. Titurel built a cathedral according to this plan with two choirs and with portals in the south, west and north. The main choir was in the east, and an organ was placed on the balcony opposite in the west. The colors of precious gems gleamed in the windows. At the height of the cupola, carbuncles sparkled against an azure ground, like stars in the evening sky. And there the sun and moon in gold and silver circled through the zodiac. The brazen columns that bore the cupola rested on the onyx floor, which appeared like an ice-mantled sea full of fish and marvelous marine creatures. The building was like a mighty etheric imagination of the macrocosm. Its microcosmic reflection lay in its midst, similar to the temple in every particular, and this would serve to house the Grail. Rudolf Steiner derives from this imagination his reference to the 'cathedral within a cathedral', for him a picture of the confluence of spirit raying back from the seventy-two apostles sent out to every direction of the compass.

"If you were to imagine the totality of human souls streaming back from every celestial direction, then you would have the earth's entire humanity gathered as in a great cathedral, a cathedral in which the yearning of all men attuned to the Christ flowed together." (December 13, 1919)

The inmost wish to unite with the divine permeated the religious life of men in medieval times. And this was necessary if the soul was to be conducted to the temple of the Grail.

"And the Holy Grail hovered in the heights above the earth. Only those on whom the divine powers had bestowed the necessary capacities could enter this spiritual temple, those who embraced the Holy Grail and the mysteries of the Bread and the Blood." (April 16, 1921)

A new impulse originates with Parsifal in the ascending evolution of mankind, and this is *knowledge* of the Grail that is derived from personal experience. This becomes a necessity for the souls of individual men.

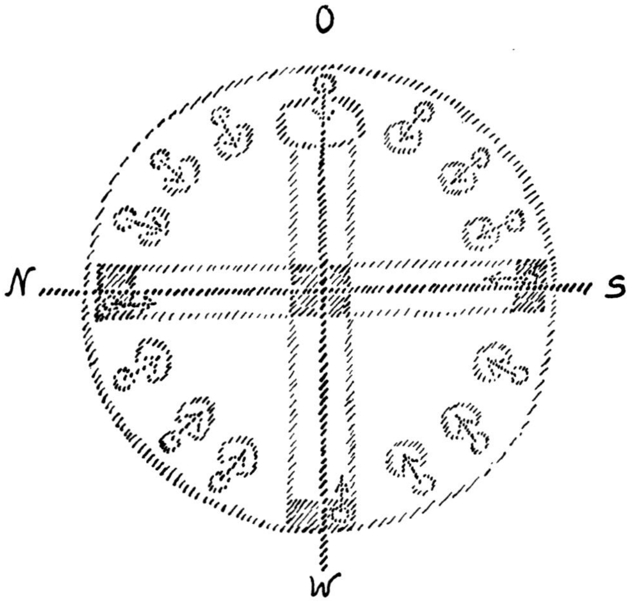

Drawing by A. Turgenieff (after Rudolf Steiner)

The Grail Temple and the Temple of Solomon

Albrecht compares Titurel, the builder of the Grail Temple, with King Solomon, at whose behest the Temple of Jerusalem arose.

> "The art rough stone to fashion
> to Solomon was granted;
> no noise of work ascended
> the city's peace to trouble,
> no ringing chisel, hammer blow
> on nail or rivet.
> Through will of God the work was ended.
> The selfsame skill and power
> was Titurel's ... ."[28]

The Grail Temple was built according to the 'art of Pythagoras', says Albrecht. This temple enclosed an inner sanctuary, just as Solomon's temple did, as described in the second book of *Chronicles.*

Behind curtains of red-violet, blue-violet, scarlet and white linen, lay the cubic space reserved for the Holy of Holies, whose measurements suggest the Pythagorean square, according to an indication from Rudolf Steiner. The Grail Temple was dedicated to the Holy Spirit, while that of Solomon served as a house for the Name of God. "Let us keep in mind above all the biblical description of the temple's use. Jehovah directed these words to David: 'A house for my name'. Thus a house for the name 'Jehovah'. And now let us make clear what the name Jehovah signifies.

Ancient Judaism at a certain period was aware of the sacredness of the name 'Jehovah'. What does that mean? The child learns at a particular moment of its life to use the word 'I'. Before this, it considers itself a thing. Just as it called other things by an objective name, so also itself. Only later does it learn to use the word 'I'. For great personalities, the moment when they experience this 'I' themselves for the first time, or first become conscious of it, is one of great significance ... .

"Men have developed themselves through many races; up to Atlantean times, they all conceived of themselves in this objective way. It was only in the course of the Atlantean races that man had developed to the point that he could say 'I' to himself. The ancient Jews took hold of this as a doctrine.

"The human being has passed through all the kingdoms of nature. His ego-consciousness arose in him last of all. Astral, etheric and physical body, together with the ego, form the Pythagorean square. Judaism attached to these the divine self that descends to us from above in contrast to the ego that ascends from below. Thus, from the square emerged a pentagon. Judaism sensed the Lord of its people in such a way; hence it was a holy thing to speak his 'name'. While other names, i. e. Elohim or Adonai, became more and more popular, only the consecrated priests, and they only in the Holy of Holies, could pronounce the name 'Jehovah'. Ancient Judaism had arrived at the sacredness of the Jehovah name, at this 'I' that can reside in the human being, in the time of Solomon. We must understand the challenge Jehovah poses mankind as this: man is to make of himself a temple of the Holy Spirit. We have now attained a new conception of the deity, namely, to make the god within the breast of man, hidden in his deepest sanctuary of self, into a god of morality. The human body became in this way a major symbol for the Holy of Holies." (May 22, 1905)

Solomon was unable to build the temple to the Name of God through his own forces. He was in possession of the greatest wisdom, but to raise this building he had to call on men who had achieved mastership in the individual arts. Thus, Hiram was installed as master-builder for the new temple. The Temple Legend speaks of his descent from Cain.[29] In these tales we come across two streams of humanity that were involved in the creation of the human race. The one – the sons of Cain – busied themselves with the arts and sciences: "through their art should the temple be built". The other – the descendents of Abel-Seth – cultivated "the truly spiritual in human nature", which was to take root in the temple. We must imagine to ourselves that according to the meaning of the legend, two streams were present on earth up to the appearance of Christ Jesus. The one built the visible temple and shaped the deeds of men, so that later the divine Word, come to earth through Christ-Jesus, might be received. A dwelling had to be prepared for the earthly appearance of the divine Word. Alongside of this, the divine should develop by itself for a time, as in a sort of tributary, in the second stream. Thus the sons of man – the race of Cain, which was to prepare the earthly side – were distinguished from the sons of God, the sons of Abel-Seth, who cared for the divine, until the time when both streams could be wed. It was Christ-Jesus who united these two streams. The temple should rise first outwardly, until He should appear who could raise up this temple anew in three days." (May 29, 1905)

In the language of his Grail epic, Albrecht describes the fashioning of the human bodily sheaths from the time of Paradise up to the reception of the immortal kernel of being.

> "Angels brought the Grail-cup
> in olden times from heaven.
> From stone of highest value
> the vessel should be fashioned.
> 'Twas called the heavenly Jaspis –
> the substance of the Phoenix
> arising from his ashes.
> The Christ took this chalice
> and smoothed it for our using."

In the course of time, man developed the sheaths which permitted him to receive the divine ego into his earthly being. The strength of this ego made it possible for him to transform and purify his bodily members, so that gradually he could win his way back to a paradisical union with the sun and moon.

The biblical story of the brazen sea, the crowning labor of Hiram on completion of the temple, points to this future deed of mankind. Hiram was to cast the brazen sea at the eastern end of the court, towards the south in a great basin borne by twelve oxen, three facing toward each of the four points of the compass.

According to the legend, Solomon had plotted with three journeyman apprentices to hinder the successful casting of the sea. In the decisive moment, as the casting was destroyed beyond hope, Tubal-Cain appeared to Hiram, demanding that he throw himself into the foundry fire. He obeyed, and arriving at the mid-point of the earth came before Cain himself, who gave him a golden triangle and hammer, with which he could save the casting.

"The brazen sea comes into being as soon as the waters of calm wisdom unite with astral fire, the fire of passion. In this way, a 'brazen' amalgam must arise, capable of being carried over into an age to come, in which the secret of Atma-Buddhi-Manas, the mystery of the sacred golden triangle, will complement it. This triangle, with all that attends it, will form the content of the renewed Christianity of the sixth sub-race. This is to be prepared by the Rosicrucians. Then what was symbolized by the brazen sea will be combined with knowledge of reincarnation and karma. This is the new occult teaching, which will be incorporated once more into Christianity. The secret that is to be revealed when the sixth sub-race is ripe for it is that of Atma-Buddhi-Manas, the higher self ... . Everything that has led to strife on the outer plane will find peace through the brazen sea, through the holy golden triangle." (November 4, 1904)

The imaginations of the Temple of Solomon and the Grail Temple both speak of the transmutation of the members of man's body and soul and the purifying of the human senses. They are pictures of the evolution of the human being, the descent of the Primal Word out of the ground of being of the world into dead, earthly ego-being and its resurrection, by means of which mankind may evolve upward to divine ego-being.

"That holy vessel from which Christ-Jesus ate and drank with his disciples, which we call the Holy Grail, and in which the blood flowing from the wounds was caught by Joseph of Arimathea was brought, so the story goes, by angels to Europe. A temple was built for it, and the Rosicrucians became the guardians of what was in the vessel, that is to say, of what the nature of the reborn God consists: the mystery of the reborn God who gains sway among men – this is the Grail mystery.

"This mystery is to be established as a new gospel. It will be said that we look up to such a sage as the writer of the gospel of St. John, who was able to say, 'In the beginning was the Word, and the Word was with God, and the Word was a God; that which in the beginning was with God, that was born again in Him whom we have seen suffer and die on Golgotha, and has risen again.' This continuity of the divine principle through all time and the rebirth of this divine principle, that is what the author of the Gospel of John wanted to represent. But all those who wished to express such a content knew this: what was there from the beginning has been preserved. The mystery of the higher human self was there in the beginning; it was held safe in the Grail; its bond to the Grail has been maintained. In the Grail lives the 'I' that is bound to the eternal and immortal, just as the lower 'I' is bound to the temporal and mortal. Whoever is acquainted with the secret of the Holy Grail knows that vivid, sprouting life proceeds from the wood of the cross, symbolized by the roses on the black wood of the cross – the immortal 'I'. So can the secret of the Rose-Cross be seen as something that forms a continuation of the Gospel of John." (June 24, 1909)

The Goetheanum and the New Revelation of the Grail

The rectangular Temple of Solomon had portals to the east, south and north.[30] The Holy of Holies in the form of a cube, lay in the west. The brazen sea was cast in the southeastern part of the court. The seventy-two altars of the Grail Temple rounded to form a circle, in whose center was the 'Little House without Compare', enclosing the Holy Grail. The first Goetheanum with its two interpenetrating cupolas – on the ground-plan they show as intersecting circles in the ratio 4:3 – reveals an approach to the Holy Grail for the men of our time.

"When we press on to our own times, we can say to ourselves that the essential impulse of the present and near future is this: to turn mankind inward. The human being, in his inner divine-spiritual nature, becomes the focus of all striving. But this inner impulse of modern striving is deadened if he does not find his place in evolution in a living way. The conception of this building arises from such an experience of the nature of modern man." (October 16, 1920)

"Why was the Temple of Solomon there?" asked Rudolf Steiner. And he answered, "It existed for the same reason that the temple of the future will exist and alone can exist ... . Our time has the task of inaugurating an art of temple building that will say clearly to the people of the future, 'The temple, that is man himself, the man open in his soul to receive the spirit!' but this temple architecture is different from all that has preceded it ... . The soul's conception of the spirit is invisible, supersensible. Yet it must take on a sensible form, must become *art*! No other period of history than our own and the age to follow will be capable of developing such an art." (December 12, 1911)

No 'temple' should be erected in the old sense. The interior spaces of the new mysteries must open the soul up, not close it off. The static forms of earlier buildings must be brought into movement. Color and light should open the way into the spiritual worlds. The entire inner surface should speak and sing, should "become an organ that speaks the language of the gods." (June 17, 1914)

Foretelling this new architecture, Rudolf Steiner says, "The god lived within the Greek temple; the congregation and its spirit were able to live in the Romanesque or Gothic building, but the spiritual world should speak through the building of the future. We have seen the house of earthly forms and of earthly forces throughout human evolution; we have seen the house where the human soul lives together with the spirit-soul throughout the spiritual evolution of the earth. Let us, my dear friends, build the *House of Speech*, the house that speaks, the house whose every wall is alive; let us build it out of love for true art, which is also out of love for true spirituality, and love for every man or woman." (June 17, 1914)

The Grail motif is not to be sought in the Goetheanum in a form suited to the Middle Ages but in a fresh metamorphosis. The architecture of the first Goetheanum had to be different from everything that had preceded it. It had to bring the striving of the individual to visibility in such a way that not simply the personal or subjective came to expression but a pure humanity. The human being in his Parsifal nature, that is, as he who builds an inner temple for his highest ideal out of his most individual cognitive powers, should become visible. The movement in feeling from the periphery to the veiled sanctuary at the center, which determined the medieval Grail buildings, is transformed into a movement of will along an axis of symmetry toward the unveiled, revealed mystery of the central motif. And this says, *Know yourself in the striving for balance between the opposing powers.*"

"As important as the knowledge was for medieval man that there was a place to gather in where something was concealed (whether it was the relic of some saint or the Holy Grail itself) and where the people gathered together could let their vague yearnings for the mysterious flow in unison, it is just as important for modern man to develop a sense for what he is as an individual; that is, as seeker for balance between two forces that are in polar opposition .... So we come back to the fact that the building will enclose something, but now it encloses the individual human being in his striving for balance." (December 13, 1919)

The forms and colors of the first Goetheanum spoke through polarities, through the reconciling of opposites: through the convexity and concavity of sculptural reliefs, through the light and dark of the etched windows, through contrasting mural colors of red and blue, warm and cold. To every beholder they cried out, 'Know yourself!' and what they showed to each was *himself*. In the column motifs, one was shown how he had undergone a planetary evolution through forces from above and below, and how he will evolve further through a fresh impulse arising out of the coming together of these polar forces. In the brightness and shadow of the windows, he could see how his path toward the spiritual heights lies between light and darkness until he reaches the building of the Temple of the Human Being where he will be received by world-transforming love. In the colored contrasts of the painting, he could experience how a Father-God had created the foundations of consciousness that made it possible for man to build up sheaths of soul into which impulses from the divine Son could be received.

Three years before the fire, Rudolf Steiner said, "If destiny permits us to complete this building one day, the person who sits in it will have before his eyes his most intimate concern: the being who gives meaning to earth evolution, the Christ. Yet this should be experienced artistically. It may not remain a mere fact established by the intellect that this is the Christ; it must be felt and experienced. Everything has been conceived artistically, and what is most important is what comes to expression through artistic forms. Thus, purely in a feeling way, I would like to say, without the intellect (which should only point the way to the feeling) what appears in the east should touch a person so that he is able to say, 'That is you'. But this is not an abstract definition of the human being for this balance can be established in infinitely varied ways. This does not imply that we have the image of a god here, for the admonition not to fashion the image of God applies to Christians as well. This is no statue of a god; what it captures is what has formed out of the group-soul nature of the human being and become the individual power of being in each human being. Account has been taken of the working and weaving of individual impulses in these forms." (December 13, 1919)

A threefold creation motif was painted above the architrave inside the western entrance to the hall. The activity of the gods in creating the human sheaths is revealed in the painting of the cupola up to the Greek era in which the human being attains the bodily foundation into which he can receive his own 'I'.

Above the architrave separating the two cupolas glowed the triple motif of the thinking, feeling and willing ego. A person can work on these himself in order to be able to assimilate the future light of mankind. In the smaller cupola this is indicated in the picture of the Slav bearing the starry cross. This possibility arises through the force emanating from the central figure in the east.

"We see that the highest ideal for human development derives from knowledge of the Grail – the highest conceivable ideal. In the end, the spiritualization of the human being appears to be a result of the harmony established in the fifth and sixth periods of present evolution, between the forces of mind and soul already achieved and the knowledge of supersensible worlds. What each person works out in the recesses of his own soul will in the end become an outer world. The human spirit lifts itself to the mighty impressions from the outer world, at first sensing and later knowing the spiritual beings behind these impressions. The human heart responds to the infinite grandeur of these beings. But a man can also attain the knowledge that his inner experiences on the level of intellect, feeling and character form the seeds for a spirit world in the process of becoming."[31]

The forms and colors of the first Goetheanum spoke of the past, present and future of mankind, or reincarnation and karma, and of the significance of human life. All that was spared from the flames was the sculptured image of 'love incarnate'.

THE HOUSE OF THE WORD

From Goethe's 'Fairy Tale' to the Mystery Dramas

One can sense that a work of art like the Goetheanum has, so to speak, descended to earth from a spiritual sphere. Pure, undisturbed, and complete, it stands before the astounded man of the present time and invites him in. As he enters the hall from the west, he discovers the movement of the columns and architraves toward the east, the streaming of colors in the motif of the creation of the world as it takes shape through time and then he goes on to the threefold motif of the 'word' IAO over the stage-opening. He experiences the caesura at the architectural mid-point – the intersection of the two cupolas. The twofold image of the Representative of Man between Ahriman and Lucifer approaches him from the east, as does the stream of blues and reds which express egohood and bring the human being and his history to light.

It will not disturb this picture in any way if we conclude by recapitulating the stages by which this building took on form, the path its creator travelled to its fulfillment. First of all there is the strand that leads from Goethe's Fairy Tale to the Mystery Dramas and hence on to the building itself. (cf. p. 12 ff.) From the year 1889 onward, Rudolf Steiner continually made new attempts to provide the key to Goethe's 'open secret'. He himself describes the long process stretching over twenty-one years by which the imaginations of the Fairy Tale metamorphosed into his first Mystery Drama, *The Portal of Initiation.*[32]

The intention to dramatize the Fairy Tale as such for the third Munich Congress (1910) could not be carried out. "When the idea arose some years ago of performing in Munich, the intention was to bring to the stage a representation of the world-shaping forces contained in Goethe's *Tale of the Green Snake and the Beautiful Lily.* This was not possible. We needed to handle this with far more realism. From this arose the Mystery Drama *The Portal of Initiation.* It is obvious that Goethe's time was not yet ready for the transition from a content that could then still be clothed in fine fairy tale imaginations to the real characters found in *The Portal of Initiation.*" (November 22, 1920)

Rudolf Steiner's concern was with the Rosicrucian impulse he discovered in the Fairy Tale, which he then worked out in the 'Rosicrucian Mystery' of his first drama. "If you take what Goethe has hidden away in *The Tale of the Green Snake and the Beautiful Lily* and try to move on to what was living in Goethe's mind, then the thought can arise: here in a human soul a new Christ-impulse is living, an impulse for the transformation of mankind such as came about through the Mystery of Golgotha, a striving for a new grasp of this mystery. The whole Fairy Tale breathes ... an air of anticipation ... . Goetheanism is at the same time a mood of anticipation for a new understanding of the Mystery of Golgotha." (January 11, 1919)

The motif of the temple appears at once. This is the subterranean temple in which the cry 'The time is at hand!' resounds. This temple then rises to earthly visibility. The imagination of this temple flows directly into the architectural idea of the Goetheanum which had lived in Rudolf Steiner ever since the performance of Eduard Schuré's *Sacred Drama of Eleusis* (1907). Marie von Sivers reported to Schuré, "If he were to have had the neces-

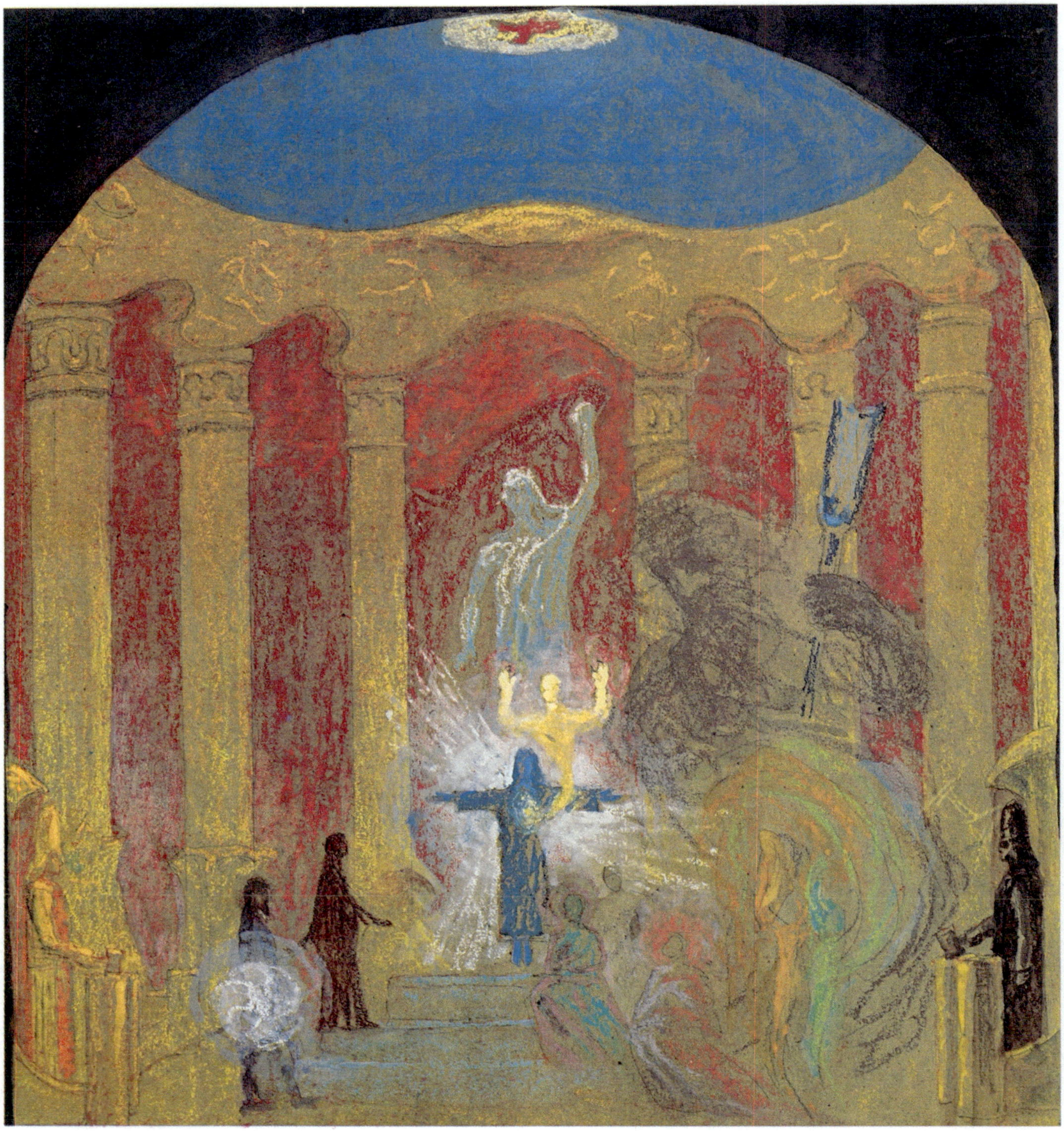

The Golden Temple, by Hermann Linde

sary materials and workers at his disposal, then in the shortest time he would have brought about something fabulous – the temple of the future. As it was, he could only sketch ideas, but they will bear fruit."[33]

In later years this relationship to the temple of the Fairy Tale was given visible expression in a work of art. The painter Hermann Linde (1883–1923), who had a leading function in the execution of the murals for the two cupolas, at the suggestion of Rudolf Steiner and with his intensive participation, painted a cycle of twelve pictures in which the motifs of the Fairy Tale and the Mystery Drama are intertwined.[34] The 'Golden Temple' is to be seen in the eleventh picture; its architecture is reminiscent of the interior of the small cupola, but it includes the pillars of the three kings. The walls are red, the ceiling blue, similar to the architectural model in Malsch and to the festival room in Stuttgart (cf. p. 24). A bird-like being hovers in the blue of the heights. Is this the hawk of the Fairy Tale? Against a background of red stands the building's central figure in a pale green, his left arm raised, the right directed to the depths. The figures of the Fairy Tale form the foreground. The signs of the zodiac can be discerned in the warm wood-tones of the architrave – to the south the Archer and Scorpion, to the north Capricorn and Aquarius.

Linde's placement of the Christ figure between the winter signs of the zodiac is representative of the cultural periods and their motifs (India, Persia, Egypt, etc.) as well as of the sun's progress through the year. The small cupola with its twelve columns reflects the cosmos with its zodiacal imaginations. As we shall see, these were cast directly into the verses, 'The Twelve Moods of the Zodiac', which we can take as a particular cosmic imagination specifically for the small cupola.

The Mystery Dramas

In the year 1907, a series of theosophical congresses began in Munich. Here Rudolf Steiner was already confronted by the inner necessity of integrating the artistic element into the planned program of lectures. As early as 1905, he requested "This should be our ideal – to create forms expressing the inner life. For in an era that has no forms to look at, that can create no forms out of what it has to see, in such a time the spirit must of necessity dissipate into empty abstraction .... Thus the work of the future must in this direction: to give the religious spirit a beautiful, meaningful form."[35]

At the first Congress in 1907, the rented hall was decorated by simple improvised means. On boards two meters high, 'planetary columns' were hinted at (cf. p. 23); between them hung 'apocalyptic seals' and on the stage front were the signs of the zodiac. The intention in unmistakable – to allow architecture to speak to man.

Eduard Shuré's *Sacred Drama of Eleusis* was performed in the translation of Marie von Sivers, brought into metrical form by Rudolf Steiner. He valued most highly what Shuré had contributed to a renewed understanding of the ancient mysteries,[36] for Shuré's was the first attempt to make the old clairvoyant mystery culture accessible once again in modern form. The Eleusinian Mysteries were of particular importance to Rudolf Steiner because of their prediction of the future times presented in the figure of the younger Dionysius. The pupil of these mysteries had before him this imagination of "a maternal figure with an infant suckling at her breast. He was then led to understand the words, 'and that is the god Iachos, who is to come.' In this way the pupil in Greece learned to anticipate the mystery of the Christ." (December 14, 1923)

The Congress opened with Rudolf Steiner's lecture on 'The Initiation of the Rosicrucians', and as if to reinforce this Christian impulse, he followed this with the cycle on 'The Theosophy of the Rosicrucians'.

Something of the mighty preparation of the Goetheanum idea can be perceived as well in the cycle on the Gospel of John, which preceded the Munich Congress the following year (1908). In the very first lecture, Rudolf Steiner spoke of the Logos mystery of Ephesus. It was here that the words introducing the John Gospel, 'In the beginning was the word', had their foundation, even if the temple of Artemis, the 'House of the Word' of antiquity, had been razed to the ground.

The years 1910 to 1913 brought the performances of the Mystery Dramas, which inspired the wish, strengthened year by year, for a building to house them (cf. p. 12 ff.). Through insight into reincarnation and karma, a renewal of the mystery drama had been achieved, together with the new art of eurythmy, which was created in 1912 and put on the stage the same year in *The Guardian of the Threshold*. It was "the first drama in human history in which the idea of reincarnation took concrete form".[37] And thus the architectural idea for a new 'House of the Word' gradually became more concrete in these years as well. At a meeting of the Building Association ('Bauverein') founded in April of 1911, Rudolf Steiner spoke quite clearly of the novel tasks posed by the building.

"We have to find the possibility, out of what spiritual science is in a position to give us, of creating an interior space that is enclosed through the effect of color, form and what otherwise is presented there artistically, yet at the same time and in every detail is not sealed off. It will ask us, wherever we look, to break through the walls with our eyes, with our feelings and senses. We are thus at one and the same time enclosed, but in this cell-like enclosure we are in contact with the universe of weaving divinity. To have walls that are no walls, that is what the temple art of the future will discover – an interior space that renounces itself, that no longer expresses the egoism of space, that is selfless in all that it displays of color, a space that only wills what allows access to the cosmos ... . It will express in colors and forms, in the language of colors and forms, in all that it is, in its genuinely living quality, what will be done and spoken here. ... And naturally the words that are spoken out into this space will find themselves so bounded that, as they meet these walls, they will encounter there something so like themselves that it will reflect back into the interior space what was given originally by the human being himself. The dynamic will go out from the center of the Word to its periphery, and this interior space should offer an echo of spiritual knowledge, of a spiritual message, not as though a window were broken through it, but as if at its borders it were both bounded in itself, in what it is, and also free and open to the breadths of the spiritual infinite." (December 12, 1911)

One can sense, through what was brought to visibility in Dornach from 1913 onward, that this did not remain an abstract request. This building was to arise according to the divine law of the Logos.

"Let us pay heed to the organs that the gods themselves have fashioned. ... Let us eavesdrop on the etheric forms of the plants and make corresponding forms for our walls. Then we are creating as nature did, when she made the human larynx for speaking. Thus are we creating larynxes through which the gods may speak to us. Let us listen to the forms on our walls, for they are speech-organs for the gods. We shall then be attempting the path back into Paradise." (June 17, 1914)

Eurythmy as Visible Speech

As the modern temple finds a voice through its sculptured forms, so should eurythmy as the language of the human form, also belong to the being of this 'House of the Word'. The very first eurythmic exercise[38] was the 'pillar' of the 'I' (ee), leading over to the experiences of A and O together with the corresponding color experience. These are the same forces at work in the 'cosmic IAO', the threefold motif to the east in the large cupola, close to its intersection with the small cupola. Those who took part in the original performance of 'The Twelve Moods of the Zodiac' beneath the small cupola on the 29th of August, 1915 could experience the union of the building, eurythmy, and speech most perfectly. This poem with its twelve verses of seven lines each, the eurythmy with its twelve plus seven performers, the sequence of twelve colors in the veils, the architecture with its twelve columns – all this called forth the impression of a ceremony in the mysteries. Marie Savitch describes this. "And when with the first upward movement of the arms, the figures stood upright, following the upward striving of the columns, and when the seven figures in the middle began slowly to move, following the direction in which the forms of the architraves were changing, their metamorphosing sculptural movements gathered into the holding strength of the cupola, one felt in this how the spiritual in the depths of man's being was uniting itself with cosmic law and finding its resonance in the building. Then one knew: the building has embraced eurythmy. That of which Rudolf Steiner spoke has come about: 'It must be built according to the same inner laws by which we speak, by which the mysteries are conducted, by which now eurythmy is performed'."[39]

Behind the symphony of the twelve stood the image of the thirteenth. Christ is the Master, but also the Brother who waits to be asked. He becomes the gardener who tends the seeds of morality and bears them on into the future. And so he speaks to souls and hearts through an artistic medium, the work of art becoming an act of creation. Nothing has permanence since the birth of the consciousness soul save what man himself wins by a free creative deed under the sign of the Christ.

"The temple stood there as man, the man as temple. Everything was inscribed in it – how worlds come into being, how man evolves and becomes active, the deeds of the gods – revealed in the color that flowed through the cupolas, in the organic growth of the motifs on columns and architraves, in the light-fashioned imaginations of the windows. Sculpture and painting surpassed themselves, overcame line and became movement. Colors created form from within, out of their own creative ensoulment. In the freshly-blossoming art of eurythmy, music and speech had become movement, stepping into visibility through the instrument of the human body. Made visible in this way, the creative powers of speech now had an enlivening effect on the other arts, kindling spiritually creative fire. The immanent inner music could lay hold of the audible tone, spiritualize it and lift it to higher spheres. Rudolf Steiner had named the building the 'House of Speech'. All the arts had their home there, together with science and mystery wisdom. The synthesis of art, science and religion had once again been achieved."[40]

Chronological List of References to Lectures cited in the Text*

*Editor's Note: Many of the lectures cited in this text have not as yet been translated into English. An attempt has been made to locate those lectures that are available in English translation and the remaining lectures are cited with their German title, publisher, etc. and the number in the Index to the Complete Works of Rudolf Steiner called in German the *Gesamtausgabe* (GA). Some of these lectures may have been recently translated by Rudolf Steiner Press (London) or the Anthroposophic Press (Hudson, N.Y.).

1. Nov. 4, 11, 1904 — Berlin, in "Die Tempellegende und die Goldene Legende als symbolischer Ausdruck vergangener und zukünftiger Entwicklungsgeheimnisse des Menschen", GA 93.
2. Dec. 19, 1904 — Berlin, in "Signs and Symbols of the Christmas Festval". Anthroposophic Press, New York 1969.
3. May 22,29, 1905 — Berlin, in "Die Tempellegende und die Goldene Legende als symbolischer Ausdruck vergangener und zukünftiger Entwicklungsgeheimnisse des Menschen", GA 93.
4. Jun. 9, 1906 — Paris, in "Kosmogonie. Populärer Okkultismus. Das Johannes-Evangelium. Die Theosophie an Hand des Johannes-Evangeliums", GA 94.
5. Oct. 19, 1906–Apr. 1, 1907 — Berlin, in "Ursprungsimpulse der Geisteswissenschaft Christliche Esoterik im Lichte neuer Geist-Erkenntnis", GA 96.
6. Jun. 4, 1907 — Munich, in "Theosophy of the Rosicrucians". Rudolf Steiner Press, London 1966.
7. May 22,26, 1908 — Hamburg, in "The Gospel of St. John". Anthroposophic Press, New York 1962.
8. Jun. 19-25, 1908 — Nurnberg, in "The Apocalypse of St. John". Rudolf Steiner Press, London 1977.
9. Aug. 4-14, 1908 — Stuttgart, in "Universe, Earth and Man in their Relationship to Egyptian Myths and Modern Civilisation". Rudolf Steiner Publishing Co., London 1955.
10. Sep. 2-14, 1908 — Leipzig, in "Egyptian Myths and Mysteries". Anthroposophic Press, New York 1971.
11. May 5, 1909 — Berlin, in "Bilder okkulter Siegel und Säulen. Der Münchner Kongress Pfingsten 1907 und seine Auswirkungen", GA 284/285.
12. Jun. 24, 1909 — Kassel, in "The Gospel of St. John in Relation to the Other Three Gospels, Particularly to the Gospel of St. Luke". Anthroposophic Press, New York and Rudolf Steiner Press, London 1948.
13. Aug. 29-31, 1909 — Munich, in "The East in the Light of the West". Rudolf Steiner Publishing Co., London and Anthroposophic Press, New York 1940.
14. Oct. 25, 1909 — Berlin, in "Anthroposophie, Philosophie, Pneumatosophie", GA 115.
15. Mar. 6, 1910 — Stuttgart, in "Das Ereignis der Christus-Erscheinung in der ätherischen Welt", GA 118.
16. Jun. 16, 1910 — Oslo, in "The Mission of the Individual Folksouls in Relation to Teutonic Mythology". Rudolf Steiner Press, London 1970.
17. Aug. 17-24, 1910 — München, in "Die Geheimnisse der biblischen Schöpfungsgeschichte. Das Sechstagewerk im 1. Buch Moses", GA 122.
18. Sep. 1, 1910 — Bern, in "The Gospel of the St. Matthew". Rudolf Steiner Press, London 1965.
19. Dec. 18, 1910 — Hannover, in "Exkurse in das Gebiet des Markus-Evangeliums", GA 124.
20. Jan. 19, 1911 — Berlin, in "Antworten der Geisteswissenschaft auf die grossen Fragen des Daseins", GA 60.
21. Oct. 14, 1911 — Karlsruhe, in "From Jesus to Christ". Rudolf Steiner Publishing Co. and Anthroposophic Press, New York 1943.
22. Oct. 10, 1911 — Stuttgart, in "Bilder okkulter Siegel und Säulen. Der Münchner Kongress Pfingsten 1907 und seine Auswirkungen", GA 284/285.
23. Dec. 2, 1911 — Nürnberg, in "Das esoterische Christentum und die geistige Führung der Menschheit", GA 130.
24. Dec. 12, 1911 — Berlin, "Und der Bau wird Mensch", Dornach 1945.

25. Dec. 21, 1911 Berlin, in "Die Mission der neuen Geistesoffenbarung. Das Christus-Ereignis als Mittelpunktsgeschehen der Erdenevolution", GA 127.

26. Apr. 3, 1912 Helsinki, in "Die geistigen Wesenheiten in den Himmelskörpern und Naturreichen", GA 136.

27. Apr. 17, 1912 Stockholm, in "Erfahrungen des Übersinnlichen. Die Wege der Seele zu Christus", GA 143.

28. May 14, 1912 Berlin, in "Earthly and Cosmic Man". Rudolf Steiner Publishing Co., London 1948.

29. Feb. 4, 1913 Berlin *Skizze eines Lebensabrisses,* in "Briefe, Band I", Dornach 1955.

30. Feb. 5, 1913 Berlin, in "Die Mysterien des Morgenlandes und des Christentums", GA 144.

31. Feb. 6, 1913 Berlin, in "Die Mysterien des Morgenlandes und des Christentums", GA 144.

32. Aug. 30, 1913 München, in "Die Geheimnisse der Schwelle", GA 147.

33. Dec. 30, 1913 Leipzig, in "Christ and the Spiritual World and the Search for the Holy Grail". Rudolf Steiner Press, London 1963.

34. Feb. 10, 1914 Berlin, in "Aus der Akasha-Forschung. Das Fünfte Evangelium", GA 148.

35. Jun. 1, 1914 Basel, in "Building Stones for an Understanding of the Mystery of Golgotha". Rudolf Steiner Presss, London 1972.

36. Jun. 17, 28, 1914 Dornach, in "Wege zu einem Baustil", GA 286.

37. Oct. 7, 1914 Dornach, in "Die Entstehung und Entwicklung der Eurythmie", GA 277a.

38. Oct. 24,25, 1914 Dornach, in "Der Dornacher Bau als Wahrzeichen geschichtlichen Werdens und künstlerischer Umwandlungsimpulse", Dornach 1937.

39. Nov. 20, 1914 Dornach, in "Der Zusammenhang des Menschen mit der elementarischen Welt. Kalewala. Olaf Asteson. Das russische Volkstum. Die Welt als Ergebnis von Gleichgewichtswirkungen", GA 158.

40. Jan. 1-3, 1915 Dornach, in "Art in the Light of Mystery Wisdom". Rudolf Steiner Press, London 1970.

41. Apr. 3, 1915 Dornach, in "Der Baldur-Mythos und das Karfreitag-Mysterium", Dornach 1981.

42. Apr. 4, 1915 Dornach, in "Geisteswissenschaftliche Erläuterungen zu Goethes Faust. Band I: Faust, der strebende Mensch", GA 272.

43. Apr. 10, 1915 Basel, in "Ein Dornacher Bau in seiner Gestaltung als Haus für Geisteswissenschaft", in *Die Menschenschule* Nov./Dec. 1964.

44. May 18, 1915 Linz, in "Das Geheimnis des Todes. Wesen und Bedeutung Mitteleuropas und die europäischen Volksgeister", GA 159/160.

45. Aug. 8, 1915 Dornach, in "Der Baum des Lebens und der Baum der Erkenntnis des Guten und des Bösen. Die Geheimnisse in der Kunst", Dornach 1936.

46. Aug. 24, 1915 Dornach, in "Die Entstehung und Entwicklung der Eurythmie", GA 277a.

47. Jan. 14, 1916 Basel, "Die Harmonie zwischen Geistesforschung und Naturforschung und die Missverständnisse über die erstere und den ihr gewidmeten Bau in Dornach", in *Das Goetheanum* Nov. 19, 1939.

48. Feb. 16, 1916 Hamburg, in "Die Verbindung zwischen Lebenden und Toten", GA 168.

49. Aug. 15, 1916 Dornach, in "Das Rätsel des Menschen. Die geistigen Hintergründe der menschlichen Geschichte", GA 170.

50. Jan. 17, 1917 Dornach, in "Kunstgeschichte als Abbild innerer geistiger Impulse", GA 292.

51. Feb. 6, 1917 Berlin, in "Bausteine zu einer Erkenntnis des Mysteriums von Golgatha. Kosmische und menschliche Metamorphose", GA 175.

52. Feb.20, Apr. 12, 1917 Berlin, in "Bausteine zu einer Erkenntnis des Mysteriums von Golgatha. Kosmische und menschliche Metamorphose", GA 175.

53. Oct. 21, 1917 Dornach, in "Aufbaugedanken und Gesinnungsbildung", Dornach 1942.

54. Nov. 16, 1917 St. Gallen, in "Individuelle Geistwesen und ihr Wirken in der Seele des Menschen", GA 178.

55. Dec. 24, 1917, Jan. 6, 1918 Dornach, in "Mysterienwahrheiten und Weihnachtsimpulse. Alte Mythen und ihre Bedeutung", GA 180.

56. Feb. 17, 1918 München, in "Kunst und Kunsterkenntnis. Das Sinnliche-Übersinnliche in seiner Verwirklichung durch die Kunst", GA 271.

57. Jun. 11, 1918 Berlin, in "Erdensterben und Weltenleben. Anthroposophische Lebensgaben, Bewusstseins-Notwendigkeiten für Gegenwart und Zukunft", GA 181.

58. Jul. 3, 1918 Berlin, in "Menschliche und menschheitliche Entwicklungswahrheiten", GA 176.

59. Sept. 20, 1918 Dornach, in "Die Polarität von Dauer und Entwickelung im Menschenleben. Die kosmische Vorgeschichte der Menschheit", GA 184.

60. Nov. 3, 1918 Dornach, in "From Symptom to Reality in Modern History". Rudolf Steiner Press, London 1976.

61. Dec. 28-29, 1918 Dornach, in "How Can Mankind Find the Christ Again? The Threefold Shadow-Existence of our Time and the New Light of Christ". Anthroposophic Press, New York 1947.

62. Jan. 11, 1919 Dornach, in "Der Goetheanismus,ein Umwandlungsimpuls und Auferstehungsgedanke. Menschenwissenschaft und Sozialwissenschaft", GA 188.

63. Aug. 23, 1919 Stuttgart, in "Erziehungskunst. Methodisch-Didaktisches", GA 294.

64. Dec. 13, 1919 Dornach, in "The Mission of the Archangel Michael". Anthroposophic Press, New York 1961.

65. Dec. 27-29 1919 Stuttgart, in "Geisteswissenschaftliche Impulse zur Entwicklung der Physik", GA 320.

66. Jan. 23, 1920 Dornach, in "Architektur, Plastik und Malerei des ersten Goetheanum", 2. Auflage Dornach 1982.

67. Jan. 24-25, 1920 Dornach, in "Architektur, Plastik und Malerei des ersten Goetheanum", Dornach 1972.

68. Mar. 20, 1920 Dornach, in "Heilfaktoren für den sozialen Organismus", GA 198.

69. Apr. 5, 1920 Dornach, "Der Dornacher Bau" II, Lichtbildervortrag (Fortsetzung des Vortrages vom 4. April 1920), noch nicht veröffentlicht.

70. Apr. 25, 1920 Dornach, in "Entsprechungen zwischen Mikrokosmos und Makrokosmos. Der Mensch – ein Hieroglyphe des Weltenalls", GA 201.

71. Jun. 12, 1920 Stuttgart, "Das Goetheanum in Dornach", Lichtbildervortrag, noch nicht veröffentlicht.

72. Sep. 25, 1920 Dornach, Ansprache anlässlich einer Zusammenkunft zur Vorbereitung des anthroposophischen Hochschulkurses, in *Blätter für Anthroposophie* 1955, 7. Jahrgang, Nr. 3.

73. Oct. 9, 16, 1920 Dornach, in "Der Baugedanke von Dornach", Dornach 1942.

74. Oct. 23, 1920 Dornach, in "Die neue Geistigkeit und das Christus-Erlebnis des zwanzigsten Jahrhunderts", GA 200.

75. Nov. 22, 1920 Stuttgart, in "Gegensätze in der Menschheitsentwicklung", GA 197.

76. Feb. 28, 1921 Den Haag, "Der Baugedanke von Dornach", Lichtbildervortrag, noch nicht veröffentlicht.

77. Apr. 16, 1921 Dornach, in "Perspektiven der Menschheitsentwickelung. Der materialistische Erkenntnisimpuls und die Aufgabe der Anthroposophie", GA 204.

78. May 6-7, 1921 Dornach, in "Colour". Rudolf Steiner Press, London 1971.

79. Jun. 29, 1921 Bern, "Der Baugedanke des Goetheanum", Lichtbildervortrag, noch nicht veröffenlicht.

80. Aug. 28, 1921 Dornach, Ansprache bei einer Führung durch das Goetheanum, noch nicht veröffentlicht.

81. Sep. 7, 1921 Stuttgart, "Der Baugedanke von Dornach", Lichtbildervortrag, noch nicht veröffentlicht.

82. Sep. 24, 1921 Dornach, in "Anthroposophie als Kosmosophie. Erster Teil: Wesenszüge des Menschen im irdischen und kosmischen Bereich", GA 207.

83. Oct. 9, 1921 Dornach, in "Anthroposophie als Kosmosophie. Erter Teil: Wesenszüge des Menschen im irdischen und kosmischen Bereich", GA 207.

84. Dec. 18, 1921 Dornach, in "Nordische und mitteleuropäische Geistimpulse. Das Fest der Erscheinung Christi", GA 209.

85. Dec. 30, 1921 Dornach, in "Stilformen des Organisch-Lebendigen", Dornach 1933.

86. Apr. 9, 1922 Den Haag, in "Die Bedeutung der Anthroposophie im Geistesleben der Gegenwart", Dornach 1957.

87. Apr. 24, 1922 London, in "Das Sonnenmysterium

und das Mysterium von Tod und Auferstehung. Exoterisches und esoterisches Christentum", GA 211.

88. Aug. 22, 1922 Oxford, in "The Mystery of the Trinity". Rudolf Steiner Publishing Co., London and Anthroposophic Press, New York 1940.

89. Aug. 29, 1922 Oxford, in "Geschichte und Überwindung des Imperialismus", Zürich/New York 1945.

90. Sep. 20, 1922 Dornach, in "Die Erkenntnis des Menschenwesens nach Leib, Seele und Geist. Über frühe Erdzustände", GA 374.

91. Dec. 23-24, 1922 Dornach, in "Das Verhältnis der Sternenwelt zum Menschen und des Menschen zur Sternenwelt – Die geistige Kommunion der Menschheit", GA 219.

92. Feb. 17, 1923 Dornach, in "Vom Leben des Menschen und der Erde. Über das Wesen des Christentums", GA 349.

93. Feb. 21, 1923 Dornach, in "Vom Leben des Menschen und der Erde. Über das Wesen des Christentums", GA 349.

94. Jun. 9, 1923 Dornach, in "The Arts and Their Mission". Anthroposophic Press, New York, 1964.

95. Oct. 5, 1923 Dornach, in "Der Jahreskreislauf als Atmungsvorgang der Erde und die vier grossen Festeszeiten", GA 223.

96. Oct. 8, 1923 Dornach, in "Mensch und Welt. Das Wirken des Geistes in der Natur. Über das Wesen der Bienen", GA 351.

97. Aug. 13, 1923 Dornach, in "Der Jahreskreislauf als Atmungsvorgang der Erde und die vier großen Festeszeiten", GA 223.

98. Dec. 14,21, 1923 Dornach, in "Mysteriengestaltungen", GA 232.

99. Dec. 28, 1923 Dornach, in "World History in the Light of Anthroposophy". Rudolf Steiner Press, London 1977.

100. Dec. 31, 1923 Dornach, in "Die Weihnachtstagung zur Begründung der allgemeinen Anthroposophischen Gesellschaft 1923/24. Grundsteinlegung. Vorträge und Ansprachen, Statutenberatung", GA 260.

101. Apr. 22, 1924 Dornach, in "World History in the Light of Anthroposophy", London 1977.

102. Apr. 27, 1924 May 9, 1924 Dornach, in "Karmic Relationships Vol. II", Rudolf Steiner Press, London 1974.

NOTES

Page

9 (1) Werner Haftmann, *Painting in the Twentieth Century*. trans. Ralph Manheim. (New York: Holt, Rinehart and Winston, 1965).

(2) Vincent van Gogh, quoted from H. Neumayer, *Fauvismus* (Vienna: 1956).

(3) Ibid.

10 (4) Sixten Ringbom, *The Sounding Cosmos.* A Study in the Spiritualism of Kandinsky and the Genesis of Abstract Painting, Acta Acadamiae Aboensis, Ser. A, vol. 38, no. 2 (Abo Akademi: 1970).

(5) Rudolf Steiner, *Four Mystery Dramas.* There are two translations available. One is by R. and H. Pusch, the other by A. Bittleston.

11 (6) Quoted from Lothar Schreyer, *Erinnerungen an Sturm und Bauhaus.* (München: 1959).

(7) In *Die neue Architektur und das Bauhaus.* (Mainz: 1965). Gropius says, "The ultimate goal of the Bauhaus was the indivisible artwork, *the* edifice in which there were no borders between monumental and decorative art."

(8) Rudolf Steiner, "Skizze eines Lebensabrisses", in *Briefe,* vol. 1. (Dornach: 1955). Refers to a lecture held in Berlin on February 4, 1913.

(9) *Goethes naturwissenschaftliche Schriften,* 5 vols, ed. Rudolf Steiner (Dornach: 1975). This is a facsimile edition of the five volumes contained in *Kürschners Deutsche National-Litteratur,* 1883–1897.

(10) Ibid., vol. 1. See also Johann Wolfgang von Goethe, *Farbenlehre.* Mit Einleitungen und Kommentaren von Rudolf Steiner, ed. Gerhard Ott and Heinrich Proskauer, "Das System der Farbenlehre" in vol. 1. (Stuttgart: Verlag Freies Geistesleben, 1980).

12 (11) From a letter from Marie Steiner to Sophie Stinde. Quoted from *Beiträge zur Rudolf Steiner Gesamtausgabe,* no. 36. (Dornach: Rudolf Steiner-Nachlaßverwaltung, 1971/72).

14 (12) In the chapter "Von den Mysterien-Dichtungen Rudolf Steiners zum Dornacher Bau", in *Marie Steiner — Ihr Weg zur Erneuerung der Bühnenkunst durch die Anthroposophie.* Eine Dokumentation. (Dornach: 1973).

(13) Ibid.

(14) Ibid.

19 (1) Assja Turgeniev, Afterword to Rudolf Steiner, *Der Dornacher Bau als Wahrzeichen geschichtlichen Werdens und künstlerischer Umwandlungsimpulse.* (Dornach: 1937).

20 (2) In an unpublished lecture given on June 12, 1920 Rudolf Steiner said the following about the seven pairs of columns supporting the large cupola: "Often when people visit they count; one, two, three, four, five, six, seven. Seven columns! Then they say, 'These are mystics; they have superstitiously used the number seven.' I can only say that nature must then also be superstitious! There are seven colors to the rainbow. There are seven tones in music with the octave being the refrain of the prime. What in nature is expressed as a self-evident structural principle becomes immediate experience when one forms something like this through metamorphosis. And I can say this: nothing could have been further from my mind than the mystical seven. My intent was rather to think of how one capital could arise out of the other, and something wondrous happened, if I may name it that; just as the rainbow has seven colors without the need of mysticism so also in the creation of these forms. When one is finished with the seventh no further artistic thought occurs to one. One knows one is finished, and so one ends up with seven forms."

(3) Assja Turgeniev, *Erinnerungen an Rudolf Steiner und die Arbeit am ersten Goetheanum.* (Stuttgart: 1972).

23 (1) The preliminary stages which led to the building of the first Goetheanum are well documented in *Bilder okkulter Siegel und Säulen — Der Münchener Kongreß Pfingsten 1907 und seine Auswirkungen.* GA 284/285.

(2) These two columns were depicted in the fourth of the seven apocalyptic seals designed by Rudolf Steiner. They also appear in one of the scenes in the drama, *The Guardian of the Threshold.*

24 (3) For more detailed information about the model built in Malsch please consult:

- Erich Zimmer, *Der Modell-Bau von Malsch und das erste Goetheanum. (Stuttgart: 1979).*
- Albert von Baravalle, "Der Modellbau von Malsch", in *Stil,* Epiphany 1979/80, vol. 1, no. 4, p. 15, and 1980/81, vol. 2, no. 1, p. 15.
- Wolfgang Pehnt, *Die Architektur des Expressionismus,* (Stuttgart: 1973).
- E. A. Karl Stockmeyer, *Der Modellbau in Malsch,* (Malsch: 1970).

(4) Hilde Stockmeyer relates how Rudolf Steiner in the presence of twenty-four friends festively laid the foundation stone to this building just as the spring full moon rose on April 5-6, 1909. See *Bilder okkulter Siegel und Säulen.*

25 (5) Concerning this he said, "When we examine what here surrounds us as luminous color, we must say that just as we enter into a relationship with particular beings through the color of a non-transparent wall so we associate with other beings through transparent and luminous color. The first beings initially spread themselves

into space but they have nothing to do with the mineral, plant, and the animal kingdoms. The second, those beings we come into contact with through luminous color, are very much concerned with these three kingdoms." October 5, 1911.

(6) They were similar to those published in the first edition (1912) of the *Soul Calendar.* They were republished in *Beiträge zur Rudolf Steiner Gesamtausgabe,* no. 37/38, 1972.

(7) Later published under the title, *Und der Bau wird Mensch – Die Ziele des Johannes-Bauvereins.* (Dornach: 1945).

(8) In this model there was a passage which led from the small cupola to a smaller building which was intended to be used for a color therapy that Rudolf Steiner wanted to work out with the phsysician Felix Peipers. See also the comment made by Wolfram Groddeck in *Das Wirken Rudolf Steiners von 1907 - 1917: München – Berlin – Dornach* (Schaffhausen: 1980).

26 (9) Natalie Turgeniev-Pozzo, *Zwölf Jahre der Arbeit am Goetheanum.* (Dornach: 1942).

27 (10) Op. cit., Assja Turgeniev, *Erinnerungen...*

(11) Ibid.

(12) Rudolf Steiner, *Das Gotheanum in seinen zehn Jahren,* (Dornach: 1961).

28 (13) See Lory Maier-Smits, "Die Anfänge der Eurythmie", in *Die Entstehung und Entwicklung der Eurythmie,* GA 227a; Annemarie Dubach-Donath, *Grundelemente der Eurythmie,* (Dornach: 1981); Tatiana Kisseleff, *Eurythmie. Erinnerungen aus den Jahren 1912-27,* (Basel: 1982).

30 (14) "In a yellow flower, that process which brings forth yellow is present in the blossom. In a blue flower, the same process occurs in the root and forces itself up against the blossom. Therefore, if I want to prepare a deep blue pigment from the indigo plant or from chicory, which has a blue blossom, I must use the root. I must treat the root chemically so that it releases its blue color." (February 21, 1923)

31 (15) Arhild Rosenkrantz, *A New Impulse in Art* (London: New Knowledge Books, 1967), p. 79f

(16) Ibid. p. 32f.

(17) Margarita Woloschin, *Die grüne Schlange.* (Stuttgart: Verlag Freies Geistesleben, 1982).

(18) See Hilde Boos – Hamburger, *Die farbige Gestaltung der Kuppeln des ersten Goetheanum.* (Basel: R. G. Zbinden & Co., 1961) p. 24.

32 (19) From a verbal account.

33 (20) Heinz Müller, *Spuren auf dem Weg.* (Stuttgart: 1970).

(21) Op. cit., Assja Turgeniev, Afterword to *Der Dornacher Bau ...*

(22) Op. cit., Heinz Muller.

42 (1) Ibid.

(2) Op. cit., Margarita Woloschin.

(3) W. Lothar Gärtner, "Auch zwei Jubilare des Jahres 1978", in *Rundbrief der Sektion fur Redende und Musizierende Künste,* no. 9. (Dornach: Goetheanum, 1979).

79 (4) The titles used for the sketches are those given them upon their publication in 1930.

80 (5) Rigveda X, 129. In the German text the translation used was that of Hermann Beckh.

81 (6) Eckermann, *Conversations with Goethe,* March 18, 1831.

83 (7) Margarita Woloschin, "Erinnerungsbilder aus arbeitsreicher Zeit", in Rudolf Steiner, *Zwölf Entwürfe für die Malerei der grossen Kuppel des ersten Goetheanum. (Dornach: 1930).*

84 *(8) Rudolf Steiner, Anthroposophie. Ein Fragment.* GA 45.

(9) J. W. v. Goethe, *Colour Theory,* Sec. 708.

(10) Ibid. Sec. 747.

(11) Compare lectures 7 and 8 in Rudolf Steiner, *First Scientific Lecture-course,* trans. George Adams, vol. II (Clent near Stourbridge, Worcs. Goethean Science Foundation, 1977). GA 320.

87 (12) Compare with the lectures, *Art in the light of the Mystery Wisdom.* GA 275.

88 (13) "The real Lucifer is a being that has remained in the Old Moon evolution. He cannot be seen amongst the physical objects of the present earth. If a painter wanted to paint Lucifer as Lucifer is, then he must paint him in such a way that he could be grasped through a type of inner clairvoyant vision as an etheric shape. Lucifer would then appear in the fashion in which he himself works into our physical organization, through the head and spinal cord. Lucifer would then have to be painted with a human head and a snake-like extension if he were to be painted after his etheric form. Therefore, a painter who knows something of spiritual science would paint Adam and Eve, the tree, and above in the tree a snake-like form with a human head .... In the painting gallery in Hamburg there is a painting by Meister Bertram out of the middle of the Middle Ages, in which the paradise scene is depicted in this way." From a lecture held on February 16, 1916, *The Connection between the Living and the Dead,* GA 168.

89 (14) These lectures were held in Dornach on May 6, 7 and 8, 1921. The first was called, "The Experience of Color: the Four Image Colors". The second, "The Image-nature and Lustre-nature of Color". The third, "Color and Matter: Painting out of Color". They have

been published by the Rudolf Steiner Press, London, under the title, *Color.*

93 (15) Rudolf Steiner, *Indications for an Esoteric Schooling.* GA 245.

94 (16) Rudolf Steiner, *Out of the Akashic Chronicle.* GA 11.

95 (17) Rudolf Steiner, *World History in Light of Anthroposophy and as a Foundation for a Knowledge of the Human Spirit.* GA 233.

98 (18) See Julius Schwabe, *Archetyp und Tierkreis.* (Basel: 1951).

(19) The primal motif of the archetypal animal appears again and again in the work of Rudolf Steiner in the blue north window of the Goetheanum, the training sketches, in blackboard drawings and graphic design. Rudolf Steiner speaks on the theme of the group soul or archetypal animal in the following lectures and essays:

- Whitsun, 1907: The Munich Congress. See *Bilder okkulter Siegel und Saulen,* GA 284/285.
- June 17 - 30, 1908: Nürnberg; *The Apocalypse of St. John,* GA 104.
- August 4 - 16, 1908: Stuttgart; *Universe, Earth and Man in their Relationship to Egyptian Myth and Modern Civilization.* GA 105.
- September 2 - 14, 1908: Leipzig; *Egyptian Myths and Mysteries,* GA 106.
- October 19, 1908 - June 17, 1909: Berlin; *Geisteswissenschaftliche Menschenkunde.*

  See especially the typescript in English of the October 29th lecture, "The Four Human Group Souls".
- December 4, 1909: Munich; "The Ego: the God Within and the God of External Revelation", in the English editions of *The Ego* and *Background to the Gospel of St. Mark* out of GA 117 and 124.
- June 24 - July 7, 1909: Kassel; *The Gospel of St. John and its Relation to the Other Three Gospels.* GA 112.
- August 18 - 28, 1911: Munich; *Wonders of the World, Ordeals of the Soul, Revelations of the Spirit.* GA 129.
- March 20 - 29, 1913: Den Haag; *The Effects of Spiritual Development.* GA 145. See in particular the lecture of March 25.
- October 5, 1914: Dornach; in *Occult Reading and Occult Hearing.* GA 156.
- July 16, 1921: Dornach; in *Menschenwerden, Weltenseele und Weltengeist,* Teil II, "Der Mensch als geistiges Wesen im historischen Werdegang." GA 206.
- October 19 - November 11, 1923: Dornach; *Man as the Symphony of the Creative Word.* GA 230. In connection with this see also the lecture, *The Apocalypse* (in typescript) of April 22, 1907 and the lecture given in Stuttgart on September 16, 1907 in *Nachrichtenblatt* 1948, 25. Jg., Nr. 23-24.

98 (20) In the *Book of Revelation* of John 4 : 7, 8 it says, "... the first living creature like a lion, the second living creature like an ox, the third living creature with the face of a man, and the fourth living creature like a flying eagle. And the four living creatures, each of them with six wings, are full of eyes all round and within, and day and night they never cease to sing. 'Holy, Holy, Holy, is the Lord God Almighty, who was and is and is to come!' "

102 (21) Rudolf Steiner. *Occult Science: An Outline.* GA 13.

(22) Compare this for example with the Rigveda X 82.2, particularly with the German translation of Alfred Ludwig, "Vicvakarman ist ausgebreitet an Geist und Grösse, Schöpfer und Ordner und höchster Anblick; dieser Menschen Gesetz erfüllende Taten werden reich an Speise dort und jenseits der sieben Rischi, wo man nur mehr das Eine nennt."

105 (23) Compare this with the translation in *Zarathustra,* Daniel van Bemmelen. (Stuttgart: 1975).

(24) In his book, *Der Gral in Europa,* (Stuttgart: 1976), Gerhard von dem Borne quotes from G. Salles' foreword to Roman Ghirshman's *Iran.* It is a description of the Iranian Highlands. "If the center of the Highlands is the driest spot on earth, it is also the focus for the most beautiful light of the world. The traveller who enters the country from the south and travels through Kazeran, Schiraz, Persepolis, Isfahan and Kum to Teheran finds he becomes bedazzled by the increasing transfiguration of the landscape. The world loses its density, becomes pure luminosity, to such a degree that even the mountains, disrobed of all substance, seem to hover immovable in the air, which permeates and carries them. One's hands seem to pass through the mountains without resistance, only their reflection is there, like jewels – blue, rose-colored, white and beige .... Then one remembers that one is in the land of Zoroastrianism in which Ahura Mazdao is the highest of all gods. He is the heavens and the light and his symbol is fire."

106 (25) Compare with the lecture given on September 1, 1910 in Bern on *The Gospel of St. Matthew.* GA 123.

(26) The basic convictions of the Persian appear in the *Avesta* in dramatic heroic fashion:

"And I will speak of the two Spirits
In the beginning of the World;
The Holy One said to the Wicked:
Our spiritual selves are not in accord,
Nor our teaching, nor our resolves, nor our
convictions;
Neither our words nor our deeds.
Our whole being and soul are without any harmony.
And always the Arch-polluter crosses my intentions
And I try to make good his evil intentions through the
power

Of truth. O, Mazdao, Just Balance, come to me,
Be my support and hold.
Decide that through the Spirit of Good the evil may perish."

(27) Rudolf Steiner, *Occult Science: An Outline.* GA 13.

107 (28) Translated by Daniel van Bemmelen in *Zarathustra.* (Stuttgart: 1975).

(29) Op. cit., Rudolf Steiner, *Occult Science ...*

109 (30) Compare with the description of W. Scott Pyle in, "Farbe, Form und Seelenwelten. Aus den Erlebnissen eines Malers", in Rudolf Steiner, *Zwölf Entwürfe für die Malerei der grossen Kuppel des ersten Goetheanum.*

110 (31) Kurt Lange, *Pyramiden, Sphinxe, Pharaonen.* (München: 1952.)

(32) The Egyptian *Book of the Dead* contains formulas and sixteen incantations which were to help the souls of the dead to find their way to Osiris. The beings they would meet and the paths they had to travel were shown. The culminating, "Emerging of the Soul into the Full Daylight" has been translated often and in many different ways.

(33) In a lecture given on December 29, 1917, Rudolf Steiner says, "These pyramids were not actually made by the Eqyptians. Whenever conquerors from Iran or that region of the middle east came to Egypt they had these pyramids built for them. The Egyptians learned how to build pyramids from those peoples that had star mysteries. They themselves had what could be described as a kind of Christmas mystery. (see, "On the Mysteries of Ancient and Modern Times", lecture 3, *Anthroposophical Movement,* vol. 6, 1929 p. 101.)

114 (34) Friedrich Hiebel gives an overview on the color perception of the Greeks and Romans in his *Die Botschaft von Hellas.* (Stuttgart: 1983).

(35) J. W. v. Goethe, "Farbenbenennungen der Griechen und Römer." *Materialien zur Geschichte der Farbenlehre.*

119 (36) A blackboard drawing to this can be found in the archives of the Rudolf Steiner Nachlassverwaltung in Dornach.

120 (37) After Hilde Boos - Hamburger in *Die farbige Gestaltung der Kuppeln des ersten Goetheanum.* (Basel: 1961). This booklet contains a descriptive analysis of the painting of the cupolas in the first Goetheanum which was the content of a lecture given by H. Boos - Hamburger. (trans.)

123 (38) Compare with the lectures in *How Can Mankind Find the Christ Again?* GA 187.

124 (39) Please compare this with the more elaborated description and quotes on p. 293f.

133 (1) Rudolf Steiner, "Das Goetheanum in seinen zehn Jahren", *Der Goetheanum-Gedanke. Gesammelte Aufsätze 1921-1925.* GA 36.

135 (2) Luise Clason, "Einige Erinnerungen an die Jahre der Malerei in der kleinen Kuppel des ersten Goetheanum-Baues", in *Mitteilungen der Allgemeinen Anthroposophischen Gesellschaft,* Juni 1950.

162 (3) The relevant section of an unpublished lecture of September 7, 1921 reads: "It is the emergence of that culture which rushes towards abstract thinking and which we still carry within the spiritual life of today. He who does not experience this, as it is commonly experienced today, but endeavors to do so as a complete human being will experience precisely within our modern mode of thinking the striving of Faust. This striving has led modern humanity to be fully aware of the I which is darkly apprehended within as the unformed and inartistically written 'I'. Only that in knowledge is endurable which, when it arises out of the complete human being, is felt to be close to the child, for joined with it is that which here (in the small cupola) has been painted out of the brown-black. Death attaches itself to our knowledge, as our knowledge only delivers to us what is dead. He who does not merely think this through theoretically but inwardly experiences how our concepts, even as concepts, are corpses, can feel that out of Faustian striving death constantly stands next to him. Therefore, he calls for birth, which on his other side appears as the child."

165 (4) Rudolf Steiner, "On the Aura of the Human Being", in *Luzifer - Gnosis.* GA 34.

169 (5) See Hans Mandl, *Vom Geist des Nordens. Studien zur skandinavischen Volksseelenkunde.* (Stuttgart: 1966).

(6) Op. cit., Marie Steiner, *Von den Mysteriendramen ...*

171 (7) In his book, *Kultur und Kunst Ägyptens. Ein Isis-Geheimnis.* (Dornach: 1975). Ernst Uehli describes the pharaoh in ritual dress as the bearer of the Word. He wore the ritual beard, which covered chin and throat ... , "when he spoke the ritual and the words of consecration during the sacrifice." This cult symbol, which he laid aside after the holy deed, was simultaneously, "... the sign of the veiling of a world mystery which he as an initiate had experienced through the death of Osiris."

(8) See also Rudolf Steiner, *Mysterienstätte des Mittelalters.* GA 233a, as well as the drawings on p. 173 of this book.

172 (9) Op. cit. Margarita Woloschin, *Erinnerungsbilder ...*

182 (10) In geographical context Rudolf Steiner speaks of this in "Gnostic Doctrines and Supersensible Influences in Europe". *Anthroposophic Quarterly.* vol. 6, 1931. "Eastward of the Ural and Volga regions, in the astral world which borders on the physical world there arose during the later Middle Ages, continuing through the centuries

to our own day, an ahrimanic form of magic practised by certain spiritual beings who in their etheric and astral development stand higher than man but in their development of soul and spirit stand lower than man. Throughout the regions of Siberia and Central Asia, in the spiritual world immediately adjacent to the earthly world, terrible etheric-astral beings are to be seen, ahrimanic beings who practise an earthly, materialized form of magic. And these forces work upon human beings who are unskilled in such arts but who are infected by them and so come under the influence of this astral world .... These beings move about among mean and carry on their activities in the astral world, using on the one hand the ahrimanic forces of decadent eastern magic and on the other the forces emanating from the luciferic, rationalistic thinking of the West. Human beings on earth are influenced and affected by these forces.

"In their present state, the goat-form which constitutes the lower part of the bodily structure of these beings has coarsened and become bear-like, but on the other hand their *heads* are radiant and possessed of a high order of intelligence. They are the mirrored personifications of luciferic rationalism developed to its highest point of subtlety. The beings indwelling this astral paradise are half bear-, half goat-like in form, with semi-human countenances exhibiting a subtle sensuousness but at the same time a rare cleverness. Since the later Middle Ages and on through the centuries of the modern age this astral region has become a veritable paradise of the Satyrs and Fauns in their present metamorphosis, and there they dwell."

179 (11) In another comment on this on June 29, 1921, in lectures on the architectural conception of the Goetheanum (GA 290), Rudolf Steiner said, "It was painted by me during the last war. Sometimes one has one's private ideas; the wretched fabric of Woodrow Wilson's Fourteen Points after all, grew out of an abstract deformation of dualism. I have, also here in Switzerland, repeatedly pointed out the world destructiveness of the Fourteen Points; that is why to my private amusement Mr. and Mrs. Wilson are immortalized in these figures. But this is, as I said, of little significance."

183 (12) By word of mouth.

184 (13) Op. cit. Margarita Woloschin.

185 (14) "And this is explained by the fact that from the ninth and tenth centuries onwards it was possible for the 'people of Christ' to emerge in a certain territory within the civilized world, a people endowed with a special inborn capacity to become the vehicle of the Christ revelation for future generations .... We mean by this that a territory has been set apart in the East of Europe in which again and again people have lived who are directly united with the Christ impulse, people in whose souls the Christ impulse continuously trickles in. The Christ impulse is ever present as an aura impregnating the thinking and the feeling of this people." In *From Symptom to Reality in Modern History*. (London: 1976). (GA 185).

186 (15) Assja Tergeniev, "Zur Malerei im ersten Goetheanum" *Rudolf Steiners Entwürfe für die Malerei der kleinen Kuppel des ersten Goetheanum.* Dornach: 1962.

(16) Daniel van Bemmelen, *Rudolf Steiners farbige Gestaltung des Goetheanum.* (Stuttgart: 1973).

(17) See Julius Hebbings' autobiography, *Lebenskreise, Farbenkreise* as well as his *Welt, Farbe und Mensch.*

187 (18) Out of Mathilde Scholl's transcript of the esoteric lesson given in Karlsruhe on October 14, 1911.

188 (19) Rudolf Steiner gave a series of 35 different eurythmy figures along with color indications. In 1922 they were cut out of flat wood and painted. Since then they have been copied over and over again. The indication for the figure of (intuitive) knowledge is white for the 'movement', yellow 'feeling', orange 'character'. See the booklet *Eurythmy and the Impulse of Dance* by Raffe, Harwood and Lundgren.

225 (1) Arhild Rosenkrantz, *A New Impulse in Art* (London)

227 (2) Op. cit. Assja Turgeniev, in *Rudolf Steiners Entwürfe für die Glasfenster ...*

228 (3) See the lecture of June 17, 1914 in *Ways to a New Style of Architecture* (London: 1927).

241 (4) Op. cit. Assja Turgeniev, as above.

242 (5) See the fourth lecture on Adam Kadmon in the cycle, *The Mystery of the Trinity.* (London: 1947).

(6) Op. cit. Assja Turgeniev.

(7) Ibid.

(8) Out of the fourth scene of Rudolf Steiner's Mystery Play, *The Portal of Initiation.*

244 (9) Rudolf Steiner, *Anthroposophical Leading Thoughts.* (GA 26). See the essays written at the beginning of January 1925.

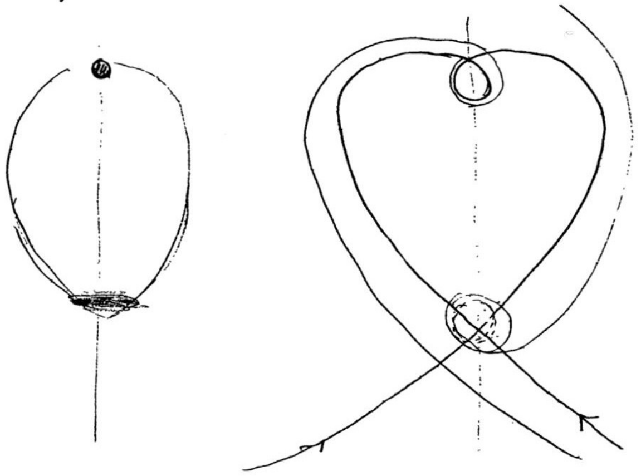

(10) Imme von Eckhardstein's drawing for Cancer was based on the following sketch of Rudolf Steiner's:

Compare this with *Beiträge zur Rudolf Steiner Gesamtausgabe,* No. 37/38 (Dornach: 1972).

(11) Hermann Beckh, *Der kosmische Rhythmus, das Sterngeheimnis und Erdengeheimnis im Johannes Evangelium.* (Basel: 1930).

(12) In another lecture Rudolf Steiner says, "All those traits that live in the hunter as he aims at an animal he wants to shoot down live in every human being. You will find that what has been depicted on the scratched glass is this inner quality of the human being poured into a figurative mold. When one comes to a particular stage of inner development one can do nothing else but to give form (*Gestalt*) to that which lives in one as desire. And if you think of this picture metamorphosed to a later stage then you have what is depicted in the right wing. Here the human being has advanced from the intention to shoot the bird down to the actual deed. He has aimed. He is shooting. What occurred previously is transformed into what has been scratched into the glass on the right window and which only becomes a work of art when it is shone through by the sunlight. Each of the windows can be treated in the same way. Here it is important that one does not come with clever interpretations but instead submits oneself with sensitivity to what is on the window. One overlooks the artistic intention precisely there where one strives for clever interpretations." In *Der Baugedanke von Dornach* (October 16, 1920).

248 (13) Rudolf Steiner, *Anthroposophical Leading Thoughts.* GA 26.

249 (14) Compare with the lecture given on February 16, 1911.

(15) Compare with Friedrich Hiebel, *Die Botschaft von Hellas.* (Stuttgart: 1983).

251 (16) Rudolf Steiner, "The World-Thoughts in the Acts of Michael and the Acts of Ahriman", *Anthroposophical Leading Thoughts.* GA 26.

(17) Compare with the detailed documentation, *Die Holzplastik Rudolf Steiners in Dornach* by Ake Fant, Arne Klingborg and A. John Wilkes, with an introduction by Hagen Biesantz. (Dornach: 1969).

(18) Edith Maryon worked on the wood sculpture (the 'Group') from the first studies made for it in the fall of 1914 until her death in 1924. Stimulated by Rudolf Steiner she worked out a few small models alone. The sixth, a two-meter high model was signed 'Rudolf Steiner/E. Maryon'. A cast of it along with other models can now be seen in the so-called *Gruppenraum* in the Goetheanum, the same room in which the wooden sculpture now stands. In the former atelier of Rudolf Steiner a second Christ-head and a head of Ahriman, both modelled by Rudolf Steiner, can be found.

(19) Hermann Ranzenberger, "Die Plastik des Ahrimankopfes", *Mitteilungen aus der anthroposophischen Arbeit in Deutschland.* 24th year, Booklet 1, No. 91. Easter 1970.

(20) The model for the middle figure was broken up at Rudolf Steiner's request.

(21) Friedrich Rittelmeyer, *Rudolf Steiner Enters my Life* (Edinburgh: 1963).

254 (22) Unpublished written account.

262 (23) Karl von Baltz, *Rudolf Steiners musikalischer Impuls,* (Dornach: 1981).

(24) From an unpublished account in which there are quotations of the lecture given on February 20, 1924.

See also *Eurythmie als sichtbarer Gesang.* GA 278.

266 (25) Rudolf Steiner, *Occult Science: An Outline.* GA 13.

(26) See also Eugen Roll, *Die Welt der Troubadours und das Reich der Minne. (Stuttgart: 1977)*

267 (27) Robert de Boron, *Die Geschichte des Heiligen Gral,* trans. into German by Konrad Sandkühler. (Stuttgart: 1977).

268 (28) Out of *Sigune und Schionatulander, Ein Minnegespräch aus dem "Jüngeren Titural",* by Albrecht von Schraffenberg, selected and rendered by Heinrich Teutschmann. (Dornach: 1972).

269 (29) Charles William Heckethorn gives an account of this legend in his book, *Geheime Gesellschaften, Geheimbünde und Geheimlehren.* (Leipzig: 1900).

270 (30) Compare with Carl Kemper, *Der Bau.* (Stuttgart: 1974) p. 201.

272 (31) Rudolf Steiner, *Occult Science: An Outline.*

273 (32) Compare with Rudolf Steiner, *Goethes geheime Offenbarung.* (Dornach: 1982) and "Von Goethes Rätselmärchen zu Rudolf Steiners Mysteriendramen", in *Beiträge zur Rudolf Steiner Gesamtausgabe,* No. 23, p. 23.

275 (33) Ibid.

(34) Published in Hermann Linde, *"Das Märchen von der grünen Schlange und der schönen Lilie", verwoben mit dem Mysteriendrama "Die Pforte der Einweihung" von Rudolf Steiner.* (Basel: 1972). The scaled down reproduction of the picture on p. 274 is made possible with friendly permission of the Zbinden Druck und Verlag AG, Basel.

(35) From a letter to Marie von Sivers on November 25, 1905 in Rudolf Steiner-Marie Steiner, *Briefwechsel und Dokumente 1901-1925. GA 262.*

(36) Compare with Rudolf Steiner, *Wonders of the World, Ordeals of the Soul, Revelations of the Spirit.* GA 129.

(37) Quoted from Max Gümbel-Seiling, *Mit Rudolf Steiner in München.* (Den Haag: 1946).

276 (38) Compare with Rudolf Steiner, *Die Entstehung und Entwicklung der Eurythmie.* GA 277a. An English translation of two of the lectures (April 5th and April 19th) is available in typescript under the title *An Introduction to Eurythmy.*

(39) Marie Savitch, *Marie Steiner-von Sivers.* (Dornach: 1965).

277 (40) Marie Steiner, *Gesammelte Schriften.* vol. 2. (Dornach: 1974).

Translator's Note

Dear Reader,
I have endeavored to keep as close as possible to the character of the original Notes to 'Das Farbenwort'. Those editions not available in English retain their original German titles. I have translated all the quotations of Rudolf Steiner anew. Scholars, please forgive the infrequent mention of publishers for many of the books. I have not had the resources available to trace them.

TD